# The Sonshine Of Our Lives

To Ann

with Best Wishes

Sheila Redgrave.

**Sheila Redgrave**

authorHOUSE®

*AuthorHouse™ UK Ltd.*
*500 Avebury Boulevard*
*Central Milton Keynes, MK9 2BE*
*www.authorhouse.co.uk*
*Phone: 08001974150*

*First published by AuthorHouse 2/8/2010*

*ISBN: 978-1-4490-6880-6 (sc)*
*ISBN: 978-1-4490-6879-0 (hc)*

*This book is printed on acid-free paper.*

To my, husband, my children and my
grandchildren
who have all so richly coloured my life
in their own unique ways.

# Acknowlegements

I would like to thank my husband Geoff for taking the time and great patience needed in helping me to complete my story. My granddaughter, Natalie, for giving up a week of her school holiday to help me to get started and typing up my scribbled notes onto my new computer - not an easy job with my hand writing, bad grammar and lack of mouse control. My daughter, Jane, for helping me to correct my computer mishaps and for having the faith in me to complete this book. My grandson, Ben, and my granddaughter, Stephanie, for their help with ideas for the book. My thanks goes to Roger, for completing the first proof reading and to my daughter Christine for her ideas, subsequent proof reading, final manuscript typing, help dealing with the publishers and the time she gave to me in collating the photographs and ensuring the book's completion to deadline. To Sophie and Zak for just being Sophie and Zak and finally to my Son Steve for being the focus of my book as without him there would be no story to tell.

# A word from Steve

I am forever grateful to both of my parents for sacrificing many hours of their time and for their unswerving support during my thirty years of rowing.

Now that I am a parent myself I can understand the devotion one has to ones children and the desire you have to help your child to be the best they can be.
If they awarded gold medals for parents, mine would be on top of the rostrum.

Sir Steve Redgrave

# Contents

# Chapter One
## The Early Years

*Growing Pains*

I was standing at the entrance to Gatwick departure lounge, looking back at my daughters Christine and Jane and our twin grandchildren Benjamin, and Stephanie.  Only an hour before they had delivered us to the airport and were here with us now, overseeing our safe departure, as we left Britain on yet another of our exciting trips.

Whenever I went away, it had always been a sort of game between Stephanie and me, to see who would be the first to cry; invariably it would be me and again this time I didn't let her down. Try as I did, tears filled my eyes as I waved goodbye and then turned to go through airport security. Once through I turned to look again but they had gone. I closed my eyes for a second and swallowed the lump in my throat, simply hoping that they would have a safe drive back to Marlow.

Picking up our hand luggage we walked through into the departure lounge. My husband Geoff turned to me and said "Whatever is the matter, we will only be away for three weeks". I smiled at him as he said, shaking his head, "You will never change." We had stayed with our children as long as possible but now, finding an airport bench seat, I sat down to regain my composure and to wait for our flights to be called.

Meanwhile Geoff went off to look in the camera shop to buy some film and also to browse in W.H. Smith and buy newspapers and books for us to read during our flight. After a while Geoff returned to say that our flight had appeared on the departure board and we were being called to the boarding gate. So, gathering our bags together, we headed off in the direction of gate 23. Thirty minutes later we were safely strapped into our seats and taxiing out along the runway destined for Atlanta, Georgia in the United States of America at the beginning of yet another Olympic adventure.

We were becoming quite used to travelling to Olympic venues, as over the last 12 years we had followed our son, Steven Redgrave, the Olympic oarsman, to three Continents. As his keenest supporters we had travelled to Los Angeles in 1984, to Seoul in 1988 and to Barcelona in 1992. Each time, Steve had returned home with an Olympic gold medal and in 1988 a bronze medal too. This time Steve's burning ambition was to win his fourth consecutive Olympic gold medal in Atlanta and we really hoped that this goal of his would once again be achieved.

Our aircraft was now in the air and levelling out at some 35,000ft. I had chosen to sit by the window, with Geoff taking the adjacent aisle seat so he could stretch out his long legs, and so we settled down to enjoy our flight. Geoff was reading his magazine but I didn't feel like reading, so I just sat and looked out of the window at the white fluffy clouds below letting my mind drift back in time to the events that had brought us on this flight to Atlanta.

*When Steve was about thirteen I can remember him coming home from school one day, brimming with excitement, to tell me that he had been invited to join the school rowing team along with his friend Craig Gibbins. Francis Smith, one of Steve's school masters, was not only the Head of the English Department at Great Marlow School but also of the Sports Department, and had recently formed a school's rowing team, calling it 'Great Marlow School Rowing Club'.*

*His original crews were already having some success so Steve was very impressed with the invitation from Mr Smith, to join an additional crew that he was now putting together. Frances, had apparently looked at Steve and told him that being so tall, with long arms and legs and with his big hands, he had the makings of a good rower. Frances, who had a great love of the sport, had always been involved with rowing going back to his own* school days and was currently also the Captain of Marlow Rowing Club. The new crew that he was putting together was a Coxed Four and was to be arranged with Steve rowing at stroke, Craig Gibbins rowing at bow and with Clive Pope and Stuart Painter in the two and three seats. Another of Steve's friends, Nicky Baatz, was yet to experience his teenage growing spurt and this therefore made him an ideal choice for the position of coxswain.

Steve had always enjoyed school sports - he was a keen rugby player and also enjoyed a mixture of track and field; he was a good all-rounder. He had never had anything to do with a water sport before though, so this new challenge would be something quite different. Although we had lived in the river town of Marlow for many years, Geoff and I knew very little about the sport of rowing - apart from watching the annual University Boat Race on TV. We were not too sure what this would entail for Steve but, as his parents, we were very pleased that he was showing a keen interest in yet another aspect of sport even though this one was unfamiliar to us all.

During their first winter together, the newly formed crew trained very hard, but unfortunately, early the following spring, the Gibbins family moved away from the area and therefore Craig was forced to leave the crew. Before he left Francis Smith gave him the chance to put all his hard work to the test by placing in an older crew that was competing in a "Head of the River" race to give him a taste of competition. A 'Head' is a long river race in which rowers compete over a twisting course of about 3 miles. It's a timed race with a staggered start. Craig's place in the crew was taken by Robert Haley. Robert was nicknamed "Bill", for obvious reasons, and was a very fit young lad who, before too long, blended in well with the rest of the crew. They soon began to gel.

During the following summer Regatta season the crew entered seven regattas and remarkably, won all seven, giving them a huge sense of achievement. The boys took great pride competing for their school and after each regatta at Prize giving they would step forward and collect their cups and tankards which really seemed to add to their self-esteem. It was the very hot summer of 1976 and Geoff and I went along to all the regattas. We really loved the riverbank settings and enjoyed meeting up with all the other supporting parents. It made each weekend's gathering quite an event. Frances worked tirelessly training the lads after school and would often tow the school boat trailers or drive the minibus to regattas, all over the country. The competition was now getting to a level where the boys were taking it very seriously; their parents too.

Geoff and I had our own business, a Garden Centre, next to our home in Marlow Bottom. We felt very guilty sloping off on 'Regatta Saturdays' as this was our busiest day of the week. Christine, our eldest daughter, was the Garden Centre shop manager and her husband Philip would often help her at the weekends. We also had our weekend helper, Julie Colligan, to rely on. She was still at school and was Steve's girlfriend at this time so between the three of them, we felt the business was being left in good hands.

The crew worked hard training all through the following winter. In 1977 they had another very successful year but at the end of the summer Regatta season they were hit by the bombshell that Stuart wanted to give up rowing as he wanted to give more attention to his other interests. All the boys understood his feelings as they knew only too well the personal time that had to be sacrificed to rowing training and competing. It was a huge commitment for a teenager. The crew became concerned that finding a suitable replacement would be difficult but Francis Smith came to their rescue - suggesting Peter McConnell, a boy from one of his younger crews. Fortunately, Peter quickly fitted in really well and the reformed crew threw themselves back into their hard winter training schedule.

The 1978 rowing season began and now presented further opportunity for them all to improve their skills. They entered and won regattas at Gloucester, Evesham, Nottingham City, Hereford and Cambridge. Then along came the opportunity for them to row at Marlow. This was a significant milestone for the lads as it would be the first time that they had entered their home town regatta. This was because, in previous years, there had not been a suitable category available for them to enter.

Marlow regatta has been the premier social and sporting event in the life of the Town since 1855 and is reputed to be the largest one day regatta in the world. Traditionally held on a Saturday in mid June, there is quite an international flavour to the event. Foreign crews come to Marlow to fine-tune their racing skills before entering Henley Royal Regatta two weeks later. A large funfair always sets up in Higginson Park, next to the river, for the four days encompassing the weekend, and everyone for miles around comes to the town.

There is nothing quite like a hot sunny regatta morning in June. Taking a stroll down Marlow High Street, decorated with bunting stretched across the high street and pretty hanging baskets adorning the lampposts; it's wonderful. The local shop keepers take the event seriously and invest their time lovingly decorating their shop windows with flags and rowing memorabilia. They know that the high street will soon be buzzing with potential customers and tourists. You'll usually find the tables and chairs outside the Chequers pub, already draped with good looking young men in striped blazers and boaters and pretty girls in their summer dresses enjoying the atmosphere. At the bottom of the High Street is the imposing All Saints Church, right on the river's edge and overlooking the famous suspension bridge designed by Tierney. Close by, The Green of the Causeway, will be dotted with the over spill of customers from the George and Dragon, sitting on the grass in the sunshine already enjoying a Pimms. This is a typically English summer scene in the beautiful town of Marlow which as the day progresses, will fill with laughter and the sounds of people enjoying themselves on the fair rides. All of this is alongside the very serious event of 'Racing on the River'.

Many of the pupils from Great Marlow School were lining the river banks this year. They had turned out to cheer on the crew that they had heard so much about during their school assemblies when, on most Monday mornings, the crew would be congratulated for winning yet another trophy for their school during the previous weekend. This success was making the boys very popular indeed.

At their home Regatta the boys decided to enter two events - The Junior A Coxed Fours and the Junior 16 Coxed Fours. It would have been hard enough for them to have entered one event really but with the possibilities of three heats to be rowed over the course in each event, a massive amount of energy would be expended in entering both. It could mean that they might have to race the rowing course five or six times over, depending on the entry numbers. This was where all of the hard work that they had put in during their winter training would be useful, and although they had built up their stamina and endurance capability, it still seemed to us to be an incredibly daunting task.

*The school and the rest of their local supporters had lined the banks of the enclosure and each time our crew raced the roar from the crowd could be heard for miles. With so many enthusiastic supporters rooting for them, it was bound to boost their confidence. They had great success that day, as the records show. In the Junior A Coxed Four event, Great Marlow School beat St. Paul's School, verdict easily - time 6:09mins and in the Junior 16 Coxed Four event, Great Marlow School beat Westminster School, verdict easily - time 6:40. With their task complete and after the prize giving, the boys had a quick tea and then went off to the funfair to celebrate. We left them to enjoy their evening and drove home feeling very proud parents. That evening, as we shared a meal, we reminisced on another very successful day for Great Marlow School Rowing Club.*

*There were two other big wins to add to their achievements that year. The National Schools Fours Cup and the National Championships "Junior 16" Coxed Fours. In the National event they came third and were duly selected to row in the Home Countries International to be held in Wales, at Llandegfedd Reservoir, later in the year. To say that the boys were pleased with their achievement would be a slight understatement.*

*The boys were all issued a special National kit. Their rowing vests were white with red lions on the front, black rowing shorts and a dark blue tracksuit with the word 'England' emblazoned across the back. The tracksuit, was the most treasured of all Steve's possessions and it went everywhere with him, until many years later, when it was stolen from his kit. Needless to say, he was extremely upset. A blazer badge was also supplied with the full kit as well and the boys all sported their England badge with great pride.*

*Their win at the Home Countries International was very special. It was a very hard fought race and they just managed to keep ahead of the Irish to win by one length; Scotland came in third place and Wales was in fourth. The cup that they proudly received was a dark green porcelain tankard with the Welsh Dragon emblem embossed on the side. Subsequently, the blazer didn't get a lot of wear, but the tracksuit had to be prized off him to be washed.*

*In March of 1978 Steve had his sixteenth birthday. He had expressed a wish to own his own sculling boat as he was now considering focusing on* becoming a single sculler. A sculler is a rower who rows with two oars, one in each hand, and a single sculling boat is a shell designed for an individual sculler. Sculling is very good for skill development, particularly for beginner, and Steve wanted to try his hand at this. We thought this seemed like a good idea and we discussed the subject with Francis. He said, he thought that Steve would make an excellent sculler but advised us not to purchase a new scull but suggested instead that he would make some enquiries and try to locate a good second hand boat, as with Steve still growing, he would soon likely out-grow his new acquisition.

Francis soon came up with a second hand boat that belonged to a chap at Cambridge University called David Sturge, an international rower who had competed at the 1976 Olympics in Montreal. Geoff and Steve, together with Francis, drove up to Cambridge all together to look at the boat and found it to be just what Steve was looking for. Geoff brought it for him there and then and as soon as they had arrived back in Marlow they collected me from home and we all went down to Marlow Rowing Club to see him try out his new boat, for the first time.

It seemed to me, that half of Marlow Rowing Club was there watching;, everyone was probably expecting to see him take a swim. Getting into a sculling boat is like stepping onto a 17ft scaffold board using only the two oar blades as a point of balance; it's all too easy to fall in. After a few minor adjustments he put the boat on the water, stepping into it. Moving off and away from the bank with a bit of a wobble, he successfully turned the boat around. Once the boat was straight, to everyone's amazement, he sculled off as if he had been sculling all his life. That year Steve won several sculling races. He would row with his crew in the Coxed Four Boat and then Single Scull in another race at the same regatta. Perhaps this amount of exercise could have accounted for the rapid build up in his level of stamina and endurance that he attained while still so young.

Geoff and I really enjoyed supporting Steve and the boys but these junior years on the river banks were at times intense and could be full of anguish. I would often take the brunt of Steve's frustration and disappointment, when things weren't going to plan and at times like these I would sometimes think to myself 'Why do I do this'. But looking back at those years now I realise that we shared some wonderful times too, as parents supporting him, watching him succeed, and seeing him mature into this amazing athlete. It was also great fun for us meeting new and interesting people and during these years we made many new friends- all of whom are still our friends to this day.

The boys were coming to the end of their school days and as Great Marlow School Rowing Club had always been affiliated to the local rowing club in Marlow, it was a matter of natural progression for the crew to go on to become club members and to carry on their rowing careers representing Marlow Rowing Club. Steve's school rowing vest though would always be his most treasured possession - never to be parted with. I have kept his original vest, darns and all.

Great Marlow School prize giving day was yet another milestone for the boys. A proud crew collected their end of school exam awards and they were given a special accolade for all their achievements in so successfully representing their school at rowing. We felt very proud parents when Steve was also presented with an award from The Rotary Club for the 'Rotary Young Citizen Award 1978'.

Serious training continued for the crew through the rest of November and December, with a little light relief for the 'Boxing Day Scratch Fours' This is an event some call an 'egg beater' that takes place every year on Boxing Day morning at Marlow Rowing club. All of the members' names, young and old, male and female, are put into the hat and drawn out randomly, to form mixed crews of Coxed Fours. This method of choosing crews will often see the lineups include coxswains as rowers and vice versa. These 'scratch crews' are raced off until they are left with a winning crew, then they all pile into the clubhouse for a much needed 'Captains Hot Toddy'. It's really good fun and an excellent way to work off the effects of the previous day's Christmas lunch.

At the beginning of 1979, the winter "Heads" were already well underway. The boys had a lot to prove this year, as the National selectors would be watching out for potential oarsmen that they could put forward for the Junior World Championships. Steve had been overlooked by them in 1978 but now the selectors seemed very interested in him. He didn't want to leave his crew though as he felt this would be letting them down. He felt that *his whole crew were good enough to be selected but the selectors had their own ideas. The selectors had a policy of not selecting pre-formed club crews instead they liked to pick individual men and would then form the crews from what they considered to be 'the best of the bunch'; Steve stuck to his guns and decided to stay with his crew.*

*In June at Marlow Regatta a 'selected' crew was put up to row against our boys and to their surprise and dismay, our lads lost by ¾ of a length and were absolutely devastated to lose at their home regatta. Steve also sculled at Marlow Regatta and won the "Senior B" sculls. A selector asked Geoff to try to persuade Steve to change his mind, but Geoff said that it was up to Steve, that his son had a mind of his own and that he definitely knew what he wanted.*

*The boys, having lost, increased their training schedule, with the National Championships looming in a few weeks time. Meantime, Steve entered Nottingham International winning the "Senior B" Sculls. The weekend of the National Championships arrived and the boys, wanting to get a good night's rest, opted to stay overnight at Nottingham University. They all felt that if they could win here and really prove themselves, they were still in with a good chance of being selected.*

*With a very positive attitude, they set off for their final race. They looked good off the start, very quickly taking the lead and then settled into the race; but then disaster struck. Clive's seat suddenly broke and he desperately tried to row with a fixed seat but it was almost impossible and the boat slowed right down. With the race now over for the crew they were forced to continue to row to the finish as Steve was imminently due to race again in his sculling boat. He had to leave his dejected crew with their boat, jump into a car and be quickly driven to the start, as his sculling event was the next but one race. A friend had already taken his sculling boat to the start for him so he took over his boat and lined up for the start. In no time at all the flag was dropped for the start of the race and off he went, as if possessed by the devil himself. He left the opposition in his wake. Strangely the official record book doesn't even show him finishing but that day he stood and took the gold medal at the rostrum. But even this success could console him; his beloved crew had failed.*

*After his race Steve was called into the selector's office and was told that only he could go to the World Championships but only as the spare man, and as a single sculler. He was also given the bad news that he would not be allowed to take his coach along. His place as spare man meant that if any of the other crew members fell sick, Steve would need to take their place but if nobody fell ill during the Championship then he would be allowed to scull in the competition. His crew members were gathered there to meet him as he came from the office and they all said how pleased they were that he had been given the opportunity to go but we could see how disappointed they all were. They would not be joining him. We tried our best to console the lads, especially Bill, as this would have been his last chance to compete as a junior. Because of the date his birthday fell he was what is known as a 'one year junior'. Francis too was equally disappointed. We felt very sad for him as he had given every minute of his spare time to these boys and he'd had great hopes for them as a crew Geoff and I had very mixed emotions that day.*

*On our return to Marlow Francis focused on Steve's future and very swiftly called in the expertise of Mike Spracklen to help coach Steve with his sculling. A long time member of Marlow Rowing Club, Mike had a very good track record himself, having won a gold medal in the double sculls with Geoffrey Baker at the Empire Games in 1958. It was arranged that Steve would go to Mike's house on the riverbank, every day for extra training. Mike thought that Steve had a good chance of making it to the final of The 1979 Junior World Rowing Championships that was being held in Moscow. This became Steve's next goal.*

*On Sunday 27<sup>th</sup> July, Steve, who was still training with his crew in his spare time, walked back from Marlow to our house for lunch after the morning's training session. With him were his friends, Bill and Steve's girlfriend, Nicola. They had planned to spend a lazy Sunday afternoon together, playing a game of pool and watching TV. After lunch I got on with my housework, and the kids went into the lounge to watch TV. Bill said that he would like a piece of fruit and got up from relaxing on the sofa to get an apple from the fruit bowl and immediately collapsed on the floor. Steve shouted for me to come. I rushed into the lounge and could see immediately that it was very serious. Geoff and my daughter Jane and her husband David arrived at the same time. Jane had just recently completed a course*

10

in first aid and with her dad and David's help, immediately started mouth to mouth resuscitation while I called the doctor and the ambulance. In no time at all the doctor arrived. Shortly after this the ambulance pulled up too and the paramedics took over, dashing Bill to High Wycombe hospital. Steven and Nicola took on the immediate job, along with Bill's sister Andrea, of trying to track down Bill's mother and father. They found them and directed them to the hospital where they joined Jane and me in a special waiting room.

Sometime later, the doctor came to us and told us that Bill had died. They said that they had done all they could, but to no avail. We were all distraught and totally devastated with this news. What could we begin to say to comfort Bill's mum Joan and Colin his dad and Andrea his younger sister? Bill had been just 17 years and eight months old and now he was gone. Steve was shattered; he had lost his best mate.

The post-mortem later determined the cause of death. His heart had gone out of rhythm and just stopped, and just wouldn't start again, nothing else was found to be wrong. His heart was slightly enlarged, but that is not out of the ordinary for a sportsman but otherwise he had been very fit. What a tragedy for such a young boy with all of his life in front of him. He was sadly missed by us all.

The funeral was held at Marlow All Saints Church by the bridge next to the river and right opposite the rowing club. His crew were the coffin bearers and the church was full of Great Marlow School pupils and Bill's college friends. People had come from all areas of rowing. Bill Mason came with his crew, the coxless four that had been selected for the World Championships. The parents of all his crew members were there and most of the boat club members too. There were simply masses of floral tributes to Bill. From this enormous show of support I think, I hope, his parents and family were able to draw a little comfort. His ashes were interred in the church yard in a small plot right next to the riverbank. This beautiful and very appropriate spot overlooks the river and Marlow rowing club and truly befits such a great rowing enthusiast and a genuinely lovely boy.

As a family we somehow managed to get through the next few weeks. This was mainly because there was so much to do. Steve passed his driving *test and then arranged a carnet and transport for his boat for the trip to Moscow where hopefully he would be competing in the 1979 Junior World Championships to be held 14th-18th August. Back in 1979, due to the Cold War, the USSR wasn't the easiest place for Westerners to visit. We had difficulty arranging our flights and our accommodation and also in obtaining the necessary visas. This all had to be done independently as there were no package tours on offer in those days. We were not even told which hotel we would be staying at until we arrived in Moscow.*

*We travelled on the Russian airline 'Aeroflot' on the same flight as the GB rowing team. On our arrival at Moscow airport we had our first encounter with Soviet officialdom. One of our boys had worn his hair long when his passport photo had been taken, and his parents had talked him into having his hair cut for the trip and he didn't look quite the same. The guard looked at the photograph, then back at him, and then back at the photograph; everyone tried to explain but the officials still held us all for half an hour or more. When they finally let us through the team boarded a waiting coach and Geoff, Nicola and I went to a central desk in the airport foyer where we were allocated our hotel. Outside the airport we were allocated a taxi driver who looked like a K.G.B. agent but, I'm pleased to say, he simply drove us into the centre of Moscow and safely delivered us to our accommodation at The Hotel Rossia.*

*It was getting quite late by then and it was very dark when we arrived at our hotel. The receptionist at the front desk asked for our passports, and it was only then that we discovered, to our horror, that we still had Steve's passport with us. The receptionist told us that Steve must have his passport with him or he would not be allowed into a hotel room that night. She was very helpful though, finding out which hotel Steve was staying in, and she got another taxi to take Geoff and the passport, back to Steve. The Ukraina Hotel was his destination on the opposite side of the city and when Geoff arrived he found Steve sitting in the foyer all alone looking extremely fed up. Geoff gave him his passport and quickly dashed back to the taxi afraid it would not wait for him) and was driven back across Moscow to the Rossia Hotel. When Geoff arrived back at our hotel he then discovered that he had no Russian Rubles to pay the taxi driver with so he had to hurriedly change some money to pay for his journey. What a start to our trip!*

*We were then shown to our rooms, and oh boy, we were glad to get to bed that night as we were exhausted. Waking the next morning we found our room to be very pleasant, painted white and very modern looking, with a large TV. The hotel window looked out onto part of Red Square. Nicola's room was a single and looked out over an inner courtyard. We all went down to breakfast, not knowing what to expect but we were, by then, starving. In the restaurant we found hard boiled eggs, cold cooked meats, dark heavy bread, and coffee and tea, both very black – we did not see any milk at all for the whole of our stay in Russia.*

*After we had eaten we went to see what we could find out about the rowing venue. We found the tourist information desk in the hotel reception and asked where the rowing course was and how we should get there. The young lady spoke good English and pointed it out on a map. She wrote down the name of our destination for us on a piece of paper as we would never have been able to pronounce it properly. She told us that it was quite a long way and that we would be best advised to go either by taxi or by metro which was about fifteen minutes walk away. We decided to go by Metro. When we got to the Metro station we showed our piece of paper to the ticket clerk and purchased our tickets which were surprisingly cheap. Geoff was first at the barrier and, as he went to walk through, a bar shot out just below his knees, and he almost fell straight over the top. Everyone was laughing as apparently he should have put his ticket in first. Helpfully, some people pointed out what we should do and we just followed the crowd on to the platform. Using our piece of paper to get the correct tube we climbed on board and sat where we could read the passing station signs, checking each one against our piece of paper each time the train came to a halt.*

*We arrived at a station that had no name so we just sat and waited for the train to move on. All the Russian passengers were looking at us again and at last a man touched my arm and gesticulated for us to get off. We followed the crowds till we were out of the station and then we had to decide whether to go right or left. We decided to turn right and in just a few minutes time, we arrived at the rowing course but it had been more by luck than judgement.*

*The course had been purpose built for the 1980 Olympics which were to take place the following year and the juniors were getting a chance to try it out first. From the grandstand where we were seated we had an excellent view right up the 2000m course. The facilities were very good with the grounds nicely laid out with flower beds and the flags of all the competing nations fluttering from the top of the stands. Shuttle buses ran between the athlete's hotel and the course so on our return journey to Steve's hotel we took the bus. As we arrived at his hotel we bumped into Steve coming out. He was just going off to the course for a training session. We talked to him for a while and then we returned to our hotel by taxi.*

*As our hotel was such a long way from the rowing course we decided that, if at all possible, we would arrange to change our hotel to the Ukraina Hotel where the British crews were staying. From there we could catch the shuttle bus to the course each day which would make our journey that much easier. We spoke to the young lady on the reception desk about this and she kindly said she would see what she could arrange. We went to our room and waited. We hadn't had a chance to unpack yet which was fortunate, as just a little while later we were told that it would be ok to change hotels and that a taxi would take us to The Ukraina in about an hour.*

*At our new hotel we were shown to our rooms. We were on the nineteenth floor of this very large and much older hotel and this time the view from our window was of a large hammer and sickle statue. The room was very comfortable though and Nicola's room was just across the hall from ours. We unpacked and settled in.*

*The day of the first heat arrived and as no crew member had so far become ill, Steve was allowed to scull. The entry for his single scull event was 19 scullers with only twelve going through to the next round. Steve had a good draw in his heat and lead off the start but, unfortunately, one of his blades caught a lane marking buoy and this stopped him dead- he was lucky not to capsize. He got going again very quickly but could only finish fourth so this meant that instead of going straight through to the next round he would have to go to the repechage. Repechage is the name for a heat within a competition during which runners-up in earlier heats have a final chance to qualify for the next round. He rowed a good race in the repechage and finished third but unfortunately only two scullers from this race went through so he was out. His hopes were dashed and further competition for him was over.*

*After the repechage Steve was taken away for a drugs test so, after the days racing was over, we returned to our hotel. At about six thirty that evening, we looked around the hotel for him but couldn't find him anywhere. I asked the other rowers we met if anyone had seen him but nobody had. So we sat in the foyer and waited. By nine thirty, three hours later, I was beside myself with worry but then Nicola spotted him leaning against a wall on the other side of the large reception foyer. We all rushed over to him and very surprisingly found that he was drunk. He had not been able to pass water for the drug test because he had been so dehydrated after the race so they had given him a beer to drink. It had taken three hours and several pints before he could pass water for the test - hence his state of inebriation. Fortunately for him he wasn't left with a hangover the following morning but he was a bit under the weather for a couple of days. At least he hadn't been sent to Siberia, where, in my imagination, the Russian officials might have banished him. Steve was understandably very upset about having been knocked out of the competition. Of course he had still to train each day in case anyone fell sick or got an injury but during this time he gave his full support to the rest of the boys in the GB team.*

*We enjoyed the rest of our stay. We watched the rowing each day and did lots of sightseeing- visiting the Kremlin, Red Square and Gorky Park. We also did some souvenir shopping in the special Russian shops that were for 'tourists only'. We brought traditional fur hats with ear flaps for the girls and their husbands and a Russian teapot for my mum, complete with Russian tea. We also made some new friends - with a lovely couple called Pat and Peter Toch. We had seen Pat around at the regattas back at home but had never spoken to her much before. Her daughter Joanna was competing in the GB women's Coxed Fours with Belinda Holmes, Kate Panter, and Jane Cross.*

*Steve made some good friends too during this week - with rowing buddies Adam Clift, who had finished 6th in the double sculls and Paul Wensley, who was in the eight and had finished third taking the bronze. At the closing ceremony the flags were lowered and speeches were made with the promise to meet again the following year at Hazewinkle in Belgium where the next Junior World Championships would take place. The ceremony was rounded off with Russian Cossack dancers, dancing girls wearing traditional Russian costumes and with loud bands playing accompanied by very unusual dancing bears- it was quite spectacular. The following day we returned to England on the same flight as the team. I felt that although Steve had been disappointed with his World Championship debut he also realised that he had gained invaluable international experience. There would always be next year.*

*Back home in Marlow Steve started on another years training schedule. We looked back over the last few weeks and mulled over what turmoil of emotion and heartache he had endured with Bill's death. All we could do was to be there to support him. We also realised that his début International rowing experience had been character building and would give him the determination to do better next time. I once read "Challenge enriches our lives and builds our character", and I think that in Steve's case, this had been true.*

*With the 1980 Olympics coming up the following year Mike Spracklen decided to start a sculling squad - to be run from his home on the river in Marlow. Ann Spracklen, Mike's wife, really deserved a medal for her part in this as having these great big lads roaming about your garden all day, eating you out of house and home, takes a bit of putting up with. But for the people who are dedicated to their sport and their supporting partners no sacrifice seems to be too great.*

*Mike's intention was to coach Steve and Adam Clift in a double scull to compete at the 1980 Junior World Championships in Belgium. He also wanted to build them into a quad for the 1980 Olympics in Moscow. With little chance of attaining an Olympic medal place at this point in their sculling career this entry would mainly be for them to gain experience at this level of competition in preparation for future events. Still, it was very unusual for a junior to compete in senior events in the same year, so with the goal of both events driving them on, the boy's training became very intense.*

*The boys would come home from their training sessions totally worn out and I worried a lot at the time that Steve was doing too much but his comment to me, as always, would be, "Don't be stupid mother". Rochdale was Adam's home, in the North of England, so he had made the considerable commitment to move south to live and to train. During this first year in the South he shared a flat with a chap in Hazlemere, near High Wycombe.*

Adam and Steve gelled so well together in the boat. They had a similar technique and they were close in height and weight so this combination really made their double scull move well. Their synchronisation was a real pleasure to watch. Their first test together in a double scull event was at the 1980 Marlow Regatta in June and they won this event convincingly.

Two weeks later came their first Henley Royal Regatta. This unique and most prestigious regatta is run over the first weekend in July where the events are raced in head-to-head knock out competitions. In 1967 moving pontoons were introduced at the start. This allowed all boats, from singles through to eights, to be aligned by the bows, precisely on the start line, so that all crews would race a course of exactly one mile and 550 yards from Temple Island upstream towards Henley Bridge. Adam and Steve entered the Double Sculls Challenge Cup.

There was great excitement as they geared up hopefully to try and take their first Henley medal- but there was a fly in the ointment. The Russians had invaded Afghanistan that year and due to this action a lot of western governments had decided to boycott the Russian Olympics. At this point Britain had not made a firm decision whether to attend or not. Many of the top rowing athletes from the boycotting countries were putting in entries for Henley this year instead, as they now wouldn't now be allowed to compete at the Olympics. The history was that Henley Regatta had always ranked alongside the best rowing events in the world. In an Olympic year the Olympic event is usually held in August or September and it's not normally considered prudent, in a disciplined build up, for a prospective Olympian to also schedule an appearance at Henley Royal Regatta. The events are too close together in the rowing calendar. However this year there would be almighty competition for our lads to contend with. Nevertheless they seemed well prepared for the challenge - both physically and mentally.

The family had managed to get tickets for The Stewards' enclosure which is situated on the Berkshire side of the river adjacent to the last part of the course and the finish line. It is only open to the Stewards of the Regatta and to members and their guests and comprises of two covered grandstands, a restaurant marquee for lunch and afternoon tea, and several bars selling Pimms and Champagne. There is also a small bandstand, where each year a military band plays delightful summer background music. All this is set *on immaculately prepared lawns running like carpets, down to the river's edge. There is also a very strict dress code. Men are required to wear a "lounge suit, blazer and flannels, or evening dress, and a tie". Women are required to wear a dress or skirt that covers their knees. Both of these rules are strictly enforced by the posting of several security gatemen stationed at the enclosure entrance.*

*Over the years I have seen many very attractive ladies in their 'Ascot-like' outfits turned away at the entrance because their dress or skirt was slightly above the knee but the men and boys never seemed to have any trouble wearing their ill-fitting old school jackets and faded school caps. That's tradition I guess.*

*Their competition in the double sculls event at Henley came in the form of the American and Canadian crews. Steve and Adam won in their heats on Thursday and Friday but on Saturday they lost to the American double by one and three quarter lengths. It was really a very good show against such senior opposition, but it was no consolation to them - in fact Adam went missing for a few hours until he could come to terms with their defeat.*

*Further disappointment was still to come in the shape of a British boycott of the 1980 Olympics. Prime Minister, Margaret Thatcher, said that she would not prevent British teams from entering the Olympics but that all government financial aid would be withheld so it would now be up to individual athletic bodies to support their own teams. The outcome of this was that (for British Rowing) only crews with medal potential could be funded. As Steve's quad was new and also, up till now untried, they weren't selected to go. Of course they were very upset but at least they had the Junior World Championships to look forward to - some of the others didn't have anything. It takes a good four years to prepare an athlete for an Olympic Games so it is very hard indeed to be told at the last minute, that you can not compete. In lots of cases that particular Olympics may have been a competitor's only ever chance to compete at that level. Personally, I think it was a very sad outcome for the affected athletes and that it had been very wrong to mix politics with sport. In my humble opinion sport brings nations together - politics seem only to divide.*

*From 13th -17th August 1980 Hazewinkle in Belgium was the venue for the Junior World Championships. The Junior World Championship is open to rowers who are 18 or younger by the end of that current calendar year and Steve and Adam were strong favourites for a medal. Clive Pope from Steve's old school crew had also been selected to row in the coxed four and Belinda Holmes and Kate Panter were rowing in the women's pair- so Great Britain had plenty of interest in this event.*

*On this occasion our daughter Jane decided to come with us to support Steve. We travelled by car and ferry to Zeebrugge, driving on to our accommodation which had been pre-booked in Mechelen which is a town near to the course. Our hotel in Mechelen turned out to be very third rate. When we checked into our room we found that it was in a very dirty condition. We even found fleas in the bed so we beat a hasty retreat feeling rather itchy. Jane and I thought it was hilarious but Geoff had not been so amused as he had to lug all of our cases up and down four very steep flights of stairs. By this time though it was getting very late and as there were no other hotel rooms to be had, we ended up sleeping the night in the car. During the night Jane got really hot, so she opened the car window and unknowingly, let in a swarm of mosquitoes. We all suffered from lots of bites and I had so many that I had to visit the chemist to get some antihistamine cream to treat them with. I'm glad to say, that the next day we found a very nice hotel in Antwerp. We made sure we thoroughly sprayed the room every night- just in case.*

*The first day of racing went well with Steve and Adam winning their heat. They also went on to win their semi-final the following day too. They were really enjoying the whole event. Two Russian girls had given them woolly hats which they wore every time they went out training. The atmosphere there was great with music being played everywhere in the enclosure. The song that seemed to be played the most was Abba's "The winner takes it all". We hoped that this was a good omen and could later become the boy's personal anthem.*

*Whilst riding his bike along the bank during a training outing with Steve and Adam, their coach Mike Spracklen, had an accident. He collided with another coach and they both ended up in a heap on the ground. Mike hit his head and was knocked unconscious. His injuries were quite serious and he had to be taken to hospital where he was kept in for a few days. During those few days someone else had to take over coaching Steve and Adam. Ann Spracklen (Mike's wife) and their two boys were camping on the course site and in their rush to get to the hospital to see Mike she hit the gatepost of the campsite with their car. Thank goodness she didn't do too much damage but chaos reigned for a while. Ann coped very well with things and a few days later Mike came out of hospital in time for our boys final. Unfortunately all he could do was to just sit and watch.*

*The race was very exciting and the boys went into the lead off the start going very fast over the first 500m. They then dropped their rate and settled to a steady pace. At the 1000m. mark they were overtaken by the Russians and East Germans but they stayed in contention and made a magnificent push with 500m to go. They pushed the Russians back to third crossing the line in second place, only losing to the East Germans by just 0:75second. This gave Adam and Steve the silver medal but later, when they came to the rostrum to collect their medals, I don't think anyone had ever seen two more dejected silver medallists. But our boys had done extremely well and it didn't take them too long to realise their considerable achievement. With their junior years now over, and with more hard winter training ahead of them, they now set their sights on making the senior team the following year.*

*The three of us now headed home. We'd had a wonderful time and, as Steve's parents we were really happy in the knowledge that now our son had achieved his first Junior World Medal. We had a good journey back, until we got to about 30kms from Zeebrugge ferry port. There we joined a long queue of vehicles waiting to make the ferry crossing. The French were on strike and all of their ports were blockaded so all ferry passengers and vehicles heading for Dover had travelled further up the coast to the Belgium ports to try to make the sea crossing there. The queues were also made worse by the fact that it was the end of the summer holidays and many holidaymakers were rushing home to get their kids back for the beginning of the school year.*

*We had pre-booked our ferry for 3pm that afternoon but with this enormous length of queue that deadline was an impossible one to meet. In the end, we finally got on board a ferry at 7.30am the following morning. Jane had phoned her husband David to let everyone at home know that we'd been held up and we steeled ourselves for yet another night sleeping in the car.*

*What a trip!*

*Back in Britain there had been no television coverage of the event (as per usual)- just a few newspaper reports, so we had a lot to tell family and friends. The local press was an exception though and carried a big article on the boys including a photo of Steve and Adam standing side by side holding their oars upright in each hand. The way the photo had been taken made them look as if they were standing behind bars. We still often have a laugh about that photo.*

*We looked ahead and thought about their senior years to come. There wouldn't be so many lovely river regattas for us to visit now. It would be a serious business for the boys from here on with hard training and even tougher competition. We could only wait and see what 1981 would bring.*

# Chapter Two
## The Senior Years

### *Onward and Upward*

My thoughts came back to my surroundings as the hostess served us with our lunch. I checked my watch and noted that we were about an hour into the flight. Good grief, I thought, the last hour had gone so fast. Our chicken salad lunch arrived and we tucked in. Geoff and I chatted about this and that but mostly about our granddaughters whom we would be looking after in Atlanta. Natalie was 5 years old now and little Sophie was just 2 ½; they were Steve and Ann's little girls. Ann, being the rowing team doctor, would be staying full time in the Olympic Village with the athletes and so we had agreed to have the girls stay with us during the Games. We really enjoyed taking care of them; it was always great fun but I just wished that Ben and Steph, our other two grandchildren, could have been with us as well. It would have been lovely to have all been together again as we had been in Barcelona for the Olympics four years before. After drinking two cups of coffee each, we stretched out our legs and settled down again, Geoff to read his book, ironically called "Favourite Son" by Steve Sohmer while I returned to my memories. Ah yes, the year was now 1981.

*The World Rowing Championship in 1981 was to be held in Munich, Germany. After the disappointment of not being able to go to the Olympics in 1980 there was now some good news for Steve; the selectors had made a decision to send some of the younger squad members to The World Championships. A new crew would be put together with Eric Sims, Julian Scrivener, Adam Clift and Steve, all good scullers with International potential. They would compete in a quadruple sculling boat, a 'Quad'.*

*Julian and Adam had moved into our home in Marlow Bottom so that they could be closer to the daily training venue at Mike's house on the river in Marlow. The arrangement worked out well for everyone and it was a pleasure for us too as they were such nice lads to have around. Eric lived in Maidenhead, so he hadn't got so far to travel and now their coach, Mike Spracklen, was back to full health after his cycle accident in Belgium.*

*Their sculling year started at the end of 1980 with the boys entering some singles and some doubles events. In November the quad was entered in the 'Head of the River Fours', a processional race held on a stretch of the tidal River Thames known as the "Tideway". It is run over the Championship course (the Oxford vs. Cambridge University Boat Race course), but in the opposite direction from Mortlake to Putney, a distance of $4\,{}^1/_4$ miles. Each crew is timed over the course, and boats are started closely one behind the other. Being one of the largest single rowing events in the UK and with more than 500 crews entering, the whole 'finely tuned' event takes just $1\,{}^1/_2$ hours from the first crew starting to the last crew finishing. There was great excitement when the final 'time' results came in and it was announced that our boys had won.*

*At Henley Royal Regatta in July 1981 Steve and Eric entered the Double Sculls Challenge Cup which they won in 8:16, verdict, easily. The quad entered the Queen Mother Challenge Cup but lost in their final to the World Champions from Germany. This was a decent result for the boys though, as it would have been a tall order for the newly formed quad to have beaten this particular German crew, RV Ingelheim & Ulm RC Donau, who had been World and Olympic champions for some years.*

*The Henley prizes that year were presented to the winners by Princess Grace of Monaco, a truly lovely lady, perhaps better known as the film star, Grace Kelly. Her father and brother had both been scullers and her brother had won the Diamond Sculls at Henley some years before, so Princess Grace was no stranger to rowing. It was such a pleasure to see Steve and Eric receive their Henley medals from her.*

*Geoff had brought a V.W. camper this year so we were going to Munich and to the World Championships in style; no more sleeping in cars. We had a great trip out there and enjoyed every minute travelling by ferry from Dover*

23

to Calais and then driving through France, Luxembourg and Germany to Munich. On our arrival we found a campsite and to our surprise soon met another family from Marlow. Jenny Pilgrim Morris, who was camping with her two children. Her husband John was out there coaching Chris Baillieu, our British sculler. We also met up with Pat Toch and her son Mark who had come to support her daughter Joanna, who was in the British women's eight. Our rowing friends Moira and Pat Cross, who were supporting their son Martin, arrived at the campsite a few days later.

The rowing course was excellent. It had been a previous Olympic course so had very good grandstands from which to view the racing. A marquee had been erected, which housed a German Beer Keller, and each day after racing traditional music was played. We particularly enjoyed the 'Umpar' bands that would often play the Birdie Song. It was great fun watching the crowds, singing along and doing all the actions. The beer was served to us in large two litre steins which we could hardly lift and would last us for hours. The beer went down well with accompanying large salty pretzels or some bratwursts and brot (German Sausage and bread); a merry time was had by all.

I had previously visited Munich when, many years before, I had come on a European tour with my American sister in law, Nadine. I remembered I had been very impressed with the wonderful clock on Munich City Hall. Every day at 11am, noon and at 5pm the, brightly painted, almost life-size, Bavarian figures of the Glockenspiel would re-enact two events in Munich's history: a royal marriage and the celebrating of the passing of the plague. These lovely little figures would appear and do a little mechanical twirl and travel back inside the clock. It was like a giant music box. At 9pm each evening, and whilst the clock is specially lit, the little monk is led to bed by the night watchman and the Angel of Peace whilst the 43 bells of the clock, which weigh about 7,000 kilos, strike up and play a lullaby. It's quite remarkable seeing the crowds of tourists gathering in the street just waiting for the clock to strike. On a trip into the city this time, I went to see it again and I found it to be just as charming as before.

Munich had been the venue for the 1972 Olympic Games and at that time the city had erected a marquee made from metal and glass; this was quite spectacular. The shops were really interesting too and there were small cafes

24

*selling gorgeous cream cakes. Of course there were plenty of Bavarian Beer Kellers too with heavy carved wooden chairs and tables, decked with colourful beer tankards and the waitresses, dressed in traditional costume. There was so much to see, beautiful statues, and many museums but unfortunately this marvellous city will always be remembered for the dreadful terrorist attack known as the 'Munich massacre' at the 1972 Summer Olympics and the killing of the eleven Israeli athletes by a group of eight Palestinian terrorists belonging to the militant group Black September.*

*While we were here we also visited Dachau, the World War II concentration camp. This was something I would never forget and I prayed that atrocities like this would never happen again. The guide told us that no birds fly over or settle there. I found this to be quite strange because the site was not far away from open countryside and I could see lots of birds flying there. How could one ever explain that?*

*Back at the rowing, the quad didn't do too well in their heat and so they went into the repechage but this race they won, putting them through to the semi final. In these Semi-finals, they only qualified for what is called the Petite Final to decide places 7 to 12. In this very hard fought final race they finished second giving them eighth place overall; not a bad result but as one might say 'back to the drawing board'. The end of Championship party gave the boys a chance to relax and to let their hair down a little after their hard work and they all seemed to enjoy themselves.*

*We went back to the campsite to pack up and say goodbye to our friends until the next year. Also we said our farewell to the field mice that had plagued everyone; they had come from the field next door into the campsite. I don't think anyone got away without a visit from them, either by accidentally running them over at night as they suddenly scampered across the road or having the food in their tents eaten by the little devils. We found one sitting in our frying pan but he was out of luck; it was empty. Our journey home this year was thankfully uneventful. We were giving a lift to a rower, who lived in the south of England and so we drove home non-stop. Our VW camper though was deemed to have been a great success.*

*Once back home and after telling our story to the rest of the family, for us it was back to work. There was some deliberation, by the powers that be, as to whether the quad in it's present form should be disbanded, but in the end it was decided to give them another year together but still to work on the principle of hard winter sculling training in all boats; singles and doubles as well as the quad. This they did, and they entered most of the Heads that winter/spring season with great success.*

*Henley Royal Regatta in July1982, this time, saw Steve and Adam enter the Double Sculls. They also sculled in the quad in the Queen Mother Challenge Cup with Eric Sims, but this time replacing Julian Scrivener with Martin Cross. In the double sculls heat on Friday, Steve and Adam broke the record to the barrier, a record which they held for over sixteen years. They won again in this boat, both on Saturday and by 3 ½ lengths in the final on Sunday in a time of 7:55. On Sunday, the quad had only to row once as there had been only one other entry and they won this race in 6:57, verdict easily, equalling the course record. The boys were as pleased as punch as this year every one of them went away with a Henley medal.*

*Lucerne, Switzerland was the venue for the 1982 World Championships. The rowing course is just outside the city on Lake Rotsee (The Red Lake). It is reputed to be the fairest natural rowing lake in Europe due to there being virtually no current and with its high bank of hills on one side shielding the course from the prevailing winds. Its length of 2400m also makes it an ideal international rowing venue. It is a really beautiful setting in unspoilt natural surroundings. The first regatta was hosted there in 1933 and it's since been the venue of a large number of international rowing events including the first ever World Rowing Championships in 1962.*

*Lucerne, which nestles on the shores of Lake Lucerne, is a beautiful city straddling the River Reuss with its famous Kapellbrücke (Chapel Bridge) the wonderful 14th century wooden bridge, the oldest in Europe. This is 670ft long and is completely covered in and has intricately carved archways. The beautiful ceilings inside the bridge were painted during the 16th century with scenes depicting Lucerne's history. All along the outside of the bridge is decked with wooden flower boxes, on both sides, full of brightly coloured geraniums. In fact, during the summer the whole town is full of flowers display with tubs and hanging baskets. During the evening, the quaint little squares all offer something different for the tourists, with buskers, fire eaters, small circuses, children's carousels and lively pavement cafes full of people. An attraction in one of the squares is a large chess board marked out on the pavement with stone chessmen about three feet high. We stayed at the campsite on the lake called the Lido and in the evening we would stroll through the street enjoying the atmosphere and the boys could always be found at the ice cream parlour just by the bridge sampling the fare.*

*This year our daughter Christine came with us, we travelled in convoy, in our camper and Steve's car. Steve wanted his car brought out to him as directly after the Championships were over, he and Belinda, his girlfriend, had planned to have a holiday driving to the south of France. They were going to stay with Sophie Ray, a friend of the family and formerly one of the many French language students who had stayed with us, during the summer school holidays at our family home in Marlow.*

*There were to be two changes made to the crew for Lucerne, Martin Cross and Alan Whitwell. Both of these men had a great deal of international experience and were to join the quad. Alan took the bow seat and Martin the stroke seat with Steve and Adam the powerhouse in the middle of the boat. They did well through the heats and went on through the repechage to the final.*

*We watched the rowing each day but also took time out to visit some places of interest. One afternoon we made a trip to Mount Pilatus. The mountain is named after a local legend which alleges that Pontius Pilate was buried there. We ascended by the world's steepest cogwheel railway and from the top the views were breathtaking. We walked down part of the way seeing lots of wild flowers, including edelweiss and then took the cable car to the bottom. We spent another afternoon on a cruise boat on Lake Lucerne calling at lakeside villages. We stopped for lunch at one of these villages; the restaurant was very quaint with heavy carved tables and a view which overlooked the lake. In a large tank on view were live fish and lobsters on which one could choose to lunch. I was glad I didn't like fish and it rather put me off swimming in the lake too.*

*It was finals day at the rowing, and all of us spectators were getting nervous. The Coxed Four finished 5th, the Coxless Pair 12th, the Single Scull 6th and the Coxless Four came in 9th. Now it was our boy's race in the Quad but it was not to be the result they had hoped for. They were not able to hold off the field in the second half of the race and so they had finished in 6th place; up two places on last year. They were moving in the right direction but were still not quite good enough. Yet another year was put down to experience gained. Our congratulations went to Alan Whitwell as while he was rowing out in Lucerne with the quad, his wife had given birth to a little girl back home in England; this showed the sort of dedication required from athletes at this level. We made our way back home to tell our tale to the rest of the family.*

*The idea of a Quad was given up and Steve decided that in 1983 he would try his hand in a single scull; a very different task to say the least. During the latter two years he had mostly been sculling in one boat or another but after training for all that time in a group; he now had to train on his own. Now, as a lone athlete and without the support of his fellow crew members, he would need a good deal of self motivation; this would not be an easy transition but Steve made a good start in the winter/spring Heads.*

*At Marlow regatta in June 1983 he won the Elite Sculls and he also won the Single Sculls at Nottingham International Regatta. His confidence was running high as he entered The Diamond Sculls in July at Henley Royal Regatta. He won on Thursday, Friday and Saturday and then he met Tim Crooks in the final on Sunday. Tim, much older than Steve, had always been one of his rowing idols and although Steve had met him at three other regattas that season, and beaten him each time, he still held a great deal of respect for him. Steve led the race all the way but in front of the Fawley stand Tim stopped sculling. Steve was so shocked that he stopped sculling as well seeing Tim slumped over his sculls clearly exhausted. Tim then noticed that Steve had stopped and, thinking that Steve had 'blown up' and was completely worn out too, gathered himself up and with a great pull on his sculls set off at a great rate of knots. Everyone was up on their feet shouting and waving, but Steve had seen him and just set off once again, picking up speed and winning by two and 2/3 lengths. Steve had taken his first Henley Diamond Sculls medal.*

*A few weeks later Steve won the Sculls at the National Championships and was then selected to scull at the 1983 World Championships in Duisburg, Germany. Belinda, his girlfriend, wasn't rowing this year so we took her and her sister Melanie with us as spectators. We also took a member of the younger school crew, Scott Poppy, who after the regatta was going to stay with his grandmother in Hamburg. The girls and Scott had tents which they stayed in on the rowing course's temporary campsite, where I must say, the facilities could have been better. Although the viewing stands were very good, the course was however, quite unfair in some lanes even when the slightest wind was blowing.*

*With the exception of our Coxed Four, who finished in 6<sup>th</sup> place, no other British heavyweight crew, men or women, made a final. Steve was unplaced getting knocked out in the repechage, as were the Double Sculls and the Coxless Pair. The only light on the British horizon was John Melvin, our lightweight sculler, who had a really good row, taking a silver medal, and the Lightweight Coxless Four, who took silver too. 1983 had not been a good year for British men's rowing.*

*We didn't get to see much of Duisburg on this trip, what with the course being out of the city. We just visited a few local shops for our groceries. I do remember a large football and athletics stadium where they put on the best firework display we had ever seen but it was soon all over for yet another year and we made our journey home. Needless to say, Steve was very disappointed with this result, and we knew that he would have some hard work to do to prove his worth for the 1984 Olympics. So, as soon as we arrived back home he and Mike got down to some hard winter training. He competed at the Heads again this season and joined the squad system which meant Steve's training would entail working against the clock and racing the other bigger boats.*

*At the beginning of 1984 Steve decided he needed a new sculling boat as he was outgrowing his present one. He wanted a racing shell made in Zurich by Stampfli, the well respected Swiss manufacturer whose exquisite wooden boats enjoyed great international success and were exported throughout the world. These boats were owned by most of the rowing elite, including Steve's rowing idol Pertti Karpinnen from Finland, who was probably one of the most successful single scullers in the history of the sport. The new boat was to be a hand crafted cedar single racing shell and was ordered, made-to-measure, to suit Steve's weight and height; we were told that it would be ready for him in March. This tied in nicely with the training camp that was planned on being held during the spring in Piediluco in Italy, and so it was decided to collect the new boat from Switzerland on the way out to Italy.*

*Mike was in charge of this training camp and flew out to Italy with the team. Steve and Geoff were to first drive the VW camper through France and Germany then onto Switzerland to pick up the new boat from Stampfli. Geoff had bought a small trailer which he attached to the camper to encompass the boat overhang when it was tied on the camper roof. Vehicle law on the continent allowed only a certain amount of overhang, so attaching the trailer would help get over the problem. They set off in quite cold and rather frosty weather to catch a night ferry from Dover and their journey went well through France. While travelling on the German motorway they were pulled over by the police for speeding. They were not aware that a very low speed limit was in force for trailers. It was an 'on the spot' fine of £22 but after some explanation the policeman phoned in to get advice from his superiors and the fine was reduced by half.*

*They continued their journey at a much reduced speed,, and they arrived in Zurich in the late evening and camped for the night in the Stampfli boat builder's yard. On waking next morning to their surprise they saw Pertti Karpinnen the world's number one sculler, twice Olympic gold medallist and Steve's sporting idol. He too was there collecting his new Stampfli boat and so Geoff decided that we had made a wise choice, even though it had been a very expensive one. Steve and his dad spent a very interesting day watching the boat building process from start to finish. Steve took his new boat out for a spin on the lake to try it, in case any adjustments were necessary but he was quite sure it was 'the bee's knees' when they eventually loaded it onto the camper.*

*Leaving Zurich quite late and taking turns at driving, they arrived at the St. Gotthard Pass at midnight. It was snowing and freezing cold and while getting out, swapping driving positions, they found that they could not close the doors again; the door locks had frozen open. They were forced to drive on with rope holding the doors shut until the locks had thawed out. Once out of the tunnel, the road descended to the Italian border. They then made a stop to try and get some sleep as they were both by now feeling exhausted and probably suffering from hyperthermia. It was so cold that they couldn't get at all comfortable so they decided after a short rest to drive on to Italy.*

At the Italian border they hit another problem; this time to do with the boat's overhang. After much deliberation, and with over an hour of arguing between themselves, the Italian police, who it was noted were sporting side arms, reluctantly allowed them to continue their journey.

The rest of the journey went without further mishap and with the weather thankfully now turning warmer; they drove around the outskirts of Rome and on to Piediluco about 57 km further south. On their arrival they found the hotel where Mike and the rest of the squad were staying. Steve booked into the hotel and Geoff found a parking space for the camper that overlooked the sea and soon got his head down properly for the first time in many hours. During his stay there Geoff spent a lot of time beachcombing. The beach was Anzio Beach which had been used for the landing of our Allied Forces in the Second World War known as Operation Shingle. During February 1944 the ensuing four-month battle saw American forces (5th Army) surrounded by Germans and suffering heavy casualties. There is a 1968 movie called Anzio about this battle which stars, Robert Mitchum, who is my 'all time' favorite movie star.

The training camp went well and Steve had plenty of opportunity to get used to his new boat. He won a regatta while he was out there and he was presented with a very large cup and a Panettone cake; they brought me a piece home but I'm afraid to say that it was a bit stale by then. On the journey home they encountered some very high winds on the motorway in the south of France which worryingly buffeted the vehicle and trailer about. With their precious cargo of the new and expensive boat tied to the roof, it all got a bit hair- raising so I think they were very pleased to get it home in one piece.

The Manheim regatta came next at the end of April, and this time Steve flew out to Germany with the team. Geoff travelled out with the VW camper, but this time he did not have to transport Steve's boat, as it gone out on the team trailer along with the other boats. In this run up to the Olympics, the selectors, were still trying out various combinations of crew in a variety of boats and because of this Steve was told that he could enter the single sculls on the Saturday but that on Sunday he would be required to take a seat in the coxed four.

*In Saturday's sculling race, Steve came third, with Peter-Michael Kolbe of Germany coming first, and Pertti Karpinnen of Finland second. It was great competition for Steve, to be up there with the 'big guns', sculling against these two top internationals, who were known as the best scullers in the world. The British coxed four won their race on Saturday, so as they had performed so well Steve thought that the national coaches wouldn't now be asking him to replace one of the crew on Sunday and he began to feel that his sculling slot would be safe. It was not to be, it was decided later that day by 'the powers that be' to include Steve in the coxed four and to ignore the single sculling event altogether. The Coxed four, with Steve included, convincingly won their race on Sunday. Their time was an incredible seven seconds faster than the day before.*

*A meeting was called by the British Rowing officials, and Steven was asked to permanently join the coxed four to train for the 1984 Los Angeles Olympics. He was told that with him in the boat, there was a very good chance of winning a gold medal. Going by his times at Manheim, if he stayed in the sculling boat, he would, at best, just make the Olympic final or that possibly, with the eastern countries boycotting the American games, there could be an outside chance of a bronze medal. Of course nothing was certain but the officials felt strongly that Britain's best chance of Olympic Gold was with the coxed four and with Steve as part of the crew.*

*Steve had a career defining decision to make and had only been given a few days in which to make up his mind. We could not advise him what to do, we discussed it with him of course but this had to be his own decision. He discussed it with Mike too and mulled it over and a few days later, his decision made, he officially joined the coxed four. I think that in the end, he had felt that he was still young enough to scull at the next Olympics. He was still only 22 years old and was getting stronger and more experienced with each passing year. Time was on his side.*

# Chapter Three
## The 1984 Los Angeles Olympic Games

### *The Unlikely Lads*

*Mike Spracklen became the official British coach to the coxed four and a new crew was put together. This consisted of Martin Cross rowing in bow position, Richard Budgett taking 3 seat, Andrew (Andy) Holmes rowing at 2, Steve was to stroke the boat and Adrian Ellison was to be their coxswain. Their training became even more intense. They all agreed to make Thorpe Park their daily training venue so that all the boys had a similar distance to travel. Steve was now back to rowing with avengance. Just for a while at least, he would put his sculling career on ice.*

*At Henley Regatta the new crew entered the Prince Philip Challenge Cup. There was only one other entry, a Dutch crew from Njord rowing club so there was just one race for them on Sunday. They beat the Dutch in 7:01 with a verdict of 'easily' but on that day, they raised some eyebrows by rowing the race wearing T-shirts with the words "The Unlikely Lads " printed on the back; this was frowned upon by the officials, as normally only club colours should be worn when competing at Henley. Their reason for this unusual display was that a few days earlier, The Sunday Times newspaper had dubbed them with this title in one of its rowing articles. I recall that the piece had something to do with Steve's supposed reluctance to join the boat. I would describe it more, as his carefully considered decision, but I think that all the crew quite liked this slightly rebellious moniker.*

*A week later it was Lucerne International Regatta. This was the last Pre-Olympic competition, and a chance for our crew to come 'face to face' with their likely Olympic opponents. All the crews were there with the exception of New Zealand, the current world champions. Hiding their light under a bushel, they had gone directly to the U.S.A for their training camp, with the rest of their team. With New Zealand out of the picture their opposition at Lucerne would now come from the East Germans. Our lads won their event without any problems, and very convincingly too, breaking the Lucerne Rotsee record; the East German crew came second and the Americans were third. We missed seeing their victory as Geoff and I couldn't go to Lucerne because of work commitments and what with our trip to the States coming so soon afterwards there just hadn't been the time.*

*The team left for America shortly after the Lucerne Regatta for their Olympic training camp in San Diego, where they would have a chance to get used to the time change and the different climate. During the next few weeks we caught glimpses of them once or twice, on the TV, during sports news reports, and it was comforting to know that they were in good health and coping well with the pre-games build up.*

*Adam had been selected to row in the eight with Alan Whitwell, and John Beatie and Richard Stanhope were in the pair. John Clift, Adam's younger brother, was rowing in the coxless four. We also knew most of the girls in the women's crews. Steve's girlfriend, Belinda, was in the eight with Martin's girlfriend, Ann Callaway, and Joanna Toch was rowing in the coxed fours. It was going to be very interesting and great fun for us to follow their progress and offer our support to all our young rowing friends.*

*Geoff and I collected our tickets from Sports World Travel. We had not taken their package deal but opted instead for 'tickets only'. This meant that our event tickets were quite a mixed bunch really, with some seated and some standing places, but at least we had tickets for every day including the Olympic rowing final. Our plan was to hire a camper from a company called 'Caravan Abroad' and obtain our air tickets through them. Looking back I remember these particular Olympics so clearly, most probably because it was our first experience of attending such a large sporting event and it was our son's first attempt at an Olympic Medal; the ultimate achievement, as he saw it, and the one that he'd always dreamed of.*

*Our flight to America was on the 24th July from Heathrow, departure time 12.15pm. Christine and Philip drove us to the airport; they were as excited as we were. They were not joining us on this trip as they were holding the fort, taking care of the business. They had also offered to keep a record of the event by videoing anything that may appear on the TV and were also intending to collect all the daily newspaper reports on the rowing. They would also be keeping an eye on Ada, my mother, who was being looked after by my brother, Brian, who had come down from Newcastle especially. My mother could only just about walk with the aid of a walking frame and therefore needed constant help.*

*Christine and Philip dropped us outside the Heathrow Departures entrance. We loaded our cases onto a luggage trolley and said our tearful goodbyes, waving to them till they were out of sight. After finding the Trans World Airline desk and checking in our suitcases, we took our hand luggage and went to look around the airport shops. We had a cup of coffee and a bite to eat and waited for our flight to be called. I remember how excited we both felt as we boarded our flight to Los Angeles; although this wasn't our first trip to the States.*

*In the 60's we had taken a 'part business, part pleasure trip' to The States to visit Geoff's brother Bill who had married a lovely American girl called Nadine, and they had settled in Florida some years before. During our time away, Christine and Jane had gone away with their school to South Germany for a holiday and Steve, who was still quite young then, had stayed at home with my mom and dad. It had been an interesting trip for us taking in New York for three days on the way out, and Washington and Bermuda on the return leg.*

*We had stayed for ten days in Florida with Bill and Nadine and their kids Denise and Bryan, and then visited South Carolina, flying into Atlanta for a couple of days to stay with the family of our friends, Bill and Betty Cline. Bill Cline was serving at that time, with the United States Air Force in the UK based at Daws Hill near High Wycombe and we had become good friends. At the airport we had been met by Betty's family, who had a farm on the outskirts of Hickory, and were kindly hosting our stay. During our stay, we also visited Bill Cline's family, who lived nearby, a very interesting family of Native American descent. We really enjoyed our weekend together; I particularly remember having lunch at Betty's mother's farm and eating unusual things like sweet potato pie and grits. They were very taken with the way we ate using both a knife and fork, as the majority of Americans use their fork to eat with, and their knife only for cutting their food. I remembered we smiled when Betty's mother said in her thick southern drawl "My old Daddy could eat like that, I never got the hang of it myself".*

*This time, our flight to Los Angeles had taken eleven hours and during this time I had watched the latest James Bond film "Octopussy". On landing we went directly to immigration and joined one of the long queues that are quite normal when entering the States. Once through we took a taxi to our hotel and then we slept; it wasn't very late in the evening in L.A. but for our 'body clocks' it was the early hours of the morning. We had been advised by the camper hire company, that it would be best to spend our first night in the States in a hotel to enable us to get a good night sleep before driving their vehicle and that the following morning, a phone call to them would bring us some transport to their depot.*

*We woke very early the next morning and so we watched some TV, but in these early hours all that seemed to be showing were documentaries about medical problems interspersed with lots of adverts. As soon as the hotel restaurant began serving breakfast, we went down to eat. We have always enjoyed the 'American' breakfast as there is usually such a wide choice; not always healthy choices but delicious nevertheless, with lots of good coffee. Geoff went out for a walk, filming with the video camera, and I returned to the room to pack our bags and wait for the shuttle bus. A phone call told us that they would be picking us up at eleven, so we went to the hotel reception to settle the bill, and to wait in the foyer for our transport. Soon a station wagon arrived and with our cases loaded into the 'trunk', we were soon being driven through downtown LA; a very interesting journey with lots to see on route.*

*Arriving at "Caravan Abroad" and after filling in some insurance forms, we were shown over our camper; our home for the next two weeks. It was a six berth 'Winnebago' so for the two of us, it was very spacious. After a quick look at a map and a reminder to ourselves that we were driving on the opposite side of the road, we set off on our adventures. We wanted to hire a TV for the camper, but we were told it would be cheaper for us to buy one, so our first stop that day was a large electrical store where we purchased a portable black and white set which we thought would be just right for watching those Olympic events that we couldn't manage to get to. A friend of mine, who's husband was a pilot on the regular Los Angeles route, had acquired maps and all sorts of other interesting information for us, on Lake Casitas and the surrounding areas, where the rowing event was being held. So armed with our maps, we soon found the freeway and were on our way to Lake Casitas.*

*It was late evening when we arrived at the campsite and it was getting rather dark. When we found the warden he allocated us a lot, number 375, saying it was just along the road. The road was just a track and after what seemed like three miles we spotted, in the headlights ahead of us, a small white sign pointing uphill to lots 365 to 375. We climbed up hill for a while and then saw number 375 up a much steeper slope, directly ahead. Once up there the area flattened out and we parked the camper and settled down for our first night's camping USA style.*

*The next morning we awoke to a beautiful day, and only then realised just how high we had climbed the previous night. The view from this camper lot was absolutely fantastic. We were really high up with a view of the whole lake. We could see the boats out training, but from this distance, it was not clear who they were. As we ate breakfast and made our plans for the day, we discussed the possibility of changing our allotted camper lot for one closer to the lake, so we could avoid the obvious trek of walking to and from the rowing each day. Our first job was to find the warden and ask if it was at all possible to change our site, then we would find the rowing enclosure and seek out Steve and Belinda to let them know that 'the parents' had arrived.*

*Changing our site was no problem. In fact, the warden wondered why we had been allocated a site that was so far away. He found us a flat site that was next to a small inlet of the lake, close to the shower block, shop and restaurant. We decided it had been a smart move because we later found that it was still a twenty-five minute brisk walk from the new site to the Olympic rowing venue. Camping Casitas was usually a venue for what the American's term 'fish camp' and there was a large sign that read that the daily quota one was allowed to catch was 10 catfish, 7 trout and one pike. Under this it stated, "No Swimming".*

*We wandered down to the entrance of the rowing enclosure where we found security to be very strict with no one but competitors being allowed in. I asked one of the guards if we would be allowed in to see our son. He said that we would have to go to Santa Barbara University which was being used as the Olympic Village for all of the water sports competitors. He told us to ask at the reception there, and that someone would then 'go' get him for us. He also told us that the boys were bussed in to the rowing venue daily being accompanied by armed patrol cars front, back and centre. It sounded a little melodramatic to us but we were pleased that so many precautions were being taken to keep the athletes safe.*

*Arriving at the Olympic Village we went to the reception and asked to see Steve. We were told that it was going to take a while to locate him and so we were asked to take a seat while we waited. The seats were comfortable and there was plenty of literature on the various Olympic events to while away our time. The hustle and bustle of the busy reception area seemed to get a little louder so I looked up from my reading and I'm sure my mouth must have dropped open. A small group of people had arrived and the man at the centre of them, was no other than film star Robert Mitchum. I couldn't believe my eyes, as a teenager he had been my favourite movie star, so I tugged Geoff's sleeve and said, "Look that's Robert Mitchum, and I'm going to speak to him." But Geoff said, "No you are not, don't be silly," so I just sat there and watched. It seemed that even Mr Robert Charles Durman Mitchum had to have the correct documentation to enter, even though he was a 'celebrity' and had obviously been invited here to meet the athletes. In the end I made up my mind, silly or not, I would go over to speak to him but as I stood up, he finally got clearance and was taken through the gates and whisked out of my sight. I never did get chance to meet my teenage idol – he who hesitates etc.*

*A little while later we were given the necessary accreditation and were shown around the Olympic Village by a very nice young lady. While we were looking around we bumped into Steve and Belinda who had been in the launderette doing their washing, which was the reason no one had been able to find them. We had a chat and a coffee together and then Mike Spracklen and Richard Budget came along and joined us. Mike was feeling a bit down because he couldn't be with his own son, who was rowing this week in the World Junior Championships at Jönköping in Sweden. His wife Ann and their younger son had gone to support him but I understood how he must be feeling, and tried to imagine how I would have felt if I could not have been here for Steve.*

*Mike told us that the 'race draw' had taken place and that the boys were scheduled to meet all of their main opposition in their first heat. If they won this heat they would go straight to the final. Steve was quite pleased because it gave them a chance to put their 'stamp' on the race. We stayed chatting with them for about an hour and a half and then moved on to see if we could track down our friend Pat Toch who had come to support her daughter Joanna. Pat had arranged a holiday accommodation exchange, swapping her own flat on the river at Twickenham for a house here in Ventura, about twenty minutes from Casitas. She had travelled, and was sharing the house, with her friend Jackie Harwood and when we phoned it was Jackie who answered our call. She told us that they had both arrived safely but at that moment Pat was out. She also said that Pat had managed to get just one of the very rare tickets for the Olympic Opening Ceremony and that she planned to go there on her own the following day. Jackie, who hadn't been so lucky, was planning to watch the ceremony on TV and invited us to have a bite to eat and watch it with her on their big screen TV at their house. It was a very nice offer which we gladly accepted and so the following day, on Saturday 28th July, we arrived in good time at 4pm. and settled down to watch the eagerly awaited spectacular. We weren't disappointed; the Americans put on a fantastic show.*

*The Games of the XXIII Olympiad opened with an amazing and extravagant show; it seemed that no money had been spared. John Williams had composed the theme for the Olympiad which was called "Olympic Fanfare and Theme". This piece later won him a Grammy award, and has since become one of the most well-known musical themes of the Olympic Games. There were eighty-four grand pianos playing Gershwin melodies, and a choir of several hundred voices assembled from singers from the region; these choir members were volunteers from nearby churches, schools and universities. There were a variety of dancing girls and thousands of balloons were released and later white doves - the symbol of peace. Hundreds of young athletes came into the arena and stood together to form the word "Welcome" and when decathlete Rafer Johnson lit the Olympic flame, it passed through the five Olympic rings on its way to the cauldron. The Games were then officially opened by the U.S President, Ronald Reagan. Geoff was especially fascinated by the man in a spacesuit wearing a jetpack on his back, who swooped down and landed in the stadium. All of it was wonderful, the television coverage was first class but I really wished that we could have been in the stadium to have seen it live. We left Jackie after the show and returned to the campsite; Jackie and Pat had both arranged to come to the camper to see us the following day.*

*In response to the American-led boycott of the 1980 Summer Olympics in Moscow, 14 Eastern Bloc countries and allies including the Soviet Union, Cuba and East Germany (but not Romania) boycotted the Los Angeles 1984 Games. For differing reasons, Iran and Libya also boycotted. LA was the only city that had submitted a bid to host the 1984 Summer Olympics; the only other interested city, Tehran, declined to bid. Many blamed this on the massive cost overruns of the 1976 Games that had been staged in Montreal. The Los Angeles Olympic Organizing Committee relied heavily on the use of area venues that were already in existence, resulting in low construction costs, and this, coupled with a heavy reliance on private corporate funding, allowed the Games to generate a profit of more than $200 million, making them by far the most financially successful in history so far.*

*On Sunday we woke up to yet another lovely day, the sun was coming up over the edge of the lake and streaming through our camper windows; it was gorgeous. After breakfast we walked down to the water edge to watch the boys training and then wandered back to our camper where we met our neighbours. They were a young couple called Kay and Fred Pisch, who were camping out at Lake Casitas with their two children, while waiting for their new house to be built on the outskirts of LA. We stood in the sun talking with them for about half an hour and when we got inside the camper we discovered that we had caught the sun quite badly as we hadn't been wearing any sunscreen. Thank goodness I had bought some after sun lotion with me, but we vowed that we would be more careful in future.*

*Steve dropped by the camper later that afternoon to tell us that the rowing would be starting early the next day. He told us that his race was scheduled for 8am and that all rowing had to be over by 10.30am due to the strong winds that blew up at that time every day which then made the course very unfair. He said that the crew were all in good spirits and looking forward to getting the show on the road.*

*Pat and Jackie came over, it was nice to see Pat again as we hadn't seen each other for a few months. We talked about rowing and mostly about the Opening Ceremony and how wonderful it had been. She told us that her husband Peter would be arriving in California soon. We all wondered where Pat and Moira Cross, Martin's mum and dad, had got to, as with the boy's race tomorrow, it was expected that they would have arrived by this time. After we had eaten an early supper Pat and Jackie went home as we all had to make an early start in the morning.*

*Even at 6am on Monday morning the weather was grand. We ate our breakfast in the sunshine, this time wearing our sunscreen, and then set off to the course and were in good time for the first race of the day at seven thirty. Our tickets today were seated and as we came through into the enclosure we were greeted with a beautiful show of flowers everywhere, in lovely pastel colours of pink, blue and primrose. It was a great atmosphere with music filling the air. The stands were wooden benches arranged in tiers giving a good view of the course, and the distant mountains across the lake. We sat in the stands taking in the scene, with Geoff recording it all on our video camera; the whole atmosphere was fabulous and filled with an air of anticipation.*

*The women's heats started the day off, and after a short break, the men's racing began. We could not yet see Pat and Jackie but guessed that they were here somewhere. We sat there feeling very nervous. Our stomachs were turning over and we were getting very restless and wishing it would all be over but only, of course, with the correct result.*

*The boats were called over to the start and Great Britain was in lane two. I almost felt that I couldn't watch. We couldn't yet see the crews, but the commentary, given by a man with a very strong American accent, told us that the boats had made a good start. At the 500m mark we heard that the boat from the USA had a half length lead over the crew from Great Britain and that a boat length further back was the crew from New Zealand. I didn't listen to the position given for the other boats. At the 1000m mark the positions were the same and if anything the New Zealand boat was moving up a little, 'Oh my goodness' I thought, my stomach still churning. By now we could see the boat positions for ourselves and the commentary continued and yes, oh yes, our boat was moving through. Just after 1500m, our lads took the lead and they went on to win. They were now happily through to the final that was to be held on Sunday 5th August; that was when, we hoped, they would row the same race as they had done today; with the same result.*

*Everyone around us was excited after such a good race and our voices were now hoarse from all the shouting. We then saw Pat and Jackie approaching us, and now able to relax with them, we sat and watched the rest of the racing. Still no one had seen Moira and Pat Cross, and it seemed like they hadn't yet made it to Lake Casitas. We all thought that this was really strange for them to have missed Martin's race today, and we discussed it as we walked back to the campsite together.*

*At the camper, with a cup of tea being the order of the day to soothe our throats, we all sat in the sun lazily chatting about today's win and the boy's prospects in the final. Pat and Jackie then left us saying that they would see us the following day at the rowing. After we had lunch we decided to have a snooze and spend a lazy afternoon soaking up the sun. Later that evening we again had a chat and a drink with our neighbours Kay and Fred once their children were tucked into bed.*

*Tuesday morning, on the way to the rowing course, we took a look around the stalls selling the official Olympic merchandise of t-shirts and souvenirs.*

*We decided to take the entire family, back at home, one of the t-shirt which were dark blue and emblazoned with Los Angeles and the five Olympic rings. We also bought large beach towels each printed with the American Bald Eagle, the national bird of the United States of America, and one of the country's most recognizable symbols. It appears on most of its official seals, including the Seal of the President of the United States, so we thought that these would be acceptable and appropriate gifts to take home from The States.*

*We met Pat and Jackie and after watching that morning's rowing, and together we decided to meet again later at the Santa Barbara beach to go swimming. Geoff and I stopped to listen to the marching bands play and watched some pretty young cheer leaders twirling batons and then we walked back to the camper. By this time it was getting really warm with the temperature already in the 90s.*

*Whilst we were sitting eating our lunch, to our surprise, Steve and Belinda turned up. They had already eaten but gladly shared some of our food too (rowers always seem to have an appetite) and then that afternoon we all went to the beach. It was only a short walking distance from the Olympic village and quite a crowd of their friends had joined us too. We all spent a really enjoyable afternoon swimming and sunbathing, and later that evening Pat Toch, and her recently arrived husband Peter, invited us to join them for a meal at a lovely little restaurant which specialised in fish dishes, down on the quayside at Ventura.*

*On our return to the campsite much later that evening, we noticed a new brown tent had been erected and was pitched quite near to our camper. There was no one to be seen and everything seemed quiet so we decided to turn in for the night and discover who our new neighbours were in the morning.*

*The next day, Wednesday 1st August, to our surprise we found the newly arrived campers to be the missing 'Cross' family, Moira, Pat and Teresa (Martin's mum, dad and sister). They had arrived late the previous night, to find their tent had been supplied and pitched for them by David Tanner. David had been Martin's coach when he had rowed in the British coxless four in Moscow at the 1980 Olympic Games, where they had won a bronze* medal. David had also acquired tickets for them for the rowing today. It was great to see them all and we chatted as we walked down to the course. I told them all about what had happened so far, and described what a great race the boys had won on Monday, and they told us about their mammoth journey. They had first flown to Vancouver, Canada, then they had travelled on a Greyhound bus to Santa Barbara, California and there they had hired a car for the rest of the journey to Lake Casitas.

We had just entered the enclosure when a lady with a vaguely familiar face passed close by, and Moira did a double take saying, "I'm sure that's Susan Hampshire, I am going to tell her about the boys." Off Moira dashed and catching the lady up said, "You are Susan Hampshire, aren't you?" Susan replied that she was and Moira continued, "I'm Moira Cross, our sons are in the British coxed four and are going to win the Gold Medal for Britain. Then pulling me forward she continued, "This is Steve Redgrave's mother, would you please give them your support." Susan was very nice, and she said that she would certainly give her support, but that unfortunately, she was only here for one day, as a guest of Christopher Davidge, one of the British Olympic officials. She added that if she managed to get back for their final, then she would most certainly cheer them on. I wished then that the ground would open and swallow me up, I was so embarrassed plus I really don't like to tempt providence in any way before such an important event; that's our Moira for you though, as bold as brass. Perhaps if Moira had been with me when I had seen my idol Robert Mitchum, I might even have got to shake his hand.

Our tickets for today were again seated so we settled down to enjoy the morning's rowing and did not see Moira, Pat or Teresa again till much later. However, we did see Pat, Peter and Jackie and informed them of the Cross family's arrival and we all arranged to meet up later at our camper.

Moira came in saying she had been everywhere for tickets, and had had no luck: "I even went to the press, but they said they only had press passes but that they would ask around for us and guess what, while I was there the local press overheard me talking and asked to interview me." Moira had told them how she had travelled to get here, and had not been able to get any tickets for her family, and that it was possible her son was going to win a gold medal, and that she wouldn't be able to see it. Also she told them *how in 1980 she had gone to Moscow, and Martin had won a bronze. Of course the press loved it, and secretly so did Moira, so we waited to see what would happen.*

*Wednesday afternoon we all took a sightseeing trip to the Old Mission in Santa Barbara. It was a lovely old building with a very beautiful fountain in front. The mission had been founded by the Spanish Franciscans in 1786. The building had been quite small at first and had been built of adobe (a handmade sun dried clay and straw brick). In 1812 it was destroyed by an earthquake, so the present day mission was rebuilt and dedicated in 1820. A further earthquake on June 29, 1925 damaged the Mission Church and friary considerably and as we wandered around we could quite clearly see where it had been repaired. The mission had been built, when converting the local Chumash Indian population to Christianity. The Franciscans had introduced agriculture to them, teaching the Indians how to grow crops such as oranges, olives, and vines for winemaking and also how to successfully farm animals. It was really interesting and we wandered in the pretty gardens, keeping cool in the intense summer heat. There was a huge palm tree that must have been over 80ft high. I guessed that this tree could have told a tale or two. After lunch we went on to the beach for an hour or so and in the late afternoon, feeling pleasantly weary, we returned to the campsite to spend a quiet evening.*

*Thursday was a 'day off' for the rowers so we all decided to go and do some sightseeing in the city of Los Angeles. We stopped off at Malibu Beach on the way, but perhaps it was too early, as we didn't see any sunbathing film stars that we recognised. The beach was superb though; in fact the entire coastline was magnificent. Geoff, being a builder, had noticed that the houses that were built on the steep cliffs had a cantilever construction to stop them from sliding when the inevitable flash floods and earthquakes came. However, basking in all this gorgeous weather, we didn't give disasters like those a second thought.*

*Moving on we drove through places with names that we remembered seeing in the films as kids; Beverly Hills, Santa Monica, Hollywood, Sunset Boulevard. These names we had held in high regard in our teenage years as after World War II we were all brought up on a diet of American movies as there was then no TV or video only the local and much visited cinema.*

45

Our first destination in LA was Long Beach where we were to visit 'The Queen Mary', the ship permanently berthed here as a tourist attraction. This Cunard ship was one of Britain's greatest ocean liners in the thirties and was used as a troop ship during the war. Her first job in peacetime had been to transport G I brides to America and, some years later, she was sold to Diner's Club, the initial lessee of the ship, to be turned into a floating restaurant docked at Long Beach. The Queen Mary has been used as a filming location for numerous films, television episodes, and commercials, the 1972 film 'The Poseidon Adventure' being among them.

The area, around where the ship is docked, had been turned into an old English village setting and there were shops here selling souvenirs, some nice English pottery, teas, jams, Scottish tartans, whiskies and shortbreads and also some fashion shops all promoting the UK. We had lunch at one of the lovely village cafes before taking a tour around the ship. It must have been a real luxury to sail on her; the cabins were lovely and looked very comfortable. Personally I am a rotten sailor, but even I might have been tempted.

The engine room was enormous, beautifully clean with shining steel, though we were only allowed to walk around the metal gantry and look down. The souvenir shop was very interesting and we spotted a Union Jack which we could use to wave on Sunday at the final. We decided that as it cost £25 for a pocket-handkerchief size we would manage with what we already had.

As it was getting late, we all decided to give Howard Hughes, "Spruce Goose" aircraft a miss. The traffic was quite heavy on the freeway and it was getting dark by the time we reached Casitas. I was getting the evening meal for us all when Moira and Pat arrived with Jackie, and Teresa. We had travelled with Peter and Pat in Peter's car and as we all sat down to eat, Moira told us how the police had stopped them because, while driving, Pat had crossed the white line and they had breathalysed him. Poor old Pat, he was so upset because he didn't even drink. The LA police were very sharp on traffic violations, and we had been warned to stick to the 55mph limit. The lanes were very narrow, much narrower than on British motorways and it was quite easy to wander a little. When they found out that he was a visitor to the Games they let him off but it was a little unnerving and made us all think twice about our driving from then on.

We chatted quite late into the evening so we were all late rising the next day. Everyone decided to make Friday a quiet day at the camp and catch up on some chores. During the late morning we hired a boat and went out on the lake for an hour. It was quite a large lake but boats couldn't get near to the rowing course as it was buoyed off for safety reasons. It was very pleasant out on the water, and it felt much cooler; I worried that I would feel seasick but I was OK. We went shopping to the local store and stocked up with food and then went back to the campsite to do a spot of sunbathing.

Rowing at the 1984 Summer Olympics featured 14 events in total, for both men and women, and Saturday, another beautiful day, was the first day of the finals so we wandered down to the lake to watch some of our other British boats compete.

That evening we all got together again to make plans for the next day, Sunday August 5th and the boys final. We discussed what to wear, should we be casual or should we dress up. The ladies decided to dress up as if we were going to Henley Regatta, the only British regatta which had a strict dress code. I had brought two boaters with me, for Geoff and I to wear, and we dressed them up by gluing on GB signs and trimmed them both with red, white and blue ribbon and I decorated my hat with flowers. The finished hats looked quite smart. Geoff wore a white pair of trousers, a shirt and tie and a lightweight jacket. I wore a blue dress with white shoes and a red, white and blue scarf, tied around my neck, which Moira had loaned me. We made pompoms and rosettes from some red, white and blue serviettes that we had bought, and we had also managed to find a Union Jack printed tea towel. We decided we would have to take care when waving it though, as it was only printed on one side. We all had a great laugh that evening making our plans for the following day. It was decided that we should all get up early and that Geoff and Pat Cross would go on ahead to the course to secure some seats with a good view down the course and situated as near to the rostrum as possible; Moira, Teresa and I would join them a little later bringing along their breakfast. Peter, Pat and Jackie would also join our 'supporters' team.

There is a sequel to Moira's "ticket story". On the afternoon after Moira's story went to press, the local campsite was swarming with newsmen from all over the States. Her story and plea for finals tickets had gone out nationwide.

*The next day, tickets arrived from all over America addressed to Moira Cross. Some people had even come into the campsite while we were out and pinned tickets to her tent. The result was that all of Moira's family had a ticket for the final with a spare one for Peter Toch; perhaps this story proves it sometimes does pay to be bold.*

*After an early night for us all, I woke at 5.30am. It was D-day but we felt shattered as neither of us had slept well. I woke Geoff and he got up, washed and dressed and had some coffee. Pat Cross then arrived and had a coffee too and then both men set off to select a good spot; armed with more coffee in a large flask. The ladies took their time getting dressed and eventually looking like smart British supporters about to 'fly the flag' we wandered down to the lake.*

*Right up until today every morning had been beautiful, but of all days today was grey, damp and cold with thick fog. Our greatest concern was that, due to this weather, the race would be put back and that any delay could disturb the boy's focus. We were shivering as we walked to the rowing entrance and we all wished we had taken our jumpers with us. The atmosphere cheered us up though and it felt rather like seeing the crowds going to a football match with everyone saying hi, hello and good morning and commenting on the terrible weather; really quite British. When we spotted the men we cheered as they had found a great spot for us all right next to the rostrum. They had put blankets down to save our seats but had been getting a hard time from other supporters so they were very pleased to see us arrive. They were also looking forward to their breakfast too and they tucked into them like bacon sandwiches had never tasted so good.*

*Moira went off to find her other daughter, Catherine, and her friends and while she was away, Pat, Peter and Jackie arrived. Moira soon brought back the rest of her family and we were all now nervously chatting to pass the time. It was now 7.45am and the fog had lifted a little but visibility was still less than 250m. Geoff spotted the boys rowing down to the start, so it was confirmed; their race was on. I was praying that the race wouldn't get cancelled at the last minute. The tension mounted and my stomach was turning over and over and I felt quite sick. Suddenly Pat Cross was missing but Moira said not to worry, he would be all right but that he got so nervous he always went 'walkabout' before an important race. I thought that if we, as parents, feel like this then what must our boys feel like at this moment?*

*Geoff had been getting his video camera ready but thought that it was too misty to record much of the race. It was now 7.55am and they were calling the crews to the start; their race really was on. If we could get through the next ten minutes it would all be over bar the shouting. I had a very strange feeling, it was as if I wanted to run away but my legs wouldn't carry me. As usual I wanted it to be over but I was also feeling anxious about what the outcome might be.*

*The time was now 8am and I knew that the race must start any second. Then the commentary started, "USA are you ready, Great Britain are you ready, New Zealand are you ready, Italy are you ready, Canada are you ready, Federal Republic of Germany are you ready," a small pause followed by the french words, " êtes vous prêt . partir," and again silence for a few seconds and we all held our breath. The commentator, who had a flat American accent, declared it had been a good clean start; thank goodness, they'd made it away first time and were on their way.*

*For a second my attention was drawn back to our crowd, I noticed Pat Cross had returned and was on his hands and knees with his face covered, every now and then he would look up and say "Oh Please". The commentary rang out, "The crew from the USA in the white vest with diagonal stripes are in the lead by half a boat length from the crew of Great Britain in the yellow shell, wearing white vests with the horizontal stripes." From Pat Cross, who was in a heap on the floor, there came a deep-throated groan of "Oh my God." We could not yet see the boats; we could only hear the commentary. "Italy third, West Germany fourth, New Zealand fifth and Canada sixth. Now reaching the 1000m mark, America still in the lead by half a boat length from Great Britain." Then it went on through the positions of the other boats.*

*The mist was beginning to lift but was still swirling round with occasional breaks. Every now and then you could just make out the dark shapes of the approaching boats. As soon as we saw them appear we all began to shout and scream, "COME ON BRITAIN". Jackie just in front of me was really going to town. We were eighteen Brits completely surrounded by Americans but we were going to be heard. I noticed one girl in front of us was covering her ears and there were still deep groans coming from Pat Cross, the heap on the ground. Then it began to happen. Now clear of the mist, the bow of the British boat was inching forward and gaining water on the USA with every stroke. With just 200m to go we could see that our boys had raised their rate and were making their final push.*

*The commentator was saying that the Americans were still managing to hold the British - when the lads came though like a steam train. Nothing was going to stop them now. With 150m to go our boys had taken the lead and in what only seemed like another second they had crossed the line to take the gold. The TV cameras turned on us, our shouts and hoots must have been heard in Great Britain. It was all over and they had won their first Olympic Gold medal in 6:18.64 a whopping 1.64secs clear of USA.*

*Everyone was shouting congratulations and jumping up and down. I looked towards the boys to see Andy and Budget with their arms waving in the air. Martin and Steve were slumped over their oars totally exhausted. It was only then that I realised what they must have put into this race, the enormous physical effort that had gone into winning this medal. Pat Cross was up now and shouting, "Wow Wee, what a great race", all the signs of his previous nervousness gone. The TV cameraman came over to film us all and we waved to the family back home in the UK. We weren't sure if they would see us but we hoped that their win would make the news.*

*My mom Ada, my brother Bryan, Jane and David had gone to Christine and Philip's home for the day to watch the TV coverage of the pre-race build up and the live race all together. It had been very exciting for them as the BBC had shown the two bows of the boats neck and neck and then the British boat edging forward into the lead and winning the gold. The family had cracked open a bottle of champagne and as they toasted Steve, Jane said, "Let's see if we can see mom and dad on telly", of course the rest of the family thought don't be silly but then I appeared on the screen and they couldn't believe it; there was our gang waving to them; it really made their day. Later the local press called round to interview them all; they'd had a wonderful day celebrating even if they hadn't been there in person to see Steve's win.*

*After the race the boys slowly rowed back along the side of the course so that they could wind down a little and dissipate some of the lactic acid their muscles had accumulated during the race. We knew that they would return in a while for the traditional row past followed by the medal ceremony. The following race was the Double Sculls and, with no British interest in this, we watched but our hearts and minds were elsewhere. I felt so elated and bursting with pride. My son, at just 22 years old, had achieved what he had been working towards from the tender age of thirteen. He'd said to me in a very quiet moment nine years earlier, "Mom, what I really want to do is to win an Olympic Gold medal." I took a deep breath and thanked God that, in our small way, we had been able to help him achieve his dream. We had helped him financially of course and we had given our unwavering support but what had mattered to him most was that we had always believed in him. His whole family had always been there for him when he needed reassuring and a little praise but we couldn't begin to express our respect and admiration for all his personal hard work which had culminated in this colossal achievement.*

*The boats were lined up in their finishing order about 250m out from the rostrum. In the near lane was the boat of Great Britain, 2<sup>nd</sup> America, 3<sup>rd</sup> New Zealand, 4<sup>th</sup> Italy, 5<sup>th</sup> Canada and 6<sup>th</sup> West Germany. The crews began their steady row towards the rostrum to the sound of a wonderfully stirring piece of music called "The March of the Athletes". Just before the rostrum the 1<sup>st</sup>, 2<sup>nd</sup> and 3<sup>rd</sup> crews came to the landing stage and 4<sup>th</sup>, 5<sup>th</sup> and 6<sup>th</sup> rowed on past the finish line and back to the boat sheds. The athletes from the three boats disembarked and walked up to the rostrum, again in finishing order. The gold medal crew walked to the centre position, the silver to the right and the bronze to the left. While this was taking place, three young female American volunteers, each carrying a medal on a velvet cushion, stood in the wings next to the IOC officials who were there waiting for the presentation to begin. Once the athletes had taken their positions, the official party walked on to the rostrum. They first went to the gold medallists and presented, in turn, a medal and a floral bouquet to each rower. Their names were announced over the loudspeakers to a roaring cheer. The silver and the bronze presentation followed. At this point the crews turned to face the flags which were rising to the sound of our National Anthem, God Save the Queen. For everyone involved this was the most moving part of the* *whole ceremony and we could see the release of emotion begin to appear on our boy's faces. The only person left with dry eyes at that moment was their Coxswain, Adrian Ellison, who had a broad grin on his face from ear to ear. We all stood, consumed in our own emotions and Geoff and I shakily but proudly sang the National Anthem. Below us the victorious British team and, high above them, the fluttering Union Jack.*

*As the strains of the anthem died away, Steve jumped from the rostrum and gave his 'victory' flower bouquet to Belinda with a kiss and then he gave his Dad and me a wonderful smile and a wave that said it all and then he returned to his crew. Martin had given his Dad and family a hug and had given his flowers to his Mom. It was a real shame though, that Andy, Richard and Adrian's families were not there to see such a memorable day at first hand. Andy was getting married on his return to England and I guess that his fiancé and his family had a lot to organise. Lots of photos were then taken of the winning crew, and they then returned to the boat where 'the four' proceeded to throw Adrian into the lake. It was this moment that was captured by the press cameras and the following day this photos was plastered all over the front page of all the British newspapers. It's a sort of tradition in rowing for the winning coxed crew to hurl their coxswain into the drink and Adrian loved it; they did remember to take his medal off first though.*

*Once back in the boat, Steve leaned over the side and promptly threw up. He hadn't looked too well on the rostrum but had thankfully managed to hold it back till then. He quickly recovered and the crew then paddled back to the boathouse and put away the boat. Steve had to go for a drugs test again, which took some time because of his dehydration following the race. It didn't take as long this time as it had in Moscow though, and this time water was used to help him produce a sample, not beer. All the crew then went off to a press conference with the BBC and other assembled media.*

*Steve and Belinda got back to us around 10.30am and he still looked a little below par. Everyone was gathering around him, wanting to talk to him and to see his medal. We did get him to sit down in the end and, after an American couple had given him a cup of coffee, he began to feel much better.*

The last race of the morning was now about to get underway; it was the eights. Our particular interests in this race were Steve's friends Adam Clift and Alan Whitwell, who were both in the crew. New Zealand was the favourite for the gold and it was a very close fought race but the result was a bit of an upset for Great Britain. Canada came in first, America second; Australia third, New Zealand fourth and Great Britain came in fifth with France bringing up the rear. It was a huge disappointment for our lads.

Our British crews had done very well overall though, the British Women's eight, including Steve's girlfriend, Belinda and a young rower, called Ann Callaway, had finished fifth. Beryl Crockford (later Mitchell) our women's single sculler and the coxless pair came sixth. Not a bad result on the whole but every athlete competes hoping to win a medal and are always very disappointed if they don't succeed. As the saying goes "It is the taking part and not the winning that matters", but I really don't think that most athletes, especially at this level of competition, would agree.

At the closing ceremony for the rowing, the promise was made to meet again in four years in Seoul, Korea in 1988; the national flags were lowered and passed into safe keeping for then. With the official ceremony over for us, it was now time to really begin our celebrations. Steve and Belinda went back to the Olympic village to celebrate with the other athletes and we made arrangements with them to meet up later at a barbecue that was being organised that evening. Our gang of British supporters went back to the campsite to celebrate. Moira's family had made a picnic lunch so, bringing our food and wine, we joined the party.

On arrival at the campsite we found our camper had been decked out with red, white and blue ribbon, a big cardboard gold medal and a large card. All of this was from our neighbours, Fred and Kay Pisch and their children. Their little boy had made the medal and their little girl the card; we were really touched that they had gone to so much trouble. We didn't see them again as they had gone out for the day, but we left them a bottle of wine and I still, to this day, exchange Christmas cards and letters with them. Stacy, the little girl, has now finished college and works at Burbank airport and Nick, the little boy, is in high school and is really keen on the sport of cycling.

*We all enjoyed our afternoon campsite party but we were aware that our time together was drawing to a close: we had really enjoyed the whole experience, watching great rowing in superb company. We made arrangements to all gather together for one last time at the barbeque party later that evening, as we slowly began to realise that perhaps the next time we would all be together like this would be a year ahead at the World Rowing Championships in Belgium. Jackie had a hotel in Los Angeles to go to, she was stopping on for the rest of the Games and Pat and Peter were staying on with their daughter Joanne. Moira, Pat and Teresa were staying a day or so with Jackie at the hotel before returning to England.*

*Geoff and I packed up our things and cleaned up the camper, as the following day we were off to San Francisco with Steve and Belinda. Once we had finished our chores, we set off for Santa Barbara and the barbecue. We called in at the shopping mall on our way to stock up on food for tomorrows journey and then we met up with everyone at the party. The food and wine that night tasted good and the music was great; the youngsters all let their hair down and enjoyed themselves. As the late evening approached, we oldies wended our way back to the camper to have a refreshing cup of tea together before saying goodbye and promising to keep in touch.*

*We parked that night on the university car park so we would be on the spot to meet Steve and Belinda in the morning, as we all wanted to make an early start. In the morning, I found that when I tried to speak, my voice was non existent, not even a croak would come out. My throat had felt rather sore the night before, due to all of my shouting during their race; now it had completely disappeared. Geoff seemed quite pleased as he realised that he was going to have a nice quiet day. While we were waiting for Steve and Belinda, we saw Colin Moynihan who had coxed the British eight. We went over to have a word with him, well let's say Geoff did, I couldn't, which he thought was quite amusing. Colin was the Member of Parliament for Lewisham East from 1983- 1992 and Minister of Sport from 1987 – 1990 and is currently the Chairman of the British Olympic Association and now holds the title Baron Moynihan.*

*Mike, Steve and Belinda eventually arrived, Mike had come to say goodbye to us and said that he would see us once we returned home. Finally we got underway and took route 101 to San Francisco. It seemed slow going with* the speed limit at only 55mph, but we stayed strictly to the rules of the road as we had learnt well from Pat Cross' experience that the traffic police here could be very strict. We made a few detours and stopped off at towns and beaches on the way so we could look around and buy our meals. It was very pretty scenery driving through the redwood country, with its enormous redwood trees, deep canyons and raging white waters, which looked scary even for the experienced canoeist that were shooting the rapids.

It had taken us ten hours to do this trip to San Francisco, and when we arrived at around 7pm that evening we found the campsite of our choice was unfortunately, completely full, and so we had to park on their overspill site which was under the motorway arches. It was a bit noisy here, but we had really enjoyed our journey and we felt happy to have arrived safely.

We decided to go out for a meal and take in China town at the same time; I had not eaten Chinese food before so we felt it was the best place to try. I really enjoyed it and finished the meal off with a fortune cookie but I can't recall now the message inside. After the meal we wandered through the brightly lit and very colourful china town. In the shops we saw carved ivory tables, vases, lacquered chests, and beautiful carpets with dragon designs on them. We could have spent hours just browsing but 'the men' soon got fed up.

We saw a Chinese Theatre and then went on to see the famous Golden Gate Bridge. By night it was a little disappointing as it was not at all well lit and by this time it was getting late and we were beginning to feel rather weary having had such a long day so we all returned to the camper and our beds.

The next day we were up again quite early and this morning, we headed out on our planned trip to Twin Peaks. This is a very high point with a spectacular view over the whole of San Francisco, the bridge and bay. The view was amazing and we took a lot of photos even though it was still a bit misty.

Our next stop was Seal Island, but that day there were no seals to be seen instead we just saw birds, rabbits and squirrels. I felt quite odd that day, a little depressed and tearful and not really myself but I hid my feelings well from the others; I was helped by still having no voice to complain with. I

55

*guess the past few days' excitement had been a bit of a shock for my system. I kept thinking that Steve, our youngest child, was growing up and might not need us any more; silly notions like that. Time would tell just how wrong my thoughts then turned out to be. A feeling of anticlimax usually follows such a high but on reflection I feel my mood was probably due to generally feeling a little under the weather.*

*Despite this we had a very interesting and enjoyable day together. First we visited the picturesque stretch of Lombard Street, the world's most crooked street. It has eight acute turns along a single block and they twist at very acute angles, making for very slow going if you are in a vehicle, as we were. Oddly enough, cars were the reason for designing the street this way back in 1922, the idea being that this design would make it easier for them to negotiate the steep 16-percent gradient. Geoff and I zigzagged down in the camper, whilst Steve and Belinda, who had already walked down, filmed us descending slowly between the sidewalks. These were planted with pink, blue and white hydrangeas in full bloom; it was beautiful, although the traffic was bumper-to-bumper with everyone sightseeing.*

*Our next destination was the Golden Gate Bridge; this time in daylight. The sun was hot and it was now beginning to disperse the mist, allowing us a much better view. We parked and walked for a while to get a close look at this six lane traffic highway and the second longest main span suspension bridge in the United States. It had been the longest one when it was completed in 1937 having a span of 4,200 feet but now the Verrazano-Narrows Bridge in New York City claims that title. It spans San Francisco Bay which opens into the Pacific Ocean and has become the internationally recognized symbol of San Francisco and California. The famous vermillion colour called 'International Orange' is used as a sealant for the bridge and to enhance the bridge's visibility in fog and there is a full time crew of 38 painters keeping it up to scratch. Its final construction cost was more than $35 million and in the 30's that was some 'big bucks'. On display is an amazing cross-section of the cable that is used to support the weight of the roadway. It's a piece of the cable (36.5 inches wide) and contains 27,572 separate wires. There are 80,000 miles of wire in each of the two main cables and the total is sufficient to go around the world 5.79 times. The bridge also has approximately 1,200,000 rivets; some feat of engineering for those days, so this morning, I was a little more impressed than yesterday.*

*From the viewing bay on the bridge, we had a good view of the cruise boats taking people around the bay and to Alcatraz Island and the now famous disused federal prison there. Many films were made about this jail and I expect that most people have seen the film about Robert Franklin Stroud "The Birdman of Alcatraz". Also held here were notable criminals such as Al Capone. The island first served as a lighthouse, a military fortification then a military prison and is locally known as 'The Rock'. It is said that no one ever escaped from Alcatraz due to the swirling tides and strong currents that surround the island and the deep water than can be as cold as 47 °F, plus the island is often blighted by ferocious winds and blinding fog. This didn't stop men trying though and 36 prisoners were involved in 14 attempts to escape with two men trying twice. Although all inmates were removed and the penitentiary closed in 1963, the prison still ranks as one of the strangest haunted sites in America.*

*The famous Gray Line trolley street cars were fun to watch, with all the people hanging on the sides as they were speedily pulled up and down the permanent tracks of this hilly city. We would have liked to have taken a ride ourselves but there was not time to do everything so we moved on to Pier 39. This is where, in all the old gangster movies, people were murdered and thrown off the pier. It was always portrayed as a dark and sinister place so I was quite a surprised to see it so bright and colourful with a big shopping precinct with lots of seafood restaurants. We had our lunch in one of these on Fisherman's Wharf and then took a ride in an open landau horse and carriage which gave us a good tour of the whole area.*

*Back at the camper Steve and Belinda said that they would like to return to Los Angeles to see the rest of the Games. This we quite understood and as we had spent two great days with them, we turned tail and headed back to LA. On this return journey we all took turns to drive, only stopping for tea breaks. It was in the early hours of the morning that we dropped them back at the Olympic Village where they had their accommodation secured for the rest of the Games. Geoff and I then had to find a place to park for the remainder of the night and we eventually found a beach car park.*

*We had just three days left before we were due to fly out of California to Florida to visit Bill and Nadine, Geoff's brother and his wife and so we decided we would make the most of our time here. The following morning* we decided to go to Disney's California Adventure Park, Disney Land and we located it without too much trouble; I was driving the camper, whilst Geoff read the map. We parked in an enormous car park and collected what we thought we might need for our day out. I locked the back door of the camper and climbed out through the driver's door and slammed it shut without giving it a second thought. As soon as I had done this however, I realised that I had left the keys in the ignition and had just locked them inside. Oh good grief, I thought, now what were we to do. We checked all round the vehicle but there was no way in and I can tell you now, I wasn't Geoff's favourite person at that precise moment. We quickly discussed the situation and decided to have our day at Disney Land and then we'd worry about how to get back into the camper later.

We had a spectacular day seeing various shows and Disney character parades. We visited Never-Never Land and Toy Town and looked around a multitude of gift shops; it was like being a child again. We took rides on space ships went for coaster rides at Magic Mountain and then stopped for lunch at Hansel and Gretel's house which was a MacDonald's restaurant in disguise. We finished the day with a quiet ride on the mono-rail before watching another parade with Mickey Mouse, Minnie, Donald, Goofy and Pluto and then we called it a day.

On arriving back at the locked camper I first rang the camper hire company who said that they'd get a locksmith to come and sort it out for us but then by chance I mentioned it to a girl at the kiosk while I was getting change for the phone and she said that this sort of thing happened all the time and that if we told her where we were parked she would send over the special squad. Five minutes later we were in, a simple flexible metal bar in the door and it was open. We did have to show them our paperwork and passports but there was no charge for this excellent quick and efficient service and it was good to know too, that it hadn't been just me.

We stayed that night on a really lovely beach park and had our meal watching the waves rolling in and the surfers in action on their boards; a lovely relaxing way to end a fun-packed day. San Diego and Mexico were going to be our destinations the following day.

We awoke and took a long breakfast looking out at the beautiful weather;

*it was a really nice morning and it made us feel like staying here for the day but we realised that we had little time left for lazing about. We had some old neighbours of ours to visit in San Diego but we decided to travel down to Mexico first as it was not too far to drive to the border. The change of scenery here was like going from riches to rags and the amount of poverty there really surprised us. The first town we arrived at was Tijuana and finding a 'safe' car park we walked to the shops where we found a huge selection of goods on sale. We settled on three Mexican blankets, nice and easy to carry home.*

*The streets were full of beggars, mostly children and I felt quite upset seeing some kids as young as five. Geoff had seen this sort of thing many times before in countries like India when he had been in the Merchant Navy. These children would come up to us saying, "One dollar Mister," but when handed them a handful of change they said that they only wanted one dollar bills. Back in the camper again we headed back to the border leaving Mexico behind. Getting through the border crossing took longer than before and all our papers had to be double-checked and the vehicle looked over and inspected inside for stowaways.*

*Back in San Diego we headed for the beach again. We parked up and phoned our friends only to be told by their sister, who had answered the phone that, they had gone out for the day. She said that they would be very disappointed to have missed us as they had watched the rowing on TV hoping to catch a glimpse of us and had seen Steve's final.*

*We still had two days left before handing back the camper so we found a lovely campsite on the beach again. The evening sunsets were magnificent to watch and we realised that we were going to really miss this wonderful climate once we were back home in the UK. There had been only one day in the whole of our trip so far that had not been so nice and that had been the day of their race when it had been so foggy that their race had almost been cancelled.*

*The following morning we went to Universal Studios where we spent five fascinating hours. Outside the souvenir shop there was a model Frankenstein with the bolt through his neck. I was inspecting this closely as it looked so real and I was about it touch it when it jumped at me. It was actually a person* dressed up but standing completely still; it was a good job I had a strong heart. We then stood back and watched while others got caught out by it; it was very funny. We listened to Robert Wagner's interesting commentary on how the movies 'Star Wars' and 'Earthquake' had been made. Then we took a tour on a train which showed us how an avalanche had been simulated for a film. The train then pulled alongside a lake where the movie 'Jaws' had been filmed and suddenly an enormous Great White Shark, with it's mouth wide open, shot out of the water and lunged towards us making everyone scream. We were also taken past 'Night Rider' the talking car, it was all fascinating.

That evening we drove back to the U.C.L.A. to say a proper goodbye to Steve and Belinda. They seemed to be having a great time enjoying what was left of the Games. The told us that when the Games were over they were going to deliver someone's car back to Florida. Apparently some people would drive to Los Angeles and then fly back leaving their car with a company who arranged for the vehicles to be driven back home for them so this is what they had signed up to do and in the process were getting a free trip to their uncles place in Florida seeing a few other states on the way. Our last night in California was spent at the beach campsite again, where we relaxed watching some people roller-skating along the prom as the evening sun was setting; glorious.

Saturday 11ᵗʰ August arrived and our flight to Florida was due to leave at 3pm so we had no time to lose. We ate a quick breakfast, cleaned out the camper, paid the campsite bill, found a carwash, filled up with fuel and were finally ready to hand our 'home on wheels' back. Our original suitcases were brought to us, plus another we had brought to take all the souvenirs plus a box with the TV that we had acquired. While we were settling our bill, we suddenly noticed a large sign above the counter saying, "Do not take campers into Mexico". We looked at each other but kept very quiet; it had been a bit late to find out but we could now understand why the company had this rule.

I sat down to check our flight tickets and to my horror I discovered we were just about to miss our flight. I had read the time as 3pm when it was actually 13.00 and so I was in the doghouse again. We couldn't get in touch with Bill in Florida to warn him either, because he was ex-directory and *we didn't know his telephone number. There were no more direct flights to Tampa that day so in the end we were routed via Atlanta. By the time we arrived in Tampa it was 1.30am in the early hours but there patiently waiting for us was Bill and Nadine. We did not expect them to be here as we had arranged a hire car but they had thought that we might need a guide to their home as it had been quite a few years since we had been there. By this time I had regained my voice so was able to apologise for myself, we then picked up the car and followed them straight back to their home in Tarpon Springs where we all went straight to bed.*

*We had a 'lie in' and made a slow start the following morning. This was a welcome change after all the early morning starts that we had experienced so far on this trip. Bill and Nadine owned a small business which they ran from their 33 acre home. It was a plant nursery and it was very pleasant to just wander around looking at all the unusual and exotic plants. We chatted together most of the day as it had been a long time since we had seen each other and there was a lot to catch up on. Brian, their son, was still living at home and was attending the local college but their daughter Denise, was living and working away in the Florida State capital Tallahassee and too far away for a quick visit.*

*We spent a lovely evening together watching the Olympic closing ceremony on their TV. We saw Joanna Toch with some of the other British girls running around wrapped in a Union Jack flag and we felt a little disappointed that we hadn't seen Steve and Belinda too.*

*The next day, August 13th, was my birthday so for a treat Geoff and I went to nearby Clearwater where there is a wonderful beach. The sea was lovely and warm and there were some large palm trees growing there which provided some much needed shade. We spent a few very pleasant hours there swimming and relaxing in the sun topping up our tans. Arriving back at Bill's, waiting for me was the biggest basket of flowers I have ever seen. It was from Steve and Belinda saying 'Happy Birthday Mom, and thanks for everything'. A lovely gesture like that makes everything feel worthwhile doesn't it and it brought a lump to my, still sore, throat and tears to my eyes.*

*Bill and Nadine took us out that evening to celebrate my birthday and we* ate at the" Kapok Tree" which was one of their favourite restaurants. The dining tables were set out in the gardens, where, growing in the centre was an enormous Kapok tree. On our arrival we all ordered cocktails and I drank a very large 'Planters Punch' in a tall glass; it went down well and also seemed to soothe my throat. We ordered steaks with salad and we were served with enormous meals much bigger than anyone could eat. That was the first time I had heard the term, "Doggy Bag" and we duly took home at least half the steak; it was a lovely birthday treat and we all had a great evening reminiscing over old times.

Over the next three days we spent most of our time lazing around on the beach. Geoff had a go at windsurfing which caused quite a laugh. He soon got the hang of it though and at one time I thought he was off out to sea but he quickly mastered the art of turning the sail and changing direction without falling into the water. We also did some shopping and we ate lunch out a couple of times.

It was now 16th August and it was time for us to move on; 'Time to go home' as the song says. Our flight to New York departed Tampa airport at midday and this time I got our departure time right. After breakfast we packed and said our goodbyes to Bill and Brian; Nadine came with us to the airport. We returned our hire car and checked in our luggage and we then sat chatting to Nadine over a cup of coffee and waited for our flight to be called. We said a tearful goodbye and then boarded our flight, this time on our way to 'The Big Apple'. We had thoroughly enjoyed our time with the relatives but the few days here had seemed to just fly by.

In New York we only had a three-hour stop over before our connecting flight to London so there was no time for sightseeing on this trip. We would be travelling through the night and were due to land at 7.45am on Friday 17th August.

Our flight was mostly uneventful and we slept on an off. Later, as we were about to have our breakfast served we were told that London was covered in thick fog and so we were being diverted to Prestwick in Scotland. We knew that the family would be waiting for us at the airport so we hoped that they had thought to check the flight ETA's before leaving home.

*Touching down at Prestwick, we stayed on the plane while they refuelled which took about half an hour. Then we were told to disembark and have coffee, as we couldn't leave yet due to there still being thick fog in London. Waiting in the long queue, I made a phone call to Christine. She said they had got up early and had called the airport and so were aware of the delay; they had now planned to go to Heathrow for about 10 o'clock. We told them our situation and carried on chatting till the money ran out; all the rest of the news would now have to wait until we returned. In the end it was nearly 12.15pm before we landed at Heathrow.*

*As we came through into the arrivals hall, Christine, Philip, Jane and David were all there to greet us with lots of hugs and smiles and full of excited chatter as they explained that they had all been given time off work to come to meet us. Coming home to them all was like experiencing Steve winning his race all over again; it was a great feeling, what a wonderful family we have.*

*As a homecoming celebration, Christine had arranged to host a family meal later that evening for us all. Geoff and I were dropped of at home to be greeted by my Mom and my brother Bryan. They had been fine and my mother, who was 81 years old, was very excited and proud of her grandson and his Olympic Gold medal achievement. Bryan made us a cup of tea, we had a quick chat and then we went to bed to catch up on some lost sleep.*

*The meal that evening at Christine's home was excellent and the champagne flowed; it was so nice to be home with them all. They had videoed every channel on the TV, showing the races, the interviews, and had collected every newspaper with any article about the rowing. They showed us the photo from the local newspaper with them all standing on the patio at Christine's home, holding raised glasses, toasting Steven with champagne just after his final. Marlow Town Council, and Great Marlow Parish Council, both wanted to know when Steve would be available to attend a town celebration to honour their local hero. 'WOWWEE', as Pat Cross would have said. It took us both a long time to get to sleep that night due to the day's excitement but I must say that I felt unbelievably happy.*

# Chapter Four
## Homecomings and Celebrations

### *Welcome Home Steve*

*We tried to settle down again to a normal routine but it wasn't easy to keep a lid on our excitement especially with more and more mail arriving everyday. There were telephone calls of congratulations and lots of pleas from various media, all wanting interviews. Marlow Town Council was pressing us for a date as they wanted to arrange a town reception. We knew how excited Steve would be about all this and we didn't want him to miss any of it but we also knew that both he and Belinda deserved their much needed holiday. Leading up to the Olympics, Belinda had been holding down a full time job as well as dedicating all of her spare time to her rowing training. This time away was going to be good for both of them.*

*About ten days after we got home, a very official looking letter arrived with Her Majesty's Coat of Arms stamped on it. Geoff and I looked at the envelope and were not sure whether we should open it; we decided to wait until the family could discuss it. Steve had told us to deal with any thing that we felt might be important, and if necessary, to leave a message with his Uncle Bill in Florida, as he planned to call in to see him and spend a few days with the family before travelling home to the UK.*

*With some apprehension we opened the letter. To our delight, we found that it was an invitation from the Prime Minister Margaret Thatcher, inviting Steve to attend a reception which was being held at 10 Downing Street for all athletes who had taken part in the 1984 Olympics. This was something very special, and a great honour, so we decided that we should get a message to him as soon as possible. We knew that Bill didn't always answer his phone, but taking into consideration the time difference, we* took a chance and rang him. To our surprise and relief Bill answered, and it turned out that Steve and Belinda were there with him having recently arrived back from their Caribbean cruise. They told us that it had been a truly wonderful experience and that everyone they had met during their holiday had been wonderful to them both, all wanting to shake Steve's hand and to see his gold medal.

The two of them were now exploring Tarpon Springs and Tampa and enjoying Uncle Bill's hospitality. We explained the reason for our phone call, and Steve excitedly asked us to write to confirm that he would be home in time to attend the reception on 4th September; they had booked their flight home for 31st August. Having had Steve confirm his ETA, I was now also able to inform the Town Council when he was expected home; they decided to hold their reception a few days later on the 8th September. Marlow Bottom Parish Council were combining their reception with the Marlow Town Council but High Wycombe District Council had decided to host their own reception for Steve later in the month. Norman Gloucester, who was in charge of organising the Town Council reception, arranged for an open top, red double decker bus to come and collect us from our home in Marlow Bottom. Steve's coach, Mike Spracklen and his family had also to be included in the celebrations as Mike was a Marlow man too.

The people of Marlow Bottom had decorated their streets with banners and flags. Liz Neighbour, our next-door neighbour, had also decorated the gates to our home at Furze Farm. They were tall black wrought iron double gates and she was able to decorate them by weaving flowers and leaves in and around the ironwork which made the entrance to our property look spectacular. Some of the local businesses had made a collection for Steve, under the leadership of his number one fan, June Heath, who worked at the newsagents; Brian Jarvis had collect money too at the DIY shop. A large card had been signed by most people in the village with 'well done' congratulation messages. A very large sign was temporarily erected at the entrance to Marlow Bottom and read, "WELCOME HOME STEVE" in huge lettering. What a smashing welcome for the local boy who they felt had done so well.

On Friday 31st August the whole family went to the airport to greet their returning hero. It was lovely to see the two of them again and they both looked really well. They had spent the journey home talking about their travels and they were filled with excitement and anticipation of their arrival. They were especially looking forward to opening the piles of letters and cards that awaited them when they got home. As we turned into Marlow Bottom, they saw the huge sign, the Union Jack flags and the congratulation banners stretched across the road; they couldn't believe their eyes. We drove them the whole length of Marlow Bottom valley so they could see for themselves the many personal congratulations and welcome home signs that people had taken the trouble to make and display outside their homes; I think they were really overwhelmed, amazed and delighted that so many local people had gone to this trouble.

Once back at home they were too excited to sleep right away so Belinda rang her mom and told her all the news and then the two of them sat down to read their mail. It was like his 'best ever' Christmas and Birthday, all rolled into one. Eventually, the jet lag got the better of them and so they went to bed; two very happy and contented people.

I had arranged a 'Welcome Home Steve' party for Sunday the 2nd September so all our friends and family could join in the celebrations. It would allow Steve to see all of those people who wouldn't be able to attend the town reception. Unfortunately, by this time my brother Brian had returned to his home in Whitley Bay, Northumberland and would not be able to re- join us with his family. Geoff's sister Doris and her family were able to attend and some of our old friends, Queenie and Arthur, Joan and Derek, Sylvia and Ken, Vic and Jane came along with all of their families in tow. These were close family friends whom had seen Steve grow up. There were also personal friends of Steve, Jane and Christine and lots of neighbours also joined us. The people who we had shared time with at The Olympics and who had experienced the same joy that day in Casitas came too; Moira and Pat Cross, Pat and Peter Toch, and Jackie Hartley. I can't remember exactly how many people were with us that day but it was a great party. It started at midday and went on till late evening; we thankfully didn't run out of alcohol but the party food was in short supply by the end.

Isabel, Jane's old school friend brought along her 90-year-old grandfather and he sat and talked to my mom all day about the 'good old days' and the things he had done in his lifetime. He was a very interesting old gentleman *who had travelled a lot and Ada seemed to really enjoy his company. The funniest thing happened a few days later when a parcel arrived for Ada from him. It turned out to be 2lb of sausages and we all pulled her leg about it for a long time afterwards but I don't think anyone really knew why he sent her sausages; still I think she enjoyed a good fry up.*

*The next event was two days later on the 4th September; the Prime Minister's reception at 10 Downing Street. Steve and Belinda both looked very smart in their Olympic uniforms as they set off to meet the other Olympic athletes. On entering 'Number 10' they were introduced to Mrs Thatcher who shook hands with everyone. Her comment to them as they arrived was, "Now didn't the rowing do something special". I don't know whether this was thought to be an amusing comment but I'm afraid the crew were quite disappointed and really felt that she really had no idea that they had won the ultimate accolade of their sport; an Olympic Gold Medal. They all enjoyed the evening though along with the other athletes and they came into tell us all about it when they arrived home.*

*What a great day Saturday 8th September turned out to be. We got up early, ate breakfast and got ourselves ready. Christine and Philip and Jane and David arrived and Belinda and Steve then appeared looking very smart wearing their Olympic uniforms once again. My mom Ada, also looked lovely and was very excited to have been invited on the bus ride and to the following reception. Mike, Ann, and their boys Christopher and Adrian were there and Mike's parents too. The open-top bus arrived and waited for us at the bottom of the drive.*

*We all walked down our drive to where the Mayor was waiting to greet us and he explained what we were to expect from the day; the crowds were beginning to collect already. We all boarded the bus, my mom and Mike's parents went inside downstairs so they could keep warm and the rest of us climbed up the stairs to the open air. Steve, Belinda, Mike and Ann all stood right at the front of the bus, our family spread out in the middle and right at the back was some journalists from the local press. Looking out from the top of the bus, to our amazement, we saw hundreds of people already gathered along both pavements either side of the road. Children were riding along the pavement on their bikes, ringing their bells and lots of our fellow villagers had come out of their homes to wave their flags and shout their congratulations from their front gardens.*

*Our bus drove to the village hall, about ¼ mile along the valley and we waved all the way, seeing faces that we knew well. There were a lot more people gathered outside the village hall and lining the street in front of the shops, shouting and cheering as the bus pulled in and stopped in front of the village store. Here the members of Marlow Bottom Parish Council and Bryan Jarvis our local DIY store owner, climbed aboard the bus to make a presentation to Steve. They presented Steve with a very smart watch and a set of French Le Creuset saucepans which he and Belinda had said they would like. A few speeches were made and Steve responded by shaking their hands and saying thank you to everyone for such a lovely welcome home.. Many people in the crowd had known Steve since he was a small boy and so everyone felt quite emotional. It was very special for both him and us. My friend Sylvia, Steve's Godmother and my childhood friends' Queenie and Joan were there with their husbands Arthur and Derek, both of whom were Steve's Godfather. All three women were armed with the bath towels, printed with the stars and stripes, that we had brought back for them from America and they were madly waving these along with everyone else waving their Union Jacks as the bus pulled away.*

*Our next stop was the old folk's flats at Patches Field at the entrance to Marlow Bottom. Steve wanted to call in and say hello and show his medal to the elderly disabled people who had not been able to leave their homes. Once aboard again and with the cheering still ringing in our ears, the bus moved on driving out of Marlow Bottom on route to Marlow. The kids riding their bicycles were still bringing up the rear, and out in front, leading the procession, was an open topped cabriolet that had been loaned for the occasion by Philip's company Saab. My friend Queenie's son, David, was using our video camera and filming for us while his wife Gill drove the car. This was to be a lasting record of the day's events which we would all be able to watch and enjoy later. The theme music from the film 'Chariots of Fire' was playing out loudly through the car's stereo speakers. The whole atmosphere was so incredible, each passing car blowing its horn, as the bus made its steady progress to the outskirts of Marlow. We stopped here and The Marlow Town Mayor, Maurice Oram, got off the bus and continued to walk out in front accompanied by a policeman for the rest of the journey into the town.*

*As the bus slowed to negotiate a traffic island, one of the photographers jumped off the bus to get a better picture. We had to laugh when later he told us that in his excitement after taking some quick photos he had mistakenly jumped back on another similar looking red bus that was on the island at the same time but going in the opposite direction back towards High Wycombe.*

*The amount of people lining the streets of Marlow was astonishing; it was packed. The amazing flag and bunting adorned streets and the throng of cheering crowds was unbelievable. At the top of the Marlow High Street our procession was joined by two waiters from the renowned Marlow hotel, The Complete Angler, carrying an enormous cake on a stretcher. The previous week, we had been asked by their head chef for a photo of Steve's Gold medal so that he could make an exact replica and so we had sneaked a quick snap and delivered it to The Complete Angler without Steve's knowledge. The resulting cake was absolutely perfect in every detail and so enormous that I think everyone in the town could have been given a slice.*

*In the middle of the High Street, strung from one side to the other, was a huge banner with the words "Welcome Home Steve and Mike, Well Done, Olympics 1984". Mike had been given a town reception when he had won his Empire Medal in 1956 but he told us it had been nothing like this. I think both Mike and Steve were overwhelmed; Geoff and I were.*

*We caught sight of Queenie, Sylvia and Margaret again waving their towels and this time wearing Union Jack hats. Right next to them and from the pub "The George and Dragon" on the causeway, were two 'Mr Men' characters. They looked hilarious, all fat and wobbly and bobbing about, squeezing through the crowds.*

*At the bottom of the High Street the bus turned right into Pound Lane and here the rowing club members had turned out in force; it was wonderful to see everyone. That day made such a huge impact on Steve. He will never forget the welcome his town gave him on his return with his first Olympic Gold Medal. Not many parents get to see such overwhelming support for their son's achievements and to feel the tremendous pride that goes with it, but we certainly did that day.*

*At the end of our journey, the bus finally turned into the car park at Court*

*Gardens, the venue by the river where the reception was to be held. There to meet us were the other winning crew members Richard Budgett, Andy Holmes and Adrian Ellison. Martin Cross hadn't be able to make it as he was attending the wedding of another well known rower, Chris Baillieu. We all left the bus and walked into Court Garden House, the beautiful Georgian mansion on the edge of Higginson Park, which overlooks the River Thames and Marlow Regatta Rowing Course. Once inside the reception room, we looked through the large French windows to see crowds of people milling around on the lawns in front of the house and there were our family friends again waving their beach towels.*

*Unfortunately, non of our friends were invited to the reception that day; it was mostly dignitaries from Wycombe District Council, Great Marlow and Marlow Bottom Parish Council, Marlow Town Council, and local teachers etc. The mayor of Marlow that year was Mr Maurice Oram who worked for Wilkinson Sword. All the guests were ushered on to the veranda of Court Garden House and then Mr Mayor called everyone to order. He spoke to the crowds saying what a wonderful occasion this was that had brought everyone together on this day and that the town would like to now present Steve and Mike with an illuminated scroll.*

*The Mayor handed Steve his scroll and Steve shook his hand and thanked him and then stepped back with a definite look of relief on his face as Mike came forward to accept his. Steve, who was rather nervous of being asked to address such a large audience, thought he had managed to get away without speaking, although he had prepared a few words earlier, with the advice of Christine and Philip who had helped him write some notes, just in case.*

*The Mayor then went on to say how everyone had watched the four men with their cox come through the mist to win gold for Great Britain and then he looked at Steve and asked him to say a few words. Steve stepped forwards with a quick glance towards Christine and looking at the microphone said thank you for the wonderful reception and the welcome home and that he felt lost for words but would like to thank everyone and then he stepped back to a rousing cheer from the crowd. No one else noticed his nervousness but I could tell that he would rather have rowed the 2000m final all over again rather than speak in public.*

70

*Steve gave a quiet sigh of relief and then Mike stepped forward and gave an excellent speech about winning gold. He said that the best part of all was to come home and share it with family and the people of the town. To our delighted surprise, all of the ladies were presented with a basket of flowers and then we all moved back into the main reception room, giving a last wave to the crowd. Young waitresses, pretty Marlow girls, dressed in Union Jack t-shirts and white shorts passed around canapés and glasses of champagne to the guests. A little while later, a wonderful buffet was revealed, spread along white linen clad trestle tables, and there, centre stage, was the enormous Gold Medal cake.*

*After we had eaten the mayor read out some telegrams of congratulations from all over the country and a speech was made by a representative of the Marlow Rotary Club who presented each crew member with a tankard which was then duly filled with champagne. The mayor then produced a gleaming Wilkinson Sword which had been loaned especially for the day for Steve to cut the cake with. Steve plunged the huge blade into the gigantic Gold medal cake to a rousing cheer. It was truly a wonderful day and one Steve will remember always.*

*A few days later we all attended another Mayor's reception, this time at High Wycombe Town Hall. This was another memorable occasion and one which we all enjoyed. This time when Steve was asked to speak, he looked a little more relaxed than the time before. Over the coming years Steve would become a very adept after dinner speaker but media attention always seems to take a sportsman a little time to get used to as it is not their most natural arena.*

*The following week, The Amateur Rowing Association gave a reception for all the Olympic rowers and Geoff and I were invited too. It was a very pleasant event and as we knew most of the lads there, we happily spent our time reminiscing with them. It took quite a few weeks for things to settle down but gradually our lives returned to normal.*

# Chapter Five
## World Championships 1985 Hazewinkle Belgium

### *Scull for Gold*

*After all the excitement, Steve settled back into the 1985 rowing season. It soon dawned on him though that there was now the added pressure of trying to repeat his previous success. This year Steve thought he would like to have another go at the single sculls. Martin Cross and Adam Clift joined together in a pair and Richard Budgett decided to give up international rowing and concentrate on his medical career. Richard was to say a few years later in an interview with the American writer Steve Seabrook, referring to the coxed four, "The boat was a decent one until Redgrave got into it; then it flew". Andy Holmes, who had been in the building trade prior to the Olympics, always admired by the others for having the strength to carry a hod and to train for the Olympics at the same time, had decided to take a year off from competing and return to 'normal life' as on his return from Los Angeles he had married.*

*Steve made his start to the rowing calendar year with a win at Marlow Long Distance Sculls in October. At over 4.5km and upstream, this is considered the toughest 'head' race on the Thames. Second place went to Joff Spencer-Jones, with Mark Buckingham coming in third. Mark was from the younger Great Marlow School crew and was now beginning to make his mark in senior rowing.*

*Steve decided not to enter the 'Scullers Head', the 4¼ mile ebb tide course from Mortlake to Putney due to take place the following Spring but instead entered The 'Wingfield Sculls' in November. This is raced over the same course and the same distance but is rowed in the opposite direction, on a* flood tide, from Putney to Mortlake. These tidal reaches of the river Thames are often referred to as the Tideway and this stretch of river is also known as the Championship Course due to the famous Oxford and Cambridge University boat race that has been held here annually since 1845. Steve won this race for the first time taking the title 'Amateur Sculling Champion of the Thames'.

That summer, at Marlow Regatta, he won the 'Elite' sculls, which led him on to Henley Royal Regatta in early July. He won all of his races here, one on Thursday and two on Friday and on Saturday he came up against the much respected sculler, Ibarra, from Argentina. In this race Steve beat the record to the barrier and continued to lead all the way to the finishing line. Steve was really impressed by the other sculler's sportsmanship when Ibarra came up and shook his hand after the race and wished him all the very best for the future. On finals day, on Sunday, he met B.A. Lewis and won the Diamond Sculls for the second time. It was an exciting day and all the family were again there to see him collect another medal. It was good weather for once and so afterwards we enjoyed the usual family picnic on Lions Meadow, the official car park and traditional Henley picnic area, behind the blue and white stripped tentage that is Henley Royal Regatta.

Nottingham National Regatta held from July 19$^{th}$ - 21$^{st}$ was earmarked as the venue where the boys from the Los Angeles gold medal crew would be honoured. Her Royal Highness, Princess Anne was coming to present each of the boys with the oar with which they had rowed in their winning race with at the Olympics. The oar blades had been specially sign written by hand with the five Olympic rings, the date of the race and with the crew member's names. All the family had been invited up to Holme PierrePoint, The National Water Sports Centre, to take afternoon tea with the Princess after the presentation. The whole crew were there with the exception of Richard Budgett who was in America and so Richard's mother was there to accept the oar in her son's absence.

Moira Cross had brought her mother with her this time but we had sadly decided that the long journey would be too much for my mother Ada. We all dressed up for the occasion and Belinda and Steve had worn their Olympic uniforms and again looked very smart indeed. We all assembled at the Tower on the Holme Pierre Pont course to see Princess Ann arrive in *a red helicopter. She was then greeted by members of the Amateur Rowing Association with the new President of the A.R.A. making all the necessary introductions. She then approached each crew member in turn, presented them with their newly painted oar and had quite a long chat with each one. They felt really honoured to meet her; she really is a lovely lady, a keen sportswoman and is, of course, no stranger herself to Olympic competition.*

*We were then all escorted to a special function room where afternoon tea was to be served. Groups of us were seated at small tables and Princess Ann was then introduced to a long line of people. Our table was very close to hers but we didn't get a chance to actually meet her. She did speak to Belinda though and said that she was very sorry that she couldn't stay to see Steven's race later that afternoon but she wished him all the best and gave her best wishes to his parents and family; we felt very proud parents but also quite sorry for poor Belinda as she seemed a little embarrassed that everyone's eyes were on her.*

*The squad soon returned to hard training as their next race meeting was at the 1985 World Championships in Hazewinkle, Belgium. Due to lack of funds, there had been no pre-championship training camp planned for this year. There would be no problems with hotels on this visit to Belgium for us as we were now planning to travel and camp in our V.W. Camper. Sadly, it was not to be good Championships for Steve. He didn't win his heat so he had to go through the repechage to the semi-final and then in this race, he pulled up with what seemed to be a back muscle injury. He paddled into last place and had to be helped out of his boat and was taken off to the physio. We, as spectators, couldn't seem to find out what had happened to him so we went to the medical area where we found him in absolute agony. A young physiotherapist had put ice directly onto his back and had fetched a layer of skin off and then on top of this she had gone on to use the ultrasound machine. The Belgian doctor had to stop her and eventually Steve received the correct treatment. Unfortunately, he couldn't recover from his injury in time to make an impression on his last race and could only just manage to row over the course to finish last in the small final.*

*Back home in England, Steve got an appointment with Terry Moule, an osteopath and a specialist in his field. Terry diagnosed a severe back condition and said that if this wasn't properly treated Steve may never row again. Terry did a marvellous job and Steve eventually recovered completely but his treatment took a long time. He had to visit Terry's clinic in Hemel Hempstead everyday for a month, then twice a week and gradually his visits dropped down to once a month over the next three months but the eventual outcome was thankfully excellent.*

*There was some good news for British rowing from Hazewinkle. Martin and Adam won a World Championship Silver Medal in the Coxless Pair, the only men in the whole of the British team to make the final. Beryl Crockford and her partner Lin Clark won gold in the Women's Lightweight Double Sculls and Steve's girlfriend Belinda Holmes and Fiona Johnson finished ninth in the women's pairs.*

*Set backs happen in life but with strength of character one can bounce right back and this was what Steve was about to do. He finished off the 1985 season with light training and a win in the long distance sculls at Marlow.*

# Chapter Six
## World Championships 1986 Nottingham
## Great Britain

### *XIII Commonwealth Games Scotland Triple Gold*

*On 5ᵗʰ April, Steve won the 1986 'Scullers' Head' a timed race from Mortlake to Putney, in a time of 21:25.08 and quickly followed this up on the 24ᵗʰ April with his second win at the 'Wingfield Sculls' which follows a course on the same stretch of river but in the opposite direction. With an uncomfortable row in rough water Steve managed to take a one length lead after just 30 seconds and went on to win the race by a substantial margin of 27 seconds, therefore retaining his title as " Amateur Rowing Champion of the Thames " with a finishing time of 23:04.*

*Steve had rejoined the squad system by now and Andy Holmes had returned from his year off so they were matched up as a pair. They were selected to compete for Britain at the 1986 World Championships being held at the Holme Pierpont course in Nottingham in August and would row as the Coxed Pair. Adam and Martin were also selected and they were put together in a Coxless Pair.*

*The Royal Regatta at Henley was, this July, extended to a five day event and Steve and Andy entered the Silver Goblets. They got through to the Sunday final and won this event for the first time. Steve defended his title in the Diamond Sculls and managed to get right through to the final where he met Bjorne Eltang, the Danish World Lightweight Champion. The race got underway with Steve taking the lead by a few lengths but at the Fawley Stand, with the race almost over, Steve stopped. We couldn't believe our eyes as Eltang overtook him and won the race. Steve finished the race but we could see he was not himself and we all rushed to the boat tents expecting it to be his back injury giving trouble again. We couldn't find him there but Andy and his wife told us that Steve was all right, just very disappointed with his performance, as he hadn't paced himself very well and had just run out of steam.*

*Feeling great relief that he wasn't injured, I got very emotional and a little tearful. It didn't help matters when everyone I met that afternoon kept saying that they were sorry to hear of his defeat. Eltang was not very nice either when speaking to the press he called Steve unpleasant names and didn't really act the gentleman. I felt rather silly taking it to heart so much and in future years I did learn to be a little more pragmatic in similar situations but I never forgot Eltang. Steve was upset too as he never enjoyed loosing a race but he realised that he only had himself to blame and was determined to put it behind him. Some consolation for him this regatta was collecting the 'Silver Goblets' Henley medal with Andy.*

*The next big event for Steve was the 1986 Commonwealth Games which were to be held at Strathclyde, in Scotland from the 25<sup>th</sup>-29<sup>th</sup> of July where rowing events were returning to the Games for the first time in 24 years. The whole family travelled up to Edinburgh to support Steve, even the three dogs. Jane and David and their two dogs joined Christine and Philip in their caravan and Geoff and I and our dog Tasha stayed in our V.W. camper. We had even brought along our T.V and video recorder so that we could tape Steve's races.*

*We all attended the opening ceremony in Edinburgh at Meadowbank Stadium and Scotland put on a wonderful show. The theme was "Spirit of Youth" and included 6500 Scottish schoolchildren taking part in a series of gymnastics routines en masse. This was the 13<sup>th</sup> Games and in the end only twenty seven nations of the Commonwealth competed due, once again, to a large political boycott. In all 32 of the 59 Commonwealth countries, mostly African, Asian and Caribbean nations that were due to take part, boycotted the Games. This mainly affected the athletic events and not the rowing as the boycotting nations didn't usually have much of a presence in any rowing events.*

*The water sports events were held in Strathclyde Country Park in Lanarkshire about 50 miles west of Edinburgh, close to Glasgow. The artificial Strathclyde*

Loch is centered in almost four square miles of beautiful parkland located next to the River Clyde between Hamilton and Motherwell and here the spectators were provided with good facilities and an excellent campsite placed at the start of the rowing course.

Steve was rowing in three events here; the Single Scull, the Coxless Pair with Andy and the Coxed Four with Andy, Martin Cross and Adam Clift with Adrian Ellison as their cox. There wasn't a coxed pair event at this regatta, if there had been, I think Steve may well have entered all four events. He was able to enter three of them as the race scheduling enabled athletes to 'double up'.

After his defeat at Henley, we were all a little apprehensive about the sculling event. There were some good athletes in this event competing from both Australia and New Zealand but we need not have worried. At Henley, Steve had learnt a hard lesson, never to be forgotten, and he now knew that he must pace himself over the whole course and row his own race. It turned out to be a three horse race with the New Zealander taking the lead followed by the Australian and then Steve. At the 1000m mark, Steve took the lead and won the race with a time of 07:28, a whole 5 seconds ahead of the Australian, Richard Powell and 11 seconds ahead of New Zealand's Eric Verdonk, who took the bronze. One down, two to go!

On the last day of racing, Andy and Steve won the Coxless Pairs with ease in 06:40 with New Zealand taking silver and Scotland the bronze; they then had only two hours to rest before the Coxed Four event. There were some very strong contenders in this race with crews from New Zealand and Australia. It was a hard slog but a tremendous race for our boys, who, leading all the way, came home to win in 06:08, taking the gold medal by 2 seconds from New Zealand with Australia only 1 second behind them. By tradition, it is usually the cox who is thrown in after a winning race but this time it was Steve who got a dunking from the rest of his crew.

Steve was ecstatic; he now had three Commonwealth gold medals to add to his collection and in the process had lain to rest the ghost of Henley. The following day, Jim Railton of The Times headlined 'REDGRAVE'S POWER AND STAMINA LAND FIRST MAJOR TRIPLE VICTORY', he then went on to write 'The ultimate achievement of becoming the first rower to win three gold medals in an international men's championships fell to Steven Redgrave yesterday - a testament to physical and mental stamina'; what an affirmation of his achievement. The Games ended with a great closing ceremony and a big party for all the athletes. We'd all had a great time even though the British weather had been mostly cold, wet and windy.

Not long after this, during the week of 17th – 24th August, the 1986 World Rowing Championships were held at The National Watersports Centre. This purpose built Watersports centre is located in Holme PierrePoint a village near Nottingham and it has a 2,000 metre regatta sailing facility which features a six lane rowing course. The World Rowing Championships, an international rowing regatta is organized by FISA, the International Rowing Federation. It is a week long event that has been held since 1962 and the competition was originally held every four years but in 1974 it became an annual event and in non-Olympic years had become the highlight of the international rowing calendar.

Steve was feeling very positive, particularly with this being his only big race left this season; he felt he could give it his all. Bolstering Steve's confidence too was a new crew member. Pat Sweeney had been introduced into their coxed pair boat. Pat was a very capable and experienced cox and he had been specially brought back from his coaching job in the States to join Steve and Andy for the championships. Things were looking promising.

The venue wasn't very far away from our home, so the whole family was able to gather together again to give their support. Chris, and Phil, towed their caravan to Nottingham, Jane, David, and their two dogs were camping in a tent and Geoff and I, and Tasha, our dog, were cosy in our V. W. camper. Steve and Belinda were having a bit of a cooling off period at this time and, as Belinda had not rowed this year either, she wouldn't be competing. Her younger sister Melanie, also a rower, was Adam's girlfriend and both couples seemed to have hit a sticky patch in their relationships.

The World Championships got underway with the Opening Ceremony which was quiet an informal event with tea being served afterwards; very British. Rowing began on Monday but Steve and Andy's first race wasn't until Tuesday. Their main opposition this time would be Italy. Carmine and Giuseppe Abbagnale, the brothers from Pompeii coxed by Giuseppe di Capua were World and Olympic Champions. Romania and Germany were also hot favourites for a medal so this was going to be tough event. In their first heat Steve and Andy won in a course record time. As it was 'first crew through to the final' we could relax for the rest of the day knowing that his first hurdle had been successfully negotiated. We watched a bit more rowing, took the dogs for a walk and then went to take a look around Nottingham. We hadn't had a chance to see the city before, even though we'd had many rowing trips up to this part of the country.

The Great Britain team were now entering the first of two days of finals and with a record eight crews getting through to this stage. The ladies events took place on Saturday and our Lightweight Coxless Four won silver, the Double Sculls and Coxless Pair took 6th place and the eight came in 5th. It wasn't really the best of results for us but as usual East Germany, Romania, and USSR had dominated the woman's rowing; some of their female crew were almost as big as the men.

Sunday arrived and the whole family was feeling slightly nervous. Philip had brought a huge Union Jack with him and had tied it to the front of the spectators stand and we all huddled together directly behind it, including Tasha the dog. The Men's Lightweights started the day with the Lightweight Coxless Four taking silver. Alan Whitwell and Carl Smith took Gold in the Lightweight Double Sculls. It was now the turn of the heavyweight men to race and first up was Adam Clift and Martin Cross in the Coxless Pair. The Russian twin brothers Yuri and Nikolai Pimenov had entered this and were already holders of World and Olympic titles. Our boys fought every step of the way down the course but could only finish a close 4th; just out of the medals. Adam had to be taken to the first aid tent directly after the race as he had passed out due to lack of oxygen. We all felt very sad for them especially as they had taken a silver medal in 1985; they were naturally very disappointed.

It was now time for Andy, Steve and Pat to go in the Coxed Pair race. We prayed that all the hard work they had put in would pay off. Italy was the favourite to win today and we had seen them take gold at the 1984 Olympics. The Italian coach had stood close to us in the spectator's stand, in Los Angeles and had loudly sung the Italian National Anthem. We hadn't imagined then that two years later Steve and Andy would be fighting the Abbagnales for gold. Steve and Andy had beaten them at Lucerne in a very good time, but that was then and this was now; they would have to do it all over again today if they were to win their first World medal together.

We sat by a TV monitor in the stands so that we could see the race closely from the very start; our stomachs were all aflutter as usual. They made a good start lying third with Italy in second place and the East Germans out in front. By the 1500m mark our boys had moved up a little and were still in third place but now only one second behind the Italians, who were still hot on their heals. The time to this mark  RDA 1.35.52, ITA 1.64 and GBR 1.63. Brazil and the USSR were about a length back but. At 1000m and with half the race now completed, the East Germans still lead the pack by 12 seconds but our lads had steadily moved into second place with Italy now trailing in third and now a whopping 24 seconds behind them. At the 500m mark Andy and Steve seemed to change up a gear, encouraged by Pat to raise their rate and keep their stoke nice and long. The tension mounted; the Italians were now just ¾ of a length behind and chasing. The Germans still in the lead tried to respond to Great Britain's final push but they had already done too much and their stroke mans head went down; they could not keep up this blistering pace. Steve and Andy swept passed them to deafening cheers from the crowd to take their first World Gold Medal with a time of 6.52.66. Italy took the silver and Germany drifted in to take bronze. The German stroke man was taken to hospital and although he eventually recovered, did not return in time to collect his bronze medal. Andy and Steve had taken 23 seconds off their own course record and they were exhausted but totally elated; they had done it. This has since been described by the pundits as one of the most breathtaking races ever.

Chris Baillieu interviewed them at this point while they were still seated in their boat and trying to catch their breath. Sticking the microphone in front of Steve, he said, "Now you are Olympic and World Champions," and Steve answered breathlessly, "And Commonwealth," to which everyone laughed. Now recovered a little, they rowed off to wind down passing in front of the stand where the roar from the crowd then erupted, equalling a stadium full of football supporters cheering a World Cup win.  We hadn't seen them that day but Steve's old school friend, Craig Gibbons, and his family had come along to support him. We didn't find out that they had been amongst the crowds till later in the week when they sent him a letter of congratulation. We were all overjoyed with happiness for him, what a wonderful year it had been.

Their race had been televised which was good news as that began to bring them into the public eye which was just what was needed for the sports future sponsorship. Christine and Philip made a move to go home directly after the race to avoid the traffic and Jane, David, Geoff and I stayed on to wait for the crush to die down. While we were waiting, Jane spent a mad half hour running round the field with her dogs. One of them suddenly ran out in front of her and tripped her up and she seemed to have hurt her leg quite badly. David took her off to hospital where she had an x-ray and was told she had broken a bone. By the time she got back to us she was in plaster so after a quick cup of tea, served with sympathy, we decided to go home; poor Jane, what a way for her to end a perfect weekend.

The pair had done so well that it was decided by the 'powers that be' to select them to represent Great Britain at the 1988 Olympics but first they had to get through '87. Steve and Andy decided to make it a degree more difficult for themselves and 'double up', going for both the coxed and the coxless pairs. In the following trials they were to prove to Penny Chuter, then Director of British rowing, that they were the fastest crew in both boats. It was agreed that with the help of Mike Spracklen as their coach, they were all sure it could be done.

Steve and Belinda, although still estranged partners, were still good friends and during their time together had always talked about visiting Australia. Her family had moved out there when she was about three and her youngest sister Rebecca had been born there. The family had moved back to England when Belinda was thirteen and had decided to make an adventure of the return trip. Belinda's Mom and Dad and their four daughters had taken a boat to India and then travelled overland the rest of the way home to Britain by campervan. Steve and Belinda decided that they would make a trip together to Australia in December. Belinda would visit her friends again in Geelong in Victoria where she used to live and Steve would visit my relatives who lived in Wollongong in New South Wales.

Steve was never a great letter writer, he would rather use the phone occasionally. I guess this had been mainly due to his dyslexia and to confirm this, the only written communication we received from him during his seven week trip away, was one 'tick box' letter which he had duly filled in and posted from Sydney. It became a family joke that the only letter he had ever written to his parents in his life was a 'tick box' letter.

In 1925 mother's sister Gladys had emigrated to Australia, on her own, at the tender age of eighteen. She had married an Australian man called Frank Gray and they'd gone on to have six children, five boys and one girl. My mom and dad had written to them regularly and when I was about twelve, I began to write too, to my cousin Joan. I still regularly write to Joan and her daughter Wendy nowadays. I had not, up to this point, had a chance to visit Australia and my relatives had never been to England either so we were yet to meet. Geoff had met them though, as in the early '50's, before we had married, while he was serving in the Merchant Navy, he had sailed to Australia and made a point of going to Wollongong near Sydney to visit them all on my behalf.

I had met part of the Australian clan though. Uncle Frank's brother Alf and his wife Edna had been great travellers and had once toured Europe visiting us in England, sometime during Steve's early senior years. At that time, they had both worked for Sydney University, Alf as a lecturer and Edna, as a librarian. Sadly, on their return to Australia, Alf had suffered a severe heart attack and had died. He was a really nice man and he had been several years younger than my uncle Frank. Edna, whose own family had immigrated to Australia, when she was just a little girl, continued to visit England every few years after that and always spent a few days with us.

Belinda went out to Australia about a week before Steve and they arranged to meet up later at my Cousin Joan's house. Steve had a friend, Paul Rushant, who rowed for the Maidenhead Rowing Club and he had won a competition in the Daily Mirror giving him a place to serve as a grinder with the crew onboard "The White Horse", the British entry in the Americas Cup. This most prestigious regatta and match race in the sport of sailing was being held this year in Fremantle, Australia. It had been arranged that Belinda would join Steve at Joan's home and then later they would both go together to offer their support to Paul in Fremantle.

*Steve flew out to Sydney and was met by my cousin Joan and all of her family at the airport. I think he was a bit overwhelmed meeting all of his Australian relatives; there were so many of them. Aunt Gladys had six children and they all had their own brood so there were quite a few of them altogether. Belinda joined Steve in Sydney and together they visited my cousin Brian who had a farm out in the bush and they really enjoyed their stay. After this they flew to Brisbane where they met up with some of Belinda's old friends. They then spent a few days at Paradise Beach before flying to Fremantle to watch Paul in the yacht race. They'd really enjoyed a great holiday together and it had been a pleasant way to draw their relationship to a close; they are still good friends today.*

*While they were away, a very official letter arrived for Steve. It was from the Prime Minister and was marked E.R. Steve had told us to take care of his mail while he was away and he would telephone every now and then to see how things were so Geoff and I opened the letter. It was to ask if Steve would accept the M.B.E. for his services to rowing and the letter told him that the honour would be announced in the New Years Honours List and that under no circumstances was he to tell anyone beforehand. We didn't know whether to tell him now or to wait until he got home. Geoff put it to the family and it was decided that we should wait for his return, in case the word got out. We were all very happy for him, we didn't know if Andy had been given a similar honour and we couldn't ask Mike either, so all we could do was to wait. I was bursting to tell everyone but we kept our lips sealed. This was really hard for us all though as he was going to be away for seven weeks.*

*He flew back into Heathrow during the early hours of the morning and went straight from the airport to visit his new girlfriend, Ann Callaway, at her flat in Fulham. Ann had been extremely ill and in hospital while he had been away so he was anxious to see how she was now and found that, thankfully, she was a lot better. The BBC Sports Personality Awards were to take place that evening which he had been invited to attend. We saw him on the TV that evening as he arrived at the BBC with the other athletes and he looked very jet lagged. This year Steve had been nominated for the award but did not win. It was awarded, controversially that year, to Nigel Mansell with Fatima Whitbread coming second and Kenny Dalglish third. Steve wasn't the only one to be disappointed that evening as I later read that Gary Lineker had felt let down too, coming in fifth, behind Ballyregan Bob, the greyhound; to date the only dog to appear on the programme.*

*The next day, when Steve arrived home, we gave him the letter from Buckingham Palace. He was so pleased it was wonderful to see his face as he read the letter and I could have cried with joy for him; the investiture was to take place on March 10th 1987. We planned ahead for a big celebration next March but we thought that it would be a nice idea to hold a party for his family and friends on New Years Eve when the Honours List would be released. We were 'pipped at the post' as just two days before the party it was leaked to the newspapers that he had been awarded an M.B.E. for services to rowing including being the only person to have won three gold medals at the Commonwealth Games.*

*We discovered, much to our surprise, that Andy had not been awarded an honour as well. This had upset Andy and also he seemed a little cross with Steve and Mike. It had not been their fault that Andy had been forgotten and we didn't know who had nominated Steve, as it was then a closed system. The Gold medal winning coxless four had not been nominated for an honour after their win in Los Angeles although more recently every Olympic medal winner seems to receive one. This took the shine off it a little for Steve as, when he received the many cards of congratulations that followed; quite a few people had written how sad they had felt that Andy had not been honoured at the same time. Andy, was awarded the MBE eventually. It came along the following June, in The Queen's Birthday Honours. It did not in any way affect their rowing together but it had caused an upset for a while and I felt it had been a real shame that it had happened.*

*Back in training once again, they now had to train in both boats every day. There was no doubt that Andy and Steve gelled well together in a boat, they made it look so easy. In fact they were working extremely hard. They would spend half a day in the coxless boat and the other half in the coxed pair with Adrian. Both of them were strong personalities and single-minded people but they also had one aim - to win in both boats. The format for Olympic racing had been changed making it now possible for them to row coxless one day and then coxed the next. The only time they would have to race twice in one day, would be for the semi-finals when there would hopefully be enough time between the two races for them to rest. Steve explained to us his differing views of the two boats he described the coxless boat as being 'lively and fast' and the coxed boat being 'heavier and harder on the legs' and that they were getting used to the change over. All we could do was to keep our fingers crossed for them; as the saying goes, 'the proof of the pudding is in the eating'*

*It was February 1987 when we got the wonderful news from Jane, and David, that they were expecting not one baby, but two. They had been told in 1986 that it was unlikely that Jane would be able to have any children so they had gone through an IVF specialist clinic. With the help of her own doctor, Hilary Walsh, and Professor Ian Croft of The Cromwell Hospital, and of course, her truly wonderful friend Jenny, who had donated her eggs, they were now expectant parents. I cannot describe how we all felt; it was fantastic and quite unexpected news. We were to become grandparents in September. Jane and David received quite a lot of media attention when the twins were born later that year because it was the first time that the G.I.F.T technique had been used with eggs donated by a 'known donor'.*

*D.A.F. Trucks, a Netherlands truck manufacturing company who had an office in Marlow, was now sponsoring Steve and Andy. They had, up until now, been putting sponsorship money into football but due to much adverse media coverage of problems with football hooligans, they had decided to sponsor rowing instead. As well as sponsoring Steve and Andy internationally, DAF were putting a lot of money into British domestic rowing through the creation of a regional competition of 'sprint rowing'. The competition split the county into four regions with the finals taking place at Peterborough, and all of it with TV coverage under the expert direction of David Goldstrum, the famous TV sports commentator and broadcaster.*

*Rowing is normally viewed as one of the most physically strenuous and energy demanding of all sports. A mixture of physical strength, endurance, aerobic power and mental determination is needed by the athlete to cover, the more usual, 2000m long course. In 'sprint rowing' however, the course, at 500m, is much shorter and this requires a more immediate and explosive performance from the competitors and therefore, makes the race much more exciting for spectators and, more to the point, television viewers. The boat* categories that were to be used for the 'sprints' were the Single Sculls, the Coxed Fours and the Eights. Also included in the competition was an ergometer test on a rowing machine.

From each of the regional 'Sprint's', the winners, and the fastest losers, of both the men's and women's events went forward to the final. Steve won both the Single Sculls and the Ergo test for his region and then went on to win a sculling boat and ergometer for his Marlow club in the finals. He was really pleased that he had been able to win this equipment for Marlow Rowing Club and it was very satisfying for him to be able to give a little something back for all the support he had received from his club over the years. The programme of the event was televised twice on Channel 4, once over the Christmas holidays; it made very good viewing.

# Chapter Seven
## The MBE

### *A Royal Engagement*

*Only two guests could accompany Steve to Buckingham Palace and Steve really wanted Ann to go, so Geoff stood down and Ann and I went with him. Philip drove us to London in his Saab and dropped us off inside the court yard of the Palace. Ann looked very nice in a black and white, small-checked, suit with a black hat and I wore a navy suit with a royal blue hat; we were both really excited.*

*We entered the main hall where Steve had to leave us to go with the other recipients and Ann and I walked up the beautiful red carpeted hallway leading to the Victorian Ballroom. The wide corridor was white marble with wonderful paintings adorning both walls. Soldiers of the Household Cavalry stood at intervals along the corridor dressed in their plumed helmets, silver breastplates and high black leather boots and never moved a muscle. As we entered the grand ballroom, the largest room in the palace, I was stunned by its beauty; this was where Steve's investiture would take place. The surroundings were stunningly beautiful and it made me feel very proud to be British.*

*We chose a tiered seat at the left of the room where we could look down on the proceedings. From here we had an excellent view of the raised platform, the throne dais, where the Queen would stand during the investiture ceremony. A short time after we had taken our seats, a band of the Grenadier Guards took their seats in the musicians' gallery, a balcony overlooking the rear of the ballroom and began playing some delightful background music; they continued to play throughout the proceedings. Everyone got to their feet as the Queen entered and she took up her position, standing just towards the* back of the small podium. To her right an Officer of the Armed Forces stood and loudly announced each recipient's name in turn. As they approached the Queen, they bowed and then stepped forward to receive their award. The Queen said a few words to each person before they took three steps back and then left the ballroom only to reappear a few moments later and take one of the seats that had been set out for them towards the rear.

Steve was one of the last, as the people receiving the M.B.E. were towards the end of the honours list. He duly did what he had been told; arriving in front of the Queen, he bowed and stepped forward. She gave him his M.B.E. and then had a long chat with him; he stepped back, bowed and left the ballroom. I can't begin to describe my feelings at this moment; I thought that I would burst with pride. With Ann being there for Steve too today; it was lovely for them both. It was just so sad that Geoff and the rest of the family could not have been here to see it too.

Once the investiture was over, we made our way back to the quadrangle where everyone was having their official photos taken. We all did the same and then Philip met us and took us back to the car. As we drove through the Palace gates, the rest of the family were waiting. It had been quite a cold day, especially for them. We slipped out of our car for a few family photographs and then we all returned to our respective cars and drove home to Marlow to have a special lunch with my mother. At 85 years old, it was quite hard for Ada to take it all in but I could see she was very proud of her only grandson.

At lunchtime Steve announced that he was going to take us all out to dinner that evening to the Complete Anglers Hotel in Marlow. What a treat, I had lived in Marlow for about thirty years and had never been to this beautiful hotel on the river. The hotel has such a lovely setting with lawns reaching down to the water, right by the bridge and opposite Marlow Rowing Club. That evening the family spent another memorable occasion together and the evening began when we were greeted in the foyer my the manager with a very large bottle of champagne, compliments of the management. We then posed with our full champagne glasses raised for the local press photographer. I think we were all feeling a little merry by the time we sat down to eat our delicious meal. But what a wonderful day it had been from start to finish, our son's special day and a lasting memory for all of us.

The 1987 World Rowing Championship was held in Copenhagen in Denmark. It was my first visit there but Geoff had been before when Steve and Adam had rowed together in a competition there when they were juniors. Copenhagen was a beautiful city but the weather was a bit mixed. We had driven here in our V.W. Camper and Ann joined us for the last few days of rowing. It was harder for her to get away now that she was a working as a doctor in London hospital. Adam's parents were there too and we all enjoyed the event together.

On Monday they won their heat in the Coxless Pair and on Tuesday they did the same in the Coxed Pair with their cox, Pat Sweeney, on board. They now had the hard task of repeating their performances on Thursday, but this time, in two semi-final races. First up was the Coxless Pairs race and they put up a good performance and won this convincingly. The Coxed Pair was next and in this race, to make the final, they had to come somewhere in the first three. They managed this and, with both semi's now under their belt, they looked towards Saturday and the Coxless Pair final.

In their first final on Saturday, they came up against the Pimenov brothers from Russia. Both Andy and Steve knew this wouldn't be a walk over, the Russians were good. They also knew that they had to race again the following day and so this race had to be a balance of doing enough to win but expending as little energy as possible. Steve sporting a full beard, eased off in mid race dropping his rate to 33and and letting the Romanians take the lead. As they approached the line the British Pair slipped into top gear and powered through to take the Gold medal with Romania 2<sup>nd</sup> and the Russians in 3rd.

On Sunday in the Coxed Pair, they would be racing the World Champions, the Italian Abbagnale brothers again. Whenever they raced this pair, the Abbagnales seemed often to make a false start; too keen to get away, I suppose. When a crew is ready and all geared up to go, false starting can take a lot out of them and it always takes time to get back to the start line to begin the race again, and today this happened. They went off cleanly the second time and by the time the race had reached the 1500m mark, the Abbagnales had a two length lead. Steve and Andy then made their move and gave one almighty push for the line and as the Abbagnales crossed the finishing line Steve and Andy had pulled enough back to take the Silver *and were just ¾ of a length behind. Our boys had done really well but they really wished that they could have made it two Gold's. Next year at the Seoul Olympics, they had already decided, would be their time.*

*Pertti Karppinen, legendary for his three consecutive Olympic Gold medals in Single Sculls and being twice World champion, came over and shook Steve's hand. This meant so much to Steve, as he thought that this Finnish rower, who at nine years older than himself and his idol, was the greatest athlete in the sport. Pertti had just been beaten into bronze third place by a young German Thomas Lange who had taken gold. Thomas also came up and shook Steve's hand and said, "You don't remember me do you?" Steve's answered, "I shall never forget you; you beat Adam and me in Hazewinkle in the 1980 junior Double Sculls." They smiled and parted with the greatest respect for each other. In the rowing world they were kings, but the general public were only just beginning to take notice of Andy Holmes and Steve Redgrave.*

*The day that we had all been waiting for had arrived, September 29ᵗʰ 1987. This was the due date for the birth of Jane and David's twins. The expectant parents had chosen the Humana Hospital Wellington in London and they were in the very safe hands of Professor Ian Craft. David was with Jane for the twin's arrival by caesarean section. We waited in eager anticipation at home for any news and every time the phone rang we rushed to answer it. The call came at 10am, our first grandchildren, a boy, Benjamin David Thomas and a baby girl Stephanie Janice had arrived and both mother and babies, and not forgetting dad, were doing really well. David told us that Jane and he had gone into the operating theatre at 7.30am that morning and that Ben was born at 9.03am weighing 6lbs 15½ oz and Stephanie at 9.04am weighing 6lbs 6oz. We rushed to London to see them and of course, we thought, they were just beautiful. There had been much media interest about the birth as this was the first time that Professor Craft had successfully used the GIFT technique which had been used in their conception. Later that morning a BBC film crew was at Jane's bedside and she and David were giving interviews while holding their new arrivals; the broadcast went out on the lunchtime news and again at 6pm and 10pm.*

*A few days later David was at work loading his car with the gifts colleagues had bought for the twins. He was going straight to the hospital from work.*

*He went back into the office to get his coat, returning immediately, to find that his car with the presents inside had vanished. He had looked around thinking that one of his work mates was having a joke but it had been stolen. The car turned up about ten days later parked out side a local policeman's house and, I'm glad to say, with all the gifts intact. As the new parents of twins they coped extremely well. Geoff and I always tried to be on hand to help if needed. They had a few sleepless nights to start with but the twins were very good babies and soon we were all getting used to and thoroughly enjoying this new phase of our family life.*

*In the autumn Steve and Ann got engaged, they had fallen in love and the world for them was looking rosy. As a doctor and a rower herself, Ann was perfect for Steve. She understood his dedication to his sport and the tunnel vision required to succeed and become the best in the world. Ann had been an Olympic rower herself in 1984, in Los Angeles, in the women's eight. Her chosen profession of medicine had meant that she had a skill that she could combine with rowing and she was being asked more and more to lend a hand with rowing injuries particularly in the squad.*

*Their engagement party was held at Court Garden House in Marlow, very appropriately, on the river Thames at Marlow. Both families and many friends were invited even our 10day old grandchildren were guests. Ann's aunt had made their engagement cake and we had caterers to provide and serve the lunch. A huge amount of work had been put in beforehand by June, Ann's mother, Christine, Jane and I, as we had been preparing food for days and had laid tables and decorated the hall that very morning. It was a great party and even Andy, the usually quiet man of rowing, let his hair down and joined the live band playing the drums. A lot of champagne was consumed that day and the party lasted from lunchtime to 7pm, although it took until gone eight o'clock for everyone to leave. I believe that a second party continued well into the night too, as Steve held an 'open house' later for all his friends at his own home in Marlow. It had been yet another very happy and memorable day in our lives.*

# Chapter Eight
## Steve and Ann's Wedding

### *Tying the Knot*

*Martin Cross was one of the orchestrators of the Serpentine Sprint Regatta along with Westminster council and London Electrics and Air France had kindly given their sponsorship. Rowing had not been held on the Serpentine in London's Hyde Park for quite a few years so this was a way of bringing it back into the public eye. It was also to be the inaugural national championships of British Dragon Boat racing with the winner going forward to the final which was being held in Hong Kong. The whole event was televised by Channel 4 with David Goldstrum organising and heading up the broadcasting team.*

*Dragon boat racing was a new phenomenon to Britain and it was such a spectacle to see twenty rowers, seated in 10 rows, two to a bench, paddling furiously aboard their 40ft boat, taking orders from their helmsman and keeping time to a drum. There was Gig racing too with 32ft traditional wooden boats, with six single-oar rowing positions and a cox. 'The Likely Lads' star Rodney Bewes had entered this event and was looking for a win. Rowing competitors from Italy, France, Russia, and Great Britain's national teams as well as junior and domestic athletes were here and it caused much excitement in the media.*

*I expect most people will remember the terrible storm that hit England in October 1987 and the rowing fraternity will not forget it in a hurry either. Trees were blown over and torn out by their roots, even enormous trees that had stood for hundreds of years. Hyde Park had been no exception and that night a huge tree crashed through a trailer of boats cutting the eights, fours and singles in half. Thousands of pounds worth of damage was done, it was devastating.*

*Most of the visiting competitors were using British boats rather than incurring the high cost of bringing their own. Due to lack of space at the event's boat shed at the Serpentine, Steve had, that night, put his sculling boat in a different place so luckily it had been spared. Despite the storm, everyone rallied round and many local clubs loaned the boats needed for the regatta to go ahead.*

*Everyone had to compete in two or three events. Steve entered the Sculls, the Coxless Pairs and the Eights and Andy entered the Coxed Four, the Coxless Pairs and the Eights. The competition was run on a points system, with points being awarded for each finishing place. Raced over a 500m course, most events were very close and exciting to watch. There was a good crowd and the atmosphere was great; a very successful event indeed. At the end of the day, Great Britain and Russia had tied for first place on points; the prize was some Waterford Crystal and I'm really not sure how they shared it. It had been a great mix of nations and a wonderful day with everyone looking forward to next year and maybe seeing themselves on TV at Christmas time.*

*The squad returned to the old task of winter training, although this time it was becoming more intense than ever with the Seoul Olympics on the horizon the following September. Knowing there was so much more to do; Mike Spracklen kept them at it. He was such a good guy and a great coach and he seemed to know Steve inside out.*

*We started to think about how we would travel to Seoul. It was difficult to plan ahead as there were as yet no secure seats in any boat until final crew selection had taken place but the air tickets and accommodation had to be sorted out soon nevertheless. I got in touch with "Sports World Travel" and managed to organise a party of 22 who wanted to go from our relatives and friends. Taking part in the British crews and from Marlow Rowing Club were Fiona Johnson, Mark Buckingham, Steve Turner and of course our Steve so, for a small town, we were fielding quite a few Olympians.*

*Andy and Pam. who had married after Los Angeles, by now had their first child, a little girl called Amy. Steve and Andy had been invited to Egypt over the Christmas period, to row on the Aswan Dam and at Luxor. They had decided to take Ann, Pam, and little Amy with them. They'd had a great time out there but their return flight gave them a little more excitement than expected. During take off, the flight had to be aborted because several tyres had burst as they were thundering along the runway. They said it had been very frightening for everyone and that all the passengers then had to endure a long delay while they replaced the tyres. We eventually met them at the airport and they all seemed very pleased to be home and still in one piece.*

*On New Years Eve and I lay awake long after the excitement had died down and amongst many thoughts I wondered what 1988 would hold for Steve. Rowing was still his life's focus and he now wanted to win a second consecutive Olympic gold medal. One would be hard enough to win but to try for two seemed almost impossible.*

*Our New Year opened with the anticipation of the twins christening; the service was to be held on Sunday 31ˢᵗ January at All Saints Church in Marlow where Jane and David had been married. It was to be a double christening ceremony, conducted by The Reverend Samuel Day. The Godparents for Stephanie Janice were to be her Aunts, Christine (Jane's sister) and Carolyn (David's sister) and family friend, Rod Schiller, and for Benjamin David Thomas they were to be Steve (Jane's brother), Alan (David's brother) and family friend, Jackie Sherry. When the day arrived David's brother Alan hadn't been able to attend the service as his own daughter had been taken seriously ill and was now in hospital; his place had been taken at the last minute by Philip, Chris's husband. Professor Ian Craft had been the guest of honour today, as it had been due to his expert professional care that the twins had been born; we had been really pleased to meet him and his wife and to offer him our thanks for being instrumental in making us grandparents. Jane and David's family doctor, Dr. Hilary Walsh, had been able to join us for the service too as she'd been the one who had initially suggested Jane and David seek Professor Craft's help and she had gone on to see Jane on an almost daily basis during the early part of her pregnancy. Jenny, Jane's wonderful friend who had donated her own eggs for the IVF procedure, was there with her own family; without her wonderful gift, we wouldn't have been celebrating this special day. The twins looked delightful in their long white christening gowns and were very well behaved while Reverend Samuel Day conducted the lovely service. Afterwards we returned to the twin's home in Marlow Bottom for the reception. A friend of the family, Tonya, had asked her mother, a wizard with sugar icing, to make and decorate the Christening cake. She had also re-iced and decorated the top tier of Jane and David's Wedding cake, in keeping with the British Christening tradition. Jane had been saving this cake for this occasion. The old cake was by now thirteen years old and had been considered to ancient to eat so both new and old cakes had been skilfully decorated with a little twin pram made from sugar paste.*

*Steve and Ann's wedding date had now been set for March 12th 1988. This was just one year and two days after Steve had received his M.B.E. so he'd remarked that he wouldn't easily forget his wedding anniversary. Some people within rowing thought he should have waited until after the forthcoming Olympics to get married but Steve and Ann had decided that the time was right for them.*

*Their wedding day was to be a very grand affair. One of the privileges extended to holders of The Most Excellent Order of the British Empire such as the M.B.E., is that their marriage and the christening of any of their children, can be held in the Chapel of The Order of the British Empire located in the crypt of St Paul's Cathedral; a Special Licence has to be granted for this by the Archbishop of Canterbury. Steve and Ann decided that it would be absolutely wonderful to make St Paul's the venue for their marriage service and the wedding reception was to be held afterwards at the Hyatt Hotel in London.*

*Paul Rushant, a rowing friend of Steve's from Maidenhead Rowing Club, was to be his best man and Adam Clift, Eric Simms, Nick Baatz, Clive Pope and Roger Hatfield were to be the ushers. Ann's bridesmaids were to be her sisters, Jane, and Susan, along with four little ones, a niece and three friends of the family. It had been decided to employ a subtle 'rowing theme' to the wedding and the six girls all wore pale blue and white striped dresses in Edwardian regatta style.*

*The bride, her mother June, and her two sisters stayed in the London Hotel on the eve of the wedding and were driven to St Paul's in vintage cars. Christine had driven to London very early on the actual day so that she could do all of their wedding make up and help the girls to get dressed. Ann's dress was made of a beautiful champagne coloured shot silk and the whole event was to be professionally videoed from begin to end and would include the filming of many of London's famous landmarks.*

*We hired two large executive coaches to transport family and friends from Marlow and Julie, a friend of Christine's, who had agreed to be the coach hostess for the day, served champagne and sandwiches on the journey to London. Everyone looked fabulous, the men in their morning suits with a tailcoat, waistcoat, striped trousers and top hat and the ladies, resplendent in their wedding outfits, wearing a variety of beautiful hats and looking lovely.*

*When we arrived at St. Paul's, Steve and his best man, Paul, met us in the car park. A coach full of Japanese female students had arrived too and were there on a sightseeing tour. One of our guests, Colin Jackson, a rowing family friend and a bit of a joker, lost no time in telling the girls who Steve was, with more than a little embellishment too, if I know Colin and subsequently, Steve was mobbed by the girls, as if he had been a pop star, and was forced to pose for photos with them, it was really quite amusing.*

*Our own vicar, Canon Dr Samuel Richard Day of All Saints Church Marlow, who had christened Steve, agreed to conduct the service and in such spectacular surroundings, their marriage was a very special occasion. As the bride and groom emerged from the Cathedral they were greeted by their rowing friends forming an archway of rowing blades as a guard of honour and the couple walked beneath them, hand in hand, down the ancient stone steps with St. Paul's as the backdrop; a wonderful photo opportunity.*

*Lots of passers-by stopped to look at us and our smartly dressed guests as we posed for the wedding photos. Then a voice from the crowd shouted, "Hello Sheila" and it was one of my mother's friends from years ago, Ivy Hands, who had come all the way from Birmingham to see Steve get married. My mother, Ada was very pleased to see her and they stayed chatting for a while. Bryan, my brother and his wife Pat were taking care of mom for the day as she was now in a wheelchair. She seemed to be thoroughly enjoying herself though even though it was going to be a very long day.*

*The weather had stayed dry for the photos and was sunny but breezy and everyone was smiling, Ann's mom, June, looked particularly radiant. My new daughter-in-law, Ann looked gorgeous, so tall and willowy in her beautiful bridal gown with its long train and my son looked so handsome in his 'top hat and tails' with a huge smile on his face.*

*The guests were coached to the reception and as they entered the beautifully decorated function room we greeted them and shook hands with everyone as they passed along the wedding family line up. It seemed to take forever but the long queue of guests seemed happy as they had been served with glasses of pink champagne and canapés. Another round of champagne oiled the conversation as the guests mingled, many of them already knowing each other, as the rowing world is fairly small compared to most sports. We then saw to our horror that the three tier wedding cake had toppled over and the waitresses were hurriedly trying to piece it together. The metal plate that the cake pillars stood on hadn't been inserted correctly and had caused the problem but it was soon fixed.*

*All the guests were then ushered into the dinning room. Once the guests were seated, the bride and groom entered together, arm in arm, to loud applause. An excellent meal was served and then it was time for the speeches. Ann's father began the proceedings followed by Paul Rushant, Steve's Best Man. He started his speech with 'Not many people know this but in 1977, I beat Steve in a coxed four at Walton regatta', then a while later he produced a huge blow-up of a picture of Steve when he was about four years old and said 'If any of you selectors want to know what a gold medallist looks like in his early years then, this is it', he was very funny. Steve's speech followed; he was getting much more used to speaking and he made a well rehearsed speech. Another hitch occurred when, during his speech, the flowers didn't appear on-cue for the 'mother's' and so he had to ad lib for a while till they were found and brought in.*

*The whole day was a great success and enjoyed by everyone. At the end of the evening the coaches arrived to take us home. Even Jane's six month old twins Ben and Steph had been very good, mostly happily sleeping throughout the proceedings, relaxed in their double buggy, dressed in their pink and blue 'baby grows' and looking so sweet. What a wonderful day, Ann's mom had done us all proud. The happy couple honeymooned on a small island in the Caribbean for just one week before returning so that Steve could catch up on lost training with the Olympics being now only a few months away.*

*At Henley Royal Regatta in July 1988, Steve and Andy entered the Silver Goblets pair race. In their first heat, unfortunately, Andy popped a rib. They did manage to finish the race but he couldn't go on to race again with this injury and so they withdrew from competition; what a disaster at this late stage, just prior to the Olympics. Usually in an Olympic year, crews that will be competing at the Olympics choose not to race at Henley as it is too closely placed in the rowing calendar and is not advised in their carefully planned lead-up to risk something like this happening. Proposed Olympics crews will use the final pre-Olympic regatta in Lucerne to judge their forthcoming world opposition instead. Steve and Andy had made the decision to enter Henley this year, mainly, to please their sponsors DAF Trucks, as it turned out unwisely so; we were concerned that this now might spoil their chances in Seoul.*

*DAF Trucks, the boys sponsor, had made Henley the venue for some corporate entertaining and had hired a Thames cruiser and marquee for the occasion. The following day Geoff, June and I were invited to spend the day with DAF and Steve and Ann joined us too as he was not racing. We all enjoyed our day, being 'wined and dined' although the weather that year had not been good but on this particular Sunday, the weather was absolutely dreadful. The field had flooded with the continuous downpour and water was lying on top of the grass. While we were waiting to board the cruiser some idiot in his Rolls Royce drove passed us and the spray from his wheels covered Geoff in mud. Geoff wanted to go home and change but he was persuaded to stick it out and anyway, by the end of the day, we were all covered in mud. That year H.R.H. Princess Ann had been asked to present the prizes and even she wore her 'green wellies'; unfortunately, no one could control the weather.*

*The big problem was now, Andy's rib. He visited Steve's osteopath, Terry Moule for treatment and Terry decided to rule him out of rowing at Lucerne. This was a shame as they would now not be able to measure their Olympic opposition but it was completely understandable in the circumstances. They tried to look at this from both angles, the opposition had not got their measure either; they were keeping their powder dry. Andy rested for a while and then went back to light training and in what seemed like no time at all they were off to the pre-Olympic training camp; they never looked back.*

# Chapter Nine
## The 1988 Seoul Olympic Games

### *The Dynamic Duo*

*It was very hard work for us in the week leading up to our departure for Seoul. I was now working as a full time driving instructor and had planned to take the week off before our trip to get ready but then at the eleventh hour, two of my pupils had their driving tests come through and so I had to accompany them to their tests although I was very pleased when they both passed. Ann had hoped to go this time to the Olympics in the Women's Eight but, due to illness in the boat, they had not done very well at Lucerne and had therefore been scratched from the British Olympic team altogether. This was really sad as they had put in so much effort and really, our girls needed this experience; a crew can't be expected to improve if they are not allowed to test themselves against international competition. DAF Trucks though, managed to get Ann a last minute ticket and she also took a job as the medical representative to the Cayman Islands, so in the end she was able to go but would have much preferred to have been one of the athletes.*

*Ann wasn't travelling with us to Seoul, she was leaving a little later in the week and was therefore able to take us to the airport where we met up with the rest of our friends and other rowing family supporters. We would all be travelling together as the British contingent and we found them there all ready and raring to go. We travelled with Thai Airways and when we boarded all the female passengers had a beautiful purple orchid, waiting for them, pinned in the headrest of their seat; a lovely touch. We were all seated in two's; Geoff and I, June, Ann's mum and Susan her sister, June's friend Patty and her daughter and Jenny and Derek Buckingham the parent's of Mark who was rowing in the four. Scattered about the plane were the Turners, the Dillons and the Stanhopes, the families of Stephen Turner,*

Terry Dillon and Richard Stanhope all rowing in the British eight. During the following two weeks we would all become good friends.

The flight took us over Denmark, Sweden, and Russia and on to India where we landed in Delhi to refuel and to take on more passengers. It was dark so we could only really see the airport buildings. Some passengers got off and few more got on and our flight took off again, this time bound for Bangkok. I recall the film shown on the flight was Bette Midler in "Big Business", it was quite amusing and helped to while away a couple of hours. We landed in Bangkok, Thailand, where we had a four-hour wait for the next leg of our journey. With not enough time between flights for any sightseeing and needing to stretch our legs, we contented ourselves with wandering around Bangkok airport looking in the shops, admiring some beautiful silks that were for sale. We then found a coffee shop and had a coffee to help to pass the time.

On the next flight, we were given another orchid which was lovely but by this time we were both beginning to feel a little uncomfortable. We landed at Hong Kong to pick up passengers and then went on to 'Kimpo' airport in Seoul, the capital city of South Korea and as they call it, "The Land of the Morning Calm". It was dark when we arrived and our journey had taken us about 30 hours so we were all feeling quite tired and a little jaded to say the least. There were a row of coaches outside the airport building to meet us but no one seemed to know which coach went to where. We were asked to leave all of our luggage in a big heap which we weren't too happy about and were then finally directed to the right coach. After a long drive, again sitting down, we finally reached what was called the "Olympic Family Town"; these words we would hear many times during our stay.

Once inside the 'Family Town', we were all allocated our apartments. June and Susan, Jen and Derek, Ann, Geoff and I were sharing one apartment and the Turners, Stanhopes, and Dillons were, in another. Patty and her daughter Tricia were allocated a nearby apartment which they were to share with a swimmer's family. The apartments did not have much furniture but they were quite large and we were all just pleased to have arrived and to get to bed. Our suitcases were finally delivered to our apartment at 2.15am. We had already arranged to meet everyone else at 7am the following day so we could begin finding our way to the opening ceremony. With the jet lag *beginning to win, we at last were able to get our heads down, even though it would only be for a short while.*

*Our first day in Seoul, September 17th 1988, started at 6am. Our apartment building looked like a very large multi-storey garage and we found out later that this was exactly what it was to become after the Games. In its very well organised 'all you could eat' restaurant there were very long counters serving every imaginable type of food, for all of the different nationalities that were attending as spectators. We just helped our selves to whatever we wanted and sat at the provided tables to eat as much as we liked.*

*After breakfast we found the 'laid on' coaches that would take us to the Opening Ceremony, which was being held in the main stadium at Songpa-gu near to the Han, a major river which flows through the centre of Seoul. The crowds were amazing; it took us a long time to get in to the stadium because of all the security measures that had been introduced. Once we had located our seats, waiting for each spectator was a large package. It contained a small radio that you could tune to your own language, a plastic Mac, a song sheet, a whistle that looked like a gold medal, a blow up cushion, a fan that looked like a table-tennis bat and a card which we would be asked to hold up at some point during the ceremony.*

*Once we had taken our seats we had time to look around us and try to take in this incredible scene. There was an enormous TV screen facing us, with the words "Gam sar Hamidam", which we later found out meant Welcome in Korean. Also on the screen was the Olympic Mascot, a cuddly orange tiger they called Hondori, which had been chosen to portray the friendly and hospitable traditions of the Korean people.*

*Jen and Derek Buckingham were sitting with us but June, Susan, Patty and Tricia's tickets had taken them to a different part of the stadium. We looked around, scanning the spectators, for our friends Pat and Moira Cross. These intrepid adventurers hadn't travelled with us and the 'Sports World' organisation; they had decided to take accommodation with the "Korean Family Association" which meant that they would be staying in a Korean home with a local family. They were getting to the Olympics by flying to Tokyo and then on to Osaka. From Japan they would be getting a passenger ferry to Pusan, in the South East and South Korea's main port, and then travelling up by train right through the centre of the country to Seoul, in the North West. Moira could never do anything the easy way, that's what makes her such an interesting character.*

*At 10.30am sharp the Opening Ceremony of the Games of the XXIV Olympiad began. It was the second summer Olympic Games be held in Asia and the first since 1964 when the Summer Games were held in Tokyo. Apparently, there were over 73,000 spectators in the stadium this morning, and it was reported that nearly three billion television viewers in more than 100 countries were watching around the world. First, up on the large screen, they showed the boats on the river Han that were bringing a special drum called the 'Dragon Drum' to the stadium accompanied by lots of small boats and windsurfers. Hundreds of Korean school children streamed into the stadium and ran in line in ever widening circles until they had formed the shape '88'. In the main arena eighty eight trumpeters heralded the arrival of the great drum which was over 2 metres in diameter and was now making an entrance through the north gate carried on a carriage pulled by 470 students wearing bright yellow robes; a man dressed in an ancient military uniform was beating it to symbolise the power of the heart beat of the competing athletes. Following behind them, was a procession of Korean farmers carrying the old 'tools of their trade'. There were then several stunning displays of traditional Korean dances and rituals by thousands of men, women and children, concluding with lots of high school girls pouring into the stadium and lying on their backs facing the sky, their bodies spelling out the words 'welcome'.*

*It was now time for the parade of the athletes. Over 8,000 sportsmen and women marched in to the stadium from 160 nations. As they filed in, the audience was prompted to blow the whistles we had been given in unison. It seemed to take ages to get the athletes into the arena and I looked out for Steve, although, he had told me he wasn't intending to be there as all of the standing about for so many hours, in the hot sun, would dangerously sap their energy and that they had come here to do a job which was to win in both the Coxed and Coxless pairs; he wanted nothing to get in the way.*

*Next Juan Antonio Samaranch the President of the International Olympic Committee gave his opening speech saying "Seoul has come so very far and has avoided so much potential trouble, but it's not done yet," he said. "On*

October 3, the day after the Games are over without incident, then we'll be able to celebrate." I assumed that he was referring to the threat of possible terrorist incidents and the fact that North Korea, still officially at war with South Korea, had boycotted the event joined by Albania, Cuba, Ethiopia, Madagascar, Nicaragua, and Seychelles. However, the much larger boycotts seen in the previous three Olympics had been avoided and this had resulted in the largest ever number of participating nations to date. The president of the Republic of Korea, Rho Tae Woo gave his proclamation in English next and with a strong Korean accent he said 'I declare the Games open of Seoul'. I'm not sure if his translator was later shot.

Eight Korean gold medalists came into the stadium holding the Olympic Flag led by an ancient Korean military band and was handed over and hoisted to the Olympic Anthem. When it reached the top of the flag pole 2,400 doves were released in recognition of this being the 24th Olympiad.

Next the torch arrived, carried into the stadium by Sohn Kee Chung the 76 year old who had been the gold medallist in the marathon at the Berlin Olympics in 1936. He had, at that time, been forced to take a Japanese name and compete as a member of Japan's Olympic team because the Japanese then occupied Korea; he was South Korea's most renowned sports hero. The huge caldron where the Olympic flame would burn for the duration of the games was perched at the top of the 'World Tree' tower. At the base of the tower was a round platform which smoothly rose to the top of the tower with the three people who were to ignite the caldron standing on it. They were two students and a teacher who, with their torches, reached over the side of the cauldron and ignited the sacred flame at precisely 12.30 pm. The whole of the audience stood to sing the Korean National anthem and when this had finished all the athletes quickly left the stadium.

Before the flame had been lit, some of the doves that had been released had landed on the edge of the caldron; we read later that a number of these doves had been burned alive by the lighting of the Olympic torch and that this would now be the last Games to use live doves during the torch ceremony.

Then suddenly out of the sky, over fifty skydivers drifted down into the arena carrying Olympic flags. The whole event had been spectacular but more was to come.

The display that followed next was amazing. A mass demonstration of Taekwondo, a Korean martial art, loosely translated as "the way of the foot and fist". The national sport of South Korea combines combat techniques, self-defense, sport, exercise, meditation and philosophy and is also used by the South Korean military as part of its training. This demonstration featured one thousand adults and children performing moves in unison. Everyone's arm, leg and foot movement was precisely in time, it was fantastic to watch.

The mascots were next to present themselves, Hodori, a tiger, was this years mascot. He was followed by all the past Olympic mascots and finally the mascot for the forthcoming 1992 Games in Barcelona, a dog called Cobi. Then 6,000 people, who had previously performed, poured back into the stadium and out of the middle rose a platform with a Korean pop group who sang the song called 'Hand to Hand'. This was on our song sheets; and we all joined in. "We lift our heads up to the sky, hand in hand all across the land, bringing down the wall for all time". The words made me feel very emotional and gave me the hope that all wars could be ended, allowing the people of the world to live happily together. When I see huge gatherings like this with everyone in such harmony, that dream seems almost possible.

The ceremony had come to an end it had been really impressive. It had taken 5 hours but the time had flown by. It was now time to find our way back to 'Family Town'. When we arrived back at the apartment I tried to find out more about the rowing venue and how to get there. It seemed that buses had been arranged to take all the spectators to every sport except rowing, and that the rowing was being held on a special man made course off the River Ham, some 35miles away. I found the Sports World representatives and told them our problem and they agreed to get a bus to take us all there but, he told us, we would have to find our own way back.

Two young American girls were standing nearby and I heard them talking about getting to the rowing venue so I gave them the information I had just gleaned to be of some help. They asked us who we were here to support and I said the British pair, Steve Redgrave and Andy Holmes. I was stunned by their reply; "Our boys will beat them, your son may be a winner but winners fall and our boys will beat them this time." I was dumbstruck, what an attitude. All I could say was; "Well, we will wait and see before we *shout about it." I was shocked. We never liked to tempt providence before a race; I'm a tad superstitious. I won't even go and look at the cups at Henley Regatta before Steve has raced, it's silly really, but I can't help it.*

*We had our evening meal and decided to have an early night. Ann arrived late that night and we got up again to welcome her and to show her to her bedroom. The next morning we were up early to breakfast, we decided to take some extra buns and rolls with us for our lunch so, armed with our lunch pack and our flags, we set off to find our bus. Sports World was 'as good as their word' and had provided us with two mini buses. We all boarded and drove to the course in relative silence; I think we were all still tired from yesterday's excitement and also that the jet lag was catching up with everyone.*

*The course facilities were very well laid out, with good views from the stands; you could see right down the course. We had to go through two checkpoints and they opened up all the cameras and of course damaged the film. The security guard dropped my camera as well so I didn't get any photos at all but there was little I could do. We all had a Sports World accreditation tag with our photo on it but I suppose they were just being extra careful.*

*Once in the stands we saw all the other Brits and put our flags up and then settled down and waited for the rowing to start. The weather was not good today with wind and rain, so we all huddled together to keep warm. Out of the blue came Moira and Pat; we were all glad to see them and pleased that they had arrived safely; we were also anxious to know how their journey had gone. They'd had a good trip to Seoul and they said that the Korean family they were staying with had kindly come to meet them at the station. The lady of the house was an Olympic official who spoke very good English and her husband was an Olympic wrestler. They had two children and they told us that the couple's elderly mother had carried the Olympic torch some of the way. Moira and Pat said that they had been made very welcome and that their accommodation was very comfortable.*

*Moira and Pat's son Martin was in the Coxed Four. That morning the crew hadn't done as well as expected but they'd got through to the repechage, so they would have a further chance later on. Steve and Andy had a good race in the Coxless Pair boat and got through to the semi-final. They had led*

106

*all the way in their heat and had dropped their rate at the end to conserve their energy as they had to do the same tomorrow in the Coxed Pair boat. Once racing was over that morning, we made our way back by bus to the 'Family Town' and went back to bed to catch up on some much-needed sleep.*

*The following day, Tuesday, we were up early for breakfast and again we took the minibus to the rowing course. We passed through the checkpoints and took up our seats in the stand, put up our flags and waited for the racing to start. The weather was a little better today but our nerves weren't too good. Andy and Steve had drawn lane 4 and were up against their main opposition the Italian crew, the Abbagnale brothers, who had been the previous Olympic and World Champions. Also they had to keep a watchful eye on the Romanian crew but at this level no one could be ruled out.*

*Steve and Andy must finish in the first three to qualify for the semi-final but tactics now came into play. They didn't want to have to race the Abbagnales again in the semi-finals and this would depend on where they finished in this race. The Abbagnales went out in front as usual but with 500m left to go both the Romanians and our boys were closing in fast. The heat finished neck and neck with Italy 1ˢᵗ, Great Britain 2ⁿᵈ and Romania 3ʳᵈ with less than one second between the three crews The result meant that our boat would avoid Italy in the semi's and, all being well, it would just be the final where they would compete again.*

*Their next challenge was going to be the toughest. On Thursday they would have to row twice in one day and they would get just four and a half hours between the two races. At least tomorrow, Wednesday, they could look forward to a rest. Wednesday was repechage day and the British eights, coxed and coxless fours all got through to their semi-finals too.*

*Wednesday evening we all decided to go out to eat at a Korean restaurant in Seoul and this turned out be great fun. We all had to sit cross-legged on the floor at a very low table. In the middle of the table was a hole containing hot coals. We had to cook our own meat on this and ate it with lots of little side dishes; it was a bit like a Chinese meal. None of us were sure what to do at first but the proprietor of the restaurant came to sit with us to show us the ropes. It was something very different for everyone and we had a great time.*

*Clothes were very cheap in Korea so Steve decided to have two suits made at a tailor shop we had found; Geoff needed a new suit too. Ann thought she would like an evening dress made and June and Patty wanted day dresses so they were all duly measured up and the tailor, a Korean called Johnie Sinn, said he would come to do the fitting at our apartment. Well, a few days passed and he still hadn't arrived so we went back to the shop. Johnie said he was having a problem with his staff but that he would come tomorrow. At the end of our stay June and Patty did get their dresses but not in the correct fabric that they had ordered. Geoff got his fitting but never did get the suit and Ann didn't get her dress either; we should have known better. Johnie explained that due to the great demand he had taken some of his sewing out of town and because of this, his regular staff had gone on strike. We only lost a small deposit but it wasn't that so much as the disappointment at not having our new clothes.*

*Thursday arrived and we went back to the rowing for semi-finals day and two important races for Steve and Andy. We had our usual breakfast and then the minibuses arrived to take us to the course. After going through the checkpoints, once we got to our seats, we tied up our flags and then began the long wait. Today 'wait' was the word as the weather was bad. It meant that there was a delay to the rowing race schedule of one hour due to the unfair conditions. One hour became two but then the bad weather started to abate. Then fate again intervened, when the American coxless pair ran into the Australian pair cutting their boat in half. It sank and so the boy's first race was put back yet again. This was going to cause them problems as the time they had to rest between their two races was now reduced to under one hour instead of the four and a half that they were originally expecting. Penny Chuter, their rowing director, had tried to do all she could to get the time of their second race altered and pushed further back in the day's rowing programme but 'the powers that be' would not agree to it. It mainly came down to the other competitors, particularly the Russians and the Czechs who refused to change; this was mostly tactical on their part but the race was set.*

*They finally got underway in the Coxless Pair and they won this semi-final in 6:45.03. Next, in the Coxed Pair and just under an hour later, they raced again. They were in third place at 1000m behind Bulgaria and Russia and had pushed into 2nd place by the finish in a time of 7:01.51,* but it had been exhausting for them. There had been less than a second between the first three crews again. They had made both of the finals, the Coxless Pair on Saturday and the Coxed Pair on Sunday. Britain now had six boats in the finals; our lad's two Pairs boats plus the Coxed and Coxless Fours, the Eight and the Women's Coxed Four.

One day we took a tour around Seoul city and were shown all the places of interest. We were taken to a lovely garden with a big pergola and a lake filled with water lilies, it was beautiful. In Victorian times, water lilies had been introduced into the lake and had now spread so much that they had become a menace in lots of the Seoul waterways. We visited some beautiful temples with many intricate carvings, a silk manufacturer and a jewellery factory. The tour also took us to the border between North and South Korea known as the 39$^{th}$ Parallel. It all looked so menacing, with rolls of barbed wire dividing the two sides overlooked by guards with machine guns. We learnt that many lives had been lost here during the civil war. It was very informative and a most interesting trip which really gave us an insight into the Korean culture.

We had been told that the Koreans like to eat dog meat so we were a bit concerned whenever meat was served to us but we found out that restaurants had been told not to serve it during the Olympics. In fact, selling dog meat has been illegal in South Korea since 1984 when dog meat manufacturing and processing were outlawed but we were told that this order is sometimes ignored. It is called Gaegogi which literally means "dog meat" in Korean; there is a soup of the same name. Even though a fair number of Koreans have tried it before, only a very small percentage of the population eats it regularly but I must say that we didn't see many dogs while we were in Seoul.

One day we did see a very funny thing though, we were out walking with Jen and Derek Buckingham in a street not far from the Family Town when we came across a street seller with an old cart with pigs heads all lined up in a row; the old man was shaving the pigs faces with an open razor. We thought we must take a picture of this interesting scene but as we pointed our cameras at him, the old man went berserk, shouting at us and waving his arms about, the open razor still in his hand and so we beat a very hasty and apologetic retreat.

*Moira and Pat would come out to see us in the Family Town in the evenings quite a lot and we would all sit and talk, we had always enjoyed their company; inevitably the conversation came round to the subject of rowing. I think that Ann really missed Steve but her pass let her into the village so she could go and visit him sometimes and he also came out to visit us on a couple of occasions with Mark Buckingham and Stephen Turner. We knew that he preferred to be quiet and left to his own devices when competing; we knew that he needed his space to focus on this enormous task that he and Andy had set for themselves.*

*Larry Tracey, a family friend, who had not planned to come out to Seoul, had watched the semi-finals on TV and could not stay away; he felt he just had to come and see the finals for himself. Larry had been a good friend to Steve and a great help to him financially in the early days. Steve had come up with the idea that he would somehow like to win both a Summer and a Winter Olympic medal so Larry had introduced him to bobsleighing. Steve had been very keen and was among the four-man team that triumphed at the national championships in 1989 where he had won a silver medal. In 1989/1990 he was a member of the British bobsleigh team but to my great relief, as it's such a dangerous sport, Steve decided that rowing was more to his taste. Larry sponsored the Irish bobsleigh team and was always helping with one sport or another. He had rowed himself so had a bit of a soft spot for the sport. Lynne, his wife, was a doctor so she and Ann had a lot in common too. Their eldest daughter Tasha had been one of the little bridesmaids at Steve and Ann's wedding.*

*Larry joined us for dinner on Friday and then we all had an early night; ready for Saturday and the coxless pairs final. We had lots of unanswered questions; we wondered what problems might befall them today? Had they used up all of their energy in the semi-finals? My stomach began to churn over now and I asked myself another question, the one I have asked so many times before, why do I feel like this? The answer is always the same; I just have to be there for my son. There were lots of people about today and I was just hoping that no races would be delayed. The minibuses were a bit late picking us up and the queues at the checkpoints had been longer than usual.*

*I was so nervous I kept visiting the loo but Geoff seemed quite calm. That's where Steve gets his composure from. Both of the men in my life show no obvious emotion on the outside, they keep 'as cool as cucumbers' and have a knack of keeping their true feelings hidden. I feel it's a little to do with the traditionally British stiff upper lip but I know that they are very sensitive underneath that façade. They both also have a talent for channelling any negative thoughts into positive motivation, Geoff with his work and Steve with his rowing. I think it was put quite succinctly, later in Steve's rowing career, by Nick Pitt of the Sunday Times when he wrote 'sentiment, for Redgrave, is always subordinate to the objective'.*

*When we arrived at the course that morning, two seats had been saved for us by our friends. This meant that we would all be able to sit together and form a much larger British supporters group; although Steve has told me that he could always hear my voice above all the others, as I shout so loudly. June, Sue, Ann, Patty and Trish were all wearing jumpers with coxed and coxless four boats knitted into a pattern around the shoulders and we were wearing our old boaters with the GB badge on the front from Los Angeles. We also had the old tea-towel flag that had been waved when they had triumphed four years before; we had taken it to every rowing events ever since. All the Brits were bunched together; Fiona Johnson's mom and dad, the Turners, the Buckinghams, the Stanhopes, the Dillons, Larry, Pat and Moira Cross; all had visible nerves in anticipation of their own son's or daughter's event.*

*Fiona's Coxed Fours race was up first; they managed an admirable 6th place. It was a very good achievement for them to have made the final; no British women had done that before. Martin's Coxed Four finished 4th, a real shame as they had missed a bronze medal by a hair's breadth. Steve and Andy's race was due now and we could see that there was some problem with one of the boats. We couldn't believe it when it was announced that their race would be delayed yet again. The Belgian pair had broken a stretcher on the way to the start and therefore the race had been postponed until 12 noon. What were the odds that it would happen again today?*

*Instead of their race being next, the Single Sculls was brought forward and this was won by Thomas Lange, the young German who had beaten Steve and Adam as juniors all those years ago, with the Silver going to Peter Kolbe, from West Germany and Bronze to Eric Verdonk, the New*

*Zealander whose parent's are Dutch; there had been no British entry. This had been a good race to watch as we knew all the lads and it had also helped to take our mind off Steve's race for a while.*

*Then we saw Steve and Andy heading off down to the start again; now their first race was on. We steeled ourselves for the outcome. They led from the start and all the way to the finishing line; what a race, they had done it, another Gold. Britain was 1ˢᵗ. 6:36.84, Romanians 2ⁿᵈ 6:38.06 with the Yugoslavs 3ʳᵈ 6:41.01. Oh boy, 1.22secs ahead of the Romanians. They did indeed deserve the Olympic Gold medal that was hung around their necks by HRH Princess Ann that day and they stood proudly singing the national anthem but I could tell that they both had their minds elsewhere. They looked slightly odd standing there in their rowing vests which were very obviously much too large, they had been given some weightlifters vests to wear, as the normal rowing kit had been just too small for them. They had a few press photos taken but quickly returned to their boat; they had to keep focussed. It had been wonderful to see them attain a gold medal in their second Olympics, but could they do the same again tomorrow we wondered, it would be a tall order.*

*The boys had not celebrated their win, they'd had to settle down, rest up and prepare for their attempt the following day - winning the coxed pairs. We too had kept a low profile on Saturday evening. Sunday came around and so, once again, did the nerves. We found ourselves back in our usual spot in the stands with our union jacks adorning the rail. Today the British interest was the Coxless Four with Mark Buckingham, the Eight with Stephen Turner, Terry Dillon and Richard Stanhope and Andy and Steve in the Coxed Pair with Pat Sweeney.*

*Steve and Andy's race was ready to start; with our boys in lane two and the Abbagnale brothers in lane three. Yet again there was some disruption with, not one, but this time, two false starts. Explosive starts are necessary to get away quickly and to do this twice in such a short space of time really saps the strength. The boats are held and aligned at the start of the race to prevent a false start but it does happen from time to time with a crew's eagerness to start. Crews are allowed one false start each while two false starts for a single crew warrants a disqualification; we couldn't then blame the Abbagnales for both.*

On the third attempt they were all cleanly away but Steve and Andy gradually slipped back into 6$^{th}$ position. The Italians got a good start and went out into the lead with Russia and Belgium chasing close behind. Steve and Andy were still doing all they could and were gradually beginning to pull it back and by the 1000m mark they were in 3$^{rd}$ position. They soon moved into 2$^{nd}$ and were neck and neck with the Germans for a while but with 250m to go the Germans pulled into 2$^{nd}$ position and that was how the race finished; Italy 1$^{st}$ 6:58.79, Germany 2$^{nd}$ 7:00.63 and Steve and Andy came in 3$^{rd}$ 7:01.95 just behind. They had a bronze medal, an enormous achievement but they looked totally worn out.

They received their medal on the rostrum and did some media interviews afterwards. They said they had done their best but the back-to-back semi-finals had taken the spring out of their legs. As they had already won a gold medal, the media were interested in doing an interview with me and Geoff and had thrust a microphone under my nose during their race. I had told them that I would speak to them once the race had finished but no one came back, I guess that bronze medal winning isn't as newsworthy; they were very soon yesterday's news. To win a gold and a bronze Olympic medal, each within 24 hour, is a fantastic achievement and I really don't feel Steve and Andy ever got the acclaim for this, they so richly deserved.

Also in the finals the Coxless Four missed out on a bronze by one hundredth of a second, what a frustration for them and the Eight also ended up in 4$^{th}$ place. All the boys were a bit disappointed but overall it had been the best ever Olympic result for British rowing with a gold medal, a bronze medal, three 4th places and a 6$^{th}$ place.

Steve and Ann came to the stands after the rowing and I gave Steve a big hug and said well done. It broke my heart when he said, "Mom, I didn't do it". He was bitterly disappointed but he soon began to realise what a great achievement it had been; he now had three Olympic medals. It was sometime later in his career when it was reported by the American News station CNN 'An obsessive winner, Redgrave would later say that he considered the bronze medal a blemish on his career'. I'm not sure that is how he really felt but I guess it didn't shine as brightly for him as gold. Later that evening and with everyone now relaxed, we all celebrated both of their wins and had a party at the Korean restaurant; all our friends and the rowers were invited.

The next day, 2ⁿᵈ October 1988, was the closing ceremony; this time it was in the evening and stated at 7pm. All the athletes entered the stadium looking casual and relaxed; some even wore native costumes of their countries. The three flags of Greece, Korea and Spain were hoisted and in turn their national anthems were played. Once again there were very colourful and spectacular displays with many performers, dancers and gymnasts. President Park Seh-jik of the Seoul Olympic Organising Committee delivered the closing remarks 'Two weeks ago we gathered here in the Olympic stadium to share the pleasure of meeting. Today we are gathered here again, but this time for the sad task of saying goodbye' he thanked everyone then said 'Goodbye everyone, see you in Barcelona' and the crowd cheered. The Olympic flag was lowered and handed to the Spanish officials to be kept safe until the Barcelona Games in 1992. With the stadium now in darkness there were 5 very loud gun salutes symbolising the Olympics rings and the flame in the caldron was slowly extinguished to the sad sound of a lone bamboo flute echoing through the stadium; everyone was moved. Out of the darkness 800 performers each carrying a red or blue silk covered lantern came in and mingled with the athletes and danced in circles. Huge inflatable mascots, Hodori and Cobi, then drifted in the dark sky to a background of an impressive firework display and the Games of the 24ᵗʰ Olympiad came to a close.

Everyone felt a little sad to be parting company and we promised to meet up again soon when we returned to England. Pat and Moira hadn't been able to stop to see the closing ceremony because they had managed to get a flight directly to Tokyo instead of their previous long train, boat and plane journey. On the return leg of our Sports World trip Jen and Derek had planned to stay over in Bangkok for a few days holiday; we were going straight home. Back at the Family Town we packed. Ann had managed to change her flight and was coming home with us but Steve had to return with the British team. We got our flight first to Hong Kong and then to Bangkok before finally returning to Heathrow: another long and tiring journey but it didn't matter we were feeling happy to have been able to make such a wonderful trip and with Steve's Olympic result, we were once again very proud parents.

Arriving back at Heathrow the family was there to meet us, it was good to see them all again. We had a meal at Christine's home that night with all the family there to celebrate our homecoming and catch up on all the news. Steve would carry on his rowing career but Andy chose to retire. With two Olympic gold medals and an Olympic bronze to Andy's name I'm surprised and very sad that he didn't seem to get the recognition at the time that he deserved.

On Steve's return from Seoul, a civic reception was held in Marlow at Court Garden House, it was a very nice affair with the Mayor and Councillors, the family and Marlow Rowing Club's President and Chairman and committee. The town' people decorated the shops and streets and so did villagers in Marlow Bottom. High Wycombe Council also held a reception to mark the occasion. It was again a great home coming celebration for Steve and gave the whole family a lot of pleasure too.

Geoff and I had flown over to Spain in November 1987 to start to investigate the possibility of retiring there. I wasn't keen at first but Geoff was very eager so when we saw a good plot of land that we liked, we decided to purchase it and to have a villa built. We sold our business and family home and purchased a tiny three bedroom link-detached just along the valley in Marlow Bottom which we would live in while the Spanish villa was under construction; it was going to take about a year to complete.

On arriving back from Seoul, Steve had sold his own house in Marlow as they were both living in Ann's house in Kingston. I told them about a house we had seen for sale in Marlow Bottom, and they came to look at it and both liked it. After a long chat with their bank manager they managed to buy it and moved in, although it took a long time for Ann to sell her property in London. They decided to name their new house "Casitas" after the lake in America where Steve had won his first gold medal, when both he and Ann had competed in The Los Angeles Olympics in 1984. They seemed very happy with their new home and we were pleased too, that they were living close to the rest of the family in Marlow Bottom. Ben and Steph, Jane and David's twins, were growing fast and we had celebrated their first birthday in September.

Steve had decided to carry on with rowing but had not yet decided which boat to concentrate on. Just three weeks after the Seoul Olympics had ended, the Serpentine Sprint Regatta came round again and as last year, Steve had *entered several events. He would race in a Single Scull, in a Pair with Andy and was a crew member in the Eight. International teams from Italy, France, Russia and Britain took part again. In the sculling event Steve came up against a chap from Russia, Yuri Jansen, who had won a bronze at the Olympics in the double scull. It was a very hard race but Steve won in the end and was very pleased with his achievement.*

*Everyone was looking forward to seeing Steve and Andy race in the pairs but when they went to collect their boat from the boat sheds they found that it had disappeared. It was later discovered that the Russians had taken theirs by mistake therefore they were forced to row in a borrowed boat. This feels like wearing someone else's shoes; not at all comfortable. Trying to make last minute adjustments, they only just made it to the start in time. The race started but suddenly something went wrong and their boat wobbled and stopped. They made an appeal to the umpire but the race carried on without them. In a normal 2000m race, should anything go wrong with the equipment within the first 100m then the umpire can call the boats back to the start but this doesn't apply in a 500m sprint race. It was really ironic that they lost this race as it was to be their last race together in a pair. They raced together later in the day in the Eight and they won, meaning that Great Britain had won overall; the Waterford Crystal didn't have to be shared this year.*

# Chapter Ten
## World Championships 1989 Bed Yugoslavia

### *Ringing the Changes*

*The media made a lot of Steve and Andy's split, saying that they didn't get on together but it was all rubbish, they were just two very different people who gelled well in a boat but had totally different lives outside of rowing. Steve had wanted a commitment from Andy to row together for the next four years, up to the Barcelona Olympics, but Andy wanted only one more year in the sport and then he wished to stop altogether, so it was mutually decided to bring their partnership to an end.*

*Steve was now looking for a new partner and this was a very difficult act for anyone to follow after having had such a successful partnership with Andy. Mike Spracklen suggested, Simon Berrisford, who had rowed in the coxless four in Seoul, and so with Mike Spracklen as their coach, Steve and Simon started a new season of winter training together. We were all really pleased for Mike too when we heard that he had won the 'Barclays Award for Support of Athletes'. Steve had nominated Mike for this and soon after this a champagne bottle was brought out once again with the news that Mike had been awarded the O.B.E. for services to rowing in the New Years Honours in 1989.*

*The training went on and as usual Steve competed in the 'Scullers Head' in April. This time Steve came 2nd he was just 5 seconds off S. Larkin of Nottingham. The following month on 4th May Steve entered the Wingfield Sculls. At Chiswick Eyot, Steve was two lengths down but by Chiswick Steps he had forced his way back into the lead and by the finish he had broken the course record by 45 seconds winning in a time of 20:16 to* retained the title for the fifth year in a row of 'Amateur Sculling Champion of the Thames and Great Britain'.

The 1989 Henley Royal Regatta was celebrating its 150th anniversary this year and for a change this year the weather was fine. The rowing was also good with Steve and Simon winning the Silver Goblets from the 32 entries and due to some good July weather we were able to enjoy our family picnic with friends in the sunshine.

The Amateur Rowing Association hadn't seemed to have capitalised on Britain winning Olympic gold in Los Angeles in 1984 or the gold and bronze in Seoul in 1988, so sponsors for the rowing team were still hard to find. DAF Trucks looked after Steve exclusively, but some other potential sponsors for the British squad wanted Steve to come under their sponsorship wing as well and that scenario ruffled a few feathers. In the end DAF Trucks withdrew Steve's sponsorship altogether, putting their money instead into domestic rowing leaving M.I. Insurance to sponsor both the British rowing squad and Steve. Steve was naturally upset because he had been with DAF Trucks for a long time but for the sake of the rowing team he was forced to agree.

The 1989 Lucerne Regatta in July saw an extremely close race for Steve and Simon in their Coxed Pair with Pat Sweeney as their cox, when five boats crossed the line together causing a photo finish. The final result was Yugoslavia 1$^{st}$. with a time of 7:1.28, RDA 2$^{nd}$ +0.01, ITA 3$^{rd}$. +0.04 and Steve and Simon coming in 4$^{th}$ place at +0.08 just 8/100$^{th}$ behind the winner. This race is still shown on YouTube as one of rowing closest finishes.

At the end of July we had just taken delivery of a new German made campervan, a Hymermobile 550. This one was going to be a little roomier than our old VW and we could now comfortably sleep four. We planned to travel through Europe to the World Rowing Championship being held this year in Bled, Yugoslavia and would take Christine and Philip with us. Bryan, my brother, was coming down from Newcastle to look after Mom and the dog and Jane, David and the twins were staying at home to hold the fort.

We took our time to get there and we really enjoyed our journey especially as Christine had made a list of places to go and things to see along the way. One of these trips was a visit to a salt mine near Saltsburg in Austria. On arrival at the mine, visitors were all given white all-in-one jumpsuits with hoods to wear. We did look funny, like little gnomes sitting astride a small bench-like train being pulled along a narrow gauge track by a small engine. The tour took us right through the mine while a tour guide explained how the salt was extracted. We went from one level to another, sometimes walking, sometimes sliding down long slides on our bottoms, it was great fun and a very interesting trip. We also visited Baden Baden in Germany and took the waters and swam in the natural hot springs.

At the Yugoslav border the guards seemed a little hostile and when they checked our passports we were held up for some time but finally waved on. We then had a very hair-raising journey through the mountain pass into Bled. The road was very narrow with many hairpin bends. I felt quite nervous especially when we met a large bus on the bend, coming in the other direction, and had to pullover to let it pass, inches from the edge of a precipitous drop. Philip had taken over the driving for a while to give Geoff a much need rest and it was beginning to get quite dark and the road looked even more treacherous in the headlights. I suddenly noticed that the brake warning light had come on, so as soon as he could, Philip pulled the camper into a small parking area and we all got out to look and investigate where the smell of burning rubber was coming from. As we walked around the side of the vehicle we saw a red glow coming from the hub of each wheel. It transpired that Philip had not taken his foot off the brake, not once, as we descended over the mountains into Yugoslavia; the warning light never did go out in all the years that we had the camper.

The hair-raising journey had been well worth it though, as when we finally arrived in Bled, we saw what a beautiful place it was. Lake Bled, in places its 30 m deep, is adjacent to the town of Bled, is a glacial lake in the Julian Alps in what is now northwestern Slovenia. The beautiful lake, which is surrounded by mountains and forests, has very good conditions for rowing being just over 2,000 m long and 1,300 m wide, and is overlooked by a 15th century, Dracula-like, medieval castle stands above the lake on the north shore. It was supposed to have been regularly used by President Tito, the Yugoslav revolutionary and statesman, as his summer residence. In the middle of the lake is the picturesque Bled Island with its pretty Pilgrimage Church. The campsite had been placed at one end of the course and had quite good facilities. Geoff and I had brought our bikes with us and Chris and Philip hired two more and we all had great fun cycling round the area.

Steve and Simon got to the final in both boats. In the Coxless Pair they lay in fourth place at 500m, managing to pull through to third place by the 1000m mark, and with 30 seconds left to go they overtook the Pimenov brothers of Russia but were just unable to reach the Germans, Thomas Jung and Uwe Kellner who were still out in front and took the gold. Steve and Simon took silver and the Austrian pair the bronze. The next day with Pat Sweeney as cox they didn't do so well and could only manage 5th place in the Coxed Pairs. Its a big mountain to climb just getting used to rowing with a new partner so we were pleased with this result, and perhaps with hindsight, perhaps they shouldn't have attempted both events so early in their partnership but Steve always has to challenge himself. The Coxed Four won bronze with an up and coming young junior called Matthew Pinsent, the Coxless Four came 4th, and the Eight also won a bronze. The Women's Lightweight Four won silver and the Men's Lightweight Coxless Four won bronze. It was a very good tally at the end of the Regatta and it was still early days for Simon and Steve.

Many of the athletes from Seoul were there too and Stephen Turner and Terry Dillon were in the Coxed Four that had taken the bronze. Pat and Moira and our old friend Pat Toch had come along, as their children were also competing and it was good to see all of our friends again. We also surprisingly bumped into a lady called Pat Tinge, and her husband, who were by chance in Bled on holiday; she worked in the local newsagent in Marlow Bottom, what a small world.

While we were there, we had another bit of bad luck with our new camper. It had been raining hard all evening and we had left the attached awning extended so we could leave our wet shoes undercover outside. In the middle of the night, we were awoken by a loud bang when, due to the torrential downpour, the awning legs had given way under the weight of the huge puddle that had formed in the middle of the canvas. Geoff and Phil had to go out in the lashing rain and got absolutely drenched trying to sort it out.

On the way back while travelling through Austria we found yet another problem with the camper, this time some of the windows seemed to be letting in water. We couldn't believe our luck and after paying so much for the vehicle we decided to get it fixed right away. We made a diversion through Germany so that we could take the camper to the Hymer factory where it had been manufactured.

The Hymer manufacturing workshops were in a very pretty little town called Bad Waldsee, 20 km northeast of Ravensburg. The manager of the factory said they would do the necessary repair the following day and we could camp on their car park overnight. The next day, while they worked on our vehicle, we all walked into the town to spend a few hours looking around. We found a delightful little lake and a wonderful bakery that sold delicious bread and mouth-watering cakes with fruit and cream. We lost time with this diversion but gained some weight while we waited. Later, with the repair completed free of charge, we headed back to Calais and caught the ferry back home. We'd had a very enjoyable holiday with Chris and Phil, even if it hadn't been quite the results Steve had hoped for.

We had put our small house in Marlow Bottom up for sale as our villa near Javea in Spain was nearing completion. The housing market had been depressed at the end of the '80's so we hadn't had many viewers. Our date for leaving the country had been set for the 29th September which was the twins 2nd birthday. The plan was to stay for their birthday party and then move off and catch the night ferry from Dover to Calais. We were taking our dog Tasha with us to live in Spain and she had been given all the necessary vaccinations and her papers were all in order. Christine was going to look after her grandmother for a few days to let us get settled in to the villa and then it was planned that she would fly with her to Spain on the 5th October.

We had employed a removal company to pack and store our furniture and belongings which they were due to deliver to the villa on the 4th October. With the final realisation that, this was it, I was really about to leave the country, I was getting more and more upset at the thought of leaving the children and grandchildren. I guessed the whole family would really miss us too but I knew that they also wanted us to enjoy a much deserved retirement. As it turned out I think I got to spend more quality time with *each of them during the following years when they regularly came on visits. When they were on holiday we would spend all our time together in the unhurried relaxation of sunny Spain.*

*My mom Ada had the beginnings of senile dementia and was quite physically disabled too and could not walk far. I had always been very close to my mother and I just wanted her to have a good quality of life so I really didn't mind taking care of her. She had lived with us for over twenty years ever since my dad had died prematurely at the age of 65, just six months after his retirement. Christine and Jane were very good with Ada too and were always there to help when needed and the twins called her 'Big Nan', I guess that meant I was 'Little Nan'.*

*The twin's birthday party was really special, they were such lovely toddlers and now that they were beginning to develop their own little characters, they were really amusing; we loved them so much. When it came time for us to leave we were all in tears, the only consolation was that I would be seeing Christine again in a few days time with mom and everyone else in the family had promised to come out to Spain for Christmas which was just twelve weeks away. I guessed I could wait that long and I knew that I would be kept busy with moving in and getting settled into our new home but I still think that I cried all the way to Spain. My family would never know just how much it broke my heart to leave them all that day.*

I become aware of my surroundings once again; we were now well into our flight to Atlanta. I took out my handkerchief to wipe my eyes and Geoff looked at me and said 'what's the matter with you now, what will people around us think'. I really felt like howling even more when he said that but I somehow managed to pull myself together. Geoff called the flight attendant who then brought me a cup of tea, the British answer to everything. I began to feel a lot better and chatted to Geoff for a while, he said that his book was very good and asked me why I wasn't reading or looking through the newspapers too but I was happy just to daydream.

I looked at my watch, we had been on the flight for about five hours now and I had been told it would take about nine, so I reckoned, half way there. I wondered how Steve was getting on at the pre -Olympic training camp in Canada. I skimmed the newspaper for a while but there was nothing really interesting; poor old John Major was going through it again, it made me wonder how politicians put up with all the stick that they seemed to constantly be given. There was trouble in Northern Ireland again too. The Irish are always such pleasant people but seem to have real trouble sorting out their problems. I looked at the horoscopes but there was nothing good there either and I wondered why I was always tempted to read them. I put down the paper and went to the toilet to wash my face. I felt a little better as I walked back to my seat and settled down and it wasn't long before I drifted back to my memories.

*We arrived in Spain on the 2nd October just after an horrific storm. We learned later that the Spanish refer to this type of storm as "Gota Fria" meaning 'The Cold Drop'. In just a few hours a huge amount of rain can fall, sometimes up to twelve inches. The ensuing flash floods cause severe damage and often result in loss of life and this often happens at the end of a hot summer usually in September or October. On the Costa Blanca the mountains which are directly behind the sea form a cold block to the evaporating water coming off the warm sea and large clouds form extremely quickly dumping heavy rain and hail in a very localised area. This year it had rained so hard that it had washed cars out to sea at Denier and Moraira, the towns either side of us, and had caused lots of damage. We drove straight to the new villa which was perched on the side of a steep hill, hoping it would still be there. The villa was luckily still standing but we found that things inside and out had not been totally finished as we had expected, and our new swimming pool was half full of very dirty water.*

*We went straight to the builder's office in Moraira and managed to speak directly to him. We explained we needed the villa to be completed in the next few days as our removal company was arriving with our furniture and he assured us that he would soon have everything in order; we were luckily fine staying in our camper on site for a few days.*

*The electric wiring was in place but bare wires hung out of the newly painted walls; we soon learned that in Spain they do thing very differently. Electricians don't fix ceiling roses but wait to fit the owner's choice of light fittings; these we did not yet have. We made a time and date with the* electrician for him to return to fit them; our first job was to purchase some. We went to the local town and found a shop that sold light fittings and then quickly make a decision about every room in the villa. On top of this, the electrician would not be available until Thursday and Christine was due to arrive with my mother on Wednesday and we would need to collect them from Alicante airport, a one hour car journey away.

The other thing making life difficult was that we had no telephone installed at the villa and this too was well before mobile phones had generally arrived on the scene; so communication was difficult if not impossible. We didn't speak any Spanish as yet and even if we'd had a smattering of the lingo, there were not many public phones around, at least not near to our villa, therefore every communication that we made had to be face to face with the local businesses and utility companies; this became a very long nightmare. When we had engaged our builder, we had been promised a telephone connection by the time we moved in but as it turned out we had to wait for six years to get connected. In the meantime, if we needed to 'phone home' to England we had to drive to our nearest town, three miles away and either visit the phone cabins, a small portacabin with 4 public coin operated phone booths inside or if we needed to speak to a Spanish company ie. Townhall, telephone or electricity company we had to rely on the help of a woman at the small Spanish builder's office who thankfully, spoke good English.

We learned, after checking on the furniture van's arrival date with our removal company, that this too was now scheduled to arrive on Wednesday, the same day as Christine and Ada, but that they couldn't be precise about the time. We decided we would just have to make the best of a bad job.

Wednesday came and we drove to Alicante to meet Mom and Chris. Her journey had been a little difficult because mom was not able to walk far but she told us that the airline had been very helpful and arranged an electric cart to deliver them to and from the plane at both ends; they had made it intact and it was good to see them both. The journey to and from Alicante went smoothly but when we arrived home there was still no sign of the furniture van; we began to worry. It finally arrived that evening at 8pm and as we had no lights still, in the dark by candle light. The removal men insisted on unloading there and then in the blackness, so armed with *just three torches, we were able to guide them across the patio, past the muddy swimming pool and up an external flight of stairs into the villa; I think Health and Safety might have had something to say about that. As the boxes were brought into the sitting room, Christine and I unpacked a few and soon came across some table lamps. The electric sockets had been already connected and so after Geoff changed the plugs to Spanish style fittings, we finally had some light.*

*It all looked much better in the morning. The cooker was fitted so we were able to have a little breakfast and with Christine's help we soon had the furniture arranged and it started to look and feel a bit more like home. Mom looked settled once she was able to sit in her reclining armchair and Tasha the dog was sniffing about getting used to the new smells. There were empty boxes and packing paper everywhere but the sun was shining again and it was beginning to really warm up; I began to relax and it felt good. Geoff and Chris set to work tidying the garden and arranging the barbeque and sun loungers; it all seemed to be fitting into place.*

*Christine was with us for a few more days and it seemed like a holiday but all too soon it was time for her to leave us and go back to England. Then it really hit me and I began feeling very homesick for my family. We had no phone yet but the telephone company had promised we would have one installed by Christmas, but they conveniently didn't say which Christmas. For contact with my children and grandchildren, I had to content myself with our twice weekly trip to the telephone cabin and even then we sometimes only got their answer phones. Those first few weeks were hard for me and I was now counting the days till Christmas.*

*The first and most important thing we had to do was to register with a doctor, especially for mom, so I signed her and myself up to the Spanish National Health system. It took us many trips to Denier and the local government offices but we finally were able to join a practice with a woman doctor who spoke good English. This meant I was able to get the correct medication for her as besides the dementia she also had a slow progressing breast cancer which doctors in England had not wanted to operate on, as at 89, they said she was too old.*

*The Spanish Medical Service treated her well and even made visits to our home, a thing not often done in Spain. The other people who lived on our complex of 62 villas were all very nice and most helpful, giving us advice and tips on dealing with the Spanish ' mañana' approach to just about everything. Jane's friend Jackie Sherry's parents lived, not far from us, in Javea and another couple we knew, Pam and Peter Plumridge also lived in the area. Jane Plumridge, their daughter, had rowed in the girl's crew at Great Marlow School and knew Steve well. Some years prior to their move to Spain, Geoff had built them a home at Shabbington, near Aylesbury.*

*These new friends all helped us to settle in and we would regularly get together at one home or another for long Spanish lunches, but we could never go far or for too long because of Mom. We only ever left her for short periods at a time, when we went out to lunch or to do some shopping, leaving her happily sat in front of the TV but we would never left her in the evening. This was just as well as if ever she heard fireworks, and the Spanish are very fond of their fiestas and fireworks, she would get very frightened and think that World War II had started again. Even when this happened when we were around we would have a job to calm her down; I guess, with the dementia, she would imagine she was back in Birmingham during the war years, cowering with her family in the air raid shelter.*

*Food shopping was a problem at first but also quite funny when we would often end up with strange looking contents of a tin because we had taken the name as meaning something else. We didn't starve though and soon leaned to shop like the Spanish locals, on the village market day, when we could buy wonderful tasting fruit and vegetables of all kinds. Our Spanish, although non existent to start with, soon became passable and we found that between us we could make ourselves understood. I learned all the names of the food items at the supermarket and the local shops and Geoff learned the names at the builder's merchants for bricks, blocks, sand and cement and all manner of hardware as he used his skills to create our new garden patios, walls and paths.*

*Christmas was almost here and it seemed as though we had been away from our kids forever, so we really looked forward to the family's arrival. Steve and Ann arrived first on the 19ᵗʰ of December but it was only a short stay as they had to get back on the 24ᵗʰ, Christmas Eve. During their short visit, Steve had to fly back on the 20ᵗʰ-21ˢᵗ as he had to go to his sponsors*

Christmas Party; it was an enormous amount of travelling just to see his mom and dad for a while but it was really nice to have them stay.

On Thursday the 21$^{st}$ December we were awakened by the slam of car doors, it was Jane, David, with the twins and Christine and Philip. We rushed to the door to find them all looking a bit worse for wear; Ben and Steph being the only bright ones. They had travelled over to Spain in two separate cars on the ferry from Portsmouth to Santander, on the north coast of Spain, in a force 10 gale through the Bay of Biscay. It had taken them 30 hours to make the 24 hour crossing and they had all been seasick, poor souls. We gave them breakfast and sent them off to bed and they didn't surface again till the early afternoon. After a light lunch we all went down to the local beach to enjoy the winter sunshine and let the twins romp in the sand. That evening, Geoff and I went to Alicante airport to pick up Steve as his return flight didn't get in till late and it was 1am before we all got to bed.

As the whole family were only going to be together for a few days we decided to make Friday 22$^{nd}$ December an early Christmas celebration. We had a wonderful turkey lunch and exchanged presents with Steve and Ann. Ben and Steph were really into singing Christmas carols and we had a great time videoing them. Their favourite was the 12 days of Christmas. Ben loved loudly singing 'five gold rings' so we always let him sing that bit on his own. They were so sweet, we played lots of party games, everybody was enjoying themselves and I don't think I have ever felt so happy with my family all around me; it was bliss. The children went to bed very tired in the early evening and we carried on playing Trivial Pursuits and card games until we went to bed as well.

The following day we all went out to lunch in the Jalon Valley which has some of the best scenery in Spain. There are magnificent mountains surrounding fertile plains of olive and almond trees, orange groves and vineyards. We came home for tea and late that evening Steve and Ann returned home to England. It was such a short visit but we had enjoyed every second that they spent with us.

The next day, Christmas Eve, we spent most of our time preparing for Christmas Day but we did find an hour to take the twins to the beach again; they loved it so much. Geoff had made them a wooden wheelbarrow each and they took these in the car with us and spent their time digging in the sand and filling their barrows to make huge sandcastles; with of course, their Granddad, being the master builder.

Christmas day dawned, and the twins who were so excited, had us all out of our beds early. They were just at that wonderful age when everything is so exciting to them. It was brilliant watching them as they opened their presents and I once again thought that I must be mad to have moved so far away from my family. Anyway I realised that these times were precious and I should make the most of them and just enjoy the moment; we had a wonderful Christmas day. On Boxing Day our friend's Maurice and Maureen, Jackie Sherry's parents, came over for lunch and we all shared another enjoyable day.

All too soon the Thursday 28th December arrived and the family had to return to England but this time they were travelling all the way by car; no more seasickness for them. In fact, Steph had asked her mum as they were being strapped into their car seats 'we don't have to go on a big boat again do we mummy?' They made an early start at 7.30am while it was still dark. We both stood on the veranda and watched the taillights of their cars until they had disappeared over the hill. The tears were streaming down my cheeks, I was so upset to see them go but I also realised just how lucky I was having such a wonderful family who had travelled all that way just to be with us; we'd had a wonderful time. I phoned them from the phone cabins on Saturday and they told me that they had got home safe and sound on Friday night after a long and cold journey with an overnight stop in France and this time a short and sweet ferry trip over the channel from Calais to Dover; much better.

New Years Eve, there was just the three of us and as the clock struck midnight we watched the fireworks from the terrace, keeping Ada calm, and listened to the church bells ringing in the distance. We all drank a toast to 1990 and wondered what the New Year would bring.

Great Marlow School crew 1978, Nick Baatz, Peter McConnell, Steve Redgrave, 'Bill' Robert Haley, Clive Pope.

Marlow Regatta 1980. Adam Clift & Steven Redgrave Double Sculls, Win

World Junior Championships Hazewinkle, Belgium silver medal. Steve Redgrave and Adam Clift Double Scull,

World Championships, Nottingham. 1986. Coxed Pair. Giuseppe & Carmine Abbagnale and cox Giuseppe di Capua (Silver), Andy Holmes & Steve Redgrave, and cox Pat Sweeny (Gold)

Lucerne, Regatta 1984 Coxed Four Gold Medal Steve Redgrave, Andy Holmes, Richard Budget, Martin Cross, cox Adrian Ellison.

Los Angeles Olympics USA 1984. Geoff Redgrave, Sheila Redgrave, Belinda Holmes, Steve Redgrave. His first Olympic Gold Medal

XIII Commonwealth Games, Edinburgh, Scotland. 1986. Steve Redgrave.
Single Scull Gold Medal

XIII Commonwealth Games, Edinburgh, Scotland. 1986. Andy Holmes,
Steve Redgrave Coxless Pair Gold Medal

XIII Commonwealth Games, Edinburgh, Scotland. 1986. Adrian Ellison (cox), Martin Cross, Adam Clift, Andy Holmes Steve Redgrave (stroke). Coxed Four

XIII Commonwealth Games, Edinburgh, Scotland. 1986 Supporters. (Left to Right) Back row- Ewan holding banner, Jane, Isabel, David, 2nd Row - Geoff, Belinda, Sheila, Steve and dog Tasha, Philip, Christine. Bottom row- Mike Ann and Chris Spracklen

Welcome Home Commonwealth Games Competitors M Cross, M Spracklen, S Redgrave, J Spencer-Jones, A Holmes, F Johnston. High Wycombe Councillor and Marlow Mayoress.

Jane and David with Ben and Stephanie .Our twin Grandchildren's Christening January 1988

Steve's M B E March 1987. Steve Redgrave, Ann Callaway, Sheila Redgrave

The Wedding of Steve and Ann at Saint Paul's Cathedral. March 12th 1988.

Seoul Olympics, Korea, 1988 British Supporters Club.

Seoul Olympics Parade of Winners Ceremony, Coxless Pairs, Romania, Neagu Dragos, Dobre Danut (silver) Great Britain, Steve Redgrave, Andy Holmes (gold), Yugoslavia, Presern Bojan, Nujkic Savik (bronze). Medals presented by Princess Ann.

Seoul Olympics 1988  Coxed Pairs,  Italy - Giuseppe di Capua (cox)
Carmine, & Giuseppe, Abbagnale (gold), Great Britain- Pat Sweeney (cox),
Steve Redgrave &Andy Holmes (bronze)

Benjamin & Stephanie, Twin Grandchildren, Their First Henley Royal
Regatta, 1988.

Leaving for Spanish Retirement - Farewell party cake 1989 Sheila, Stephanie, & Ben.

# Chapter Eleven
## World Championships 1990 Lake Barrington Tasmania

### *Iron Man and Wonder Boy*

*A few days later, in early January, we took Tasha to the stony beach near us, where dogs were allowed of the lead. She loved playing with stones and would paw at them and trying to catch them in her teeth as the waves washed them in. On this particular day she jumped out of the camper onto the stones and landed on a piece of glass and cut her paw very badly. We had noticed a veterinary surgery not too far away so we rushed her there. The vet was a Spanish young lady who spoke really good English. She cleared the surgery and took Tasha in. She had lost a lot of blood, as she had cut a main artery so she put her on a drip and after a struggle managed to close the artery. She kept her there for two hours to make sure she was ok and then we took her home. We had to carry her back to the car and then into the villa, but she was ok; animals are so stoic.*

*I was quite worried about mom while we were away as we had been gone for four hours. When we returned, she seemed not to have noticed how long we had been gone but she did say that she was feeling very hungry and where was her lunch. Tasha took about three weeks to heal properly and to regain her fitness after the heavy blood loss. After this incident, we never took her to that beach again although it didn't seem to stop her from playing with stones. The months that followed had some bright spots and we saw our friends regularly but I was always waiting for Sunday so we could go down to Javea and the phone cabins to make our calls to the family.*

*Simon, Steve's new partner, had been training alone around Christmas time in his sculling boat and another boat had accidentally rammed him and the collision had injured his back very badly; it looked like he might never row again. Everything possible was done but it was decided by the medics and coaches that he should stop rowing for the whole year in order to recover. From this point, Steve seemed to generally lose some interest in his rowing, and this year he lost his Wingfield sculls title for the first time in six years. Geoff and I were quite concerned about Simon and Steve but there was nothing we could do but wait and see what transpired.*

*It was then decided to try out a young rower, Matthew Pinsent as Steve's new partner and immediately their combination seemed to work remarkably well. They were well matched in size and strength and they made the pair really move; everyone was really excited by the new pairing. Then bad luck struck again. Steve went down with what was thought to be salmonella poisoning. He wasn't aware what he was suffering from, he thought it was just a bug and he didn't pay attention to Ann's advice to rest, he just went on training all the following week. He then suddenly got much worse so Ann took him into hospital. He was given tests but was given no definite diagnosis; he was put on a drip and kept in hospital for five days to rehydrate and rest until he felt better. Jane and Christine had visited their brother in hospital and both reported to us that Steve was ok but that he had lost a lot of weight and looked a little washed out. When Steve returned home he still felt very weak. It was thought his illness may have come from a piece of undercooked chicken he had eaten at a barbecue the day before he became ill. No one else at the gathering became ill, just Steve, so it had been really just a bit of bad luck.*

*Steve gradually regained his strength and soon returned to training. With Matthew now confirmed as his new partner they began their preparation for the big annual event, the World Championships, which this year, was being held in Tasmania, Australia. Due to the fact that this event was to take place in the Southern Hemisphere, The Championships dates of 24th October-4th November were much later in the year than usual. Almost everything seemed to change around this time as they now had a new coach too. Steve's previous coach, Mike Spracklen, had been offered a job as coach to the Canadian National Team and he had taken this, inviting Steve over to Canada on a couple of occasions in late summer for extra training. Their new coach wasn't too unfamiliar though as it was Pat Sweeney, the cox from Steve's previous coxed pair with Andy Holmes had been given Mike's job. On their way out to Australia, Steve, Mathew and Pat had taken up a kind offer from Mike Spracklen for some last minute coaching and had visited Canada before going on to Tasmania.*

*The 1990 World Rowing Championship was to be held on Lake Barrington. The lake, which had been built to provide a head of water for hydroelectric power generation, is protected by the state government as a nature recreation area and is the site of a world-standard rowing course. This would be the first World Championships of our son's that we had ever missed and we were both really upset that we couldn't be there to cheer him on as usual. During the competition, we had tried all sorts of ways of obtaining news of how things were going for the boys but we had no satellite TV and, by the time they reached us in Spain, the British newspapers were then about two days old. The Spanish TV networks were not covering the Championships, so that all we had to rely on was a small portable radio with a weak signal from the world service that constantly drifted in and out.*

*After staying with Mike in Canada for a few coaching sessions, the boys had flown on to Geelong in Australia for the rowing squads pre championship training camp and then onto Tasmania.*

*In their heat they had finished 2nd to East Germany and had gone on to win their semi-final. In the final they made a bad start and at the 1000m mark the East Germans were leading by a length. Although our boys rowed a good middle course, the German pair Thomas Jung and Uwe Kellner took gold (07:07.91), Nikolai and Juri, the Russian Pimenov brothers, took silver (07:10.20) and Steve and Mathew took bronze (07:12.38). It had been just too much after all Steve had been through. His hospitalisation so late in the build up and with so many changes to the boat taking place they had done extremely well to manage a bronze this year.*

*For us listening on our small radio in the early hours of the morning we had heard the commentary until the 1000m mark, and then we lost the signal. We didn't know the final outcome of their race until we spoke to Jane the next morning, which we did as soon as the phone cabins had opened. We caught up on all the news as usual and Jane told us that while Steve and Ann were away, she had been looking after Steve's Old English sheepdog Thea and his African Grey parrot William. She made us laugh when she*

141

told us that the twins, Ben and Steph, had eaten some of the parrot's food when she hadn't been looking but that she didn't think it would do them any great harm as it had been mainly sunflower seeds.

Two days later one of our neighbours, Doug Reilly, came over to tell us that he had seen an article in The Daily Telegraph about The British Pair winning Bronze so Geoff rushed out to buy the paper. Steve and Ann faxed us the result too and said that all was well with them but that also took two days to get through to us as we had to collect any faxes from the local phone cabins as well. Before returning to the U.K. Steve and Ann had taken a short holiday break in Australia as they were so close and they visited my relatives in Sydney.

We had a visit from Christine and Philip at the end of September. They had decided to look for a plot of land to purchase on which to build their own villa. Geoff spent a lot of time with them and various agents viewing different properties and locations and they finally settled on a large plot near Cocentaina some 40 miles inland from where we lived on The Costa Blanca. It was a five acre hillside with beautiful views to the distant City of Alcoy and had masses of potential for building several villas which they were regarding as a long term project. They met with the local Mayor of the village, made their purchase using local Spanish solicitors and spoke to architects about their design ideas before returning to England to await the drawing up of initial plans and for the agents to obtain the various permissions from Valencia.

Sylvia Ray, Steven's god mother and her husband Ken came out to Spain for a week to stay with us. They brought with them a video of Steven and Matthew's race and letters from the kids and friends back in the UK. We spent a lot of time chatting and showing them the local area and we really enjoyed their stay.

We also met Barbara and Alan Penny who lived just a few villas away. They came from Nottingham and were both retired school teachers. Alan had been headmaster at West Bridgeford School near the National Rowing Centre at Holme PierrePoint so we had a lot in common and had loads to chat about with them. They came out to Spain for three months during the summer each year so weren't permanent residents like us but they were

142

*super company and we would get together for drinks and barbeques and Barbara would kindly sit with my mom Ada sometimes if we had to go out anywhere; we became good friends.*

*We had settled down to our usual routine when we were surprised on Monday 19th November by a sudden visit from Christine. She walked in and immediately we could see that she was very upset. She broke down and told us that her marriage to Philip was in trouble after eighteen happy years. They had a wonderful home, the building of which they had recently project managed themselves, Philip had a good job with the Swedish automobile company Saab and Christine ran her own beauty business; life seemed perfect for them. Philip had said that he had met someone else in the course of his work and he didn't know what he wanted to do and trying to make a decision 'to go or to stay' which was making him mentally ill. Christine's knee-jerk reaction was to show him the door but in the cold light of day she had realised that she loved her husband and had not wanted her marriage to end. They had met while at school and had married in their early twenties and up till then they had never needed anyone else. After a great deal of talking and forgiveness they had decided to give it another go.*

*Philip was about to take up a new post at his company's European headquarters' and had been asked to move to Brussels in Belgium. He wanted Christine to go with him and had suggested it would be a new start for them both. Christine closed her business, they sold their wonderful home and they moved to Europe 'lock stock and barrel' to a very nice flat in the leafy suburbs of Brussels. Devastatingly, Christine later discovered that Philip had been deceiving her all along so that he could remove all of their joint money and property out of the UK and away from British jurisdiction. After another eighteen months of emotional ups and downs Christine, who couldn't take the constant deception any more, finally threw in the towel, left her home in Brussels and went for a divorce. Christine stayed with us for a while in Spain and then she returned to England. She experienced another dreadful year of financial struggle due to her ex husband's managing to evade a fair divorce settlement and somehow managed to purchase our small house in Marlow Bottom by taking on a huge mortgage. She soon began to rebuild her beauty business by working all hours and just got on with her life. Geoff and I were so proud of the way she got though this very hard time of her life; she showed such great emotional strength managing to get through such devastating life changes.*

143

My brother and sister-in-law Bryan and Pat came over for two weeks to look after Mum. This enabled Geoff and I to travel back to England in the camper to spend an early Christmas with the family. We shared our early Christmas lunch at Steve and Ann's home with all the family and here we got the good news that Steve and Ann were expecting their first baby. What great joy after what had seemed like such a bad year, we all felt very happy for them both.

All too soon it was time for us to return to Spain. The winter weather had been bad and our midnight ferry couldn't sail until 2am and so once docked, we stopped for the rest of the night at Calais so that we could get a few hours sleep. The following morning we got under way again but we ran into deep snow at Lyon. Although the motorway had been reduced to only one lane we managed to get through ok and drove on through France to Spain, with the weather rapidly improving, back home to Javea.

While we had been away, Brian and Pat had managed very well looking after Mom and the dog even though Ada had been giving them the run around, constantly asking where her handbag and pension book were, even though her bag was right by her chair all the time. It can be very wearing indeed dealing with an elderly relative with dementia but we all knew that she couldn't help it. The following day we took them back to the airport to catch their flight to Newcastle and the cold of a Northern English winter. That Christmas past by uneventfully for the three of us and on Christmas Day we received some good news from Steve and Ann. They had decided to take a little break and fly over to Spain to spend the New Year with us, from the 28th December to the 3rd January; this cheered me up no end.

It was lovely to have them staying with us and we went for long walks, relaxed playing cards and Steve would go running each day to keep up his fitness. The weather was good for early January and on New Years Day, Geoff, Steve and Ann decided to get some real exercise by climbing a nearby mountain. The mountain is called 'Mongo' a Spanish word for elephant, as the mountain's outline resembles an elephant's head and trunk. The summit is about a two hour walking distance from the bottom and there are several paths each marked in a different colour denoting the difficulty of the climb to the top. It's not a difficult climb for the first 90minutes but the last 30minutes is much harder. I was a bit concerned about Ann but she coped *very well and they all seemed to enjoy their selves. Geoff was a bit puffed out as they had all done it in a very quick time but he had managed to keep up with the young athletes.*

*All too soon it was time for Steve and Anne to return to England and after they had gone we gradually settled down into our usual routine again. We both really hoped that this coming New Year would bring happiness to all of our family and particularly for Christine as the previous year, 1990, had been so dreadfully hard for her.*

# Chapter Twelve
## World Championships 1991 Vienna Austria

### *Who's the Daddy*

*In February 1991 Steve went to Boston, Massachusetts in America to compete in The CRASH-B World Ergo Championships an indoor rowing competition using ergometers. Ergometers, or Indoor Rowers as they are now known, are calibrated to measure the amount of energy the rower is generating and they simulate the action of watercraft rowing. CRASH-B initially stood for Charles River All Star Has-Beens. This is the name the group of originating rowers gave to themselves, and they are still the official governing body of indoor rowing which has now become established as a sport in its own right. Steve became the 1991 World Ego Champion when he won this event in a time of 7:27.1 then raced over 2,500m on a Concept 2 Model B ergometer. After this event, he went on to Australia for 10 days; life was becoming very busy for him.*

*Jane asked me to go back to England to look after the twins while she studied and took her Beauty Therapy exam. It was to be for six weeks so the only way I could do this was to take my mom Ada with me. The journey was quite difficult but the airline was very helpful and we made it back to England without too many problems. Jane had rearranged her home giving Ada her own bedroom/living room downstairs so she was very comfortable. Ada was beginning to experience bouts of aggression due to the dementia but we managed her all right and Jane worked hard and passed her exams with flying colours so it had all been worth the effort.*

*On Easter Saturday, Ann and Steve were busy working in their garden and William, their African Grey parrot, happily wandered about the lawn while they worked. They had done this many times before but on this occasion a flock of birds flew overhead and William suddenly thought he would take off and follow them. Steve and Ann were in such a panic and so we all joined in the search to look for him asking everyone we met if they had unusually seen an African Grey parrot flying past, but to our disappointment no one had. Word spread locally and most of the neighbours started looking for him too. We had to give up our search when it got dark but early the following day, and after many calls of sightings, we all went back out to search again. A man whose garden backed onto the land that we still owned at Furze Farm had seen him in his garden so we went to Furze Farm and found him sitting high up on a branch in a tree.*

*I telephoned Steve and Ann who had gone to Ann's mother's for Easter Sunday and they rushed home and we all went back to see if he was still there. Ann and Steve talked to him and he almost came back to them but at the last minute he flew away again. It was now getting dark and it was beginning to feel much colder too so we had to give up yet again but were worried that he would not survive the chilly night. The following day he was sighted in the village playing fields so off we all rushed again. Steve had gone out training but Susan, Ann's sister, came with us to help and she and Ann brought Williams cage along with them. David leaned a plank on the tree trunk and we tried to entice him with some parrot food and very slowly he started to waddle down the plank.*

*Ann, and Steve who had now come home, began to talk to him again and William, standing just out of reach, put his head to one side and said 'Hello' and then immediately flew off once again only to land on another tree but still just within our sight. Steve finally caught him in the playing field when William just waddled up to him and calmly stepped up onto Steve's arm. I wouldn't forget that Easter in a hurry and neither would William, as he didn't venture out of his cage for some weeks after his little adventure.*

*The following Saturday the 6th April was the 1991 Scullers Head of the River.*

*Christine drove me to Putney and we had an interesting day together watching all the competing boats. This year Steve won the Head by a huge margin of 19 seconds. Making up for last year defeat, he seemed to be back on course once again.*

*A few days later Mom and I returned to Spain and Geoff and the dog met us at Alicante Airport. We were home, once again, and in the sunshine with mom seemingly none the worse for her trip away.*

*On the 26th June, Pat, and Bryan arrived again to look after Mom while Geoff and I went back for our annual trip to Henley Regatta, Lucerne regatta and the 1991 World Championships, this year in Vienna, Austria. All the family were fine and it was lovely to see them all again even though I had only been away from them for a few weeks. Ann seemed to be keeping quite well and this year was to be the doctor for the crews at Henley Regatta. I felt she might be doing too much what with being pregnant but she said she felt fine and said she enjoyed being busy. Henley started on the 3rd July in good weather and this year Steve and Matthew won the Silver Goblets, the Coxless Pair event.*

*We took the camper to Henley for the week and our five year old grandchildren, the twins, stayed with us on the Saturday night so that they could have a 'sleepover' and see the firework display at 10pm. Ben managed to stay awake but Steph dropped off to sleep and so we had to tell her all about it the next day. We also took them to church on Sunday Morning to a really lovely service held in St Mary's Church by the river, the ancient Civic Church of Henley-on-Thames dating from 1204 that dominates the skyline of the town. Jane and David came by later to collect the twins but returned for the family picnic at the end of finals racing. We spent Monday cleaning the camper and getting it ready for our trip to Lucerne.*

*We hadn't seen Ann and Steve at all on Monday but early morning on Tuesday 9th July we had a call to say Steve had taken Ann to hospital when she had started her labour pains at 4.30am although the baby wasn't expected for another few weeks. It was a day of concern for us all but at 9.23pm the wonderful news came that a baby girl, Natalie Ann, had joined our family; we were grandparents again and we couldn't wait to see her and drove to the hospital. Natalie Ann was lovely and looked very much like her dad. Steve was still decorating her nursery as her arrival had been so sudden. He needed to get a move on so Geoff helped and it was all nearly finished by the time Ann arrived home with the baby.*

It was Lucerne regatta the following weekend so Geoff and I left on Wednesday to drive to Switzerland; Steve flew out with the team. We arrived on Friday just in time to see Steve and Mathew's first heat which they won taking them safely through to the semi-finals on Saturday. The Swiss weather was not at all special and after watching their race we went off to book the campsite.

On Saturday we met Ann Spracklen, Mike's wife, who was very excited to hear the news of the new arrival. It had been a dull start to the day but by the afternoon the weather had turned really nasty. Steve and Matthew won their semi-final going through to Sunday's final. That evening we met the boys in Lucerne at the ice cream parlour where all the crews seemed to be gathered. As the weather was so bad we didn't stay long and we returned to the campsite and went to bed early hoping that the weather would improve by the morning.

On Sunday morning we awoke to find that the weather had not improved much at all and it continued to rain all day. We got quite wet watching the races that day but it didn't really matter as the boys won their race setting themselves up nicely for the World Championships the following month. The crews flew home and we set off to Bad Waldsee and the Hymer Camper factory, where we had booked in for our annual check over and service on the camper. We had always loved Bad Waldsee which is such a lovely, typically German, little town. As usual while the camper was being put through its paces we spent a relaxing day strolling around the lake and picnicking on the warm bread and delicious cakes from the town's wonderful bakery. Later that day, when the camper was ready we set off back to Calais and took the ferry back to England to once again visit Ann and our lovely new granddaughter. We found both mother and baby well and Ann seemed to be coping admirably on her own with her new charge, as Steve had already left for training camp; Natalie seemed to be a settled and happy baby.

We spent the next few weeks in England before leaving for the World Championships. During this time we decided that it would be great fun to take Ben and Steph to the seaside. The English summer seemed settled so

149

we spent a long weekend on the south coast leaving on Friday evening and coming home on Monday evening. The twins absolutely loved it and so did we; Jane and David didn't like to be away from the twins for too long, so we could only manage short spells away with them.

About ten days later we were planning to go up to Preston in Lancashire to collect some parts for the camper so we again took Ben and Stephanie with us and the four of us spent a couple of days in Blackpool. The weather could have been better but we did manage to get onto the beach with the children and they had their first donkey ride at Pleasure Beach. Due to the bad weather and endeavouring to keep the twins amused, the trip ended up costing us a small fortune but it was worth it as altogether we'd a lovely time. On the way back South, we stopped at Warwick Castle where there was to be a display of knights on horseback which we thought the children would enjoy but unfortunately, by the time we got there, it was all over. Arriving in Marlow Bottom later that day we dropped the twins off and they were excitedly greeted by their parents who seemed very pleased to have them back.

The next few days were spent cleaning out the camper and stocking up with food for our trip to Vienna and The World Rowing Championships. Steve returned home from training camp to find his wife and daughter doing fine. On Sunday morning, 11th August, Steve and Ann asked us to visit their house to lend a hand catching up with some household chores and we gladly obliged. On returning to Jane's home for lunch we were stunned to find the house filled with all my friends; the kids had planned a surprise party for my birthday. I was really shocked and surprised and I must have looked quite a state but I soon had a quick shower and tidied myself up and I really enjoyed my 60th birthday party. However, that evening ended with a trip to Wycombe Accident and Emergency as Ben cut his foot quite badly and had to be taken to hospital; we had a long wait but they finally put him right.

We left the next evening for the World Championships taking a night ferry and stopping the rest of the night to sleep at Lille in France. The following day when I was driving the camper on the German Autobahn and I suddenly felt the camper swerve with a puncture in a rear tyre. We were in the middle of some road works and the traffic had been reduced to one lane *so I couldn't stop immediately as I would have completely blocked the road. I eventually was able to pull over and soon the German police arrived to help us out and called someone to give us a hand to change the tyre. We used the spare but had to drive on to Vienna hoping for no more punctures as we only had the one spare tyre. Next we had a problem finding the course and camping ground and by this time it was getting late and it was also quite dark. Beginning to feel the stress of our day, we had missed the correct slip road off the motorway and so in the end had to find somewhere just to park for the night.*

*The following morning, in the daylight we had no trouble locating the rowing venue on The Donauinsel (Danube Island) on the Neue Donau, "New Danube" just north of Vienna. The main purpose for this manmade island was to be part of Vienna's highly sophisticated flood protection system and consists of a long, narrow island, between the Danube River and the parallel excavated channel 'Neue Donau' but it had now also become an attractive and well used recreational area. We got settled into the campsite there which was nice and close to the course. It was the first time we had come away without our bikes which would have been ideal as there was a cycle track which ran right along side the course, still we thought; the walking would be good exercise and wouldn't do us any harm.*

*I sent a fax to Ann giving her the route and directions to the venue. She was due to travel out by car, accompanied by her mother and baby Natalie, as she had been asked to work as team doctor to the rowing team and had decided to bring her mother, June, to look after Natalie while she did her job. They hadn't planned to leave the UK until Sunday the 18th because Ann's sister, Susan, was getting married on the 17th August.*

*The opening ceremony was on Sunday 18th August. It was a small affair with all the nations presenting their country's colours. We spotted Steve and Matt out on the water on a training outing but we couldn't get to speak to them. On the campsite were several people that we knew and amongst others we had a good chat with Richard Phelps' cousin who was taking in the Championships to support Great Britain while holidaying in the area. Richard was a Cambridge rower and part of the British team; he would later go on to be an Olympic oarsman in Barcelona and a well known freelance sports journalist working for the BBC and on the 'Five Live' commentary team in Sydney 2000.*

When the Championships started on Monday we had a good day watching all of the races. On Tuesday we saw Steve and Matthew win their heat putting them into the semi-final on Thursday. While watching the rowing on Tuesday, Ann arrived with her mum, June, and baby Natalie, who seemed none the worse for the long journey despite being just 41 days old. They'd all had a good journey and had arrived on Monday night and had found their hotel without any problem.

On Wednesday we went to watch the rowing again and were on hand to support June with baby Natalie while Ann worked. We met our old rowing friends Pat and Moira Cross and had a good chat; their son Martin was rowing in the Eight this year. Mike Spracklen, Steve's previous coach, and his wife Ann were there too, as Mike was coaching the Canadian Eight who, this year, were in with a good chance of winning the gold medal. After rowing had finished for the day Moira and Pat came back to the campsite to share a meal with us and to reminisce over old times.

Thursday was semi-final day and Steve and Matthew raced that afternoon and won without any problems. We continued to watch the rest of the day's racing and Moira and Pat once again came back with us for a meal; we really enjoyed their company as they both had such a good sense of humour.

Friday was a rest day for Matt and Steve so we decided to try and find somewhere we could buy a replacement spare tyre for the camper and then we would carry on into the city of Vienna to do a little sightseeing. We visited the fashionable shopping centre near the Hofburg with beautiful clothes shops, porcelain and glass stores, goldsmiths and jewellers, book, music and antique shops; it was fascinating and lovely to window shop but we couldn't afford to do much more than that. We toured the Hofburg, which for over 600 years had been the official residence of the Austrian sovereigns. Originally it was a medieval fortified castle dating from the 13th century and it had been extended by each emperor until eventually coming to resemble a 'city within a city'. The now sprawling complex which extended over 240,000 $m^2$ consists of 18 wings, 19 courtyards and 2,600 rooms in which nearly 5,000 people still work and live today. We felt that most of the buildings in the city were absolutely magnificent but particularly the museums and the very famous opera house 'The Vienna State Opera.

*Towards the end of World War II the opera house had been set alight by an American bombardment. Another remarkable sight was St. Stephan's Cathedral with its beautiful ornately patterned and richly coloured roof which is covered by 230,000 glazed tiles. Probably, Vienna's most famous historical citizen is Mozart and we saw the house where he had lived and where he had composed the Marriage of Figaro. Geoff and I both found Vienna to be a very impressive and a most interesting city and we felt really pleased we'd had the opportunity to stroll amongst its historic buildings.*

*We also took a trip to the well known Spanish Riding School that uses highly trained Lipizzan stallions in public performances that demonstrate classical dressage movements and training. We found the tour very interesting but unfortunately, in August, the Lippizaner horses did not perform. The breed is relatively rare, with only about 3,000 horses registered worldwide. Most Lipizzans are gray. Like all gray horses, they have black skin, dark eyes, and as adult horses, a white hair coat. Gray horses, including Lipizzans, are born dark—usually bay or black—and become lighter each year as the graying process takes place, with the process being complete at between 6 and 10 years of age. Contrary to popular belief, Lipizzans are not actually true white horses. A white horse is born white, has pink skin and usually has blue eyes. The horses that we saw had their manes and tails plaited with gold ribbons and we were told that they are trained to dance the quadrille, gavotte, polka and slow waltz; full training apparently takes an average of six years for each horse. I made a promise to myself that one day I would come back to see them perform.*

*Saturday 24th August was the Final day for our boy's event so we got to the rowing course early to secure some good seats. The lightweight men and women came first. Our Men's Lightweight Coxless Four found gold first, which was wonderful and then the Women's Lightweight took bronze in the Coxless Pair. This was a terrific boost for the British women. The men's Coxed Four had a hard race and unfortunately, right at the end, they slipped back into fourth place.*

*Steve and Matthew's turn was next and now as usual all our stomachs were beginning to churn, even little Natalie began to stir. Steve had taken Silver in 1989 and a Bronze medal in 1990, what would this year hold, we wondered. The race got underway and the French seemed to be making headway with Steve and Matthew, hot on their heals, and still in contention. Then our lads came past them and went into the lead, winning the race in 6:21.35. Matthew had taken his first World Senior Gold and Steve his third. As they had crossed the line Mathew's face was a picture, with a wide smile, he flung both this arms in the air and almost leapt out of the boat; Mr Cool just sat there calmly behind him. It was their first World victory together with the Slovenian Junior world champions Istok Cop and Denis Zvegelj taking Silver 6:24.18 and Austrians Karl Sinzinger and Hermann Bauer taking Bronze 6:24.51; the famous Pimenov twins from Russia come in a close fourth. Ann ran up to the rostrum with Natalie and gave her to Steve, she was so small, when he held her in his arms, she looked totally lost. What a proud mom and dad they made, not to mention the three proud grandparents in the background Geoff, June, and me.*

*On Sunday Great Britain was victorious again when Martin Cross in the Men's Eight took Bronze which made Pat and Moira's day. Mike Spracklen's Canadian Eight had taken silver loosing to the Germans by a very small margin. The Germans were always going to be the crew to beat and the Canadians had given them a good race. One of the German crew had broken his arm and had been substituted at the last minute so they had deservedly taken gold.*

*That night Geoff and I went out to celebrate our boy's victory with Jean and Ewan Pinsent, Matthew's parents, and with Matthew, Steve, Ann, June and baby Natalie. We had a tasty Chinese meal and that made a pleasant end to an extremely good week.*

*Steve, Ann, June and Natalie had planned to visit us in Spain for a short holiday after the Championships so the following morning we set off first and they had caught us up by the time we got to the Brenner Pass, the mountain pass through the Alps along the border between Italy and Austria. The scenery here was beautiful and we would have taken our time and done a little sightseeing but the weather was so hot that we decided to travel quickly back to Spain and after just two days journey we arrived home and all fell straight into the pool to cool off. Pat and Bryan stayed with us all for another week and we enjoyed a great family get together. Steve's ten days with us passed quickly by but I'm happy to say that my mom really loved little Natalie and seemed not to have forgotten her only Grandson.*

*Natalie Ann was to be christened at St. Paul's Cathedral on the 14th December 1991 and I had to think of a way to get mom looked after while we were away. My brother Bryan could come out to Spain again but his wife Pat couldn't. A friend of ours knew of a local nurse who would visit each day to take care of mom's personal needs and this was arranged with Bryan coming over on his own to take general care of Mom and Tasha the dog. Geoff and I then flew back to England for ten days. Our first job was to find Natalie a Christening present and we settled on a delightful picture of three children playing on a beach, a boy and two girls which made me think of our three Grandchildren, Natalie, Ben and Stephanie.*

*The 14th December arrived and what a lovely day we had. The Christening service was to be held in The Crypt in St. Paul's Cathedral, where Steve and Ann had been married. Steve organised a coach to take us all up to London which was ideal as it would mean that all of our relatives and friends would be together and would allow us all a chance to chat. Matthew's dad, The Reverend Ewan Pinsent conducted the service and the godparents were Matthew Pinsent (Steve's rowing partner), Ann Spracklen (the wife of Steve previous coach) and Joan Haley (Steve's late schoolboy friend Bill's mother). The service was really lovely and afterwards we were all bussed to the Christening reception which was held at the Watermans and Lightermans Guild Hall. Due to the rowing connection, Steve had been made an honorary member of this association and had been offered the use of the hall for his daughter's christening.*

*The Company of Watermen and Lightermen was established by Act of Parliament in 1555 to control the Watermen on the River Thames responsible for the movement of goods and passengers. Indeed it remains the only ancient City Guild to be formed and controlled by Act of Parliament. Today the Watermen and Lightermen still work on the River Thames, the former being concerned with passenger transport and the latter with the carriage of goods. The young Freemen of the Company who serve their apprenticeship are eligible to participate in a special sculling race for the Doggett's Coat and Badge and this race has been held annually since 1715. The gruelling boat race is held each July and goes along the river from London Bridge to Chelsea. The winner has the honour of wearing the scarlet coat, breeches and silver arm badge that are based on the original costume of an eighteenth century Watermen. The Hall was a lovely old historic London building dating back to 1780 and remains the only original Georgian Hall in the City of London. Inside there were replicas of boats and displays cases with the bright red Dogetts Coat uniform and Badges worn through the ages. This year's winning apprentice was standing at the entrance wearing his full regalia, his sculling oar standing to attention beside him; he made a very impressive doorman.*

*Everyone enjoyed the party, even Natalie seemed to know that she should be on her best behaviour; she was such a good baby. On the way home the coach drove back through London so we could see all the city lights and Ben and Steph seemed to really love it. This was a really special day for the whole family.*

*We had a last minute rush to get our Christmas shopping before we flew back to Spain. On our arrival in Javea, we found that Bryan had managed well with the help of the nurse but he was very glad to see us again and to hand back the reins. What would we have done without him? She was his mother too but not all families help each other out and I couldn't sing his praises enough for the regular respite care that both Bryan and his wife Pat gave to me when taking care of Mom. My gratitude also goes to my wonderful husband Geoff, not a lot of people would let their mother-in-law burden their lives so.*

*Bryan returned to Newcastle to his family for Christmas and we prepared to spend Christmas in Spain. We had a lovely last minute surprise as Steve, Ann, baby Natalie and Christine came over to spend Christmas with us. They had taken it in turns to drive non stop, with two hours on and four hours off, and had arrived in record time with Natalie sleeping most of the way; Steve always had to have a challenge. It was so good to have them with us but we realised that it was still a hard time for Christine but she said that it felt comforting to have her family around her. She seemed to be coping so well and getting on with her life. We all phoned Jane, David and the twins on Christmas evening; they'd had a fun day but missed us all as much as we missed them.*

*On New Years Eve our local friends Pam and Peter Plumridge came over and joined us to see the New Year in and in true Spanish tradition, we all tried to eat our twelve grapes, one on every strike of the clock at midnight;*

*it's surprisingly hard to do and bad luck if you can't manage to swallow them all but happily no one chocked this year. After a very pleasant evening together and once everyone had gone to bed we eventually went to sleep hoping with all our hearts that Christine would find happiness again in the coming year and that the whole family would keep fit and well. Steve, Ann, Natalie and Christine went back to England on the 1st January and we watched them drive away, wondering when we would next see them.*

# Chapter Thirteen
## Lucerne Regatta 1992 Switzerland

### *Motivation Inspiration Respect*

*January came and went for us quite uneventfully really. Steve went off to South Africa for the very first time to get some 'good weather' winter training in. Now that Apartheid was over, the former restrictions had been lifted and it was now deemed acceptable for sportsmen to visit.*

*My Mom, Ada, was having quite a few bad days and by mid-February we had to fetch the doctor out to see her. Her breast cancer had become much worse and she needed the nurse to visit every day. The doctor thought that the longest she would live would be perhaps another two months. So it was with deep sadness that I gave this news to Christine, Jane and Steve. They all loved their Nan so much and even though she was, by now, a very old lady, they still didn't want to lose her. Bryan was very upset too and said that he would do anything he could to help but there really wasn't much anyone could do. She was getting exceptionally good treatment from the Spanish medical system and after a few weeks she seemed to markedly improve so the nurse dropped her visits down to twice a week; Ada was proving that she was a tough old bird with a strong will to keep on fighting.*

*Steve and Matthew went to the 1992 Cologne Regatta and had a convincing win there on the 2nd May; there was little report of their success in the newspapers. They then followed this up with another good win at Essen Regatta on the 16th May; Ann had gone with the boys, leaving Natalie with her grandmother, June. When we went to the phone cabins to call Steve the following week, he told us that he had picked up a salmonella type bug, yet again, while in South Africa and he hadn't been well since. He told us that in fact he had been ill for sixteen consecutive weeks and had now been* put under a specialist. It seemed that the salmonella infection had led to ulcerated colitis and he had lost a lot of weight. We felt very concerned and really sorry for him but also quite helpless too.

Pat and Bryan arrived on the 3rd June and brought a message from Jane that Steve would not be rowing this year at Lucerne International Regatta which would have been a regular event for him under normal circumstances. She told us not to worry though, it was just that he wasn't yet back to full fitness after his recent illness and he had been advised by the doctors not to race just at the moment. With this news we felt a little better. Pat and Bryan had come over to Spain to take care of Mom and the dog while we went to Germany for the usual annual camper service. We had then planned to go on to Lucerne and then return to England for a few weeks prior to our trip to the Barcelona Olympics.

Mom was holding her own now and on some days she was quite good. I had a few days with Pat and Bryan before leaving, to explain Ada's routine and pass on instructions on how to get the doctor or the ambulance to come out if it was necessary but I knew that our neighbours would help them if need be.

We left on the 5th June hoping that the situation with Ada would remain stable. We decided to go to Lucerne Regatta as we had originally planned, but mainly to meet up with old friends and to get some measure on Steve's competition for the coming Olympics. No one seemed to understand why we had come to the regatta especially with Steve's absence but we explained that we really enjoyed our annual visit to Lucerne and we were here also to check out the opposition as this would be the final international event that would be held before the Olympics.

We left Lucerne on Sunday afternoon after the finals had finished and headed for Germany. We had been invited by our friends, Barbara and Alan Penny, who spent their summers at a neighbouring villa to ours, to visit their daughter's house in Kirchzarten just outside Freiburg, a delightful little town not far from the Black Forest. Their daughter Sarah had three children, two boys and a girl called Mafanwee aged seven who was a very talented violinist. Mafanwee could speak very good English and so she constantly translated for us; the whole family made us feel very welcome.

*During our stay, the town of Freiburg held their annual festival, which Mafanwee translated as, "Happy Dead Body Day". The townsfolk would all meet at the central Cathedral Square in the town and would walk in procession together with their elected church members through the town being led by local dignitaries, followed by the butchers, the bakers and other tradesmen all dressed in their traditional costume. The various churches of several different religions came next and the children scattered rose petals along the way from little baskets that they were carrying. It was a very interesting experience for us to take part in the procession and at the same time have an enjoyable tour of the town.*

*On Monday, Barbara and Alan took us into Freiburg to browse the city shops and to meet up with Mafanwee and her father, Matthias. They were busking with Mafanwee and her friend playing violin; her father the double bass and they had been joined by another friend, a very talented accordionist. They were all playing such wonderful music; we could have listened all day. As we wandered around sightseeing, every square we came across seemed to have some entertainer or other and it gave a real vibrancy to the city.*

*The following day we said our goodbyes to this lovely family and headed for Bad Waldsee for the camper service; Barbara and Alan were leaving too, for their villa in Spain where they would be staying until November. We had made plans to meet up with Steve, Ann and Natalie in Silvretta in the Austrian Alps at Lake Silvrettasee, Europe's highest lake, where they were all staying while Steve shared an altitude training camp with rest of the Great Britain rowing squad in preparation for the Olympics. We were going to help them out by looking after our granddaughter while Steve rowed and Ann worked as the team doctor.*

*After a lovely stop getting the camper serviced and filling ourselves up on cake and bread from the town's superb bakery, we made our way via Ravensburg, to Friedrichshafen on Lake Constance. Bodensee, as it is known locally, is a lake on the Rhine at the northern foot of the Alps. This huge freshwater lake is 63 km long and borders Germany, Switzerland and Austria. We were both overwhelmed by the beautiful scenery here and decided to stay the night in this quaint little town.*

The next morning we rode our bicycles along the lake shore exploring the area. The water in the lake is amazingly clear. The Germans, who are known to prefer their coffee really dark and strong, have a saying that refers to these pristine waters, they say that if you can see the bottom of your coffee cup then the coffee is sneeringly referred to as 'Bodensee Kaffee'.

That afternoon, we drove the camper on to the old Roman city of Bregenz in Austria for our overnight stop. Here we met a fellow Englishman who had attended a vintage car rally and was on his way home, travelling at a sedately pace in his beautiful old car. We then slowly climbed our way up in the camper to Landeck a Tyrolean city at an elevation of about 820 m. and as we continued up through the Silvretta mountain range to Lake Silvrettasee, the road was clear but there was deep snow on either side. The scenery here was stunning. The majority of the peaks that we could see were above three thousand metres high and being surrounded by glaciers, this area was known as the 'Blue Silvretta'. During our stay here, as the snow slowly melted in the summer temperatures, it raised the level of the lake producing some quite spectacular waterfalls.

In the wake of German reunification on 3 October 1990 and towards the end of 1991, a new coach was employed by Leander Club and the Amateur Rowing Association. Jürgen Gröbler from Magdeburg in the former German Democratic Republic had been appointed as Steve and Mathew's new coach. He came with a first-class pedigree, having coached the East German rowing squad to success since 1972. His English was not too good at first but he soon leaned to make himself understood very clearly when coaching, and the boys quickly developed enormous respect for this very firm but extremely pleasant man and they all got along very well.

Altitude training began and it was Ann's job to keep the squad fit and healthy. The squad were all staying in ski huts and so we parked our camper close to Ann's hut so she wouldn't have far to go with Natalie. It was so good to see them all, Steve had lost a lot of weight but he said he was feeling ok, although to us, he really didn't look too well. Natalie was now nearly one year old and she was a real delight. We would take her for walks near the lake each day to watch her dad training and to fill our lungs with the pure Alpine air. One day while walking, we came across a very large greyish shaggy-looking dog; he looked a bit like a wolf and appeared to be on his own, then as we got closer, we noticed a lady who appeared to be his owner with another similar looking dog. The owner turned out to be an English woman who made had this wonderful place her home and she told us that the dogs were Irish Wolfhounds. We chatted to her for a long time and I told her about an Irish wolfhound we had known of called, Finbar, an Irish boys name meaning 'fair head' and an Irish version of the name Barry. He had lived with his family at the top of our road in Marlow Bottom and although huge, was extremely well behaved with a placid nature and wouldn't have hurt a fly. He would play out in the quiet country lane with the other smaller dogs that lived nearby and one day he accidentally knocked over a woman who reported the incident to the local police. An ensuing court case was held in Marlow Court House and Finbar was made to sit in the dock; his owners had employed a barrister from London to defend him. The Judge ruled that from now on he would have to be kept in and not allowed out without his family, who would have to keep him on a lead at all times. All the local kids and villagers loved Finbar and we were all pleased that he had been reprieved.

A few days later Natalie went down with tonsillitis and she was quite poorly, so much for the Alpine air, so we had to go down the mountain to find a chemist and get her some antibiotics. I'm glad to say that it was only a few days before she was feeling much better again.

With the training camp now over, the Great Britain rowing team including Steve with Ann and Natalie left Austria to fly home to the UK and we slowly made our way back through Germany in our camper. We chose to drive 'The Romantic Route' going through the Fern Pass. This 1,212 m high alpine pass was created by an entire mountain collapsing thousands of years ago, filling part of the valley and we really enjoyed a lovely picturesque drive on the well-maintained Swiss roads over the pass to Landeck, on our way, viewing Germany's highest peak 'Zugspitze'. The passing landscape was marked by a series of lakes that are believed to have been created by the same mountain slide. Our scenic route took us through Augsburg a city in the south-west of Bavaria and many other wonderful old German town's along the River Danube; it was really lovely.

The weather had been good but now it was beginning to change so we decided to make a dash along the autobahn to catch the ferry back to

*England and the family. It was Natalie's first birthday soon after we got back and we had a family barbeque to celebrate and it felt good to be in the heart of my family once more. There was no time to be lost though, and it was our job in the following days to clean the camper and fill the cupboards with provisions in readiness for our trip to Barcelona to once again support Steve in his third Olympic competition.*

# Chapter Fourteen
## The 1992 Barcelona Olympic Games

### *Fly the Flag*

*Steve, Matthew, and the rest of the rowing team had left early for their pre-Olympic training camp in Varazze, in Italy. Steve seemed to be much better now although he was still very thin. He said that he had returned to his previous level of fitness but only tough competition would prove that. Jane and the twins were travelling with us in the camper and we had decided to take our time, calling into seaside places along the way, so that the two children wouldn't get too fed up with the long journey. David, Jane's husband would be coming out later by car and ferry and Christine was travelling over with her new friend Edward by car. They had planned to make it their summer holiday destination and were sightseeing and camping on route; we had all planned to meet up at Banyoles where the Olympic rowing was to be held. We had booked ahead and were all staying together renting the complete upper floor of a very large old farmhouse close to the rowing lake. Steve had sussed out this location for us all during one of his visits to Banyoles sometime during the previous year when he had viewed the farmhouse during its renovation. It was a very old building and had been used as a military base years before and was being re-constructed by the owners to, he was promised, a high standard and would be ready in plenty of time for the Olympic event.*

*Leaving England on 15th July, we spent a wonderful time with Jane and the twins getting to Spain, taking a route through the Picardie region of France from Calais, to Abberville. On the road between Dieppe and Rouen we had a puncture on a back wheel of the camper which Geoff blamed on the copious amount of tinned food that I had stashed away; he thought that we were overloaded. The twins thought this was great fun and they looked* up the French word for tyre in their school books. Once the puncture was repaired we carried on our journey through Caen and Bayeux following the coast round to Saint-Malo. This ancient and very picturesque walled city in Brittany is most interesting with its château and harbour full of boats and yachts. We walked around the wall and browsed the shops and everywhere we went we found the streets decorated with flowers displays. We then drove through Nantes to La Rochelle a seaport city on the Bay of Biscay, where we camped overnight and here the children enjoyed the sea.

The following day we drove on to Bordeaux and then we took the motorway to Toulouse stopping off at Carcassonne the fortified French town on the way. Jane wanted to visit the sparkling wine vineyards so we took a slight detour to Limoux, in the Languedoc region of southwestern France, an attractive market town located in the eastern foothills of the Pyrénées. We took a tour which showed the viticulture and the wine production in this area that included a tasting. The wine was exactly like Champagne and was really delicious so we brought a few bottles of Blanquette just in case we needed it after Steve's last race at Banyoles. Later that day we drove on to Perpignan and stayed in a camp site right on the beach at Cannet Plage, the weather was fabulous and the twins enjoyed a swim and of course it was a much deserved rest for Geoff who had, up till now, done all the driving.

The following day, we continued our journey into Spain heading for Lake Banyoles in the province of Girona in northeastern Catalonia, the venue for the Olympic Rowing. Lake Banyoles is a natural lake and is named after the nearby town of Banyoles which is about an hours drive from the City of Barcelona. The lake is approximately 2,000 m by 700 m with an average depth of 15 m but in several points gets down to almost 40 m and it had become a regularly used rowing location and is ideal for racing.

We arrived at Banyoles Lake in the afternoon of Thursday 23rd July, parked the camper and enjoyed a cup of tea. Geoff and I then decided to take the twins for a bike ride into the village leaving Jane in the camper. Along the way we bumped into Mike Sweeney, a rowing official, with a small group of FISA members. FISA is the "Fédération Internationale des Sociétés d'Aviron" in French, or the English equivalent International Federation of Rowing Associations and is the governing body of the sport of rowing.

*Mike said to me in a very serious tone, "Have you heard about Steve" and my heart missed a beat. I shot a glance at Geoff and really for an instant thought the worst. We had been on the road, and therefore completely out of touch, for the last eight days, and it had been even longer since we had last spoken to Steve, anything could have happened. The Romanian lady in the group said to Mike, 'Tell her then, you can see she is upset.' Mike laughed and told us that Steve had been chosen to carry the flag for Great Britain during the Olympic Opening Ceremony; I didn't know whether I would laugh or cry. I think tears came into my eyes and I looked back at Geoff and I could see by the expression on his face that he too was relieved that our son was alright. At the same time we felt excited and really pleased for Steve as we knew that it was something he had always dreamed of doing; it would be an enormous boost for British Rowing as well. I managed to control my emotions but it wasn't easy.*

*We had promised the twins an ice cream so after a short chat with the group, we moved on. With my mind in overdrive we found a shop and I held the bikes while Geoff took the children in to get their ice creams. They came back all excited saying, "Guess what Nan we have just seen Steve." I couldn't believe it and then a few minutes later Steve and Matthew joined us and I gave them both a big hug. It was wonderful to see him and he was looking so well. Jürgen was with them too and he heartily shook our hands and we both could see that he too was very pleased about Steve being chosen to represent his country and the sport of rowing. By the time we returned to the camper it was getting dark and Jane was beginning to worry but when we quickly explained what had happened she was over the moon too.*

*The Olympic Opening Ceremony is usually a very long and protracted affair, great for the spectators sitting in the stands but for the athletes standing around for hours, sometimes in the heat as well, it could be draining. At the previous two Olympics Steve hadn't attended an Opening Ceremony due to the fact that his first race was always the following day and he needed to rest before competing; therefore this time we hadn't bought advanced tickets either, particularly as the main arena, where the ceremony was to be held, was in Barcelona, about 150km away from Banyoles. Consequently, we had no tickets, and very little chance of getting any at this late stage, to see Steve carry the flag.*

The following morning Friday 24ᵗʰ July, we drove up into the hills above Banyoles to find the farmhouse that we had rented. The farmhouse property had come to Steve's attention through Terry O'Neill, a British rowing coach who was coaching the Spanish crews; he knew the people who owned it. Terry later went on to be a British and International rowing coach, who nowadays works for Concept 2 developing and promoting indoor rowing training.

The ground floor of this very large property was rented out to a group of rowers and spectators from Thames Tradesmen, the first floor was where the owners themselves lived and the top floor was for our family and friends. Our floor had a very large kitchen with seating area but there was only one toilet and one shower and as there was going to be nineteen of us once they all arrived; it wasn't looking too good. It was not all that clean either so, rolling up our sleeves, Jane and I and got to work. Even after several hours of elbow grease it still didn't look a whole lot better. At least we had a working TV on which to view Steve at the Opening Ceremony.

The worst thing about the farmhouse was the flies; it was a bit like Alfred Hitchcock's, "The Birds", but with flies. It was, we found out too late, a working cattle farm, and in the middle of a Spanish summer, it didn't help. As soon as we got rid of one lot, another lot would somehow get in. We sprayed and we cleaned but they still kept coming. Our only option was to keep all the doors and windows closed but with no air conditioning available; the inside of the farmhouse soon became a sauna. To top all of this the beds, which were mostly like children's camp beds, were made up with nylon sheets. With the combination of closed windows, summer heat and nylon sheets, no one could sleep. Outside there was a large garden and a large swimming pool which we were really looking forward to utilising, especially for the children but we found to our dismay that the pool cleaning pump was broken and so within a few days the clear blue water had turned to a murky green; no one fancied a swim. I felt so sorry for Terry O'Neill, he explained that he really hadn't known that the conditions inside the farmhouse were so bad; it looked lovely from the outside We had no option but to stick it out, where else were we going to find accommodation for 19 people in this small town this close to the start of the Games; we gritted our teeth, and tried to make the best of it.

On Saturday 25<sup>th</sup> July we all sat glued to the telly and watch as Steve walked into the arena, leading out the team from Great Britain, holding the Union Jack out at arms length. What a proud moment for us all.

Steve and Matthew arrived to visit us at the farmhouse on their bikes the following day. Steve said that they were both feeling ok due to the fact that they had stayed in Barcelona overnight so were not feeling too tired. They both took a good look around the farmhouse and Matthew, helpfully letting in some fresh air, pulled the blinds up and flung open all the windows and promptly let in another swarm of flies. He wasn't to know, but we were trying to keep to the Spanish tradition of keeping out the heat of the day along with the flies by keeping the windows shut and the blinds closed; never mind.

Monday 27<sup>th</sup> July 1992 was the start of the Olympic Rowing at Lake Banyoles. In their heat, Steve and Matthew had drawn the Slovenians, who were known to be good. As it turned out, the strong opposition posed no problem at all and Steve and Matthew took the race with apparent ease. But believe me, no Olympic race is easy, crews don't get to this level for no reason. Steve was looking better now and by putting their stamp on their first race they had scuppered any rumours about Steve's fitness. Hugh Matheson wrote the following day in The Independent 'Steven Redgrave and Matthew Pinsent were absolutely dominant in their heat of the coxless pairs. After 1500m the Slovenes gave up the chase and the British pair dropped to a cruise rate and still came home in the fastest time of the day'.

We all returned to 'Fly Castle' as we were beginning to call it and had a swim before the pool had gone completely green. Later, Geoff and I went for a gentle bike ride around the lake. It was very pleasant cycling in the warm sunshine and watching the crews training; afterwards we headed back to the farm. It was a bit of a hard ride going back as it was all uphill and as we puffed up the slope we were passed by a car that had an English number plate; there was someone shouting and waving out of the window. It was Pat and Moira Cross, it was so good to see them here; no Olympics would be complete without them. They came back to the farmhouse with us and of course they knew everyone else; we all had a cool drink and shared our news.

On Tuesday morning, we all went to the rowing again and watched some of our other crews racing and later in the afternoon we went to the supermarket and stocked up on food as we knew that we'd be feeding the proverbial five thousand. Wednesday morning, June and her family went into Barcelona; Ann went to the rowing while Geoff and I took care of Natalie.

Christine and Edward made it to Banyoles on Wednesday evening and they said that they had really enjoyed their camping trip, slowly meandering their way through France. They too were not impressed with the farmhouse flies; it remains a joke to this day. Where we lived in Spain on the Costa Blanca, not far from the sea, we didn't seem to suffer from flies in the summer months like this but I guess that we were staying on a cattle farm and the cow sheds were right next to the farmhouse; we were stuck with them it seemed.

Thursday 30th July was the day of the semi-finals. Steve and Matthew had all their tough opposition in their race. My tummy started to churn once again while we waited for his race to begin. We suddenly spotted Audrey and Harry Payne in the seats a little way in front of us, they had known Steve since he was a little boy and were great fans of his. Audrey had been the post lady for Marlow Bottom and we hadn't seen them since we had moved to Spain. It turned out that they spent their holidays each year at Estartit, which was not too far away, at the northern end of the Costa Brava and they said that they weren't going to miss the chance to see Steve row; it was lovely to see such support for him.

Now it was finally time for their semi final to begin. They absolutely flew off the start and in no time at all were leading the race. They led all the way making their win again look easy. We all hoped that they would find it as easy on finals day when they would have to race the course again on Saturday.

As we left the rowing venue that day we met Julie Colligan with her Spanish boyfriend, Luis, and her sister Susan. Julie had been Steve's first girlfriend when he was still at school and she had also been our weekend helper at our garden centre. Julie's mother was Spanish and so Julie, having a good grounding in the language, had moved to Madrid to live and work. They had all come to support Steve; it really was becoming a big gathering of old friends and supporters.

*The temperature of the Spanish afternoon was rising well into the 90's and we felt so hot after the rowing had finished that we went back to the farm to try to cool off. After our complaints, the owner had worked on the pool so despite the flies we all got in for a swim and shared a good laugh with the boys from Thames Tradesman and Lea who had taken over the ground floor of the farmhouse; they were so fit that they had cycled all the way to Spain. We were settling in and making the best of a bad job, the nights were a bit noisy but we thought that if we were coping with the flies then we could cope with a bit of noise at night from the lads having a little fun.*

*Matthew's mom and dad, Jean and Ewan Pinsent, were staying with us at the farmhouse and David, Jane's husband, had now arrived, having made his journey to Spain by ferry across the Bay of Biscay to Bilbao, driving the rest of the way to Banyoles. That afternoon Lynne and Larry Tracey had unexpectedly turned up too, with their four children. They had planned to book into a nearby hostel but after inspecting it, found that they didn't like it and had come to see us at the farmhouse and had ended up camping on our floor. Julian Scrivener, one of Steve's rowing friends, and his girlfriend, had also come out to Spain to support Steve and the British crews and were camping on the other side of the lake. The number of British supporters was growing by the day; we felt like one big happy crowd and comrades-in-arms.*

*During the middle of that night, Ann knocked on our bedroom door and woke us to say that she had just discovered some strange man in the kitchen, who apparently was very drunk and was eating food from our fridge; we all went down to the kitchen to see who it was. We didn't recognise him but he appeared to be a foreign rower who was the proverbial 'three sheets to the wind' and lurching about like a drunken sailor. Geoff escorted him outside and saw him safely back to his tent. We all assumed that he must have been a friend of The Thames Tradesmen on the ground floor. I later found out, much to my annoyance, that it had been the Danish sculler, Bjarne Eltang who had been so un-gentlemanly after Steve's Henley defeat in 1986.*

*Saturday the 1ˢᵗ August dawned and it was the day of the boy's final and Steve's third Olympic bid; our nerves began again and we wondered if he would be able to reach his goal, one more time. Of course, looking at it logically, we knew that there was a very good chance Steve and Mathew would come up trumps once again but as always there was that nagging little doubt that crept into the back of my mind; would their luck hold out. Steve would say to me that it wasn't down to luck at all but to sheer hard work, the right preparation and the positive belief in ones ability to win; even so, all the family know how superstitious I am.*

*It was a bit hectic that morning, getting everyone out of the farmhouse on time. There were now so many of us that there was the inevitable cue for the loo and shower but we all managed to get some breakfast and made it to the rowing venue on time. We all settled into our seats in the stands with the Spanish sunshine already feeling hot on our faces. We tied our faithful old Union Jack to the back rails and sat in front of it, posing for photos with friends and family; the excitement and tension was beginning to build and there was a buss in the crowd around us. The British supporters were ready.*

*Finally, their race started and immediately Steve and Matthew took control. It was a tremendous race which they dominated throughout, all the way to the finish line. The roar from the crowd was enormous, they had done it again, a third Olympic gold for Steve and Matthew's first; absolutely wonderful. Their golden time was recorded at 6:27.72 with Germany's Colin Ettingshausen and Peter Holtzenbein taking Silver in 6:32.68 and Slovenia's Iztok Čop and Denis Žvegelj taking the Bronze in 6:33.43: they had won by almost five seconds.*

*It was fantastic; our friends and family were all ecstatic. After the medal ceremony Ann fought her way through the crowds to the rostrum carrying Natalie in her arms. Natalie had been dressed in a British all-in-one rowing kit just like her dad and she looked so cute. Mathew and Steve posed for the press, wearing their Gold medals and with Natalie held in between them in Steve's arms; it was such an excellent shot that it made the front page of every British newspaper the following morning.*

*On their return to the Olympic Athletes Village, Steve and Matthew received a fax from the British Prime Minister, John Major, expressing his sincere congratulations and good wishes. Pertti Karppinen, the Finnish rower and former three times Olympic champion in the single sculls event, had wished the boy's all the best as well; Steve was really chuffed with that as Pertti had always been his rowing idol.*

*After racing we all walked round to the official reception area and met the two boys there. It was such a great feeling for us to see our son achieve another victory despite his recent illness. I spotted Thomas Lange, the German who had just won a Gold medal in the Single Sculls, and went over to offer my congratulations. I introduced myself and shook his hand, then thanking me he said, 'I already know who you are'. He had been in the double scull that had pipped Steve and Adam to the post in the 1980 World Junior Championships; he had just taken his second Olympic Gold medal here in Barcelona.*

*When all of their interviews were done, we all trouped down to the café by the lake for some lunch. We tried to decide where would be the best venue for a proper celebration that evening. Some of us thought that it might be nice to continue the festivities by eating out at a local restaurant in the village, but in the end, and mostly due to there being so many children; the decision was made to have a barbeque back at the farm. It was to be a big mistake for we had forgotten the dreaded flies. Everyone lent a hand and' with the money each family had put into the kitty' we managed to buy some good meat to barbie, a selection of salads and copious amounts of beer, wine and champagne. Sadly it turned out to be a never ending battle and a race to see who could get to the food first, us or the flies. We had to keep all the food in boxes with the lids tightly closed and we had to constantly keep our hands over our glasses or we would find a dozen flies doing the backstroke in our Rioja but we were all in such a jubilant mood that we didn't really care.*

*On Sunday 2nd August, British hopes lay with the young Coxed Pair of the Searle brothers coxed by Gary Herbert; we were also routing for the British Eight. There was a dramatic finish to the Coxed Pair race when, the young pretenders, Jonny and Greg, suddenly came from behind in the last few seconds of the race to snatch victory from the Abbagnales, the previous double Olympic gold medallists; what an unbelievable finish. The Men's Eight didn't do so well but they put up a brave fight nevertheless. Their race had been won by the Canadian eight, coached by Mike Spracklen; a great day for Steve's old coach.*

*It was the end of yet another Olympics for us all and it had definitely been an excellent result for Steve and an exciting time for the whole family.*

Christine and Edward left the farmhouse early on Sunday, headed for our home in Javea, on the Costa Blanca, where we would all be meeting up again in the next few days. Jane and David drove off to Barcelona for a few days on a business trip, leaving the twins with us; they would come on to our villa in Javea early the following week. Steve, Ann and Natalie were flying back to England with the team, whilst June and her family were taking a steady drive back through France. As usual, I felt the inevitable anti-climax that always accompanied the moment of parting with good friends and family but this time wasn't so bad as I now had at least ten days to look forward to, having all the family join us at our villa, for the rest of their summer holiday; and of course there was the enormous bonus of not having to constantly fight 'the battle of the flies'.

When we got to Javea we learnt from Pat and Bryan that my Mom Ada had been a bit up and down during our absence but they had managed well. My brother and sister-in-law returned to England and we busied ourselves preparing for our daughters to return and meantime we thoroughly enjoyed our grandchildren Ben, and Steph, taking them to the beach and swimming with them each day in the clean and sparkling water of our own pool.

We received a message informing us that Marlow Town Council was planning to give Steve and Matthew an official reception on 17th October and they were asking us if we would like to attend. We were faced with a huge dilemma as I felt that I couldn't really ask Pat and Bryan to come back to Spain so soon. A friend kindly recommended a good nursing home near Alicante that would be ideal for a short stay solution to Ada's care and so I made a visit to inspect it. I was pleasantly surprised at how nice it was, especially, as it overlooked the sea. The rooms were very clean and well furnished and most of the members of staff were English; those that were not seemed to have a good command of the English language. I felt much happier and made my decision.

It was decided that I would go back to the UK for five days on my own and, on the way to the airport, we would drop Mom off at the nursing home leaving plenty of time to settle her in; Geoff had decided to stay at home with the dog. I carefully explained all this to Ada but she soon forgot what I had told her, poor soul. We delivered Ada in plenty of time for me to settle her in and then catch my flight but I did feel very guilty leaving her and in *the end almost missed my flight as I had stayed with her too long; we had a last minute dash to the airport. After what seemed like a very short flight to the UK, I was met at Heathrow by Jane, Ben, and Steph.*

*Saturday 17th October was a very sunny day but with an Autumnal feel to the air. First there was an open-top bus ride through the streets of Marlow for Steve, Mathew and their families, accompanied by the councillors of Marlow and High Wycombe and followed by a reception, held at Court Gardens as before. It was a very enjoyable gathering with a buffet lunch and champagne during which a presentation was made to the boys followed by speeches from both Steve and Matthew. It was all over by about 3.30pm and later that afternoon I rang Geoff, and Pat and Bryan and told them all about the day's events.*

*On Sunday we had a family dinner at Jane's and on Tuesday I flew back to Spain; it had been a bit of a whistle-stop visit but I had really enjoyed it. Geoff met me at the airport and on our arrival at the nursing home, the attending nurse told me that for the last five day's, Mom hadn't stopped asking where I was. As soon as I saw her she said accusingly, 'where have you been?' and I had to smile. I gathered her things together and Geoff drove us back home.*

*Steve, Ann and Natalie had promised to visit us at Christmas so with this to look forward to we settled back into our usual routine. Unfortunately, when Christmas arrived they had to cancel their visit due to Steve being ill again and we all thought that it was better for him to rest at home. Christmas 1992 came and went with just Geoff, mom, the dog and me. We went to the Phone cabins and telephoned all the kids on Christmas day and we found Steve still wasn't at all well. On New Year's Eve we called everyone again and discovered that Steve was still suffering. That evening Geoff and I saw in the New Year together and discussed the events of the fading year with its highs and lows; we were particularly worried about Steve and I wondered what 1993 would hold for us all.*

Geoff stirred in his seat, he had been asleep for over an hour. He asked me if I had slept at all but I said no, that I had just been thinking about Steve's rowing career.

Passengers started to move about the plane again as members of the cabin staff prepared to serve everyone with food. We began to tidy ourselves up, Geoff folding the blanket that had covered him and we both lowered our tables looking forward to the new distraction of the imminent arrival of a meal. We talked about this and that as we ate. I checked my watch; we had been in the air for about six hours now. Geoff was beginning to feel a bit fidgety but he eventually settled down with a rowing magazine; I went back to my cloud gazing and 1993.

# Chapter Fifteen
## World Championships 1993 Račice Czech Republic

### *Czech out the Facilities*

*1993 started with the news that Steve was still not at all well, he was still experiencing a lot of stomach pain, his current medication had been changed yet again and he was expecting to undergo further tests; we were beginning to really worry now and at the end of January I rang and spoke to him. He said that he was just about to go into hospital as it seemed that now he had sugar in his blood too. He told me that he was getting some good care from the specialists and they had asked him to come in while they tried to find the cause of all these problems in this hopes that they could begin to treat whatever it was.*

*I phoned again two days later to see if there was any news and I spoke to Ann. It seemed that he had now been diagnosed with diabetes and would have to learn to check his blood sugar level regularly throughout the day and correct it by injecting insulin into himself. Ann told me not to worry and said that Steve was coping well with this news and she gave me the telephone number of the hospital so that I could speak to him directly. Steve said he was all right, but then again, I knew that he would say that, but it was a relief to talk to him myself and even though I wasn't exactly familiar with this disease, I needed to know just how much something like this would affect his future health. He seemed fairly positive and I felt greatly relieved that the news hadn't been much worse but I was also not sure whether this diagnosis would mean the end of his sporting career.*

*Barbara and Alan Penny came out to Spain on the 6ᵗʰ February and brought with them a letter from Jane saying that Steve had come out of hospital two days before but that she didn't know much else. We received a fax a few days later to say that Steve and Natalie would be coming out to visit us for a week so that he could rest and get used to his new medication; Ann was unable to come due to work commitments. It was so nice to have both my son and granddaughter to stay. Steve looked very thin and quite strained but he said that he was feeling much better. He was learning to test his blood sugar level and was beginning to master his own insulin injections. We were relieved that he seemed to be coping well with this new regime and I watched his diet, cooking meals of protein and complex carbohydrates and keeping him off his favourite sugary foods. Natalie was as good as gold and was no trouble at all whilst Steve trained on the ergometer twice a day and in between slept and relaxed watching TV. By this time, we were feeling a little more civilised and in touch with the world at large as we had recently installed satellite TV; we still had no phone line. Steve loved watching television and would avidly watch any sport so it was a good way for him to relax. We took Natalie to the beach every day as, for early February, the weather was good.*

*Towards the end of the week Steve was beginning to look a lot better. I watched him as he had sat outside in the sun and he seemed to have lost the grey pallor that he'd had on his arrival; the Spanish sunshine was good medicine. While at the airport, waiting for their flight to be called, Natalie looked so cute in a pale pink dress that I had put on her that morning. I thought that it would be lovely for her mum to see her looking so pretty on her arrival at Gatwick. Steve brought Natalie some Smarties and she promptly proceeded to cover her face and her clean pink dress in chocolate; I didn't think Ann would mind though as she would be so pleased to see them both again.*

*On the 28ᵗʰ February I phoned Ann and Steve and received the good news that Steve was now off insulin and was beginning to stabilise. Thank goodness, we had been so worried about him; we had prayed so hard that he would recover and at last it was looking possible. However, all was not well in Spain, as Ada had hit a bad patch and was very agitated during the night calling out for me every so often. I had to get up many times each night to settle her down and I was beginning to feel exhausted. She was not really ill but seemed to be suffering from hallucinations and getting panicky and frightened. After a week of this the district nurse gave her some mild sleeping tablets so we could all get some much needed rest.*

*The post that week brought us the news that Great Marlow School was to honour Steve, their former, now famous pupil. I would have loved to have gone back for this event but I could not leave Mom at the moment as her health problems were so unpredictable. Christine and Jane went to represent us and afterwards they told us all about it. They said it had been a super day meeting all the teachers and governors and that it had made them feel so very proud of their little brother, particularly since it had been their senior school too.*

*Matthew, and the rowing brothers, John and Greg Searle, all received the MBE in March. We were so pleased they had been honoured too, it is such a great reward but it also made us think back to the 1984 Olympic gold medal winning crew who rowed with Steve, of Martin Cross, Richard Budgett and Adrian Ellison who had never received an honour; it didn't seem fair. Steve had received his in 1987 after winning his three Commonwealth gold's and Andy Holmes had received his later for his Olympic wins but those three never did receive their just recognition. We thought that it must be hard for them and their families when they had achieved so much as well.*

*Moira Cross came out to Spain to visit us for ten days, she hadn't been well recently so had come out to the sunshine for a bit of rest and recuperation; it was great to see her. She was a good Catholic who liked to attend mass each day so we would drive her to the church at Benitachell, a nearby village, and arrange to pick her up later. One day she decided to go off on her own but she didn't tell us that she was going out, I just happened to see her disappearing out of the garden gate about 2.30pm. I thought she had gone for a short walk and took no more notice. Later, at about 5.30pm, having not seen or heard from her all afternoon, I went to check her room; Moira was nowhere to be seen there. I told Geoff and we both considered whether*

178

we should sent out a search party but came to the conclusion that, as we didn't know where to start, that we should wait a bit longer. I got on with preparing the evening meal and was beginning to imagine the worst; had she collapsed from the heat somewhere we didn't know. At 6.45pm, just as we were getting in the car to go and look for her, up drove a taxi and out climbed Moira and paid the driver. She said, "Oh Sheila, I walked to the church at Benitachell, attended the usual service and then on my way back down the hill I must have turned the wrong way. When I got to the golf course, I asked a man where I was, as I hadn't seen this place before. He told me that he didn't recognise your address but that he would give me a lift to the main road. From the crossroads where he dropped me I walked back into Javea town and asked a policeman to call me a taxi." And here she now was, looking all hot and bothered. She must have walked about 6km or more and so that night she slept well. The rest of her holiday went by quite uneventfully and we all enjoyed her stay.

Steve's birthday was on the 23rd March so we went to the phone cabins to call him and he seemed much better. He was still on tablets for the colitis but he said he was feeling much better. He told us about the event at his old school, where they had erected a plaque in his honour. It seemed like he'd had a very interesting time chatting with pupils, staff and governors.

The boat race was on the 27th March this year. Matthew was president of the Oxford crew but unfortunately Oxford didn't win, it was Cambridge's turn this year and we really felt bad for him but, as they say, you can't win them all.

My mom, Ada, had not been well for a few weeks now and so the doctor kindly arranged for her to go for a thorough check up to the teaching hospital in Denia which was a 40 minute drive from our villa; we had to take her there by car for an 11am appointment. We arrived on time and then had a long wait in the hospital reception but eventually a doctor called us in. This was followed by another long wait while they found a doctor who could speak a little English. He arrived and spoke to us saying that his only option was to remove Ada's breast; I was really unsure what I should do. Over a year ago *the doctors had then told us that she was very unlikely to live another two months, and here she was, still with us. She still seemed quite strong physically but the growing breast cancer was making her very uncomfortable so I decided, to give her the best quality of the life she had left, that he should go ahead with the operation. I explained all this to Mom but I could see that she really wasn't taking it in.*

*After an x-ray, we went up to the ward and I tried to ask the ward sister when they would be expected to operate and that I would have to go back to the villa to get Mom's things as we had not been prepared for her to stay in hospital immediately. It was very difficult for me as my Spanish wasn't good and the ward sister didn't seem to understand me, so, in the best way I could, I told her where I was going and I left. The time by now was around 4pm in the afternoon and I had left Geoff and the dog in the car in the car park at 10am this morning. I quickly explained the situation to Geoff and we dashed back home, had a quick sandwich, fed the dog, packed a bag with a few of Mom's things and dashed back to the hospital.*

*The journey both ways took us about an hour so by 7pm I was back on the ward, this time armed with my Spanish dictionary and a notepad. I saw the same ward sister and was about to speak to her when she said in very good English, "Your mother has had her operation and she is ok but you will be expected to stay with her tonight." I was absolutely speechless. I went to see Mom and she looked to be ok so I went to explain to Geoff what had happened. He was again sitting in the car park with the dog in the car. I explained that Ada had already had her operation and that I was expected to stay with her overnight; I waved him goodbye and went back to the ward. Two hours later Geoff appeared at Ada's bedside saying that he had driven all the way back home only then to realise that I had the key to the house in my handbag. What a day; it had been a nightmare.*

*I sat in a chair next to Mom's bed and she thrashed about all night trying to pull out her drip. The nurse came every few hours to check on her and to alter the drip. All night, I could here the wind whistling around the building and the lady in the next bed constantly calling for her husband, who was curled up in a very comfortable chair and was fast asleep. She kept calling, "Ramon, Ramon," and I just wished that Ramon would wake up and that the morning would soon come. When daylight dawned, mom wasn't looking too bad and she asked me for a cup of tea. The nurse said that she couldn't have anything until the doctor had seen her.*

*The previous evening, I had asked Geoff to come back to the hospital at 9am and this he duly did and arrived bearing a very welcome flask of coffee. I was able to have a drink, the first I'd had since returning home yesterday afternoon. The doctor came at 11am, examined her and said she could go home. I asked if she was to go home by ambulance and he replied that she could but she would have to wait until 7pm when one might be available. I asked if we could take her in our car and he replied that we could but we would first have to wait for her release papers. The papers didn't come until 2pm but arrived with a lady who spoke good English. She said that a nurse would attend Ada everyday at home and that a doctor would occasionally come and check her as well. It seemed that the hospital's policy was to send 'old folk' home as soon as possible as they seemed to settle better in their own surroundings, so that's what we did. Ada was very pleased to be back in her own bed and seemed none the worse for her amazing ordeal.*

*During the following three weeks, the district nurse came out everyday to dress her wound and the doctor visited her twice. In just a few weeks Ada seemed fully recovered from her operation and was better than she had been for a long time. When I phoned home to give them this good news about their grandmother, Christine was really pleased but she also told me that her father-in-law had died in Wycombe Hospital on the 1st April. Although Christine and Philip were no longer together, she had gone with Philip to the hospital, as he had asked for her support, to be with the rest of his family at this emotional time. I wrote to Philip and his mother offering my condolences and sending my apologies for not returning to the UK for Eric's funeral as I couldn't possibly have left Mom. Steve and Jane had gone with Christine to offer their support to the family that they had all known for such a long time.*

Ann and Natalie came out to spend a short holiday with us in Spain at the end of April. It was lovely to have them visit and we went regularly each day to the beach, paddled and made sandcastles and then swam in the pool at home in the afternoons. Bryan and Pat couldn't manage to get out for Ada's respite care until the 29th June this year and, as we did not want to miss any of the summer events back in the UK, we decided that Geoff should drive back on his own in the camper and I would fly over to the UK a few days later, when they had arrived. I collected them from Alicante airport and on their arrival at the villa I could see that they were very pleasantly surprised to see Mom looking so good. I settled them in and then I left Spain the following day on a schedule flight to Heathrow. Jane met me at the airport and I stayed with her that night and then the following day joined Geoff in the camper at Henley for this summer's Royal Regatta.

The British summer had not been good so far this year but Henley saw the weather change for the better and it was nice and dry underfoot; the sunshine continued throughout the week which was lovely. Steve and Matthew were rowing this year in the Silver Goblets (Coxless Pair) and Steve was also entering The Stewards Cup (Coxless Four) with Rupert Obholzer, Richard Manners and Ben Hunt Davis. Steve and Matthew had a bye allowing them to advance to Thursday in the Goblets and the four had a bye till Friday and in both cases the boats made it through to the final on Sunday.

On Saturday evening, Ben, and Steph, came to stay with us in the camper to see the fireworks. Unfortunately only Ben saw the display as this year it was Steph who couldn't keep awake. Sunday morning arrived and Ann, brought Natalie, to us early and we went with all the children to the church service; I always liked to go to this if possible. It was a lovely day, the sun was shining and the children looked lovely all wearing their Sunday best. Jane collected the children after the service and it was arranged that she would bring them back later for the traditional family barbeque after the prize giving.

Steve and Matthew won the Silver Goblets & Nickalls Challenge Cup by one length from WM Coventry and CI Clayton-Greene of Waikato RC

New Zealand in 7:22, and Steve and the other lads won the Stewards' Challenge Cup by two thirds of a length from Rc Hansa Dortmund of Germany in 6:44, therefore bringing Steve's Henley medal tally to twelve in all. Hugh Matheson wrote of this race in *The Independent*, 'Redgrave also won the coxless fours event as a spare man. The ruse paid off, because the four had their first victory over the German crew who had been their bogy opponents this season, beating them by narrow margins at three European regattas'. It seemed Steve was an asset to any crew.

At this year's Henley a new race was added for women and the Women's Single Sculls was won by Maria Brandin the Swedish sculler. The Diamond Challenge Sculls was won by Thomas Lange of Germany as was expected but it was a very tight race with Vaclov Chalupa, the Czech Olympic Silver Medallist, coming in second but by only one foot; we had seen some great racing.

This year's prizes were given by Peter Coni, the Chairman of Henley Royal Regatta; he was the man who had made Henley the success that it is today. He had been forced to resign in January due to ill health but he gave a very memorable speech this year and sadly died just nine days later. He was a remarkable man and would be sadly missed by everyone. Our Henley gathering concluded with our usual family barbeque, this time on a delightful summer's evening; it had been another memorable regatta.

The next few days were spent, once again, getting the camper ready for our trip to Lucerne in Switzerland. We travelled through Europe with Natalie in the camper having arranged to meet Ann and Steve there, as they we re travelling out with the rest of the team and on our arrival in Lucerne booked into our usual campsite. We were really looking forward to our stay here and for this trip we'd had a little seat for Natalie fitted on the back of Geoff's bike so that we could all go cycling together. The following day, July 9th, was Natalie's 2nd birthday. I had made her a cake in the shape of a rabbit and after she had gone to bed Geoff and I blew up lots of balloons and hung them all around the camper so that when she woke up we could sing Happy Birthday to her and she could open some of her presents. After Natalie's Birthday breakfast we went to watch the rowing and afterwards met up with Steve, Ann and Matthew. Steve and Matthew had won their heat and had gone straight through to the final on Sunday so they all came *back to the camper for some Birthday cake. Back in the camper and out of the rain, Natalie got to blow out her candles and opened the rest of her presents with her mom and dad.*

*It was Julian Scrivener and Tabitha's wedding day today and the ceremony was being held in Jersey. We all should have been there but they understood that it wasn't possible for us to attend as we would all be in Lucerne; we sent our best wishes. It had started to rain here in Lucerne and we hoped that the bride and groom were getting better weather in Jersey.*

*On Sunday Steve and Matthew won their race and in the process we all got very wet. We were then quite pleased to return to the camper and after packing up, we made our way through Switzerland to Germany for our annual camper service in Bad Waldsee. As usual we fed the ducks on the lake, bought some lovely cakes and bread from the local baker and then later, once the camper had finished having its 'health check', we made our way back to England.*

*Natalie was very pleased to see her mom and dad again and was looking forward to her proper birthday party which was to be a 'Teddy Bears Picnic'. This was held at Radley College on the 18th July and was called 'Music at Oxfords Teddy Bears Picnic' and everyone went in small parties, taking their own food and joined the rest of the picnickers at this outdoor event. There were about eighteen of us in all, aunties, cousins, grandparents and a few friends; we all had a wonderful time. For the concert, an orchestra played all sorts of children's songs, like Puff the Magic Dragon, songs from the Sound of Music and the like. The children could sing and dance, shout, run around and drop their food and no one minded; it was a marvellous idea for a children's party. We picnicked on sandwiches, jelly and cakes and then Ann produced a big teddy bear cake with candles. There were lots of people dressed up in animal costumes like rabbits and teddies walking around us. We all had song sheets and later sang all the way home, it was the best children's party I've ever been to. The weather was not that good but the rain held off till we were on the way home so it didn't spoil our fun.*

*A few days later Ben and Steph broke up from school and so we took them down to the south coast in the camper for a few days, firstly stopping off at Bournemouth. There was a lovely sandy beach with nice sand for them to* play in making sand castles. We went for a ride along the esplanade on a special train and came back on the bus which was the most hair-raising ride I'd ever been on but it just seemed to amuse Ben and Steph. We moved on to Weymouth and the following day took them to see an "Iron Age Farm" which turned out to be very interesting. The tour we had was conducted by the people who lived and dressed as if they were in the Iron Age and we all learned a little about the history of Iron Age Britain. Later that day we moved on to Lyme Regis for an overnight stop and then made our way back to Marlow and delivered the twins back to their mom and dad.

The next two weeks were spent at Steve and Ann's house looking after their dog and parrot and taking care of Ben and Steph during the day as they were on school holidays. Steve, Ann and Natalie were away at their altitude training camp with the rest of the team. William, their African Grey Parrot, spoke very well and would continually ask questions in Steve's voice and answer himself in Ann's. He also called the dog all the time and it was really very funny. The dog would run around the house like a mad thing trying to discover who had called him.

The 13th August was my birthday, I was 62. I woke up that morning beside Geoff but he didn't say Happy Birthday to me. I got up, made our breakfast and still Geoff didn't say anything. Breakfast was eaten in relative silence and I thought that he must have forgotten but then the phone rang. It was Ben, Steph and Jane all singing Happy Birthday. Geoff laughed and told me that he had arranged to take us all out for the day; Jane had taken the day off work. My cards arrived before we left on a visit to the zoo at Oxford and afterwards we had a lovely meal in a nearby restaurant; it turned out to be a very nice birthday. Christine was away on holiday in Spain with Edward and she rang to wish me Happy Birthday and Steve, Ann and Natalie who were due home the following day had sent me flowers. My good friend Sylvia and her husband Ken hosted a party for me on Sunday; they had invited all of my old friends especially the ones I didn't get to see very often, it was great.

On the 24th August we packed up the camper again, said our goodbyes to everyone, which was always hard, and set off with Natalie for the 1993 World Championships, this year being held at Roudnice Czechoslovakia about 40 km north of Prague. We took the night boat from Dover to Calais *where we stopped to sleep for the remainder of the night. The next morning we made our way through Holland heading for Dortmund into North Germany and then on to Kassel where during World War II severe bombing had destroyed 90% of the city centre; here we stopped for the night. The next day we drove into what used to be East Germany. It was so different, the countryside was pleasant but during the German Democratic Republic, many apartment blocks had been built and these mostly remained giving most towns the appearance of consisting of concrete tower blocks and not much else.*

*I was looking forward to seeing Dresden the Germany city which lies on both banks of the river Elbe. I knew it had been bombed badly during the war when RAF and USAAF bombers had let loose some 650,000 incendiaries, 8,000lb of high explosives and hundreds of 4,000lb bombs in three waved attack, almost one bomb for every two people. Huge residential areas of the city were destroyed; a recent report has claimed that there were around 25,000 civilian casualties. The city still bore many wounds from 1945 and not much significant reconstruction seemed to be underway; I was very disappointed to see that more progress hadn't been made. The Baroque-style architecture of the old buildings that remained was very fine but nothing else was in keeping, it all looked rather run down and the major roads were in really bad repair. From here we took the E55, crossing the border into The Czech Republic at Altenburg, heading for the famous north-western spa town of Teplice. As we approached the border there were lots of lorries parked up at the side of the road waiting to go through customs and every bar and car park seemed packed with local prostitutes, it really was unbelievable.*

*It was dark by now and we needed to stop somewhere so the next lay-by we saw we pulled in and parked. No sooner we had stopped and before we realised what was happening, a large crowd of youths were all over the vehicle, cleaning the camper windscreen etc. It was quite unnerving and we weren't sure what to do. We had no local currency so we found whatever German marks we could put our hands on, and quickly handed it out of the door to them. We then drove off again as quickly as possible; I don't expect they would have hurt us but we didn't want to take the chance. We drove on for a while but Geoff was feeling extremely tired. Just then, we spotted a sign for a campsite that said 'Rowing' underneath it so we followed the signs until we came to what looked like a football stadium. We parked up and, as all seemed quiet, we bedded down for the night but first, due to our earlier experience, we made very sure that the camper was secure. What a journey.*

*In the morning, the daylight revealed that we were camped in the middle of a football ground; the facilities were dismal. There was a small hut housing two very disgusting toilets and a single washbasin. It must have been really bad as Geoff wouldn't even let me go and take a look. Luckily we had our own toilet and shower in the camper but we needed to top up on water and this we got later from the rowing course. Soon the football stadium began to fill up and a young couple that pitched camp next to us were from New Zealand, Lawrence Hill and Fay Wilson. We became quite friendly with them during our stay as Natalie very quickly made herself known therefore breaking the ice.*

*The rowing course at Račice was opened in 1986 for the World Rowing Junior Championships after six years of sand quarrying. The purpose built eight lane course at the Rowing Centre had a restaurant, finish towers, boathouse, changing facilities and showers and toilets for competitors; much better than the campsite. The World Championships this year consisted of lightweight and heavyweight men and women events and some disabled rowing events. Rowing began and Steve and Matthew won their heat and went straight to the semi final on Thursday.*

*We met Pat and Moira as they were here to support Martin in the British Eight and also Andrea and Terry Dillon whose son Terry was rowing in the British coxed four. Mr and Mrs Foster were here too but their son Tim had been pulled out of the Coxless Four fourteen days prior to the championships with a back injury. This had been a disappointment to them all but we all knew that if he had rowed with an injury he could have done even more damage. He had a good track record to date, having already won two gold medals; as a junior in a Coxless Four in 1987 and in a Coxless Pair with Matthew in 1988. Mr and Mrs Hunt-Davis were also here supporting their son Ben who was in the Coxless Four; we were becoming quite a large crowd of British supporters, which we were told by our boys, was always a huge boost to them as they raced and we shouted our encouragement. On race mornings, all the supporting parents would meet up at our camper to share a hot pot of coffee before braving the weather as it had been very cold and wet.*

*Ann and Mike Spracklen joined us too and we had a long chat. Since the last Olympics, Mike had left Canada and had taken a job as chief coach for the USA rowing team and they were now living in Santa Barbara, California. Ann sounded like she was really enjoying her new home in The States but she said that she was missing all the good friends that she had made in Canada. She had taken up golf and was getting into the swing of it, as you might say. We also bumped into Julian and Tabitha Scrivener who told us that their wedding in July had been wonderful and that they had come over on Julian's motorbike to watch the championships. They were also camping on the football ground in a tent; I didn't like to mention the toilets.*

*Thursday was semi-finals day and all went to plan with Steve and Matthew going through to the final. We decided that on Friday, the rowers rest day, Ann, Natalie, Geoff and I would visit Prague "The city of a hundred spires" and that we would travel in by train. We found the local station without any trouble and bought our tickets and after a short wait we boarded the train for Prague.*

*For 41 years, from 1948-1989 Czechoslovakia was a Communist state within what we knew as the eastern bloc. On January 1, 1993 Czechoslovakia peacefully dissolved into its constituent states, the Czech Republic and Slovakia. Compared to what we had seen so far, Prague, situated in central Bohemia, the capital and largest city of the Czech Republic was very different. It had beautiful old buildings and wonderful old squares. The city was so big that we decided to take a bus tour so that we could take in all the sites and we found one that suited our needs. It's always nice to know a little about the history of a city and we were told that Prague had suffered considerably less damage during World War II than some other major cities in the region allowing most of its historic architecture to stay true to form. This amazing and beautiful city now contains one of the world's most pristine and varied collections of architecture, from Art Nouveau to Baroque, Renaissance, Cubist, Gothic, Neo-Classical and ultra-modern.*

*We travelled through the Jewish quarter and saw the cemetery. We were told that the numbers of grave stones and numbers of people buried there are uncertain, because there are layers of tombs. However, it has been estimated that there are approximately 12,000 tombstones presently visible and there may be as many as 100,000 burials in all and no one was sure just how many Jews from this city had perished in World War Two.*

*Geoff and Ann went to look around the Gothic, Saint Vitus's Cathedral which is inside Prague Castle; I didn't get to see the inside as Natalie had fallen asleep and so I'd stayed with her on the coach; I didn't mind much as the coach was warm and it was quite cold outside. When they returned, they said that it was very beautiful, especially the Chapel of St. Wenceslas, where the relics of the saint are kept. The trip came to an end in Wenceslas Square named after Saint Wenceslas, the patron saint of Bohemia. Natalie now woke up and so we found a nice restaurant and had some lunch. Afterwards, we wandered through the square looking at all the stalls selling all sorts of things. Glass and crystal was a very good buy but I found a wooden toy stall. It had lots of jigsaw puzzles made of wooden cubes and I found Snow White and the Seven Dwarves. The cubes made six different pictures of scenes from the story of Snow White. When I had been about eight years old, I had been presented with a puzzle like this at school for coming first in a running race at Sports Day and I hadn't seen one like it since so we decided to buy it for Natalie. We also bought some lovely wooden skittles made to look like soldiers for Ben and a Russian Doll for Steph. The weather was beginning to worsen with heavy rain so we headed back to the train station; Ann returning to her hotel and the three of us to the camper.*

*Saturday was the boy's finals day and as usual excitement was running high. It opened with Peter Haining who won the Lightweight Men's Single Sculls, the first ever gold in this event for Britain and making him Scotland's most successful oarsman. It was nice to witness success for rowing coach Bill Mason too when his Lightweight Women's Coxless Four won gold; we had known Bill since Steve was a junior.*

*We met John Beatie in the crowd; we hadn't seen him since Barcelona. His international rowing was now over but he still rowed at club level and was still an avid supporter of rowing. John and Martin Cross were good friends* and in our 1984 video from Los Angeles, Moira's voice comes over very clearly saying, "Hello John, have you phoned your dad?" Geoff and I always smile and think about that whenever we meet John.

Steve and Matthew's race was the last of the day so we had plenty of time to get ourselves into a tizzy and as we approached their event our stomachs started to churn. The race started and the commentator came over the tannoy saying that all the crews were level. As the race progressed our boys seemed to stay with the pack, which did concern us a little, but then, with 500m to go they put in a really strong burst and broke away. It was as if they had changed down a gear and they went on to win the gold by clear water from Detlef Kirchhoff and Hans Sennewald, of Germany who took silver, and last years silver medallist, Denis Zvegelj and Iztok Cop, of Slovenia who took the bronze.

What an incredible row they'd had and in my excitement I rushed down to the rostrum with Natalie in my arms and kissed Steve and congratulated them both. I didn't think about it at the time but I didn't usually get the chance to do that; in fact I think this was the first. On the way back to the camper I bought commemorative T-shirts for the family back home; Steve and Ann joined us later. Ann had recently told us that she was pregnant again and so she was taking things steady and didn't want to go out wildly celebrating so we were all happy to stay in the camper and have our meal in. After we had enjoyed our meal and chatted about today's rowing, they returned to their hotel and I settled Natalie down for the night.

Sunday was the last day of the Championships and it was dreadful weather in fact it steadily rained for most of the day. Today there was success for the disabled rowers as Derek Irvine took gold and Geoff Spencer took silver; a wonderful achievement in this special sculling event. The Searle brothers still coxed by Gary Herbert this year again took gold in a very good Coxed Pair race, beating the Italian Abbagnale brothers, who took silver. The British Eight came in 6th place but Mike Spracklen's American crew came 3rd to win a bronze medal. We also had a Coxless Pair and a Coxless Four in the Women's events but neither made the final. I felt really sorry for these girls as they hadn't had much financial support along the way which made it very hard for them.

*At the end of rowing today, we said goodbye to our friends for another year and went back to the football ground for the last time. We didn't see Julian and Tabitha again today as the majority of people were heading home due to the weather. We exchanged addresses with the New Zealand couple who had camped next to us and settled down for our last night. Natalie was returning to England with her mom and dad in the morning and we were heading back to Spain and hopefully a little more sunshine.*

*The following morning after breakfast, we took Natalie to the hotel where Steve and Ann had been staying; the entire team was travelling to the airport by coach. I got a little emotional as we said farewell; it was made all the worse for me due to the fact that Natalie wouldn't say goodbye; she stubbornly refused. I knew how children could be sometimes and so I didn't push her but I did feel upset. Finally just before they departed she relented and kissed us both and said goodbye just as they were getting on the coach.*

*Mike and Ann Spracklen were staying on in Prague for a short holiday, which was nice for Ann as she didn't get to see much of her husband while he was busy with the regatta. We would see them again next year so we said our goodbyes and set off on our journey to Spain.*

*We left Teplice behind, turning south west and crossed into Germany at Cheb. As we drove through the border, I looked back and wondered how long it would take these towns to catch up to the standard of Western Europe. Once in Germany, we followed the River Danube to the Black Forest, a very beautiful and wooded mountain range, famous for its cherry schnapps gateau and for clock-making. We continued to travel by Lake Titisee with its crystal-clear water and finally arrived in Kirchzarten, where Sarah lived, the daughter of our friend's Barbara, and Alan and where we had stayed last summer. Here we booked into a campsite, washed and dried our wet and muddy rowing clothes and did some food shopping and later we spent that evening with Sarah and her family.*

*Getting on the road again the following morning we left Germany behind us and travelled via Mulhausen into France; here we joined the motorway and headed South for home and some sunshine. We decided that this time we would go through the eastern Pyrénées, stopping off at Andorra for some shopping before descending into Spain. Andorra is a small but very*

*prosperous country mainly because of tourism and its status as a tax haven.*
*The people of Andorra have the highest human life expectancy in the world,*
*and live to an average age of 85; must be the air. I was pleased to feel it*
*getting warmer as so far this trip we'd had more than our fair share of rain.*
*We re-joined the motorway at Tarragona and travelling non-stop to Javea*
*arrived at 3.30pm; it was the 11th September. We were pleased to see Pat,*
*Bryan, Mom and the dog, all looking well, thank goodness, and we spent*
*the next few days with them catching up on all the news before they flew*
*back to Newcastle three days later.*

*We soon settled back into our routine once again. On the 29th September,*
*the twins were six years old, how those years were flying by and we got to*
*speak to them on the phone. On the 9th October, Mom was 91 and she*
*had cards from all the family and we had a few of the neighbours round*
*for afternoon tea. She seemed to enjoy her day and was quite happy. Geoff*
*travelled back to England at the end of the month as Ann and Steve had*
*brought an old house in Bourne End, which needed lots of attention. They*
*had asked him to help with the building work as they had permission to*
*turn it into a Clinic so that Ann would have somewhere to work from. He*
*was away for a long time and I began to feel quite isolated especially when*
*Barbara and Alan left their villa to return to England. I had plenty to do*
*though looking after Mom and walking the dog. I made our Christmas*
*cake and wrote Christmas letters and cards so I kept myself busy. During*
*this time Mom was very up and down and quite restless and one night*
*she fell out of bed. It was very difficult picking her up on my own and I*
*struggled to haul her back into bed; she seemed to suffer no ill effects from*
*her ordeal but as a precaution I barricaded her in by pushing heavy chairs*
*against the side of her bed in the hopes of avoiding another tumble.*

*About mid-December I managed to get to the phone cabins to call the UK*
*to see how the building was going and Geoff said that Ann, Natalie and*
*Steve were coming back to Spain with him for Christmas and would be*
*there for about five days. I felt so excited and pleased that I wouldn't be*
*spending Christmas alone, just me and Mom. I busied myself for the next*
*few days preparing for their arrival. I managed to buy a real Christmas*
*tree, which isn't easy in Spain, and decked it with decorations and lights; it*
*looked lovely and very welcoming placed by the glowing wood burning fire.*
*They arrived at the villa at 8.15pm on Christmas Eve and were all very*

*tired with only enough energy left to eat the meal I had prepared, before going to bed.*

*On Christmas morning I got up early, made up the fire, walked the dog and got Mom out of bed and washed and dressed her in her best clothes. Natalie woke up next so everyone else got up for breakfast and to open their presents. Later that morning we all went to phone Jane and family and Christine and Edward to wish them a Happy Christmas and afterward we had a stroll along the beach before retuning to the villa for a light lunch. We had already decided to have our Christmas meal in the evening so that, after an afternoon nap, Natalie would have a chance of staying awake longer. We all sat down to eat together at 5.30pm; it had turned out to be a lovely day and it was really wonderful to have at least part of my family with me on Christmas Day.*

*Over the next few days we played with Natalie as she became familiar with her new toys, visited the beach and all played board games and cards in the evening. Our good friends Pam and Peter Plumridge had invited all of us to their home in the Jalon valley on the 28th December and we enjoyed a fun day with them. While we were away that day, the lady from next door kindly came over and looked after Mom, enabling me to enjoy the day and not have to worry about her. We all ate and drank too much as usual, as Pam is a very good cook and Peter an excellent host.*

*The following day Geoff, Steve and family left our villa to start their homeward journey at about 3pm. Their idea was to drive straight through taking it in turns to drive and sleep. I packed them up with food for the journey and flasks of tea and hoped that Natalie would sleep through the night. I watched them drive away until the car was out of sight and then began to tidy up the house to keep my mind off the fact that now it would be just Ada and me. I phoned the next evening and they'd made it home safely in just 20 hours which was pretty good going.*

*On New Years Eve, Mom was suffering from a chesty cough, so I put her to bed early and saw in the New Year on my own. It was my first New Year's Eve alone since Geoff had been in the army some forty years before; I guess I couldn't really complain. I had managed to eat my twelve grapes before the last stroke of midnight and I sat staring out into the darkness of the Spanish night, watching the occasional firework explode and wondering what 1994 would bring for us all. I hoped for good health for Steve and happiness for Christine, Jane and family. It would be Indianapolis in Indiana, USA this coming summer for the World Championships, if we could afford it. I downed my glass of sherry and went to bed.*

# Chapter Sixteen
## World Championships 1994 Indianapolis USA

### *The Arrival of Sophie Jayne*

Drifting back to reality, I looked around the plane. Most of the passengers appeared to be asleep. Geoff was dozing too, his book resting in his lap. I always feel that flying is always rather boring, especially on a long flight with nothing much to occupy your time apart from watching a film or listening to music through those awful headsets at least with train travel you get the sense of movement as the fields go rushing by and it's a little more stimulating. Most of the time an aircraft feels motionless, if you were lucky, I supposed; at least this way we'd soon be there.

I stretched out my legs and accidentally woke Geoff. He asked me if I was OK, I replied that I was but that I could do with a cup of coffee. He said that he would like one too so we buzzed the hostess and asked for two hot coffees. Before long we were sipping our drinks and having a quiet chat. Geoff asked where I had got to in my daydreaming, 1994 I replied. "That's the year Sophie was born isn't it? You'll be up to date by the time we land." Then we both lapsed back into our own silent thoughts.

*Geoff returned to Spain on January 25th 1994; the building work for Ann's Clinic now completed. He had converted the first floor into a self contained flat, which they were planning to rent out and the ground floor of the 'Old School House' he had turned into two consulting rooms, a toilet and reception area. He had lived in the house while he worked on it and said it had been rather cold at times before the new central heating had been installed; he seemed very pleased to be back in the sunshine and away from the British winter. It felt really nice to have him at home again and I had really missed him; our dog Tasha was really pleased to see him too.*

*Ann's baby was due in February so it was agreed that I would go back and look after Natalie while Ann had the baby. Pat and Bryan were coming out to look after Mom and this time Geoff decided to stay behind in Spain too as he had lots of jobs around the villa and the garden that he wanted to get on with. Pat and Bryan arrived on the 9th February and I left the following day. Jane, Ben and Steph where there at the airport to meet me as usual, it was so good to see them; they always seemed so excited to see me and would make me feel so welcome.*

*Once back in Marlow Bottom, I went to Steve and Ann's and that night slept on a new spare bed which had been put into Natalie's room especially for me. It wasn't long before Natalie had taken to sleeping in the new bed, leaving me to sleep in Natalie's much smaller bed; I really didn't mind though. A few days later I heard Ann get up several times during the night and then at 4.30am Steve came in to tell me that they were off to the hospital as the baby seemed to be on its way. Natalie didn't wake up until 7am the following morning and I told her that her mummy and daddy had gone to the hospital and we might hear soon that she'd have a new brother or a sister; we ate our breakfast and waited.*

*Steve rang very excitedly at 8am to say that the baby had arrived and that it was a little girl and he asked me if I would bring Natalie to the hospital as soon as possible as they wanted her to be the first to see the new arrival. We soon arrived at the hospital and Natalie was the first to hold her new baby sister, who again looked very much like Steve; Ann looked really tired but said that she felt fine. Sophie Jayne Redgrave came into the world on the 19th February 1994.*

*Later on that day, Ben said that he was a bit disappointed that it wasn't a boy as now he was really outnumbered 3:1. Those initial feelings seemed to disappear when he held her though and Steph took her turn holding the new born too and said that she thought she was lovely as well; it's funny how children seem to like babies.*

*I sent a message to Geoff, via Maureen Sherry, another of our friends in Spain who had got a telephone line, and she kindly said that she would drive over today to give him the good news that he had become a grandfather once again, this time to a very bonny baby granddaughter. I stayed at Steve's house in Marlow Bottom till the 1ˢᵗ March and then returned to Spain as Pat and Bryan were due to leave on the 2ⁿᵈ. They had managed Ada very well but we all wondered how long we would be able to cope with Mom.*

*Once again life settled down quickly and we made our regular calls to the family every Sunday and all seemed fine. Ann and Steve booked our flights and hotel to go to the 1994 World Championships Indianapolis for September. Our accommodation was going to be at the Holiday Inn so this time, it would be a first class stay and we were really looking forward to our trip to The States.*

*Pat and Bryan returned to look after Mom and the dog in about the third week of June. We decided to make our summer trip back to England for Lucerne and Henley Regatta a little more interesting this year by going off the beaten track. We took our time on the journey and enjoyed ourselves driving inland at Valencia to the remote and rural province of Teruel in north-east Spain, up in the mountains. Pig farming is a popular industry in this area with the production of the famous Serran ham, Jamón de Teruel, and we were most surprised to see hundreds of hams hanging up to cure on giant, wooden racks where they had been left to mature; it was quite an impressive sight. We then made our way to Zaragoza which lies in a valley surrounded by mountains. This area of Spain has a dessert-like appearance with a semi-arid climate. There's little rainfall here and the summer temperatures often get up to 40°C. We eventually reached Pamplona, a city in the north most famous for 'the running of the bulls' fiesta held each July, when brave young men run in front of bulls that have been let loose on a course of some sectioned-off streets of the town. Injuries are common with many youths getting gored or trampled; the Spanish can be mad. We climbed up through the Pyrenees descending into France near Bayonne. We hugged the coast where we could, travelling through Bordeaux, Poitiers, Tours, Le Mans famous for its 24 Hour sports car race and Caen in north-western France about nine miles inland from the English Channel.*

*This year, 1994, was the 50ᵗʰ Anniversary of the D. Day landings. We had watched the coverage on TV in early June, when the Queen, US President Bill Clinton and other representatives of the countries that had taken part in the landings, attend a memorial service for the people who lost their lives in the battle. I was 13 in 1944, and Geoff was 14 and we both remembered it all so well, everyone was saying then that it was the beginning of the end of the war. I was eight when war had broken out and was living in Birmingham with my family. We soon got to know about bombing, sleeping in air raid shelters, half day schooling and being excused from attending school if there had been a bad raid the night before; it's all still so clear in my mind.*

*I remember what it was like the first time the air raid sirens sounded, my mother gathered us up, also telling the milk man to tie his horse to the fence and come and share our air raid shelter which was at the top of our long garden. One of our neighbours, a very large lady with eleven children, had no shelter so had gone up to the end of her garden and sat under the apple tree with eight of her children, four tucked under each arm; three of her boys were away in the forces. My mother shouted to them across the garden fence, saying that they couldn't stay out there and she invited them into our shelter too. Round they all trouped and we all squeezed into our small shelter like sardines. Just after the last one of them got in, the 'all clear' siren sounded so we all scrambled out again. We were all quite frightened really as we hadn't known quite what to expect but this incident has always stuck in my mind and was really quite amusing.*

*Geoff had lived in Marlow at that time and being in the heart of the countryside they had lots of evacuees from London and he had to share his school with many of these displaced kids. They could see London being bombed from where they lived in Marlow Bottom and had a few dropped close by. Geoff had told me that during this time a bomb had dropped in a field about a mile from their home and he and another lad had rushed off on their bikes to see if they could spot where it had landed. On this occasion he had arrived first at the edge of the deep crater and had jumped in on top of the bomb and had quickly ripped off one of the fins which were such collectable items. He only then realised that the bomb was still intact, it hadn't exploded. The two boys raced away and never told a soul as they assumed that they would be in big trouble with their parents. Steve may never have been born if things had been different and the UXB had been unstable. Geoff's father, Edward (Ted), was a carpenter and had been put to work on manufacturing wooden aircraft propellers so he was doing what was known as 'essential war work' and so didn't see active service. He was in what nowadays might be called 'Dad's Army' though, the Territorials. Just before D. Day on June 6th, 1944, Ted became involved, when many of the troops who were to take part in the landings were held in the woods and country lanes around Marlow, hiding until the final push to the coast came. It must have been a logistical nightmare getting all those men and machines to the coast, into their boats and across the channel to their destination undetected; a really remarkable feat. So, for us to see Normandy and the places where they had landed was really interesting, as, up until now we had only heard on the radio when we were kids about our brave soldiers who had fought so valiantly.*

*We hadn't been to this area of France before so we made a detour and stopped to look at the war memorial and cemetery. The flower wreathes still lay where the Queen, The Duke of Edinburgh and President Clinton had placed them. We wandered around the graves, each a cross with the name, age, and regiment and most of the boys had been between 17-21 years old when they were killed. We stood at this beautiful spot, a part of England, forever. We moved across the road to the museum and there read newspaper cuttings from the period, and saw the vehicles that had been used and the uniforms these men had worn.*

*We then moved on to Aramanch where our troops had landed in France undetected. Here we saw the great concrete caissons of a Marlborough Harbour that had possibly been built in Southampton, and then towed out to sea and across the channel by British tugs. These floating harbours had been used to land tanks and other vehicles. One piece had beached and had broken, fifty years before; we stood beside it on the beach, feeling very small. Aramanch hadn't changed much at all since those days, a small French village with narrow streets; we took a look around.*

*We then drove on to take a look at the five main beaches on this Normandy coast line, where the troops had landed in 1944. The D-Day operation, officially named Overlord, was scheduled to take place on June 4th, but a storm caused General Dwight D. Eisenhower, to postpone it by one day. Omaha beach was where the allies lost 2,400 men while successfully landing*

34,000 troops. Utah beach was much less defended by the Germans and the allies only lost 300 men here. Gold beach is where the British had lost 400 men successfully landing 25,000 and Sword beach was the other British destination where 29,000 men landed but in the process 700 men had been killed. Juno beach had been assigned to the Canadians, but here natural off shore reefs took their toll on the landing craft and 1200 out of the 21,400 troops that landed perished in taking Juno beach. We drove back to Calais pondering the massive loss of life that had taken place here and elsewhere during the war and felt thankful that Geoff hadn't been ten years older and in the thick of it. We boarded our 1am ferry to Dover, parked for the rest of the night to get some sleep and then we drove back to Marlow the following morning. We had travelled 2,300km from door to door and we had enjoyed every minute of it but it felt good to be back in the UK with our children and grandchildren.

The 1994 Henley Regatta was held 29th June - 3rd July and this year we took several of our friends on Wednesday, the first day of rowing. Steve and Matthew had entered the Silver Goblets and had been given a bye until Thursday, so today we were able to relax and entertain our friends without our usual anxiety. Geoff had been staying all week at Henley in the camper and I commuted from Marlow each day during the week but stayed overnight at the weekend. Geoff would meet Ann and Sophie each morning and then take care of Sophie until Ann had finished her work with the athletes. Jane and Chris came on the Thursday and we had a lovely day with them; Steve and Matthew won their races comfortably, on both Thursday and Friday.

On Friday night the twins and Natalie stayed with us in the camper after first being taken to the fair. Jane collected them on Saturday morning and brought them back in the evening so they could watch the fireworks and they all stayed with us overnight so that we would be ready to go to church on Sunday morning; we really loved this Henley tradition. Steve and Matthew had made it through to the Sunday final and didn't disappoint the crowd, when they won the Silver Goblets & Nickalls Challenge Cup, beating J Van Dreissche and L Goiris, of Belgium in 7: 22 by 1¾ lengths. It was the sixth time that Steve had taken this cup and the third time for Mathew. After rowing we had our usual family barbeque and went home about 8.30pm after the crowds had died down, feeling pleasantly weary but very contented.

*Lucerne regatta was the next event on this summer's agenda. This year, Ann decided to stay at home with Sophie, asking Richard Budgett to stand in for her as the team doctor. We took Natalie with us in the camper; she always enjoyed travelling with us. It was her birthday on 9<sup>th</sup> July, while we were away, and we celebrated on the day with Steve and Matthew her Godfather, all enjoying a large slice of cake. Steve and Matthew had a very successful row on Sunday to win yet again when they knocked three seconds off their own world record and nine seconds off the Lucerne course record beating a new German pair of Peter Hoeltzenbein and Thorsten Strepplehoff. Hugh Matheson of the Independent newspaper said afterwards 'Pinsent has said that his tactic is to 'wap them all, each time we race, so that when we get to Atlanta no one believes he can beat us.' The Lucerne Regatta proved that the rest of the world is getting faster, but it also showed that Pinsent and Redgrave have deeper resources than anyone believed.'*

*We went back via Bad Waldsee for our usual camper service and to visit the local baker there for the lovely German bread and cakes. We made our way back to Calais where I took Natalie, on the hovercraft across the channel to meet Ann and Sophie in Dover; they were sitting in the sun waiting for us. We all ate some fish and chips together and then Ann and the girls drove back to Marlow and I returned on the hovercraft to France to meet up with Geoff.*

*Our plan was to wait in the Calais area until Ben and Steph broke up from school for their summer holiday, then we were to meet Jane, David, and the twins, when they travelled over for the day on the ferry to France. We would take the twins back to Spain in the camper and Jane and David would join us out there later. They duly arrived with their friend's Jackie and Rod who were going to do some shopping in the French Hypermarket at Calais with Jane and David before returning to England. Meeting up with them, we had a great day, swimming in the cold English Channel at Calais beach and sharing a meal together before the twins said goodbye to their parents and we set off to begin our journey to Spain. We stopped at Le Tréport just above Dieppe for the night, it was all very crowded as by now, we had now run into the French holiday season but we found a spot to park and bedded down for the night.*

*The next morning Geoff took the twins for a walk and they came across a*

*B.M.X. bike park so they excitedly rushed back to the camper to collect their bikes and both Geoff and I were dragged along to watch. Round and round they went, only just missing each other. Then Ben decided to test his skill further by attempting one of the jumps and ended up in a heap on the floor. I immediately rushed over to him but, thank goodness, he had just a small cut from the bike pedal; Nan soon fixed that. After that we retreated to the beach and the much safer game of beach ball and then they both went for a swim. After an early evening meal we moved on again. We found that by travelling this way, the children didn't get bored with the long journey and this is how we managed the whole trip.*

*One night after just passing Bordeaux, we stopped just south of the Arcachon bassin area and settled down for the night. The following morning Geoff, took the twins for their usual walk while I prepared breakfast. They came rushing back looking very excited to tell me that they had found a sand mountain. Geoff was smiling, so I thought they were joking but he then said it was true. After breakfast we locked the camper, and walked up a hill passing some shops and restaurants, then suddenly it was there in front of us; the biggest sand dune I have ever seen, no wonder the twins called it a mountain. It was incredible and when we had managed to reach the summit, the view from the top was breathtaking with an amazing panoramic view over the Atlantic Ocean; it seemed an awful long way down to the sea. Ben and Steph begged us to go down and, after running out of excuses, we gave in and almost had to slide down the slope on our bottoms it was so steep. Once we made it down to the beach, it was a "natural amusement park" and the twins began to play in the sand and then they swan in the sea. The sunshine was nice and warm and the kids soon got thirsty so Geoff had this great idea of going back to the camper to fetch us all a packed lunch. Off he set, climbing up the slippery sand dune, trudging all the way to the top and then disappearing out of sight. He took ages but eventually returned with our lunch and some drinks, looking totally exhausted; his comment, "It's a long long way." And he flopped down for much needed rest.*

*We stayed until mid afternoon and then we all made our way back. It was extremely hard going; Ben seemed ok but Geoff, Steph and I struggled. For every step forward we took, we would take two steps back, sliding on the sand underfoot; it was a real heart attack job. Slowly, slowly, we made it* to the top, lots of people were having the same problem as us and we passed one woman struggling along with her three children, carrying one, with the other two crying by her side; we did feel sorry for her. In the end we made it back to the camper, with Geoff having completed the journey twice that day, and needless to say, we all slept very well that night. We found out later that the place was called The Great Dune of Pyla and is the largest sand dune in Europe at 107 metres high.

We crossed into Spain, and travelled south via Pamplona, Zaragoza, and Teruel once again, where we stopped to show the twins the hanging hams. That evening, we made the Mediterranean coast and stopped for a few hours on the beach, before making the final push for home. To our relief, we found that Mom, Pat and Bryan and Tasha our dog had all been fine while we had been away. Bryan was most excited to tell us that a lot of telephone poles and reels of wire had been delivered; we couldn't believe it, it had taken, Telefónica, until 1997, the only telephone company in Spain, six whole years to supply us with a simple telephone line; and everyone thought BT was bad. Pat and Bryan returned to Newcastle a few days later and we promised to keep in touch regularly once we had the phone installed.

We slipped nicely into a routine with Ben and Steph. They would eat their breakfast, and then read to their granddad for an hour, and then the three of them would swim in our pool while I showered and dressed Mom. We'd then take the twins and the dog to the beach and while we were out we'd go to the local town to do our shopping before coming home for lunch. After lunch we would see that they both did their homework while they digested their meal and afterwards we would all swim together and the twins would play for the rest of the afternoon. A week later Jane and David arrived and we all had a great holiday together laying in the sunshine and cooling off in the pool; at the end of their holiday they all sported a lovely tan, looking healthy and relaxed. We returned them to Alicante airport; the time had passed so quickly. I consoled myself with the fact that I would soon be seeing them all again when we returned to England just before our trip to Indianapolis in September for the World Championships.

The next few days I spent washing, ironing and packing for the trip and Geoff did some jobs around the house and garden. Pat, and Bryan, arrived back again on the 4th September and we left two days later. My Mom *hadn't been too bad in herself but just lately she'd been waking up again during the night several times so I felt that, unfortunately, they wouldn't find this visit without its problems.*

*Steve, Ann, Natalie, and Sophie, had now been out in the States for three weeks already. They had been staying in Tallahassee, Florida for a training camp, then they were moving on to another training venue in Bainbridge, Georgia before going on to Indianapolis; Steve had left our tickets with Christine. We flew in to Gatwick from Spain stayed the night with Jane and David and then the following morning Christine took us both back to Gatwick for our flight to The States. We were flying with Delta airlines and the flight took us to Cincinnati where we would change flights for Indianapolis. With an hour and a half to wait for the flight we decided we had time for a quick coffee and toasted tea cake before boarding. We arrived into Indianapolis at 9pm, collected our baggage and made our way to the area where we could pick up the transportation to our hotel. Asking for a ride to The Holiday Inn, we quickly discovered that there were in fact three in this city, so we had to rummage through our bags to find our paperwork; we were booked to stay at The Holiday Inn Union Station.*

*We were driven there and, as the name had suggested, we found it was an old station that had been tastefully re-modelled so that each floor looked like a railway carriage. The Indianapolis Union Station was one of the first union stations in the world, opening in 1853 almost 150 years before; that's pretty ancient for America. We checked in, and after being shown to our rooms and tipping the porter, we took a good look around. We had been given a lovely spacious room with large en-suite bathroom, a huge king size double bed with a small table and chairs arranged in a sitting area. There was also a single bed for Natalie to sleep in and plenty of room for her to run about. Steve and family were not due into Indianapolis until the following day so, feeling quite tired from our journey, we had an early night.*

*In the morning we found a restaurant for breakfast with a very good self-service selection. We thought we would have a look round for Steve and Ann's hotel which was called the Omni Severin Hotel. We asked at our hotel reception and they told us that it was on the corner of the next block. It looked like a luxurious hotel so we went inside to take look round and bumped straight into David Tanner, the rowing team manager. He said that the team wasn't expected until 3pm that afternoon, so we wandered off to do some shopping and have some lunch.*

*At 2.30pm we returned to their hotel and sat in the reception lounge to wait for their arrival. Natalie spotted us first; we hadn't seen them all since July and there was great excitement while, three year old Natalie, enthusiastically told us all about their flight from Bainbridge. We thought how much Sophie had grown since the last time we had seen her; at 7 months old, she didn't talk much yet but Natalie said enough for them both put together. I was pleased to see that Ann and Steve both looked really well too. Sophie was staying with her Mom overnight as Ann was still breastfeeding and so it was arranged that Ann would bring Sophie to our hotel early in the morning as, between our two hotels, was the large square where the athletes would be catching their bus each day taking them to the course located at Eagle Creek about 12 miles out of town; Natalie would stay with us.*

*The next two days we spent amusing the children. There was much to see and do at the Union Station Mall. We found the most wonderful model train shop that had freight trains, old rocky mountain trains, modern trains and every other sort of locomotive and a working model track ran all the way around the shop. There was a Thomas the Tank Engine lay out too that the younger customers could play with and the shop sold engine driver's outfits, books, station master's whistles and just everything one could think of to do with railways. Natalie loved it and she would persuade us to take her there everyday. Another shop that she liked sold soft toys; there were cats, cows, lions, crocodiles and horses. A very large cookie shop that sold every type of cookie imaginable was located in the centre of the mall which, of course we regularly frequented; there was also an amazing Christmas decoration shop. All of this in a train station setting which was dotted with several statues of individuals who might have been seen in the railroad station in years gone by; with so many shops, to interest both young and old alike, it was a child's paradise.*

*The biggest fascination for the children was in our hotel. There was a real train and with several carriages which had been made into hotel rooms. They had been dedicated to film stars like Rudolph Valentino, Betty Davis,*

James Cagney and Joan Crawford and other old movie actors. On the platform there were statues of passengers waiting for the train; men, women, children, soldiers and sailors. Natalie loved this and had her photo taken with them more than once; there was always something to amuse her.

The opening ceremony was held a few days later in a nearby park, it wasn't quite an Olympic Opening Ceremony, but it was lovely with bands playing and things that were particular to the state of Indiana; Sophie slept through most of it. While we were there we found an official stall selling tickets to the rowing and we asked about transportation to Eagle Creek. They told us that there wouldn't be any laid on for spectators and that we would have to take a taxi. I got quite cross and told them that I had attended many world championships, all over the world and that some form of transport for spectators had always been made available free of charge; they said they would look into it and let Ann know. Later that day we received a message that we would be permitted to use the athlete's transport; we were really pleased as this would be very convenient even though it would mean an early start.

On the first day of rowing, Steve, and Matthew's, heat was scheduled for 9.30am so we needed to catch the bus by 8.15am. It was a bit of a dash but we made it on time. Ann travelled with us and, on our arrival, left both of the children with us when we reached the athlete's gate. We had arrived at Eagle Creek Park, one of the largest municipal parks in the United States. It encompassed an enormous 3,900 acres of land with a huge reservoir covering 1,400 acres. It had about ten miles of paths and served primarily as a nature reserve; I think this was the biggest rowing venue we had ever encountered.

Three large stands had been erected but there was no shade from the hot sunshine. It was already quite hot so Geoff kept Sophie in her pushchair underneath the stand and I sat with Natalie nearby so we could swap our charges from time to time as the heat of the day increased.

We met Andrea Dillon with her daughter and grandson. Terry, her husband, was coaching the women's pair. Jean and Ewan Pinsent were here too, having taken a flight to New York and then hiring a car had driven the rest of the way to Indianapolis. As we took our seats we caught a glimpse of Steve and Matthew's boat as they rowed down to the start. Soon the commentator was telling us the race was underway and by the 500m mark, Redgrave and Pinsent had taken the lead. A surge of excitement rose within me but I managed to keep a lid on it as I knew that there was still a long way to go. Natalie was asking, "Nan, are they winning?" and I told her that yes, at the moment, they were in the lead. At the halfway 1000m mark, we heard that they had maintained their lead and then suddenly we could see them and remaining seated we began to shout our usual encouragement. With just 250m to go we were all now standing up and yelling but there was really no need, the boys put in a final burst and finished comfortably. What a good win, they had put themselves safely through to the semi final, on Thursday. Jean Pinsent and I exchanged glances of relief; we could now relax and enjoy the rowing for the next few days. Natalie was very excited but by now she was very used to taking all this in her stride and we took her to buy a celebratory ice cream and then returned to the bus for our ride back to the hotel; a good days racing.

Martin Cross was in the Coxed Pair the following day so we'd probably see Moira Cross tomorrow; I wondered how she would be travelling here, via China knowing her. In the afternoon we took both of the children to the hotel pool for a swim and then afterwards, as usual, we went to their favourite place, the train shop, before having a meal then taking them to bed.

The following morning we followed the same routine, having an early breakfast and then catching the bus up to Eagle Creek. Today we met Moira, it was good to see her again and we had a good long chat. We watched the rowing together and then we met up with Steve and Ann for lunch. After taking both of the girls back to the hotel for a rest, we again paid a visit to the train shop and this time also found a shop selling puppets that kept them both amused for most of the afternoon.

On Wednesday we decided to give the rowing a miss and instead to take the girls to see 'The Children's Museum of Indianapolis'; we'd heard this was the largest children's museum in the world and was well worth a visit. Ann brought Sophie over to our hotel and we decided to take a bus to the museum. At the stop, a bus pulled up and as the doors opened, I asked the driver, a rather large and very friendly black woman, if this was the *right bus for the museum. She confirmed that it was, so I got on with the girls, leaving Geoff to try to collapse the pushchair; you needed a degree in engineering to get the thing up and down. Once we were all aboard the driver shut the doors and pulled back out into the traffic. She started a conversation with us, constantly looking over her shoulder for what seemed like several minutes at a time, the bus seemingly on autopilot, "Where y'all from?" she said turning almost completely towards us. Geoff, and I, looked at one another, concerned about the traffic so Geoff moved closer to her so that she could converse whilst looking in the right direction; at the oncoming traffic. He told her that we were from England and that we were here to support our son at The World Rowing Championships. She asked if we thought he'd win and we said that we hoped so. Another woman near me, told me that we needed the next stop, so I gathered the girls and all their things together and got ready to get off. The driver then drove the bus straight past the official stop and right into the museum driveway, especially for us. We got off, thanking her very much, and as the doors were closing she said, "Y'all have a nice day" and then drove off.*

*Geoff and I were still smiling as she pulled away and then we struggled again to get the pushchair back up and popped Sophie back in. We had a wonderful day in the museum and both the girls loved it. The museum was situated on 19 acres of land and the huge 400,000-square-foot facility housed eleven major galleries that explored the physical and natural sciences, history, world cultures and the arts. It was an incredible place 'to learn and to do' and whenever possible, exhibits were "hands-on" There were costumes available so that children could dress up as a crab or an octopus and then stand in a Perspex tank and look out at people passing. They were also taught to take brass rubbings and they were allowed to dig in sand for archaeological finds. After lunch we wandered around a dinosaur exhibition and learned how they had evolved; the entire place seemed to support kid's intellectual curiosity and love of learning and every exhibit was extremely well done.*

*At the end of the afternoon we headed back to the hotel. Natalie fell asleep on the bus exhausted by her exciting day out. We carried her for a while but on the way back to the hotel, refreshed, she woke up and asked to go to the train shop again; she seemed to have so much energy, we could hardly keep up. At the mall we listened to some karaoke and Natalie, loving to sing joined in. Finally we walked back to the hotel and all dropped into bed.*

*Thursday, was semi-final day and Steve, and Matthew were due to race at 9.16am which meant a very early start for us. We met Ann and Sophie at the bus stop and taking Sophie, left Ann to do her job. We managed to get a good seat in the stand but as Sophie was asleep in the pushchair, Geoff couldn't join us in the stands. We must have missed the boys at they rowed to the start because all of a sudden the starter was calling out the race order: Lane 1 – Italy, Lane 2 – Germany, Lane 3 – Australia, Lane 4 – Great Britain, Lane 5 – Poland, Lane 6 – Lithuania, and the race was underway. I cuddled into Natalie, and said a quiet prayer. Natalie, was already shouting, "Come on daddy" and at 500m into the race, Great Britain were leading followed by Germany, Australia, Italy, Poland and then Lithuania and this was the order to the finish; they were safely through to the final on Saturday. We had our lunch and I got some official souvenir t-shirts to take home and then we headed back to the hotel. After a rest, we took our usual train spotting trip before having an early tea and heading off to bed; I think that, added to the excitement of their race today, we were all still feeling a little exhausted from our exciting day out yesterday at the museum.*

*Friday was an official 'day off' for the rowing so we decided to take a visit to the zoo with Ann whilst Steve, and Matthew, had a quiet day doing some light training. We had breakfast and Ann joined us with Sophie. The hotel porter kindly said that, as he was on his way to the airport, he would drop us all off at the zoo. This was a great help and when we arrived we hired a little cart for Natalie, as we knew that today, there would most likely be too much walking for her to cope with. With Sophie, in her pushchair, and Geoff taking charge of Natalie, who thought that being pulled along in the cart was great fun, it was much easier to handle the two children. We did all the things one does at the zoo; we saw monkeys, lions, tigers, snakes and Ann and Natalie went for a ride on a camel. After lunch we watched as the sea lions were being given their lunch too. Other animal the kids really liked, were the polar bears; they had a very large pool with high rocks that they would dive off making a huge splash. There was a tunnel underneath their enclosure where we watched them swim underwater and they would dive down and come right up to the glass where the kids could see them up close. They had been named Frankie and Johnny, and we watched for ages as they showed off to the crowds. We saw a dolphin show that included a killer whale; it was great fun. The zoo was very clean and the animals all looked to be well taken care of. Natalie loved every minute but Sophie was a little young to appreciate it all although she was very good sitting in her pushchair just watching, and sometimes, taking a nap.*

*The porter had said that we could ring him when we were finished and he would come and collect us, so we gave him a call and returned to the hotel in style. The children had a swim and then we had our meal but of course Natalie didn't want to go to bed without paying our, now daily visit, to see the trains and the puppets; she never forget them. We all had an early night as the rowing would be starting early the following morning. We had seen Steve and Matthew earlier in the day and they seemed to be in good spirits with no outward signs of tension but I felt quite sure that there must have been a little there somewhere.*

*Saturday 17ᵗʰ September 1994 dawned and we were up with the lark and quickly off to breakfast. Natalie said, "After today Nan, will daddy play with me?" and I said that I was sure that he would but her words pulled at my heartstrings. She did love her daddy and was so very sweet most of the time, but, this very bright three year old, could also have her moments. Yesterday, she had been lying on the bed next to her sister Sophie when suddenly Sophie had let out a yell and was holding up her hand. Geoff checked Sophie's fingers and could see little teeth marks and said to Natalie, "Did you bite her?" Natalie replied without any hesitation saying, "She put her finger in my mouth so I bit it." There was no real damage but Natalie was told it was very naughty and if she ever did anything like that again we would bite her back. Poor little Sophie, she was very brave and didn't make much fuss.*

*After breakfast we got our things ready for the day ahead and caught the bus to Eagle Creek, this time for the big race. Everyone was wishing us luck and wanted to have a chat but really I would rather have been quiet and left to my own thoughts until the race started, however, knowing so many other spectators and when sitting in the stands amongst them, being solitary just isn't an option. Geoff spotted the boys boating up to the start. Natalie came over and sat on my lap and Sophie did her usual thing, she fell fast asleep. We saw Larry Tracey who had flown over to The States to support Steve and Matthew in their final race and also to watch Mike Spracklen's, USA Men's Eight; he was then going on to do some business in Canada.*

*There had been a lot of false starts to races during these championships and the Canadian Women's Single Scull, who was a dead cert for a medal, had been awarded two false starts and disqualified; nothing, after all the hard work she had put in, poor girl, we really felt sorry for her. This was making us a little concerned; we were hoping this wouldn't happen to our lads. Once again, their race was called to the start and then they were off but a few seconds later, the bell rang signalling another false start. We strained to hear whom it had been given to and, oh my god, we heard the words, Great Britain, I felt sick. I glanced at Jean Pinsent, and she too had gone quite white. I knew just how much energy it would deplete and my nerves immediately got worse, because I knew if they did it again; they would be out.*

*The next few minutes for me, were really tough. Natalie was asking me why they weren't coming so I had to try to explain calmly what had happened, when all the time my own feelings were in disarray. The boats were called to the start once again and then they were off, this time cleanly, thank God, but Steve and Matthew were now in last position. My sinking feeling lasted almost throughout the race, my heart pounding, as they gradually clawed back to lead. Natalie and I were on our feet shouting and they came in for a clean win proving they could come from behind as well as lead from the front. In the fast tail- wind conditions they had taken the gold in 6:18.65 with Germany's Peter Hoeltzenbein and Thorsten Streppelhoff taking Silver in 6:19.75 and Australia's Robert Walker and Richard Wearne taking the bronze in 6:20.25. Hugh Matheson again wrote a piece in The Independent newspaper saying 'Matthew Pinsent and Steven Redgrave took their fourth pairs title with a devastating last 500 metres when they passed the Germans, Peter Holtzenbein and Thorsten Strepplehoff, who had used the fast conditions to build a three-second lead. They hung dead level for a tantalizing 10 strokes before the sheer strength of the British carried them through'; it had been a really exciting race.*

*The feeling of great joy and total relief overwhelmed us all. Geoff had gone down from the stand to be with sleeping Sophie who was still in her pushchair so Natalie and I went down to talk to him and found him standing with Larry Tracey, looking as pleased as punch. Natalie and I went to the rostrum to see Steve and Matthew presented with their medal and as usual Steve came over and gave Natalie a hug and a kiss and then the boys got back into the boat to row off for their interviews and photos, saying they would see us later.*

*We watched the rest of the rowing and then met up with the boys and Ann for a light lunch and then we took the children back to the hotel by taking a lift with Matthew's, girlfriend who had brought her car. We had made arrangements to go out with them all that evening to celebrate but not before we had taken our trip once more to the train shop, in fact on this occasion Steve and Ann came along as well.*

*On Sunday we returned to Eagle Creek for the last day of rowing, only to find that Steve was unexpectedly to partner Martin Cross in the coxed pair due to the fact that Martin's original partner was ill and couldn't race. As Steve, and Martin, had rowed together in the past, notably in the Olympic Gold Medal Coxed Four in Los Angeles, he was allowed to take the sick man's place in the small final, the race to determine the 7th-12th place. I don't think Steve had rowed a coxed pair since 1989 and so they had a small outing to get used to the feel of the boat, then they went straight into the race and won in 6:55.84 coxed by Haydn Bass, therefore claiming 7th place. The American press made quite a big deal out of Steve, getting into a strange boat at the eleventh hour, with an old partner in the small final and with no medal hope; in fact he became quite a sporting hero. I think that Steve enjoyed the challenge and a chance to row again with Martin.*

*When the rowing was over, Steve, Ann and Matthew stayed on for the end of regatta party and had a great time celebrating with the other competitors and guess where we went, that's right, to the train shop with Natalie one last time. We were all going our separate ways the following day, Matthew was flying to Canada with his Canadian girlfriend, most of the other parents and crew were returning to England and Steve, Ann, Natalie, Sophie, Geoff and I were off to Atlanta to take a look at the venue lake for the 1996 Atlanta Olympics and to meet a few people there.*

*On Monday we all departed Indianapolis and took a flight to Atlanta. On our arrival, Steve hired a large car which was big enough for the whole family and we headed off to the city where we were booked in to The Holiday Inn Plaza. Steve had recently completed some promotional work for Holiday Inn Britain and our accommodation had been booked ahead* by their promotions team. It was a very luxurious hotel and Steve and Ann were taken to a suite which had two bedrooms and a sitting room and they found a huge bowl of fruit on the dining table to greet them. Geoff and I were on the floor below and also had a complimentary fruit bowl in our room. The hotel was attractively decorated with an ultra-modern appearance with a glass lift that rose in the centre of the hotel giving views over the lounge areas and large garden with terrace. In the garden was a large aviary with lots of birds which the children regularly asked to go and see. There were several restaurants too; their breakfast was our favourite.

On the Tuesday we all went to 'Six Flags Over Georgia', a 100-acre theme park, billed as having, awesome rides, great shows, and incredible attractions. We spent the whole day here and all had great fun. Wednesday we spent shopping for things to take home and Steve bought some golf shoes. The following day, Steve had to meet up with an Olympic official and his family to discuss the forthcoming Olympic rowing venue.

The Olympic lake was originally going to be at Stone Mountain but it would have meant moving a small island which the conservationalists didn't really agree with and so the venue had been changed to Lake Sidney Lanier south-west of Gainesville in Georgia. Lake Sidney Lanier with an area of 74 square miles was formed by the building of Buford Dam on the Chattahoochee River in Forsyth County, Georgia and, completed in 1958, was now used for flood control, hydroelectric power and recreation purposes; it would be a perfect venue for the 1996 Olympic water sports.

We swam most days in the lovely hotel pool and soaked in the warm jets of the Jacuzzi but soon it was Monday and time for us all to return to the UK. We left Atlanta on a night flight so the children would sleep most of the way and we arrived back at Gatwick and were met by the family.

We spent a couple of days back in Marlow, preparing for Sophie's Christening which was to be held in the crypt of St Paul's Cathedral on 1st October. Matthews's father, the Reverend Ewan Pinsent, had been asked to conduct the service and Sophie Jayne's Godparents would be Melanie Clift, Alison Hall and Eric Sims, one of Steve's rowing buddies from the early years. Coaches were laid on for the guests to travel from Marlow Bottom to London on this lovely autumn day and the service was really nice and *was made very personal with Ewan presiding at the font; eight month old Sophie had been as good as gold. Afterwards we returned by coach to The Leander Rowing Club in Henley by the river for a delicious champagne buffet to wet the baby's head in style.*

*Returning to Spain, we discovered that Pat, and Bryan, had experienced quite a trying time with Mom, having had more than a few disturbed nights to deal with; they were quite pleased to see us back and they returned to Newcastle a few days later. I had to adjust once again to my old routine of looking after Mom and Geoff returned to his odd jobs around the house and garden. Mom was very up and down nowadays but we coped and the time passed quickly. Christine and Edward were coming out for Christmas but could only make it for five days as they both had work to get back to. It was wonderful for us to have them stay even for such a short while and we spent a really lovely Christmas together. On Christmas Day we never thought we'd get to the end of all the presents she had brought from all the family. Later that morning we spoke to everyone, this time on our own telephone, and Pat and Bryan rang in the afternoon to speak to Mom. We enjoyed an enormous Christmas Dinner and that night we all went to bed feeling like stuffed turkeys ourselves.*

*On Boxing Day the four of us drove over to Pam and Peter's villa for lunch in the Jalon valley and Mom stayed at home with lots of food and sweets to eat; the lady next door kindly promising to pop in and out regularly to check on her. It was really nice to get out for a while and to have a break; Pam and Peter were always such good hosts. The next couple of days flew by too quickly and before Christine and Edward left for the airport I gave them almost half the Christmas turkey, some mince pies and some Christmas cake to take home which Christine duly packed in one of their suitcases. When she got home she rang us to say that the airline had lost one of their cases, the one with the food in. It had mistakenly been put on a flight to Paris and when it turned up a couple of days later they could only give the turkey to the cats.*

*On New Years Eve, we stayed at home and saw in the New Year, with our twelve grapes and a glass of champagne. We wished each other a Happy New Year and then went out onto the veranda to watch the fireworks and listen to the church bells. At one o'clock the phone rang and it was the whole family who were all still enjoying a New Years party at Jane and David's house. It was so lovely to speak to them all and I thought what lucky parents we were to have such caring children. Geoff and I then went to bed but I found it difficult to sleep as usual I was pondering what the following year might hold for us all.*

# Chapter Seventeen
## World Championships 1995 Tampere, Finland

### *Gold, Wet and Windy*

*January 1995 in Spain was much colder than usual. I didn't get to see 'The Three Kings' procession because Mom wasn't too good and I didn't feel that I could leave her. In every town and city in Spain there is a Procession of the Three Kings which is known as Cabalgata de los Reyes Magos which is usually held on the 5th of January to welcome the Reyes Magos (The Three Wise Men) who shower the crowds with sweets. According to Hispanic traditions gifts are exchanged on the Feast of Epiphany the 6th of January rather than on Christmas and these gifts are borne by the Reyes Magos who perform the duties of Santa Clause in the Latin world.*

*Christine had a knee operation during January to trim a torn cartilage. She worked as a beauty therapist and keep fit teacher and years of standing all day and teaching her exercise classes meant that her joints had begun to suffer from some wear and tear. She had been told to rest for ten days afterwards and I wondered if she really would. Steve left at the end of January for a warm weather training camp in Australia and I didn't get a chance to chat with him before he left.*

*On the 26ᵗʰ January I got up and made Mom a cup of tea and took it in to her. I was alarmed as I couldn't seem to wake her. She seemed to be breathing normally but I couldn't rouse her. Geoff went to get a doctor and he arrived back at 11am with a male nurse. He could speak a little English and after he had examined her said that she was a very sick lady and he would call in again tomorrow. I made her as comfortable as I could and then just sat with her, moistening her lips now and then. I rang Bryan and*

Pat who wanted to fly straight out but I told them that I felt we should just wait and see. I also rang the children and told them. I sat in a chair by her bedside all night and at about 10am the following morning she came round, asked for something to eat and drink and seemed perfectly ok. The nurse came about half an hour later and was really shocked to see her sitting up in bed. The next day she sat in her chair for a while in the afternoon and then had a good night's sleep but after that she didn't seem to be well again. Her voice got very weak; in fact, she would laugh with me because sometimes I couldn't understand what she was saying. She died very peacefully on the 5th February 1995, her long life over.

She'd had a very hard life as a girl, her own mother had died when she was just fifteen leaving her to bring up her six younger brothers and sisters. She married my father Harold Stevenson in 1924 and had a very happy life with him until he died of cancer aged 66. It was in her nature to be happy, loving and giving to Bryan and me, as well as her grandchildren and her great grandchildren who had called her "Big Nan". All of us would miss her very very much. I phoned the news to the family telling them that I had decided on a cremation here in Spain. I then planned to take her ashes back to England and to hold a service of remembrance so that all the family would be able to attend. Her ashes were to be scattered with my father's at Amersham Crematorium.

The phone didn't stop ringing; first Steve from Tokyo on his way back from Australia, my friend's Queenie, Joan and Sylvia, even Christine's ex-husband Philip rang, he too had been very fond of Mom. Christine and Bryan notified the people who needed to know and the memorial service was planned for the 18th February when all the family could gather at Jane's home.

Geoff didn't go back to England with me; he stayed in Spain to take care of Tasha our dog. Geoff had been really wonderful to my Mom, having housed her and provided for her for 30 years and I know she had very much appreciated that. I flew back to England with the ashes and spent a busy few days making the final arrangements. Bryan and Pat and their daughter Janet and her daughters Nicola and Kim came down from Newcastle on Friday, Bryan's eldest daughter Susan and her four boys came on Saturday. Susan lived in Hythe in Kent and could make it there and back in one *day. It was so nice that they could all attend the service. It was a very sad occasion but all her family celebrated her long and generous life.*

*My friend Sylvia and her husband Ken had come to the service too but we could see that she wasn't well and she said that she was awaiting the results of some tests. She came back to the house but didn't stop for long and I didn't get to see her before I returned to Spain as I had developed a nasty cold and didn't want to pass it on.*

*I flew back to Spain, still not feeling too good especially as my flight was delayed for six hours. Luckily, I was able to get a message to Geoff so he didn't have to hang about at Alicante Airport. Once I got home, the following day I threw myself into cleaning and decorating the house to keep myself occupied; I was really missing Ada; she had been such a prominent part of my life for so many years.*

*On the 20th March I received a phone call from my friend Sylvia that knocked me sideways. She had received the results from her tests and she had been diagnosed with terminal cancer. She said that she would fight it and didn't want anyone's sympathy and that she had done it to herself by smoking for so many years. She was so brave, we had been friends for 40 years and as Steve's godmother, she was so proud of his achievements. I tried to keep a bright side to the conversation but after coming off the phone I sat and wrote her a letter because I felt I could express myself better that way; I was devastated she was the youngest of my group of close friends.*

*I returned to the UK at Easter but by this time Sylvia had been taken into Windsor Hospice. I visited her as much as I could while I was there and on my last visit, Steve joined me. She was so pleased to see her Godson and we all had a good chat and we laughed a lot, she seemed so bright. We both knew it would be the last time we would see each other as I had to go back to Spain the following day. We said goodbye and as I walked away I couldn't look back and show her how upset I was. On the 24th April 1995 I had a phone call to say that she had died.*

*I tried all the airlines but I couldn't get a flight that would get me back to the UK in time for the funeral. I wrote to Ken and his two daughters, Judy and Sally, to say how sorry I was but I knew that, with the slow*

Spanish postal system, they wouldn't receive my letter in time. Chris, Jane and Steve went to Sylvia's funeral and it pleased me to know they would be there. We'd said our goodbyes when I was last in Marlow; Sylvia had been a good friend, she'd had a good sense of humour and could always make me laugh and I'm sure that's the way she would have liked to have been remembered.

Life goes on, as they say, and in the next few weeks we had lots of visitors that kept me busy. We made a decision to rent out our villa while we were away this summer so I arranged to hire a caravan on a campsite in France in which Pat and Bryan could stay while they looked after Tasha our dog; it would make a nice change for them. We met them in Calais and delivered them to the campsite and got the three of them settled in. We then drove back to England arriving at Jane's home in time for Sunday lunch. All the family were there to greet us, except Steve, who was away. Poor little Sophie had gone down with the mumps, and Steve, with Lucerne only a week away, had decided that it would be wise to move out of the family home and temporarily stay at a hotel in Henley, to avoid catching the infection. Geoff moved into Henley with the camper and the forecast for the weather over the next few days was good; Steve's campaign for The 1995 Henley Royal Regatta was to win a record seventh Silver Goblet title and as it was also to be Steve's Henley swan song, the boys intended to go out with a bang.

The lads had a bye until Thursday 29th June when Dan Topolski wrote in The Independent newspaper, 'The reigning Olympic and world champions will face huge enthusiasm but limited resistance from 16-year-old Robert Sanders and 17-year-old Richard McElroy, two eager schoolboys from Newcastle Royal Grammar School'. Steve and Mathew had ticked their first box that day when winning by 2 ¾ lengths in a time of 8:10. Dan wrote the following day of their win, saying 'They dealt kindly with the youngsters, dropping to a majestic nine strokes a minute by the end. Redgrave is seeking to surpass Guy Nickalls' six-win total in the Silver Goblets and Nickalls' Challenge Cup and there is no one in the world, let alone at Henley this week, who can stop him'. Friday saw Steve and Mathew beat Korb and Fugel by 1 ½ lengths in a time of 7.46 and go comfortably through to the next round on Saturday.

*The Saturday of Henley Regatta always drew the largest crowds and this year was no different. Gillard and Kettle of the Queen's Tower Boat Club. were their opponents today and both men were experienced rowers. Dave Gillard, was a Cambridge Blue and former winner of the Silver Goblets, and Martin Kettle was a Commonwealth Games medalist. This race was amazing, everybody in the crowd was expecting a show and they got one. Norman Fox wrote in The Independent newspaper 'The record came against the experienced Dave Gillard and Martin Kettle, but after only a quarter of a mile they knew the worst - Redgrave and Pinsent had already taken a one-length lead. They held on until the Barrier, but at Fawley they were three lengths beyond redemption. But the multi-champions decided that this was the time for something special, and increased their stroke from an already impressive 36 to a fierce 41 per minute to win by a margin that by tradition had to be called "easily" but in reality was nearer a horizon'. Their time was an astonishing 6min 56sec, taking 13 seconds off the previous best time which had been set by Steve and Simon Beresford in 1989. What a cheer went up as they crossed the line, it made this Henley crowd realise what our boys were capable of and Guy Nickalls' title, previously held between 1885 and 1907 passed to Steve. I remember Matthew saying, "It will take a long time to beat that one".*

*Later that afternoon the boys rowed again, this time joining with the Oxford Blues, Laird Reed and Jo Michels, to enter a Coxed Four in the Prince Philip Challenge Cup final as members of the Leander Club beating the Belfast Rowing Club by 1¾ lengths with records at the Barrier (1min 57sec) and Fawley (3min 18sec). What a superb day's racing.*

*The Sunday Final by contrast, was a bit of an anticlimax when they beat Everington and Partridge by five lengths in a time of 7 minutes 18 seconds; it had also started to rain. The whole family gathered after prize-giving for our traditional barbeque. David had brought the 'kit and caboodle' down in the late afternoon and set it all up for us. It was great fun, a huge celebration but I must say it was a little damp; that's British summers for you. I felt quite sad too that this was the last time that we would have one of these gatherings but we'd all take away some fabulous memories of wonderful times here over the years seeing Steve compete in some extraordinary races . I expected that this one would stay in his memory for some time though, along with such highlights as the race in 1983 against*

*Tim Crooks in the Diamond Sculls, when Tim stopped rowing and in the Double Sculls Challenge Cup with Adam Clift when they broke the record to the barrier, 1 minute 58 seconds, set in 1982 this record still stands.*

*July 3rd Monday and the following day, Tuesday, we spent cleaning the camper and making sure we had enough provisions for our trip to Lucerne. On Tuesday night we set off with Natalie and Sophie, mainly to give Ann a break as she hadn't been well either. We caught the ferry to Calais early on Wednesday morning, driving straight to the campsite to find Pat and Bryan and to collect Tasha, our dog. The weather for them had been a bit mixed really and they said that they had missed the guaranteed sunshine of Spain but they'd had a good rest, my brother Bryan reading his books and walking the dog and they had both enjoyed a visit from their daughter Susan who had come over from Hythe in England and taken them out and about. We saw them safely on the ferry back to Dover, where Susan would be meeting them; we were very grateful for their support in taking care of the dog. We drove straight through to Lucerne, went straight to our usual campsite and settled in. With their record-breaking glory of Henley now behind them, Steve and Matthew were turning their attention to international racing on the Rotsee Lake; this year Great Britain was fielding twenty crews.*

*Sunday would be Natalie's 4th birthday but we had already decided to have the celebrations on Saturday as her dad would be involved in his finals race on Sunday and wouldn't have time to join us. When she woke up Saturday morning, we gave her our cards and presents. After some breakfast we got the children ready and went to the Rotsee Lake rowing course where we met Steve. He had bought Natalie a cake with four candles, we all sang Happy Birthday as she blew them out and we each had a large slice to celebrate. Later on Steve and Matthew rowed and won their race getting through to the final the following day.*

*We awoke on Sunday to find that the Swiss weather had taken a turn for the worse, so Geoff went to watch the rowing while I stayed in the warm and dry camper and played with the girls. After lunch we got them dressed up in their wet weather gear and braved the storm to see Steve and Matthew's race. We met a few friends along the way but it was so wet and cold we didn't stand around chatting for long. We had been to Lucerne many times over the years and we had learned that the weather could never* be guaranteed, it could be one extreme or the other; galoshes or flip-flops. When Steve and Matthew's finals race started, Natalie and I shouted our heads off as usual but they didn't really need our encouragement as they had a very convincing win. They waved to us as they paddled back down the course to the boat sheds and we returned to the camper to dry off and to prepare for our journey home.

We called in at Le Touquet the elegant holiday resort and playground of rich Parisians in northern France and found the beach so that the children could have some fun playing in the sand and collecting sea shells; the French weather now much better than in Switzerland. I had made prior arrangements to meet Ann in Dover so she could collect the children; Geoff stayed with the camper and the dog as before. The three of us travelled over the channel on the hovercraft and Ann was there to meet us. We spent a short time together before I returned to Calais saying that I would see them all soon at the World Championships in Finland. We had a few weeks ahead of us to look around this unfamiliar part of Europe. When planning the trip we had considered travelling to Finland via Germany, Poland and Russia but on good advice from Jürgen, Steve's coach, we were now taking a route through Holland and Germany and taking a ferry to Helsinki across the Baltic Sea.

Leaving Calais we made our way into Holland where we stopped at Arnhem. We got settled into a campsite and used it as our base to look around. I had seen the 1977 film 'A Bridge Too Far' directed by Richard Attenborough about Allied forces in World War II trying to capture a number of important river bridges in Holland in order to secure a route for our troops to pursue the fleeing German army and I wanted to learn more about it. Operation Market Garden, as it was code-named, launched September 17–25, 1944, was the largest operation since D-day and involved putting thousands of troops 60 miles behind enemy lines in order to capture the bridges. Geoff and I went first to the Airborne Museum at Hartenstein and here we found the story depicted using a large model of the area with spoken commentary and slides illustrating the course of the battle with a large collection on display of both Allied and German weapons. This museum was founded in 1949 as a tribute to the many British and Polish Airborne troops who lost their lives. At Arnhem the British 1st Airborne Division encountered far stronger resistance than anticipated. In the ensuing battle only a small force *managed to hold one end of the Arnhem road bridge and after the ground forces failed to relieve them they were overrun on the 21st. The rest of the division, trapped in a small pocket west of the bridge, had to be evacuated on the 25th. During the battle Dutch railway workers went on strike in order to aid the Allied assault. In retribution Germany forbade food transportation and in the following months thousands of Dutch citizens starved to death, a time known as the Hongerwinter (Hunger winter). It was really interesting and also deeply moving to learn of the real human tragedy that had taken place here.*

*We moved along the northern German coast to Hamburg, then on to Lubeck, the largest German port on the Baltic Sea, finally arriving in Travemünde Germany's northernmost city and the closest port to Finland in mainland Western Europe; here our Finjet Ferry would take us to Helsinki. We spent five days exploring the lovely seaside town of Travemunde with its seaside museum, light house, the beautiful golden sand beaches and the historic 'Altstadt' old town district. Here we saw, for the first time, a large wind farm with its group of wind turbines being used for the production of electric power. After our short stay, we boarded our Finnjet Ferry and were very impressed to find that it was the fastest, longest and largest car ferry in the world and powered by gas turbines it had a top speed of over 33 knots. The ferry would takes us across the Baltic Sea, known as the Viking Sea, the world's second-largest body of brackish water, a unique mixture of sea water and fresh water and our journey would take 24 hours. As we were traveling with the dog, we had been advised to take a cabin which turned out to be very comfortable indeed and we walked Tasha on deck where there were large gravel pits provided for dogs to use. As we sailed into Helsinki, dozens of islands escorted us on our way into Vuosaari harbour.*

*On arrival, taking a quick drive around, we were quite impressed with the spacious city of Helsinki with its wide cobbled streets and lots of parks and squares before driving on to Tampere and the World Championships venue. Tampere, a city in southwestern Finland, is a two hour drive from Helsinki and has been dubbed the "Manchester of Finland" for its industrial past as the former center of Finnish industry, giving rise to its Finnish nickname "Manse". It was known for its textile and metal industries although nowadays, telecommunication and technology has taken over. Tampere is located between two lakes, Näsijärvi and Pyhäjärvi and since the two lakes*

223

*differ in level by about 18 metres, the rapids linking them, Tammerkoski, have been an important power source throughout history, most recently for generating electricity.*

*It had been pre-arranged that we would collect the two girls in a few days time from Steve and Ann's hotel, once they had arrived with the team but first, we had a few days to find a campsite, settle in and get the lie of the land. Steve and Mathew had just returned from three weeks of exhaustive training at their camp in Varese, northern Italy and Steve had told us on the telephone that although the training had been hard, they were now feeling confident of success. We found a campsite on Lake Kaukajärvi close to the rowing course and spent the next few days getting our bearings before we picked up the girls from the hotel. The Finnish summer weather had been good and, once we had collected our granddaughters, we had no problem keeping them amused as they happily played together on the sand at the lake's edge.*

*The opening ceremony of the 1995 World Rowing Championships was held at the Kaukajärvi Rowing and Canoeing Centre on Friday 25th August and was very different to any we had seen before. Due to such an abundance of water and with over 188 thousand lakes in Finland, for centuries, the local people had travelled to church using traditional Finnish 12-meter wooden boats as their transport. These craft were called Churchboats, Sulkava or Viking boats and were modelled on the large boats of Scandinavian Vikings. Since the Reformation in the seventeenth century, the church had demanded the maintenance of these boats, which were used almost everywhere in Finland to travel to holy mass on Sundays. It was replicas of these traditional boats that were used at the opening ceremony to carry the flags of the competing nations and it was quite a spectacle. There was also a demonstration of a traditional Finnish sport, and a mock battle, in which the two competitors each stood on a huge floating log and used a long wooden pole to maintain their balance and to combat their opponent; the winner knocking his opponent into the water. One of the two competitors today was Pertti Karppinen the Olympic and World Champion Finnish single sculler.*

*Steve and Matthew's heat was on Monday morning the 21st August and, easily winning, even in the tricky headwind conditions, they went straight through to the semi-finals on Thursday. Hugh Matheson wrote the following day in the Independent newspaper 'Steven Redgrave and Matthew Pinsent opened the World Championships here by easily winning the first heat of their coxless pairs yesterday. Though the winning margin over the Dutch pair, Vos and Simon, was only one and a half seconds, the Britons had cut their pace to a cruise after 500 metres and still finished almost a minute ahead of new entrant, Kazakhstan'.*

*British rowing had formed a supporters club this year and, to us, there seemed to be a lot of new faces. The competitors were all staying in the same hotel which meant that their parents could all easily get to meet one another too. Initially, we seemed only to know Jean and Ewan Pinsent, Matthew's mum and dad, and Heather and Brian Foster, Tim's parents, but within a very short time we got to know all the other supporting parents too.*

*The campsite had plenty of room for the children to run about and, with us being camped beside the lake, it made it really interesting for the girls watching and feeding the many ducks and wild geese there. We'd had some rain but a break in the weather had given me a chance to get some washing done and with no washing machine or tumble dryer available for use, everything had to be washed by hand and hung out to dry. Natalie helped me to do the washing and, while keeping an eye on Sophie, Geoff had rigged up a small clothes line. Soon with all the washing done and hung out to dry, we settled down with a cup of tea. Sophie, the energetic toddler wearing her wellies, had other ideas and thought it would be great fun jumping in the muddy puddles next to the washing line and in her excitement managed to completely cover all the newly washed clothes with mud. This meant that most of the clothes needed to be washed again but thankfully we managed to get it all dry before the rain came down again.*

*Thursday was semi-final day for the boys and we set off to the rowing lake and took our seats in the stand to wait for the racing to start. Once their race was underway, Natalie and I went to the water's edge and as usual shouted our encouragement. The boys won a good race and Jean Pinsent and I exchanged glances and breathed a sigh of relief that they were through to the final on Saturday; we watched the rest of the day's racing in a much more relaxed state and finally returned to the camper. Once again, the following day Hugh Matheson wrote in The Independent, headlining, Cool*

*Redgrave and Pinsent in control. 'Steven Redgrave and Matthew Pinsent led their semi-final from the first stroke in the World Championships here, and allowed the field to sort itself out in their wake. "Everyone else expects us to win and we expect to win. But we still have to do it," Pinsent said'.*

*The following day we went into Tampere to look around the shops and, amongst other interesting stores, we found the most beautiful Christmas shop that I have ever seen; Natalie and Sophie loved it too. It had various sized models of Santa Claus, fairies, elves, reindeer, gnomes, rabbits, trees and tinsel, and every kind of bauble, candle and fairy-light imaginable. It was a wonderland for the girls and we made several visits there during our stay in Finland. I would usually take back official rowing merchandise T-shirts for the family at home but this year I took Christmas decorations instead from this gorgeous store dedicated to all things 'Christmas'. Natalie was asked later what the best thing about her trip to Finland was and she replied, 'The Christmas shop'; it seemed a shame that she wouldn't remember it much when she grew up as she was still just four years old.*

*Saturday arrived with all the tension of a usual finals day and to accompany it, the rain was bucketing down. Sophie was cosy and dry, covered up as she was in her pushchair and Natalie, Geoff and I had on our waterproofs and wellies. Lots of the other parents had brought black plastic dustbin liners to wear over their coats which helped a little but the rain still seeped its way through eventually, leaving everyone bedraggled.*

*The line up for their race was; lane 1 – Belgium, lane 2 – Australia, lane 3 – Great Britain, lane 4 – Italy, lane 5 – France and lane 6 – Croatia, and by the 500m mark they seemed to have the race under control. Steve and Matthew came through this dreadful weather to take their fifth World gold together in 6:28.11 with Australia's Robert Walker and Richard Wearne taking silver in 6:29.87 and France's pair Michel Andrieux and Jean-Christophe Rolland taking Bronze position in 6:30.63. The boys rowed in to receive their medals and after the ceremony Steve came across to speak to Natalie and Sophie saying that he would see us all back at the hotel later on. Ann joined us back at the hotel too and we waited for Steve to return. I'd had a very uncomfortable feeling just lately about him, he had taken his Grandmother's death quite badly earlier in the year and his health problems seemed to be constantly worrying him but I also had the feeling that there* was perhaps some tension between him and Ann. Steve did eventually turn up and we celebrated the boys win with Matthew and his parents; we had champagne out of paper cups while we tried to dry off our clothes. Later that day, I managed to have a quiet word with Steve and he assured me that he and Ann had sorted out their differences and that everything was now ok. Ann was a good wife and mother and she was trying to keep her career going too and she really didn't need this added hassle but I guess that's marriage for you; it's certainly never all smooth sailing.

The following day was the last day of rowing and today the parking at the Kaukajärvi Rowing Centre was really bad with nearly every vehicle getting stuck in the thick mud. That night we decided to stay on the hotel car park so we wouldn't get stuck in the mud too in the morning, as we had to make an early start getting the girls ready for their parents to collect as they were all flying back to the UK; they collected the girls from us at 5.30am and after saying our goodbyes they left for the airport.

After breakfast we set off for Helsinki and started our long journey home to Spain; it had been well worth the several thousand mile round trip to see our son take another World Championship Gold Medal. With the weather improving, we had a very pleasant journey to Helsinki and by the time we had arrived in the city it was really feeling quite hot. Helsinki has a temperate continental climate and owing to the Gulf stream, temperatures in winter are much higher than its northern location might suggest; rarely dropping below  −5 °C for more than a couple of weeks. Although due to its latitude, during the depths of winter, the days lasts less than six hours, in summer, the city enjoys long days, almost nineteen hours at the summer solstice and temperatures can average around 20°C.

We took a stroll along the quayside and had an interesting time browsing all the stalls which were full of all manner of goods, from exotic fruit to woolly hats and puppets. We spent several hours looking around and came across another couple who were from New Zealand and were also travelling in a camper and they invited us to join them for a cup of coffee. They were a very pleasant couple and we enjoyed chatting. They told us that they were from the North Island and owned a chain of motels and that he'd recently had a heart attack so they had decided to come away for a long relaxing trip travelling through Europe.

227

While we were waiting to board our ferry, we watched part of the German Navy fleet come into port; they must have been on a goodwill trip. There were two battleships, a cruiser and five U-boats and there was what seemed like an official welcoming ceremony. We had never seen a U-boat close up before but had heard a lot about them during the war and we were both surprised to see how small they actually were.

Later that day we boarded the ferry to Travemunde and we were told that due to the tides our journey back would take us a little longer this time. We sat up on deck and watched the scenery as the boat left Helsinki harbour and then we returned to our cabin and slept until morning. I'm not a very good sailor at the best of times and the weather had taken a turn for the worst so when we awoke, I stayed in our cabin while Geoff walked the dog.

When we arrived in Travemunde, before continuing our journey, we had to return a gas bottle and while we were in this part of the town, we took a stroll around the shops. We found a very quaint old antique shop and discovered some 1952 Olympic ceramic plates and an old Christmas plate dated Christmas 1849. There were also some lovely bakeries and confectionery shops but we resisted temptation.

We drove on again to Hamburg and thought that we would try to find Scott Poppy and his parents who now lived here. Scott had been in the younger Great Marlow School crew and had moved back to Hamburg some years ago but we had no current address for him. We found a telephone box and leafed through the local telephone book. We found two Poppy's but the first one we rang turned out not to be him and there was no reply from the second one so we decided to give up our search and move on.

We took a pleasant route straight through Germany, directly from North to South, travelling through some towns which we hadn't visited before. When we entered the city of Ulm, the birthplace of Albert Einstein, with its cobbled streets, the camper began to make a dreadful noise. We limped on a few more miles into Bad Waldsee, where our usual Hymer camper factory and Mercedes repair shop looked it over telling us that the engine mounts had gone and also something in the drive shaft. They said they could repair it but that they would have to keep it at the garage overnight and do the work early the next day. The following morning they started work and five hours and £800 later we drove on again heading for the coast feeling totally devastated with the bill. This was going to be our most expensive rowing trip to date, but of course there was the Atlanta Olympics on the horizon next year and perhaps that might top the lot.

We took the car ferry from Meerburg to Constance situated on the German side of the Swiss-German border and on the southern shore of Lake Constance. This saved a good deal of travelling time as the lake is so large to circumnavigate; we then travelled on through Switzerland, France and home again to Spain, arriving, feeling in need of a good rest.

We just had a quiet time for the next few months leading up to Christmas when our old friends Queenie and Arthur Johns would be flying over to Spain to join us for the holidays. Queenie arrived with a bad cold but she was thankfully better in time for Christmas day. We all phoned our respective families on Christmas morning and our local friends Pam and Peter Plumridge joined us for Christmas lunch; we all had a very enjoyable day eating too much and making each other laugh.

On New Years Eve we stayed at home on our own together to reflect on the past year. It had not been one of our best with so many sad events and although Mom had been a lot of work for me, I really did miss her very much.

# Chapter Eighteen
## The 1996 Atlanta Olympic Games

### *Just Shoot Me*

*On February 28ᵗʰ Steve and Matthew came out to Spain to do some winter training in Seville, and as we had never been to this Spanish city before, we decided to travel down and meet them there; it was about 750km. On our way, we stopped off at Benidorm to see Ken Ray, my late friend Sylvia's husband. He was taking his first holiday since her death the previous spring and we called in to see him. He seemed very lonely and was missing her desperately. He said that he hadn't wanted to return to any of the places they had visited together and therefore he hadn't wanted to stay with us, although, he said, he knew we would have welcomed him; his memories of happy holidays shared with her were still hard for him to deal with. We stayed a few hours with him and had lunch together before saying farewell and getting back on the road to Seville.*

*On our arrival we met Steve and Matthew and we were happy to see that they were both looking well. We watched them rowing and afterwards they came and had a meal with us. The following day a TV crew did a piece on them and they filmed Steve and Matt at the camper with us and it went out a few days later.*

*We had heard that Seville was a beautiful city so we decided to do some sightseeing while we were here. We had parked the camper and had walked around for perhaps twenty minutes or so before returning. As we approached the camper we could see a strange man looking into the side window and we could hear that inside our dog Tasha was barking like mad. Someone in a car on the opposite side of the road sounded their horn and the man started to run. Geoff immediately gave chase but lost him in a nearby building*

230

site. *Looking through the camper we found that the thieves had taken a bag that contained our passports, our bankbooks and our video camera. We had stowed the bag under the seat by the front door, thinking that it would be safe there out of sight, especially since the dog was left to roam free in the camper. One of the thieves must have distracted the dog at the window at the back of the camper while the other had broken into the driver's door and snatched the bag before quickly closing the door again. We reported it to the police and had to fill in forms and also cancel our chequebooks. There were no branches of our banks in the area so there was little chance of them drawing any money but the lost passports could present a problem. We did have copies of our passports at home as, in Spain, one is asked to copy all official papers. We also checked our bikes on the back of the camper and it appeared that they had tried to take those as well but that the padlock had stopped them. It was very unsettling being robbed but after all the miles we had travelled, in both Europe and the rest of the world, I guess that it was surprising that it hadn't happened to us before now.*

*We watched as Steve and Matthew won their regatta event in Seville and after saying goodbye we decided that on our way back to Javea we would make a stop off at the city of Grenada in southern Spain. Here we visited The Alhambra, a beautiful 14th century palace and fortress complex of the Moorish rulers of Granada which exhibits the country's most famous Islamic architecture. It was the place where artists and intellectuals took refuge as Christian Spain won victories over the Arab and North African Muslim governors. The Alhambra mixes natural elements with man-made ones, and is a testament to the skill of the Muslim craftsmen of that time. The name Alhambra meaning "red fortress" reflects the color of the red clay of the surroundings from which the fort is made. The buildings were beautiful and very well preserved and the gardens were filled with the sound of running water from several fountains and cascades; most refreshing on a hot Spanish afternoon. We could have spent much longer there wandering about admiring the architecture but all the time, in the back of our minds, we kept wondering if the camper and dog were safe.*

*The backdrop to all this was a magnificent view of the Sierra Nevada's snow covered mountains and the clear blue sky. We decided we would drive up into the mountains and take a look and it wasn't long before we found the road to the summit. It seemed really strange that it was so warm in* the town below but up here people were skiing. We stopped at 1700m at a vantage point to gaze out over the town and the surrounding mountains and then we drove on until we reached the snow. The summit was about 3400m high and we ran into cloud and mist; the snow here was about 6ft deep on either side of the road and it was very cold. We descended again to where it was warmer but felt very glad we had taken the time to reach the top, especially as the views had been so breathtaking. We spent that night in our camper on a lovely warm beach by the blue Mediterranean with the gentle sea lapping on the shore.

The next day we travelled on up the Eastern side of Spain hugging the coast. Here the beaches are really good but the scenery is spoilt by the many torn and tattered polythene tunnels covering the surrounding hills that offer shelter to growing crops of tomatoes and the like. We moved on to La Manga that night and camped by the Mar Menor which lies right at the most southern part of the Costa Blanca. The Mar Menor or 'little sea' is a salt water lake and is almost totally separated from the Mediterranean Sea by the "La Manga del Mar Menor" which means "the sleeve of the little sea". This very narrow strip of land, around 13 miles long, makes up the lagoon of Mar Menor which at it's deepest spot is only 8 meters deep and so maintains a lovely water temperature of around 17 °C. On returning to Javea we worked out that we had made a very interesting 1422km round trip which had only been slightly marred by the break in.

Our next trip away from home was in early April to Lake Banyoles where we had arranged to take the children off Ann's hands as she would be working as the rowing team doctor while Steve and Matthew trained with the rest of the British squad. We collected the children and took them to spend a week at Estartit which was once a sleepy fishing village but now a family beach resort, 40 miles south of the French border. It was late spring and surprisingly, for Spain, was not yet all that warm but the children loved it playing on one of the longest sandy beaches on the Costa Brava; we enjoyed seeing our granddaughters having so much fun. At the end of the week we drove inland to Banyoles and returned the children to their parents and then headed back to Javea.

The next thing on the agenda was to collect our replacement passports which all took time; in fact we had to make the journey back and forth to

*Alicante twice. We were fast running out of time, as we were also to meet Pat and Bryan in Calais on the 6th July. We rented out our villa again for the entire summer, in late May and then spent all of June roaming France in the camper. We didn't go to Lucerne this year because Steve and Matthew weren't rowing due to an injury and they wanted to 'keep their powder dry' for the Olympic Regatta in Atlanta.*

*We met Pat and Bryan on the 6th July and settled them into our camper on a campsite, with Tasha our dog, as they would be taking care of her for the duration of our trip to the States. All four of us spent that night together in the camper; it was a little cosy but we managed. We got up early, had some breakfast together, said our goodbyes and then got a taxi to the ferry for our journey back to Dover where Christine and Edward were to meet us and drive us back to Marlow. The following few days were busily spent getting ready for our trip to Atlanta. Steve, Ann and the girls had already left England on the 4th July for their training camp in Buffalo, on the eastern shores of Lake Erie and at the head of the Niagara River, close to Niagara Falls and the Canadian border where they would be staying at Brook University.*

Geoff gently nudged me back to awareness and told me that our aircraft was nearing Charlotte airport and that we would be landing in about 30 minutes. Light refreshments were now being served by the cabin crew; it really hadn't seemed like eight hours since we had said goodbye to Christine, Jane, and the twins at Gatwick. I went to freshen up, and then returned to my seat for coffee and muffins; there would be no time for dreams now.

The pilot made an announcement asking the passengers to fasten their seat belts for our approach to Charlotte airport, North Carolina and just half an hour later we were back on terra firma, collecting our suitcases and making our way to the hire car desk to collect our car. The young woman who took our details, asked for our address and we gave Jane's home address which we had used when making the booking, she said 'oh where is that, New York State?', Geoff and I smiled at each other and said no, it was in the United Kingdom. We packed our cases into the boot and then bought some maps to help us find our way to Atlanta, in the adjoining state of Georgia. It was over a two hundred mile drive away from where our flight had landed at Charlotte airport in North Carolina. It had been pre-arranged with Steve and Ann that we would collect the children from them in two days time when they flew in to Atlanta with the rest of the squad. The weather was very pleasant and we took our time enjoying the journey, stopping now and then for snacks and coffee. Around 5pm we saw a suitable motel and decided that it was time to stop for the night. We booked in, had a meal and then went straight to bed as we were both beginning to feel the effects of jet lag after our long journey.

The following morning we awoke feeling quite refreshed, enjoyed our breakfast and then set off for Atlanta to collect the children. Their flight was due in around 3.30pm on an internal flight from Buffalo where they had been staying at their training camp. The accommodation that we would share with the children, this time, was going to be quite different, as we had arranged a 'Home-Stay', with a local American family. Our hosts were to be Mr and Mrs Fuller. Mr Fuller was the youngest judge in the county and he and his wife had two children, both girls, aged about 10 and 13 years old. They lived in Gainesville, which was a city right on the shore of Lake Lanier, which had been named after Georgia author and musician Sidney Lanier and was where the Olympic rowing was to be held.

Their flight arrived on time and we stood at the gate waiting to meet them. The children both ran out to greet us; it was lovely to see them all again. Geoff, Steve and Mathew gathered all of their cases together and we all headed for the lift. Once inside the lift, a woman with two small boys asked us if we knew Steve Redgrave who was with the British Team. Steve stepped forward and introduced himself. She said that her name was Anita Bennet and that she would be looking after his parents and his children for the next ten days as the Fuller family were away on holiday and that she had gladly agreed to be a substitute host until their return. Anita Bennet took care of us and the children from then on. Steve, Ann and the rest of the team went to the Olympic village, where no children would be allowed.

Anita turned out to be a really nice person, and her home, in which we would be staying, was in Gainesville right beside the lake. Her husband, a dentist, had died about a year before and she had thought that she would enjoy keeping busy during the Olympics as a volunteer helper. She had two grown up children, a girl with two children and a Spanish American husband and Brett, her son, married but with no family as yet. Brett's passion was a large boat that he had moored at his mother's house on Lake Lanier. Anita's lovely house was on two floors and it had gardens which ran down to the lake shore and private boat house.

Gainesville is a city in Hall County in Georgia and because of its large number of poultry processing plants, is often referred to as the 'chicken capital' of the world. Nestled in the foothills of the Blue Ridge Mountains, parts of the city lie along the shore of one of the nation's most popular inland water reservoirs, Lake Lanier. This enormous lake which encompasses 38,000 acres of water, and has 692 miles of shoreline was created in 1958 when The U.S. Army Corps of Engineers dammed the Chattahoochee River near Buford, Georgia and flooded an Appalachian mountain valley. Although created primarily for hydro-electricity and flood-control, it also served as a reservoir providing water to the city of Atlanta and had in turn become a very popular recreational attraction for all of North Georgia. We learnt that Gainesville also sat on the very fringe of Tornado Alley, a region of the United States where severe weather is common. Supercell thunderstorms can sweep through any time between March and November, but we were told, to our relief, that these were mostly concentrated in the spring. Tornado Watches are a frequent issue in the spring and summer as Gainesville was the site of the fifth deadliest tornado in U.S. history in 1936, when the city was decimated and 203 people were killed. Fingers-crossed, we hoped we wouldn't have to deal with that as well as the anxiety of Steve going for his fourth Olympic medal. The area close to Anita's house was well served too with nearby shops and restaurants, a library, the town hall and several churches. Each day we would take a special bus to the lake that had been laid on for spectators; things seemed to be really well organised.

The first event that we attended was to line the streets with all the local residents to watch the Olympic torch as it was carried through the town; Anita's daughter was in the torch relay. In attendance was the

Olympic mascot for Atlanta which was a large mouse like creature, the design for which had been computer generated, called "Izzy"; it was great fun to see and we all enjoyed it. We were grandly entertained by Anita's family and we all took trips out and enjoyed picnics on the lake in Brett's boat. We were also regularly invited to Anita's daughter's home so that Natalie and Sophie could swim in her pool, and play with all her children's old toys, which they absolutely loved.

One day, we took the children on a trip to visit Babyland General Hospital in Cleveland, Georgia the "birthplace" of Cabbage Patch Kids. This special doll brand was created by Debbie Morehead and Xavier Roberts in 1978 and Roberts had converted an old clinic into a retail unit and mini theme park dedicated to providing a birthing, nursery, and adoption center for his Cabbage Patch Kids. These dolls had been all the rage in the UK during the 80's and I remember one Christmas when stores everywhere had sold out and the dolls couldn't be bought for neither love nor money. Cabbage Patch Kids were funny looking dolls with large, round vinyl heads and soft fabric bodies. The large shop there was full of toys, mostly cabbage patch dolls, of all shapes and sizes. There was also a very large display of fabric cabbages, arranged in tiers, attended by two women dressed as nurses who would announce, every now and then, the birth of another cabbage patch doll as they plucked it from underneath one of the cabbages. They then proceeded to give the new doll a name and a date of birth; the children absolutely loved it and played with the dolls for a long time. Geoff and I thought it was a bit 'over the top' but it seemed to be a good sales gimmick, and they were selling plenty of premium merchandise.

On another day, we were taken to the Baptist Church that Anita regularly attended; all the visitors staying at" Home stays" had been invited. The service started with a Gospel choir singing a very up-beat number; it was really very good and then the minister welcomed everyone. He asked each visiting family to say who they were, where they hailed from, and who they were here to support. As we were sat in the front row, I was asked to start this off, I said, "We are Sheila and Geoff Redgrave and this is Natalie and Sophie our granddaughters. We are here to support our son Steven Redgrave, their father, who is rowing in the Great Britain, Coxless Pair". One by one the other families of athletes, swimmers, cyclists, and other rowers from all over the world made their announcement. When it came to the turn of an Australian man at the back, he stood up and said, "I think the Redgrave's are being a little bit modest about their son, Steve, he is perhaps the best rowing athlete in the world," Geoff and I both looked at one another as tears welled up in our eyes, Natalie cuddled into us and every one clapped; it was a most emotional experience for both of us. There was more Gospel singing and prayers and afterwards tea and cakes were served to us all while we mingled and chatted to the rest of the congregation.

On Friday 19th July, we watched, on a large screen TV at Anita's home, the Opening Ceremony of the 26th Olympiad which was taking place at Centennial Olympic Stadium, the 85,000-seat main stadium; it was packed to capacity. The event was officially opened by President Bill Clinton and the following spectacular displays honoured southern US culture and the one-hundredth anniversary of the modern Olympic movement. The official theme, "Summon the Heroes", had once again been written by John Williams, making it the third Olympiad for which he had composed. The song "The Power of the Dream", was emotionally performed by Céline Dion accompanied by the Atlanta Symphony Orchestra and Centennial Choir and Gladys Knight sang "Georgia on My Mind", Georgia's official state song.

Steve had again been selected to carry the British flag, and he held the Union Jack at arms length as he proudly entered the arena, leading the United Kingdom contingent. Both of the girls had been allowed to stay up to see their Dad on TV and both Geoff and I felt very close to the rest of the family who we knew would also be watching too, at home in the UK. A record 197 nations were to take part at these games, twenty-four countries were making their Olympic debut, giving a combined total of over 10,000 athletes.

Once the athletes had entered, the following scene was dedicated to Atlanta's favourite son: the late Dr. Martin Luther King, Jr. famous for his "I Have A Dream" speech in 1968. This was followed by the entrance of former celebrated Olympians, Dawn Fraser the Australian swimmer, Bob Beamon the American long jumper, Mark Spitz the American swimmer, Nadia Comaneci the Romanian gymnast, Teofilo

Stevenson the Cuban boxer, Carl Lewis the American track athlete, Greg Louganis the American diver, Vitaly Scherbo the gymnast from the former Soviet Union and lastly Leon Štukelj, a sprightly 97 year old and the oldest living Olympic gold medallist gymnast from Slovenia.

Then local boy, Evander Holyfield, who was an Olympic boxer in 1984, carried the Olympic flame into the area and we were then very moved to see Muhammad Ali, the world's best-known sports figure and former World Champion and Olympic boxer, now sadly stricken by Parkinson's disease, igniting the Olympic cauldron; he later received a replacement gold medal for his boxing victory in the 1960 Rome Olympics, due to the original one having been lost. The Opening Ceremony had taken over five hours from start to finish; the whole event had been very moving to watch and we felt extremely proud parents to think that our son had been a part of it.

The following day, Saturday 20th July, the rowing started. We took the official bus to the rowing centre at the lake and here we met lots of people we knew and chatted to them while waiting in anticipation for the boy's heat. Eventually they lined up and in a few seconds they were off. The winning crew would go straight through to the semi final but the rest of the crews would have to race again in the repechage. Natalie clung to me and Sophie to Geoff, who had the binoculars, but he really couldn't tell at this distance, which crew was out in front. Finally he told me he could see them clearly and that they were leading the bunch; they made it look so easy but we knew that it wasn't. A few minutes later they crossed the line first and the cheers went up; we all hugged and felt immense relief. Hugh Matheson for The Independent, headlined 'Redgrave and Pinsent on Song' and wrote, "As usual Matthew Pinsent took the British pair off at a high pace to spread the opposition and quell any irreverent dreams they might have of victory. They reached the 500 metres and 1000m marks a second faster than the leaders of the other heats and, only when the message was clear, did they ease off and drop the rate well below 30 strokes to the minute and press the cruise button". After Steve's race, Ann had managed to make her way through the crowds to see the children and we were able to relax and continue watching the other rowing events. Later we wandered around the stalls looking at the T-shirts and other rowing souvenirs on our way back to catch the bus back to Gainesville.

We had not seen Steve and Mathew to speak to, as immediately after their race they'd had to return to the athlete's village; the security here was very tight. We returned to Anita's home for the last time, as today, we were to move to the Fuller's home as they had returned from their holiday. As we packed our suitcases we felt just how privileged we had been to have shared a home with such a lovely lady; we were really going to miss Anita she had been a wonderful host. We consoled ourselves a little knowing that we would probably see her each day at the rowing lake, as she had now started her job as a volunteer/helper at the rowing course.

We once again, felt really fortunate; the Fuller's were a lovely family too. Our two girls played with their two girls beautifully. Their children had lots of toys and in fact the basement of the house had been turned into a dedicated playroom. In their garden was a very large tree house that had been built to span the dividing fence between their neighbour's house and theirs and there was also the biggest trampoline I had ever seen; there were no problems keeping the girls entertained.

We received a message from Steve to say that Radio 5 Live wanted to interview us, together with Mathew's parents. The Pinsent's were staying with one of Anita's friends, Lois, so we all met at her house. Martin Cross, Moira and Pat's lad, was working at that time with Radio 5, and he arrived at Lois's home with Eamonn Holmes the Irish journalist and media personality from Northern Ireland to do the interview. It was still early in Eamonn's GMTV career and he was still presenting the The Eamonn Holmes Show on BBC Radio 5 Live on Saturday mornings; I don't know if our family ever got to hear our interview as there was no time to warn them that it was to be aired.

Steve and Matthew had been having a lot of hassle getting to the rowing course each day as it was about a 60 mile drive from The Athletes Village in Atlanta. Busses had been laid on for the crews but the whole transport system had been extremely disorganised and drivers were getting lost and not turning up on time which meant that the boys were often late for their outings. This could have been disastrous for them on a race day so they decided to up sticks and move into a local hotel near to the course.

One afternoon, we took both of our host families with us to a reception being held at the hotel where most of the supporters were staying. It had been organised by David Tanner the GB Rowing Senior Team Manager so that we could all meet the rowers and each other and have a general get-together. We all had a lovely time and Steve, Ann, and Mathew were able to join us too.

Thursday 25ᵗʰ July was Semi-final day, and as usual, we all felt the tension rising. The first three crews would go straight through to the final and the last three crews would compete later in the petite-final; the petite final would decide places 7-12. This morning was surprisingly cool and a little cloudy but we thought that this might suit our boys. Their race was very exciting; they paced themselves well, doing just enough to ensure they got through to the final but conserving precious energy in the process. Their winning time was 6: 50.30 ahead of New Zealand and Italy. The US crew had led by one length up until the 1000m mark which had worried most of the supporters but they had gone too soon and came in fourth; one of the crew had collapsed and needed medical attention. After their race an American reporter had rubbed Steve up the wrong way and he replied when asked why he and Mathew hadn't led all the way '. "If a crew wants to race like nutters at the beginning, and end up in a B final it is up to them, Australia and France are our main opposition but we knew that the USA and New Zealand had real potential. If we'd been sucked in by the US, raced them to 1,000 metres, then we might have ended up in the B final ourselves. The Americans were fast enough to be in the final but they paced it badly." We knew that our two boy's long experience had taught them well.

After racing we went to the Olympic Village to see Steve and Ann but we had a bit of a job to get in; there was so much security. Finally Steve and Ann were called to the entrance and we followed them through. Just then we caught sight of Princess Ann getting into her car, and Steve seeing her, called us over and introduced us all. When Natalie was introduced, all she could do was to make a grunting noise and then buried her head in the father's jacket. I don't think Princess Ann really noticed but we did pull Natalie's leg about it later. Steve had been on a fund raising trip with the Princess to the US the year before the Atlanta

Olympics and they seemed to be quite well acquainted. An Olympian herself, she had always offered great support to rowing and had been called upon to make a few presentations to Steve over the years.

The boy's Olympic Final day, Saturday 27th July dawned with the news that a terrorist's bomb had ripped apart a peaceful Friday evening in Centennial Olympic Park where thousands of people had gathered for a late-night pop concert. A security guard Richard Jewell had discovered a suspicious knapsack left at the base of a concert sound tower and had alerted authorities who were preparing to evacuate the area when the package exploded at 1:21am. The knapsack contained three pipe-bombs surrounded by a deadly load of nails which ripped through the concert crowd. A Georgia woman, Alice Hawthorne, was killed by a nail that struck her in the head. The bomb wounded 111 others. Turkish cameraman Melih Uzunyol died too from a heart attack he suffered while running to cover the blast and the entire world was reminded of the terror and tragedy of Munich in 1972. It took five years to bring Eric Robert Rudolph to justice and he is currently serving four life terms in the supermax federal prison in Florence, Colorado. Geoff, the girls, and I were on our way to the course when we heard the dreadful news so we didn't know till we arrived at the course if the racing would be cancelled; Olympic officials decided that the Finals would go ahead but we wondered if the awful news would distract the boys from their task.

Ann had managed to come over to be with us for their race and we all knew that their biggest challenge today was expected from the Australian crew, David Weightman and Robb Scott, a comparatively new partnership. The race got under way and at the 500m mark, the crews were tightly pack; at 1000m they were still quite tight but I remembered Steve saying to me earlier, that if they were still in contention at 1000m, we were not to worry. At the 1500m mark and with a quarter of the race left, they seemed to change gear and came powering through to take the gold; mission accomplished, as the TV reporter had said, with the result being 1. Great Britain, 6:20.09; 2. Australia, 6:21.02; 3. France, 6:22 and as they crossed the line Matthew punched the air in delight. .

It was really wonderful, our son had won his fourth Olympic Gold medal; it was a second Gold for Matthew. We could see that Steve was being interviewed by the BBC's Chris Baillieu, while he was still sitting in the boat, and we later found out that it was during this interview that he had uttered those immortal words "If anyone sees me going anywhere near a boat again, they have my permission to shoot me. I do not want anybody to see me in a boat again. I've had enough". We could see that he was absolutely exhausted.

It had been reported that Jürgen his coach had said "I'm just proud to have been involved with a moment of history for Steve. When the ceremony finished Steve came up to me and said 'you're the greatest'. I just said 'No, you're the greatest'. There's nothing better you can hear from any sportsman to a coach but it shows the sort of man he is. He doesn't compare with anybody else". Apparently, as well, David Tanner had admitted that Redgrave's departure was a sad day for British rowing. One of the Australian pair, Robb Scott, had said "If we're going to be beaten by anybody you don't mind it being Steve, he is an absolute legend in rowing"

Every one around us was shouting that they were the heroes of the day. Later we would realise that Great Britain would only win one Gold Medal at the 1996 Atlanta Olympics and it belonged to our son. The British Olympic web site later remarked that in Atlanta 'Many underperformed, and it was left to two of Britain's most committed Olympians to salvage some national pride. The duo found themselves under mounting pressure before they even got out onto the water. Unbeaten in some 58 races stretching back to 1992, Redgrave and Pinsent made no secret of their belief that they would defend their title, but as the winless run in Atlanta extended through the British team, the importance of achieving this ambition became paramount. These two giants of their sport rose above all difficulties, and exploded out of the blocks in the final as a nation held its breath'.

Despite the mayhem caused by the terrible bomb in the park the officials decided that the Olympic Athletes Village party should go ahead. Our family hosts Andrew and Gaynor Fuller were 'over the moon' for us too and on the evening of the boy's final they had given us a really lovely dinner. They had decorated the table all in gold, the girls loved it; what a nice thought. This amazing trip of ours had gone by like a flash and all too soon it was time to take leave of our wonderful hosts and, sincerely thanking them for having us, we drove back to Atlanta and handed the girls over to their Mum and Dad. We returned our hire car and flew back the UK.

On Monday morning, 29th July we read, amongst other reports, an article by Hugh Matheson in The Independent newspaper that, for us, summed it up well. The article was headlined 'Old Golden Oars Waves Goodbye'. "Steven Redgrave rowed majestically into history in Atlanta. Rowing requires a rare combination of strength and endurance. Redgrave was born strong and from 16 years old he was bigger than most of those around him. In the next 18 years he proved endurance beyond anyone else in his sport and the equal of only three others in Olympic history. He has toiled for these years with no state support, for most of the time entirely dependent on his family, who are not rich, and on small grants from the Sports Aid Foundation, a British charity. Redgrave himself does not know what the future will bring and he remained modest about his phenomenal achievement". Steve also paid tribute to Matthew "He is the best partner I've had and I've had some outstanding partners in my career."

Within days of his win Steve had a job offer to coach at Australia's Academy of Sport - an offer made all the more tempting by the suggestion that Ann would be offered a post too; they had given this serious consideration. Ann said later to reporter Mike Rowbottom "The Australians were gutted when he said he was not going to accept the job," Ann said. "But they said the opportunity would still be there in four years' time."

We knew that we would all just have to wait and see.

Spanish Villa 1989 -1999

Four Generation's Sheila Redgrave, baby Natalie, Ada Stevenson (big Nan) and Steve

Tasha our lovely dog

Ben and Stephanie (aged four) at the park

World Championship 1991, Vienna, Austria. Gold Medal Coxless Pair  Left to Right - June Callaway, Sheila, Ann, Steve, baby Natalie (four weeks old) Matthew Pinsent.

Natalie's Christening Reception 1991 – back row – Matthew (godfather) and Steve.
front row - Ann Spracklen (godmother) Ann holding Natalie and Joan Haley (godmother).

'This is your life' TV Show BBC studio Left to Right - Bryan (my brother) Lawrence , Susan, Pat (Bryan's wife), Kim, Nicola, Janet.

'This is your life' TV Show BBC Studio. Lynne and Larry Tracy

Sophie Jayne's Christening October 1994 (2nd child) Ann holding Sophie,
Natalie cutting the cake.

My Daughters (left to right) Christine and Jane

Natalie watching her Dad on TV carrying the flag for the British Team at
Atlanta Olympic Opening Ceremony

Moria and Pat Cross Atlanta Olympics 1996

Natalie with winner's bouquet at Atlanta Olympics 1996

Home coming from Atlanta Olympics 1996 Bus Ride through Marlow.
Matthew, Natalie and Steve

Steve cutting Cake at Marlow Home Coming Celebration 1996 on lookers
Natalie, Laura, Ben Stephanie, Edward and Christine

World Championships Aiguebelette France 1997. Natalie, Sheila and Sophie - Standing in front of our camper.

Christine's Christmas Show- Michael Jackson's Thriller. Sophie, Chris, Ben, Natalie Stephanie.

Steve with a few of his trophies

Natalie and Sheila visiting the train shop at Indianapolis World
Championships 1994.

Zak Robert Redgrave's Christening Saint Paul's Cathedral 1998 -Cleanliness
is next to Godliness

Steve CBE 1997 Outside Buckingham Palace Steve with sisters Christine & Jane and his daughters Natalie & Sophie.

Natalie and Sophie  Support their Dad at Atlanta Olympics 1996

Steve's children Zak, Natalie & Sophie

# Chapter Nineteen
## World Championships 1997 Aiguebelette, France.

### *Coxless Four Debut*

Another wonderful reception for Steve was given by Marlow and Wycombe town councils. As the open top bus drove us through the town, we were amazed at the thousands of people that had turned out to line the streets, waving their flags and holding up the banners that they had made, congratulating the boys. Steve and Mathew were getting the adulation that they really deserved; it was fantastic to witness and we all enjoyed another wonderful day feeling enormously proud of our son.

Ann told us a few days later that she had a secret to tell us and that it was something that Steve did not yet know about; he was to be the subject of the BBC programme 'This Is Your Life'. The programme researchers at the BBC wanted to visit us all during the next few weeks so that they could surreptitiously record a short VT clip from each of us, which they planned to playback during the actual programme. A great deal of planning, research and preparation must have gone into putting this one programme and we were all really excited to see Steve reaction.

Steve and Matthew had been asked to appear at the live draw on the National Lottery show, so that they could alternately read out the numbers on the winning balls as they came out of the lotto machine. This had been chosen as the venue to spring the surprise. Bob Monkhouse, the host for The National Lottery show, had been in on the surprise. When Michael Aspel came on to the set with his Big Red Book, just as the boys had completed their task, Steve was absolutely gobsmacked and Bob Monkhouse looked at the audience, and raising one eyebrow, gave his famous grin. With no time to recover from the shock Steve and Mathew, who had been already primed, were then whisked off to the BBC studios where all of us were already waiting on set for his arrival.

It was a fabulous, and at time extremely touching show, as many people appeared to say how proud they were of our son. The producers of the show had been in touch with Steve's old school friends and masters, fellow rowers, all of his coaches, both past and present and key family members, ending the evening with a personal appearance from Pertti Karpinnen, the famous Finnish Olympic Gold medallist rower who had always been Steve's idol and roll model; it was incredible that we were sitting here witnessing these huge accolades for our son.

As the show ended we all gathered around Steve on stage as Michael presented him with his own Big Red Book to keep. After the show, the BBC put on a wonderful buffet and we were then able to chat to everyone who had appeared. As the evening wore on Steve's three children all fell asleep lying amongst a pile of coats in the corner of the room and had to eventually be carried back to the waiting coaches that then retuned us all to Marlow Bottom; a superb evening and a really fitting tribute.

Soon after we returned to Spain we were really shocked by some bad news of yet further health problems for Steve. He had been undecided as to whether he should continue international rowing. His ulcerated colitis was now being well controlled by medication and he was learning to adjust to his condition but the news we received was of something much more serious. Ann hadn't liked to tell us of her earlier suspicions, until they had been confirmed by a specialist, but she now informed us that Steve had been diagnosed with Diabetes Millitus; a life threatening disease, if left untreated.

In short, his pancreas was not doing its job properly. Or at least the part of the pancreas called the islet cells. These cells produce insulin, a protein hormone, necessary so that the insulin 'receptor' cells in his body could use the glucose released from his food. If this didn't happen, then his body couldn't repair its cells, used for energy and growth. In a nutshell, insulin helps the cells in your body to efficiently utilise food. With this devastating news Steve's spirit was really low for a while, he thought that, this was it; his body was making the decision for him. The specialist had been more optimistic though and he had apparently told Steve that there was no reason to quit rowing but that if he had the resolve to carry on rowing at his level then he would just have to learn to cope with his new condition; it could be done.

He suffered many high's and low's trying to get his sugar levels right. He had to now inject Insulin again but this was unlike the previous time a few months back when it had been a temporary state from which he'd made a quick recovery. His pancreas had still been producing some insulin previously just not enough but this time the Diabetes was a permanent condition that he would have to deal with for the rest of his life; it took him a while to get his head around that.

Now the regular delivery of artificial insulin via injection had became vital and this had to be combined with careful monitoring of blood glucose levels constantly using blood testing monitors. Low levels of blood glucose, called hypoglycemia, could have led to seizures or episodes of unconsciousness which may even have resulted in coma and so they absolutely had to be treated immediately; he needed to be on the ball with his monitoring.

For an athlete like him requiring, at times, extreme levels of energy, getting it right wouldn't be an easy task. With improvements in medical science, in later years, it would become possible for him to deliver his insulin by a pump, which would allow continuous infusion of insulin 24 hours a day at pre-set levels, and give him the ability to program doses of insulin as needed at meal times; the small cassette insulin pump he now has permanently attached to his body allows him much more freedom from the previous laborious need to inject and he has adjusted well; it now just part of his life.

Mathew had wanted a change from rowing in the pair, and so it was decided to put together a new coxless four and serious training for the rowing squad had restarted at the end of October 1996. After their summer break, following Atlanta, Steve had not been able to train with them as he was still adjusting his insulin intake to deal with the exhausting regimes. He had not rowed for some months now and with the total exhaustion he had suffered after Atlanta, with his energy levels all over the place; it was going to take him some time to regain his fitness. Jürgen Gröbler, his coach, was more than fair and had said he would give him the time he needed as long as he was back training by 1$^{st}$ December; Steve met the deadline.

On Thursday 28$^{th}$ November 1996, Steve held a press conference at The Leander Club in Henley. The riverbank was absolutely packed with television crews and cameramen. He made the announcement that he would be trying for a fifth Olympic Gold in Sydney 2000, exactly four months to the day when he uttered those now famous word "If anyone see me anywhere near a boat". Ann told reporter Mike Rowbottom "I would have liked him to have stopped but my instinct told me for a long time that he would carry on. He has the chance to be the best Olympian. That's what I think he wants in his heart of hearts. He wants to be the best, and he's not quite there yet." Earlier in the morning, Ann had said one of the reasons she had wanted him to stop was that it was always better to do so when you were at the top. Steve had apparently overheard her remark and replied, with a steely little smile, "Can I just add one more thing to that? I still plan to stop at the top." Mike went on to report, 'Inevitably, the question of age was raised. Redgrave will be 38 by the time of the next Olympics. "The age of successful athletes is going up now because there is more professionalism," Steve responded. "If you can put in the time and effort in training, you can stay at a high level. Anyway, the oldest man to win an Olympic rowing gold was 42, so I might have another couple of go's." At this point, the ghost of a smile did not flit across his wife's face. Sydney beckoned, and he could not resist the call.' It was settled then he would go for gold one more time.

It was now January 1997 and the British Rowing team was off to South Africa for a warm weather winter training camp. Steve had gone along but had found it very difficult to keep up the pace and he would get quite despondent at times. He would phone Ann and she would talk to him and help settle him again, trying to boost his confidence. We admired her dedication and self-sacrifice in helping our son achieve his goals. I think she had hoped that he would give up after Atlanta. I think that she really wanted her husband to spend some time at home with her and the children but instead she supported him in every way; we hoped that he appreciated the sacrifices she had made, not many wives would have done the same. Little by little he re-gained his fitness; it was a long uphill struggle. As parents we felt so helpless, we were so far away and couldn't offer much practical help from this distance but we tried to encourage him when we spoke to him on the phone and we prayed that he would again recover his zest for life; this had hit him very hard indeed.

We didn't make our decision straight away, but gradually we then began to think very seriously of selling up and returning to England. The estate agents told us that it was not a good time to be putting the house on the market, but we took a chance anyway and began to market our villa.

On March the 21st Prince Charles invested Steve at Buckingham Palace, this time with the C.B.E. Commander of the Order of the British Empire. Steve took his eldest daughter Natalie and his sisters, Christine and Jane as his guests; it was good of him to include both of his sisters on this occasion as they had always been such a good support to him in our absence. We watched the television all day waiting for any news programmes that might report from the palace. Steve rang us at 8.30pm that evening to tell us all about his day and suddenly, as we spoke on the phone, there he was on the news, on our TV, with Natalie, and his two sisters. It was so nice to see them all and they all looked so smart in their special outfits; we were so proud of our son.

We'd had a few people to view the villa, but the market was really dead. It was now May and Tasha the dog had not been at all well. We had taken her to the vet, but she hadn't improved much and so on the 28th May we had to make the decision to have her put down. Antonia, our Spanish vet, had looked after Tasha since we had come to live in Spain and she was very upset when she had to tell us that Tasha had found a tumour and that she could do no more. Tasha had been Steve's dog originally, a good old Heinz 57, but she had been so very faithful to us since we had adopted her, and she had also been such good company for my Mom when she'd been alive. Even with her failing health and dementia she had never once forgotten who the dog was. We were both distraught and we brought her body home from the vets and buried her in the garden then we phoned all the family to pass on the sad news. Some people would think that it was silly to get so upset over loosing a dog, but Tasha had been more than just a pet to us, she had been more like a dear old friend.

A few days later Jane, David, and the twins, came out for a holiday, followed by a two week visit from my brother Bryan and his wife Pat and then Christine and Edward came out for a week too, so we were kept really busy. Ann, Natalie, Sophie, and Ann's Mum, June, came to stay a little while later and we both thought that Ann was looking extremely tired but while she was with us we tried to give her a good rest by taking the children off her hands as often as possible and leaving her to relax. Her slightly peaky appearance was later explained when Ann gave us the good news that she and Steve were expecting another baby next February; we were so pleased for them.

The 1997 World Championship 31st August -7th September was to be held in Aiguebelette, on a lake just west of Chambéry in the Savoie area of France, not far from Grenoble. We left Spain during the last week in August, driving the camper into France and we collected the girls from Ann and Steve on our arrival at Lake Aiguebelette. Finding a really nice camp site right beside this magnificent emerald green coloured lake, we settled in. Nestled at the foot of the Alps, with the protection of the surrounding mountains, the Montagne de l'Epine, and being renowned for the tranquillity of its waters, the lake made an ideal rowing venue. In such beautiful and calm surroundings, with its pretty houses on palisades, little boathouses lining its reedy sides, watching the little fishing barques plied by local fisherman, we felt really relaxed; it was also quieter than the other great lakes in this area, as motor boats weren't allowed on its waters. Aiguebelette claims to have the warmest waters of Savoie's great lakes, up to 28°C in summer and its beaches have excellent facilities watched over by lifeguards. It was a very safe environment too and the girls could ride their cycles around without fear of passing motorists. Natalie and Sophie made friends with a little lad who was staying with his parents in the Eurotent camp nearby and they had great fun joining in the activities at the children's club there.

On Sunday 31st Aug, the Championship's Opening Ceremony was to be held in the local town, and on our way there we made a chance meeting with an old rowing friend, Terry Dillon; he had sadly lost his lovely wife to cancer a few months before. He had decided to cycle from England, crossing on the ferry to Bordeaux and then cycling across France to Aiguebelette. He was staying at a very nice, nearby hotel, with the rest of the rowing supporters, so he was in good company; we had not seen him since last year. On meeting us he said, "That's terrible news about Diana", not having heard the news we asked him to explain, then he told us how Princess Diana had been killed in a car crash in Paris with Jodi Fiad. We were shocked, it was unbelievable. He went on to tell us how the majority of the people in the UK, and the rest world for that matter had been stunned by the news.

We walked on into the town feeling quite affected by the information we had just received. We attended the opening ceremony which was very good quite different from previous occasions. There were men dressed as clowns walking around on stilts and ladies prettily dressed in traditional costumes; Natalie and Sophie loved it. We'd really had the wind knocked out of our sails with the awful news and felt strangely detached from the jovial atmosphere surrounding us. All of the Brit's that we came across and that we spoke to that day were really shocked too. Jane rang us later that afternoon to pass on the news and told us just how the shocking information was reverberating right across the county and the world at large; everyone was feeling a real bereavement.

The Coxless Four that had been selected from this year's British squad was made up of Steve and Matthew from the previous pair and joining them in the boat were James Cracknell and Tim Foster, both with excellent international experience; they were still being coached by Jürgen Gröbler

The rowing started on Sunday afternoon and for the first time ever we had no tickets. We had thought that we would be able to get them on our arrival at the course. We discovered that getting tickets for their heat today wasn't any problem, but we were told that, for the Semi's, and most importantly, for the Final, there was going to be great difficulty in obtaining any at all. There was no time before racing began for us to try to get this problems resolved so we just purchased our tickets for today and decided to try again later. In their heat they came up against Slovenia, Italy, Poland, and Korea. And they won easily in a time of 6: 0.55; the fastest fours heat of the day.

The sports headlines the following day spoke for themselves, they read, 'Redgrave's Four Hit Form' and went on to add "Steve Redgrave led Britain's Coxless Four to an impressive opening victory in the qualifying heats on the first day of the World Championships on Lac d'Aiguebelette in France yesterday. The four-time Olympic gold medalist, along with team-mates Matthew Pinsent, James Cracknell and Tim Foster, left the rest of the field trailing in their wake". We were very pleased that he seemed to be back on form once again.

After racing had finished, we started to look round for those important tickets and finding the main ticket office, were once again told that none were available for either race. I was really upset and I began to explain that we had not been able to buy any tickets in England; the reply was still sorry, none available. Pushing both girls forward, I explained that these were Steve Redgrave's children and how upset they would be to miss their fathers' race. I had never done this sort of thing before in the whole of his rowing career but I was desperate. It seemed to do the trick, we were sold some tickets; the seats turned out to have obscured views of the course but at least we were all able to see Steve race on both occasions.

Semi-finals day was Thursday 4ᵗʰ September where they would be meeting Poland, Russia, Germany, Italy, and Lithuania. We couldn't see very well from where we had been seated but we could hear over the tannoy as it was announced that they had taken the lead. The finishing order was Great Britain 5:57.85, then Italy, then Germany, the first three through to the final. We then watched the other semi-final which confirmed that France, Romania, and Slovenia would be joining our boys in the final on Saturday.

Saturday 6th September dawned and with the usual mixture of eagerness and anxiety, we got to the course early, staking our claim with our Union flags. With our fingers crossed, we huddled together waiting for their race. Their biggest opposition today would be the French who were the Olympic Gold Medallists from Atlanta. During their race the crews were all quite closely matched but our lads eventually pulled away to take the Gold in 5:52.40, France took Silver in 5:56.34 and Romania the Bronze in 5:57.10. It was a great outcome for this new British crew but their mood was sombre when they came to the rostrum.

Hugh Matheson gave a great insight to the atmosphere that day when he later wrote, "Steve Redgrave led his team-mates Matthew Pinsent, Tim Foster and James Cracknell in a silent tribute to Diana, Princess of Wales, after they won the world championship coxless fours here yesterday. The British four wore black ribbons on their uniforms and started the race just after a moment of silence was held at the request of the British, Australian and Canadian teams at the time of the conclusion of the funeral service in Westminster Abbey. Redgrave, who won a world title for the seventh time, seemed especially upset during the awarding of the medals. Then, during the playing of the national anthem, the four bowed their heads and stood silently with their hands behind their back as the Union Flag was raised to half-mast; below the flags of second-placed France and third-placed Romania. Redgrave explained the team's feelings: "Back at the hotel, we saw the Princess's coffin and the thousands and thousands of people lining the streets. It made what we were doing a little bit insignificant in some respects. It was a last-minute decision to keep our heads down. It seemed to us the least we could do given the circumstances."

In fact, for Great Britain it had been a really successful Championship all-round; the final medal haul had been 8 in total. As well as our lad's Gold, for the Men, there had been, Bronze in Men's Single Sculls, Bronze in Men's Coxed Four, Silver in Lightweight Men's Eight and our British woman had put in a supreme effort winning Gold in the Women's Coxless Four, Silver in Women's Double Sculls, Bronze in Women's Eight, and Bronze in Lightweight Women's Coxless Pair; over all it had been a good week.

Natalie and Sophie had enjoyed their time in this delightful place, riding their bikes and playing with the other children. After the rowing was over we handed our Grandchildren back to their parents and on Monday 8th September we set off on our journey back to the UK in the camper, taking our time and enjoying our meander through France.

We stayed in Marlow for a while. Geoff was helping Christine to build an extension to her house by digging the footings and doing the brickwork. While Chris moved barrow loads of soil and mixed the mortar, her partner Edward worked on the carpentry, the electrics and the plumbing. I spent my time sitting with Steve's children and helping out where I could. Our home in Spain was rented out until mid October, so on the 18th October I took a flight back to Alicante to re-occupy our villa, re-arrange our stored belonging and get the home ready for us to settle back into.

Pat and Brian were staying in Mallorca this year for two weeks holiday and then their plan was to join me in Javea to spend some time with me and to give me a hand sorting out the house while Geoff was in the UK with Christine. On Monday, I had an urgent phone call from my niece Janet, Brian's daughter in Newcastle, telling me that Brian had suffered a massive heart attack on Sunday 19th October and had died. They had only been at the hotel a few hours having just arrived at the beginning of their holiday and were getting ready to go down for dinner, when he had collapsed. Pat had immediately called for a doctor, but apparently Bryan had died instantly; I was devastated, I couldn't believe it. Poor Pat was out there on her own so I immediately phoned her hotel and spoke to her saying that I would fly out to Mallorca straight away. She said that I shouldn't come to Mallorca as the doctor and the other officials had told her that they would be flying her home the next day with his body; so I flew straight back to the UK instead as soon as I could get a flight and then went up to Newcastle to stay with Pat and her girls. Pat had returned but Brian's body had needed to remain in Mallorca until all the paper work was completed. The funeral was arranged for Friday 31st October.

Geoff, Christine, and Jane, came up to Newcastle by train, but Steve was not able to get there till the day of the funeral, as he wasn't going to be the U K till the 31st. The service was lovely and Susan, his eldest daughter gave a very touching eulogy, giving tribute to her father; I would really miss my brother, he had been such a kind and caring husband to Pat, a wonderful father to Susan and Janet and a lovely Grandfather to their children. In my eyes, he had been a good son to our mother. He had been my older brother and we'd been very close; I would dearly miss him. I stayed on for another week with Pat and the girls before returning to Marlow. As the year was flying by so fast, and with now no need to rush back to Spain, Geoff and I made a decision to stay in the UK till after Christmas especially as Christine was going into hospital in early January to have a hysterectomy, I felt that I wanted to be around when she came home to give her a helping hand; as it turned out she made a remarkable recovery and was up a ladder decorating her new extension within five weeks of her major surgery.

Steve and Ann took their girls for a short trip to Lapland as a pre-Christmas surprise to see Santa Claus. It had been extremely cold and bad weather had delayed their flight home and at the last minute their flight had been diverted to Manchester. They had finally arrived in London at 5.30am the following morning when they should have been home by 10.30pm the night before; they were all exhausted. On the 19th December, Steve and his family flew off again, as soon as Natalie had finished school, this time on a skiing holiday. Over the following few days I managed to finish my Christmas shopping and we spent a delightful Christmas day this year at Jane and David's home celebrating with the rest of the family. Steve rang and spoke to us all on Christmas morning saying that they were enjoying their holiday and had plenty of good powder snow; Six year old Natalie was leaning to ski in the Kindergarten ski school, three year old Sophie was sharing in the fun of Steve's skiing, as she was strapped to her dad's back and Ann was thoroughly enjoying herself, skiing on the green runs even though she was, by now, seven months pregnant.

New Years Eve was spent at Steve's home with all the family. Some of our friends had been invited to the celebrations too including our old friends Joan, and Derek. Joan had not been well; she had lost a lot of weight and was looking quite poorly. Early in January she had visited her doctor, and had been taken into hospital suffering from cancer of the kidney. She had major surgery right away and was really ill for a long time but, being determined, soon fought her way back into remission.

As with every passing year, I wondered what the New Year had in store for everyone, particularly my family. Steve, who was still a little up and down with his diabetes, was winning the battle and had proved with his performance at The World Championships this year that nothing could stand in his way.

# Chapter Twenty
## World Championships 1998 Köln Germany

### *A Son is Born*

We left Marlow early on Sunday 11th January 1998, drove to Dover and boarded the 8.30am boat to Calais. We had a good trip back and arrived in Javea once again on Wednesday and within a few days our life had settled back into its normal routine.

We had a phone call early on Monday16th February at 8am from Steve to say that Ann had gone into labour and that he had taken her to High Wycombe hospital; we waited in eager anticipation. At 2pm that afternoon the phone rang and it had been Steve again telling us that we had a new grandson Zak Robert Redgrave who had been born a healthy 8lb 13oz; we were over the moon. I was really looking forward to seeing the new arrival and I managed to get a flight back to the UK just two days later; at the airport to meet me were Steve, Natalie, and Sophie.

Zak was beautiful and looked just like Steve had done when he had been born. Christine told me that on the morning of Zak's birth she and Jane had taken the two girls into the hospital to meet their new brother. Sophie, whose fourth birthday was due just three days later had been told that the new baby was expected sometime around her birthday and from this information she had come up with her own idea that this new bundle was her present. A very proud Dad had given Zak to Natalie to hold but Sophie had insisted that she wanted to hold him first as he was her birthday present. Early afternoon, the same day, his new family had taken him home but not before they had all visited McDonalds for a Big Mac and fries. June, Ann's mum and I took it in turns to help with the washing, the housework and helping Ann with the baby. I really enjoyed my stay with all the family and returned to Spain on March 4th.

Pat, my sister-in-law, came out to Spain to stay with us a few weeks later and Geoff and I took her out and about as much as possible. During her stay, on 19th March, we took her to Denia a town near to where we lived to see a Spanish fiesta, celebrated in the Valencian Region, 'Las Fallas Day'. On this day huge Fallas are set alight. Las Fallas literally means "the fires" in Valencian (a provincial language somewhere between Spanish and Catalan). The origin of this fiesta is unclear but one explanation is that it celebrates St Joseph, the patron saint of carpenters. It all started back in the Middle Ages when carpenters used to hang up planks of wood called 'parots' in the winter to support their candles while they were working. At the onset of spring these pieces of wood would be burned, as a way of celebrating the end of dark winter working days. After a while, they began to put clothing on the parot, and then started to try to make it identifiable with a well-known local personality. These became the forerunners of the contemporary Ninots, the enormous cardboard, wood, cork, plaster and papier maché figures of today that can take up to six month to construct and can cost thousands of pounds. It's a spectacular sight to see with literally hundreds of these Ninots set up in different squares around the town. The parades of these figures start at the crack of dawn accompanied by brass bands and end with a loud, smoky, rowdy fiesta where the whole town seems to be set ablaze. It creates a hug headache for the local firemen, the 'bomberos' but everyone has such a good time; the Spanish really know how to celebrate.

Having had no luck to date, with the house sale, we decided to rent the villa out again for the summer while we went away for our usual trips to the rowing events. After more visits from the family during the early spring, on 16th April, we once again departed for the U K. Jane, David, and the twins, travelled back with us this time and it was a pleasant three day journey with the twins sleeping in the camper with us at night and Jane, and David, over-nighting in motels.

On the 28ᵗʰ April St Georges Day, Steve was awarded the St Georges Day Trophy for Outstanding Achievements in Rowing; it was a beautiful statue of St George on horseback, slaying the dragon; we once again felt really proud parents.

Henley week started on Wednesday 1st July. Steve was not rowing until Saturday this year when he would be entering the Stewards Cup, the Coxless Four event, with Mathew, James and Tim. Today, we had invited three couples to be our guests in The Stewards Enclosure, our old friends Queenie and Arthur, Joan and Derek and Vic and Jane Tuhill. The weather kept fine for us, but a brisk cold wind was blowing off the water and the ladies were obliged to hang on to their hats as we watched the racing from the Grandstand before enjoying our picnic champagne lunch.

On Saturday the boy's, rowing for their Henley club Leander, came up against a crew from Melbourne University and Mercantile Australia and Leander had won by 1 length. That evening Ben, Steph, Natalie, and Sophie, came to stay the night with us in the camper so that they would be able to see the usual HRR firework display. They were all growing up now and it was a bit of a squash but they were all well behaved and thoroughly enjoyed the fireworks even though the weather was very wet and windy that evening. Sunday morning we made our annual trip to the Henley church service. When we all stood up to sing the first hymn, four year old, Sophie, said to me, "Nanny, I don't know the words", I told her not to worry and just to sing La, La, La along with the music. This she did with great gusto and as the hymn came to an end, much to our amusement, she simply carried on seemingly oblivious to the now silent congregation around her; she was so sweet and we managed to conceal our laughter till after the service.

It was Finals day today and Steve and the boys were up against the Danish Lightweight Olympic Champions. It was a very exciting race with Leander winning by three quarters of a length and leading all the way. After prize giving, that evening, we attempted to have our usual barbeque but due to the worsening weather, Geoff had to cook the meat on the grill outside while sheltering under a large umbrella. We all managed to cram into the camper to eat and to keep warm but we didn't stay late. We're a stoic lot us Brits, readily showing patience and endurance during all adversity but we often need to with the British weather.

We left for Lucerne the following Thursday 9th July, which was Natalie's seventh birthday. Due to her still being at school, it was the first time in five years that she wouldn't be coming with us; we had often in the past celebrated her birthday whilst away at the regatta in Lucerne. This year we had given her a Spanish guitar as a birthday gift and we had given it to her before we left. We arrived in Switzerland on Friday 10th July at about 1.30pm, much later than we had expected and therefore, missed the boys first race; they had won and gone through to the semi final on Saturday. For the semi-finals they had an easy draw and were through to the finals on Sunday with no problems. Here they would meet Australia and Romania their biggest opposition. Sunday's Final race was for some reason put back by one and a half hours but despite this disruption they had a brilliant race, winning by one and a half lengths, with Romania, second and Australia third.

This race was also the final one in the three international rowing competitions organized by FISA (the International Rowing Federation) and raced during each summer, known as The Rowing World Cup. The other regattas this year had been at Oberschleissheim a district in Munich, Germany during May and Hazewinkle, Belgium, held in June; Lucerne was the third. The World Cup first began in 1997 and in each event points are awarded to the top seven finishing boats and an overall winner is determined after the last world cup regatta each year. During the regattas the current leader in each event must wear yellow bibs. The nation with the most points overall from all boat classes is declared winner of the Overall Rowing World Cup; this year it was Germany once again and they would go on to win for the next eight years too. With racing over we headed back to the UK, driving through heavy rain most of the way.

Ann left the UK on the 22nd July, as she had been asked to be the team doctor for the British under 23's rowing competition held at Ioannina, in north-western Greece; she took five month old Zak with her. We looked after the girls while she was away for the week and when she arrived home, the following weekend, Ann, Zak, the girls and I, drove up to Newcastle to attend Pat's Granddaughters wedding. It was a lovely day and it was good to see that Pat was keeping well. While we were in Northumberland we visited Seahouses and Hadrian's Wall, and in County Durham, we spent the day at Beamish the Victorian replica village set in 300 acres of beautiful countryside that vividly illustrated life in the North East of England in the early 1800s and early 1900s. Buildings from throughout the region have been brought to Beamish, rebuilt and furnished as they once were. The costumed staff welcomed visitors and demonstrated the past way of life. The girls had great fun here as at The Colliery Village a guided tour took us underground and we saw a real 'drift' mine and we visited a row of pit cottages showing how pitmen and their families had once lived. We travelled by tram along the cobbled street of The Town and went inside an old school house where we sat at the old desks, imagining that we were pupils and wrote with chalk on slate as the children in that era had done; we ended the day with a visit to the old fashioned sweet shop.

We left for Germany on the 2nd September heading for the 1998 World Rowing Championships that this year were being held at Lake Fuehlingen near Cologne from 6th -13th September; our journey there was good but with mixed weather. When we arrived in the local area we had a problem at first finding the course and a campsite for our stay but eventually found the Esso Parking Platz and as not many people had arrived we were able to secure a good camper site. Lake Fuehlingen is a disused gravel pit located at the northern-most border of Cologne City and it has been turned into a landscaped reserve for water sports.

We spent a few days cycling around the area, finding the rowing course and the local shops. On Sunday the 6th September the opening ceremony started with a row past of boats carrying the flags of competing nations; it was very well done. Steve's heat was the last of the day to be rowed and his crew had drawn against Egypt, Lithuania, Norway USA, and China, this they won putting them in the semi-final where they would be lining up against USA, Romania, Australia, Germany, and Belarus. On Thursday 10th September they won their semi-final comfortably, in a time of 5:58.95.

With a few free day's we travelled into Cologne to look around the city. Cologne, the fourth largest and the oldest city in Germany is also famous for Eau de Cologne. At the beginning of the 18th century an Italian expatriate Johann Maria Farina created a new fragrance and named it after his hometown Cologne, Eau de Cologne (Water of Cologne). In the course of the 18th century the fragrance became increasingly popular and it was the house number 4711, given to the factory at Glockengasse, which became the brand name that still exists today.

We took a conducted tour around the beautiful cathedral which is one of the world's largest churches and the largest Gothic church in Northern Europe. The cathedral suffered seventy hits by aerial bombs during World War II. It didn't collapse though and stood tall in an otherwise flattened city. Some of the stained glass windows had been stored away, during the War, in the vaults but most had been destroyed. The most celebrated work of art in the cathedral is the Shrine of the Three Kings, a large gilded sarcophagus dating from the 13th century. It's traditionally believed to hold the remains of the Three Wise Men, whose bones and 2,000-year-old clothes were discovered at the opening of the shrine in 1864.

The river Rhine, one of the longest and most important rivers in Europe flows through the centre of the city. It runs for over 1,320 kilometres from its source in the in the Swiss Alps and flows through four countries, Switzerland, Germany, France and Holland, before emptying into the North Sea at Rotterdam. It very busy with cargo boats, barges, and passenger boats and it was pleasant to sit outside a little German street café and watch the boats chugging by whilst drinking coffee and eating some chocolate torte.

We also visited The **Imhoff-Stollwerck Chocolate Museum** and factory where the smell was divine. We wandered around looking at the machinery where the chocolate is actually produced and learned about the history of chocolate production. Then the best bit came when we sampled the liquid chocolate on wafers from a chocolate fountain which tasted delicious; it was the first time we had seen one of these. Then we went into their shop and spent a small fortune.

Ann, Natalie, Sophie and Zak were coming over for the finals, it would be a bit cramped for us all in the camper but we thought we could manage for a couple of days; she arrived with the children about 8.30pm on Friday evening. The weather hadn't been good and when they arrived it was pouring down. We prepared a meal, ate, then put the kids to bed; they were very good and slept right through. We awoke to more rain and after breakfast we put on our raingear and set off for the rowing. We managed to get some seats under cover but it was still very wet and cold. We made friends with a French lady sitting near to us, whose son was rowing in the French four against our boys. She was very friendly with Zak, giving him lots of hugs but when it came to their race, we both became totally partisan; she shouted for her son and we shouted for the Great Britain crew. The outcome was Great Britain, first in a time of 5:45.06, France 2nd 5:49.44 Italy 3rd 5:49.46, Australia 4th, 5:49.63, Romania 5th, 5:55,62, 6th Norway 6:00.47, what a race, Steve's crew had set a new World Championship record; the French lady was the first to congratulate us.

We all went to the press conference; we had some lunch, and then went back to the camper feeling pleased that we had witnessed another one of Steve's great races There would be one more World Championship next year before the 2000 Olympics in Sydney, Australia. The following day, Sunday, was the last day of rowing, the weather was beginning to improve and after breakfast we went off to watch the racing feeling quite relaxed knowing that our crew had rowed yesterday; today we could just enjoy being spectators. By the end of the competition Britain had won three gold medals and one silver. Miriam Batten and Gillian Lindsay had won gold in the Women's Double Sculls, Dot **Blackie** and Cath Bishop had taken silver in the Women's Coxless Pair, and the Lightweight Women's Coxless Pair had also won gold; it was another great achievement by the British women who had, this year, been coached by Mike Spracklen.

We said our goodbyes to the Terry Dillon and his family, our rowing friends. And after lunch we said goodbye to Steve, Ann, and the kids who were returning to the UK. We stayed that night at a campsite on the Rhine, and watched a man fishing and then cooking his catch on the barbecue in the rain. The following morning we set off on our trip back to Britain stopping for a night on a campsite near Lille in northern France. As the weather was still bad, there seemed no point in taking our time getting back, so we headed for the boat at Calais, and then drove back to Marlow Bottom.

We stayed in England with the family until the 2$^{nd}$ November then took a relaxing journey, steadily driving, back to Spain; we arrived at the villa about 8pm in the evening, three days later. It was really nice to see the sun again especially after what had seemed like a very wet summer. We spent the next few days tidying up the garden; having to buy some new plants as quite a few had died off in the summer heat. Three weeks later, with everything spick and span, we got ourselves ready for yet another journey back to England as we had been asked to take care of the children while Steve and Ann went to Australia, for a winter training camp; they were leaving at the end of November. We had a busy but very rewarding time being Grandparents and it didn't seem long before Ann had returned, this time alone as she hadn't wanted to miss the children school Christmas plays. Steve was involved with training till the 13$^{th}$ December when he returned feeling really pleased with his progress having had a successful squad camp.

I spent the next week doing my Christmas shopping but managed to buy and wrap all the gifts in time for Christmas day. We spent the morning at Steve and Ann's, watching the little ones open their presents, then we all went to Jane and David's for a wonderful Christmas lunch. It was lovely to have all of my children and grandchildren around me during this holiday. A few days before Christmas, Christine, with all the children, had put on a special concert party for us all to watch. She managed to get them all to put on little sketches, some singing and dancing on a little stage in her lounge. She and Edward had spent a lot of time and money making props and buying costumes and wigs for them to wear; a lot of effort went into the show and all the kids had a marvellous time performing in front of their parents and grandparents. Even toddler Zak climbed up on the stage and joined in the dancing. They performed Michael Jackson's thriller, with Ben as Michael and all the others as the Zombies; it was fabulous. Steph sang a Marlene Dietrich song "Falling in Love Again" perched on a bar stool, wearing false eyelashes, dressed in black fishnets, a black basque and a pink feather boa, while holding a long cigarette holder, which I think shocked her father. Natalie did "My old man said follow the van" and Sophie sat on a wooden horse and sang "Horsey Horsey Don't You Stop", dressed up in a cowgirl outfit; it was a really wonderful afternoon, ending up with a Christmas tea served by the artists. Steve Ann and the girls left for their skiing holiday on Boxing Day; this time both of the girls were going into ski school and Zak would be strapped to his dad's back to enjoy the excitement of the slopes with Steve. Geoff and I spent the rest of the holiday looking after their dog and visiting our family and friends.

The New Years Eve celebrations this year were spent at Jane and David's home; at midnight Steve and family phoned to wish us all a happy new year. As usual we again entered the New Year eating our twelve grapes, one on each strike of Big Ben and making our wish in the Spanish tradition. My wish was for good health for all the family but especially for Steve, still battling with Colitis and Diabetes.

# Chapter Twenty One
## World Championships 1999 St Catharines, Canada

*Ed? Tim? Baldrick?*

We left England on the 7<sup>th</sup> January; we had decided to return our villa to the market again this coming spring. On our journey home we ran into really bad weather while travelling over the Pyrenees Mountains and found ourselves driving through a dreadful snow blizzard but once over the border, the weather markedly improved and gradually began to warm up on our decent into Spain; it felt really good to see the sun again.

After putting the villa once again in the hands of the local estate agent, we were kept reasonably busy with a steady stream of viewers. Some of the viewers seemed very keen, but in the main, we would hear no more. In March a very pleasant couple, a Mr and Mrs Dean, came to view the villa, bringing along their twelve year old daughter. They took a good look around and happily said that it was just what they had been looking for. They enthusiastically put down a deposit with the agents the same day and we agreed to their request for an extended completion date of 6<sup>th</sup> September. We felt that this would suit us too as it would allow us to rent out the property again this coming summer, whilst we were away in the UK and Canada.

Geoff flew back to England in April, after a request from Jane and David to stay at their home and look after their dogs while they took the twins to Disneyland in Florida for their Easter school break. While Geoff was away, I busied myself packing away our belongings in preparation for the villa's summer rental. On his return, we entertained our last lot of visitors this spring, when Ann brought her three children, her Mother June, along with Ben and Steph who had just returned from their trip to the States.

Although our un-heated swimming pool hadn't yet been fully warmed up by the Spanish sunshine, the kids didn't seem to mind at all and spent much of their day diving in and hauling themselves out, only to stand around shivering, blue lipped, wrapped in big fluffy beach towels. Meanwhile, Geoff and I carried on with our packing, leaving just enough furniture in the villa for the rental period.

We had taken a gamble and bought another vehicle from a local garage, an ancient, long wheel base, blue, Mercedes van. This, we both agreed, would enable us to take a load of our belongings back to England on this trip, in order to lighten the load when we finally moved out on completion in September. So, with some trepidation, on the 8th May, we left the Spanish villa, each driving a vehicle; I drove the camper and Geoff was at the helm of the old van. We, thankfully, had a good steady run back to Marlow, only encountering one small problem during the 1500 mile trip; one flat tyre on the van.

On the 1st June we took the four older grandchildren on a seaside trip to the south coast. We finally pitched up in Seaford, near Brighton and camped right next to the beach and were lucky enough to experience a few days of unusually good British weather. We had taken all of the kid's bikes with us, tied on the back of the camper, and so they were able to get some great exercise riding their bikes along Seaford's very long and flat promenade. They thoroughly enjoyed the beach too, spending hours paddling in the gentle surf, searching for starfish and crabs and unusual looking shells. They all insisted taking home their catch to show their parents; not the best things to be transporting, at close quarters, in the hot weather we were experiencing. Geoff had his birthday during this trip away, so it was a good excuse, on 2nd June, for us all to visit McDonalds (or Mick Donald's as Ben had always insisted on calling it), for the kids favourite, a Big Mac and fries, accompanied by various dips.

Once home, and having returned all of the grandchildren to their parents, looking rather scruffy and sunkissed but still in one piece, to our delight, we discovered that Christine had organised a trip for Geoff's birthday to the 'Royal Military School of Music' at Nellor Hall, in Twickenham, the famous training school for English Military Bandsmen. We were to attend one of Nellor's summer evening concerts being held in the school's grounds. Christine and Edward organised a delicious champagne picnic for the four of us and drove us up to London. We spent a lovely warm evening watching a variety of Bands march past us playing some very stirring Military music (Geoff's favourite). Taking part in the parades that evening were the Coldstream Guards, The Welsh Guards, The Grenadier Guards, The Jamaican Defence Force, The Royal Tank Regiment, and also a guest band from the German army. The finale was a very rousing performance of Tchaikovsky's '1812 Overture', complete with cannon fire, well at least, accompanying fire works; a perfect end to a wonderful evening.

This years Henley Royal Regatta was held from 30th June to 4th July and Steve, and crew, were entered this time in the Stewards Cup. Instituted in 1841, The Stewards' Challenge Cup for fours is considered second only to the Grand Challenge Cup (for eights) in seniority and is subject to the same rules of entry. In the early days of this race, the boats carried coxswains and, according to Henley Royal Regatta official history, in 1868 W. B. Woodgate competing in the Brasenose four event thought that such an encumbrance seemed unnecessary and instructed the coxswain, F. E. Weatherley, to jump overboard on the word "Go". Lightened by the ejection of this passenger, the Brasenose four went on to win easily - only to be later disqualified. Presentation prizes for a race for fours without coxswains were offered at the next Regatta, but it was not until five years later, in 1873, that the Stewards' Challenge Cup became a coxless race.

On Saturday Steve's opponents were a crew made up of Molesey Boat Club and Star Boat Club and our lads won easily by two and a half lengths. That evening, as usual, we had invited all the children for a sleepover with us in the camper so that they could enjoy the fireworks. During that night we had an horrific storm, with strong winds violently shaking the camper waking up the children. The noise of the storm was accompanied by some loud knocking on the door from some drunken revellers looking for shelter; quite an exciting experience for our youngsters. When at last Sunday morning dawned, the weather was thankfully beginning to clear but it was still very wet under foot. Wearing our Sunday best, we all gingerly picked our way through the wet grass and the puddles to the other side of the river to attend the church service being held as usual at **St Mary's Church** on the bridge at the bottom of **Hart Street** in Henley. After the service, and when the children had been collected by Jane, Geoff and I went into the Stewards' Enclosure to watch the regatta finals.

That afternoon the lads came up against a crew from Denmark, and again won comfortably, this time by one length and later that day, at prize giving, the cup was presented to the boys by Princess Ann. Steve's winning crew had contained a 'new boy' Ed Coode, who was taking Tim Fosters seat. Tim had recently had an operation on his back, and was currently trying to get back to full fitness. We felt very sorry for Tim as this was also a crucial time in the build up to the 2000 Sydney Olympics when all the athletes were looking for Olympic qualification and vying for a seat in a selected boat; we hoped he would soon recover.

In the middle of the following week, we left for Lucerne, with the European weather still generally very unsettled. We arrived on Friday but were too late to see their first race, a heat, but later learned that the crew had gone safely through to the semi-final on Saturday.

In order to secure a parking spot at the rowing venue, we left the camp site relatively early on Saturday, taking our lunch and folding camping chairs with us but more importantly our rain gear, as it was still looking very overcast and dull. The weather in Lucerne in mid summer could be at one extreme or the other, and today, with a strong likelihood of more rain to come, we settled down in a spot close to the lake and huddled together sipping hot coffee from our flask to try to keep warm. The lads were due to row at 3.38pm that afternoon and we began to feel, as the rain started to pour down on us, that it was already beginning to seem like a very long day.

The boys had a hard race that afternoon but they had made it to the final and so, as the rain was still pelting down, we made or way back to the campsite to dry out and to try and get our circulation going once again; we felt damp right through to our bones. Back in the camper as we ate our meal, I remarked how much I was missing the grandchildren being with us. Yesterday had been Natalie's eighth birthday and we had spoken on the phone. For many of the previous years she had accompanied us on this trip to Switzerland and had celebrated her birthday here with us in Lucerne, but she was now of school age and like all the others, had not broken up for her summer holidays yet.

Sunday morning arrived and for today's finals the weather was looking a little better. Our lads were due to row against Norway today at 3.30pm this afternoon. The last time they had met this Norwegian crew, Norway had come in 6th place. The Scandinavians put up a tremendous fight; it was an exciting race, real nail biting stuff, but our boys won by half a length. We began to wonder what other opposition they would be likely to meet at the 1999 World Championships later this year in Canada; it seemed to be getting stronger. We took a leisurely drive back to England, visiting Bad Waldsee and the Black Forest on the way but as the weather was still very changeable, we soon decided to head back to Calais and the return ferry to Britain.

For my birthday this year, Christine and Edward had arranged another trip to Nellor Hall, as we had so enjoyed our last visit here in June. This time they had arranged for us to bring our good friends Queenie, and Arthur along too. On this occasion, as the six of us watched the Military Band play, we enjoyed a fish and chip supper with our champagne. It was 1st August today and we were celebrating my birthday early this year, as on 13th in two weeks time, we would be in Canada.

On the 5th August, Steve and Ann and the children flew out to the pre-World Championship training camp in Canada. We had made arrangements to rent a cottage that was positioned right on the lake, 'Martindale Pond' as it was called, in St. Catharines the largest city in Canada's Niagara Region. This was a large urban area in Ontario and where the rowing championship would be hosted this year and we were due to follow Steve and family out on the 14th August.

The excitement in Britain this August was the forthcoming total eclipse of the Sun, due to take place on 11th August. Jane, David, Ben, and Steph, had gone down to Cornwall to stay with David's brother Alan and his family, as this was apparently the best place in Britain to see it. Edward, being extremely fit, had taken this opportunity to cycle down to Cornwall too and would be joining them there. His four day cycle/camping trip had been quite hard going with a lot of rain on the way. Christine had planned to drive down to meet him there for a few days break afterwards; she had been working and had also felt that to join him on the actual cycle trip would have been just too hard on her legs. Although a little cloudy on the morning of the eclipse, Geoff and I went down to Christine's house in Marlow and the three of us stood together in the her garden and waited for the event. Peering through some protective cardboard glasses that had been given free with newspapers, like millions of others that day, we looked skyward and witnessed a total eclipse of the Sun as the moon passed directly between the Sun and the earth, casting its full shadow over our planet. It became strangely hushed all around us as it became dark for those few seconds; an event I'm pleased to have experienced.

Our flight to Canada on the 14th August was a bit cramped, but bearable. When we arrived in Canada we were met at the airport by Steve, Ann, and the three children, and they took us straight to our rented cottage. It was 32 miles south of Toronto and just 12 miles from the American border, just outside the town of St Catharines, known as 'The Garden City', due to its 1,000 acres of meticulously groomed parks, gardens and trails.

When we arrived at our temporary home, the owners of the cottage, a Mr and Mrs Kelly, showed us around their beautiful house before handing over the keys. Our rented cottage was in a delightful spot with a view looking directly up the rowing course and only yards from the finish line. The Kelly's had a son called Broderick, who Sophie had insisted on calling 'Baldrick', we couldn't help but smile and we hoped that the Kelly's hadn't seen the British comedy series 'Black Adder'. The girls wanted to stay with us that night but Steve and Ann had insisted that we were left alone for one night to get a good rest before taking on their three children for the rest of the World Championships.

The house was very well equipped and of course its position on the lake couldn't have been more perfect. The view through the lounge window, was of the full length of the rowing course, we could almost have watched the racing from our armchairs; what a luxury. The following day, after breakfast, we drove out in our hire car to try to find the University campus where Steve and Ann and all the rowing athletes were being housed and we found it without too much trouble. Ann was working as team doctor again this year and was being kept busy that day, so Steve took us off for the day to see Niagara falls which was only about an hours drive away; a few of the other rowers came with us too. It was a magnificent sight and we all took a boat trip on the "Maid of the Mist" to 'Explore the Roar' as they put it, which took us right underneath the falls. The first Maid of the Mist has been launched here in 1846 and here we were aboard the 7th vessel of the same line, over 150 years later, wearing our Blue plastic Macs, supplied for the trip as some protection against the incredible spray. The Canadian 'Horseshoe Falls' are 170ft high with a massive brink of 2,500 ft, the water coming from four of the five great lakes. Originally 5.5 billion gallons of water per hour flowed over Niagara Falls but nowadays over half of this is diverted for power generation for Canada and The States. We noticed that passengers on other boats from the American side were wearing Red plastic Macs. Looking up at this torrent of water it was almost impossible to believe that anyone had ever wanted to climb inside a wooden barrel and be swept over the falls, as Ann Edison Taylor had done in 1901 and had lived to tell the tale. After our exhilarating trip we returned to our cottage with the three children, we had a meal and after putting Zak to bed, sleepily played some board games with the girls till it was their bedtime; their boundless energy seemed inexhaustible.

The following morning, after breakfast, we went grocery shopping and took a look around the area. Port Dalhousie, where we were staying was a community in St. Catharines which was well known for its waterfront appeal. It was the site of the annual Royal Canadian Henley Regatta, a world-class event that brought over 3,000 athletes from various nations to the city each year, and this year, 1999, it was this site that was hosting the World Rowing Championships. 'The pond', as the locals called it, was also home to the St. Catharines rowing club.

The city's most popular beach was, luckily for us, here too, on the shore of Lake Ontario, located in historic Lakeside Park and where the kids loved playing. The park was also home to an antique Carousel which was carved by Charles I. D. Looff in 1905 and brought to St. Catharines in 1921 and it continued to provide amusement for young and old alike, at just 5 cents a ride. This became a daily outing for the three children along with a regular stop at one of the many ice-cream parlours.

Usually for us, when on one of these trips, we would have first embarked on a fact finding tour, discovering the where, when, and how of the rowing event but this year, everything was on our door step; it could not have been simpler. The cottage was just a short walk from the enclosure and grandstand and each day Geoff would take the three children off early, with Zak in his pushchair and the girls walking , they would enjoy timing their trip; by the time the rowing event was underway, they had got their journey down to a slick two minutes brisk walk from cottage to grandstand. Also at the cottage were lots of toys for the girls to play with which belonged to Broderick, and on the days when their dad wasn't competing, the girls would often prefer to stay at home rather than to go to the rowing enclosure. I didn't mind this either as I could follow the races I was interested in watching from my armchair; we were so near to the finish line.

The 1999 World Rowing Championships started on the 22nd August and would run till the 29th August. On Saturday the 22nd the opening ceremony was held in St Catharines and a large parade marched through the town. The girls were very excited and so we set off early with Zak in his pushchair, hoping to secure a good spot from which to view. The parade consisted of vintage cars, shiny fire engines, marching bands and a variety of floats which had been made by local schools and businesses. It was really interesting and while we were there we saw a few rowing people we knew and would stop to have a quick chat. The kids spotted their mother in the crowd and Ann was then able to spend a little time with her three children as the evening drew to a close, before she had to return to campus and her work and we made our way back to the cottage to put the children to bed.

Monday 23rd August was the start of the rowing. We were up early this morning and of course this is when the 'two minute trip' to the course came into play. After all the practice they'd had with their Granddad, the children loved it, the girls running ahead of Zak's pushchair, showing me the way. Our boys weren't due to row till 11.49am., when they would be rowing in their first heat. They had drawn Lithuania, New Zealand, Poland, Croatia and Uruguay and they led all the way going through to the semi final, all the others would go to the repechage. The lads seemed quite pleased with their row with Ed Coode still in the boat. Tim had managed to reach full fitness but, for this World Championships, he had been put into the eight, I guessed this was to gradually get him back to competition racing after his long lay off. With the days racing over, we returned to the cottage for our lunch. Later that afternoon we took yet another trip to the beach, including enjoying rides on the Carousel and a visit to the Ice cream parlour.

On Wednesday, as there was no rowing today for our boys, we decided to take the children to 'Marineland', Niagara, which was a theme park built around a marine centre. The centre kept Dolphins, Killer and Beluga whales and the children could touch and feed the sea creatures and make contact with the wildlife in the surrounding park. As we entered the grounds, we saw herds of Deer and Elk and a stall selling small bags of feed for them, which visitors could buy. Natalie excitedly ran over to buy a bag of deer food but before she even had time to open her bag, a group a Deer had rushed up and were jostling   to be first in line for a meal. She was so shocked by their sudden rush at her that she dropped the bag and came running back to us looking petrified. Her close encounter was soon forgotten though, after a few rides on the roundabouts and we spent the rest of the day having fun watching the wide variety of animals and sea life.

Thursday 26th August was Semi-final day and again we were up early for breakfast and soon off to the course. The coxless fours race was at 12.30pm with their opponents today being, Belarus, Egypt, Italy, New Zealand and the Netherlands. As their race concluded, amidst great roars from the crowd, having led all the way, they came home to win with the first three crews going straight to the final. The rest of the day was taken up with our usual trip taking Natalie, Sophie and Zak to the beach, the carousel and the ice-cream parlour; tomorrow would be a rest day for the rowers and for us too.

Saturday 28th August was the boy's big day. With our fingers crossed, at 8am we made an early start as we wanted to be sure of a good seat. It was a little bit hectic getting the three children and ourselves out on time but with a scramble we made it to the enclosure: their race was due to start at 10.30am. There in the stands, we again met the French woman who we had first met at last year's World Championships. Once again she made a huge fuss of Zak, whom she said she couldn't believe had grown so much in just one year. She was here again to support her son who was this morning racing again against our lads. We chatted a while with some of the other supporting parents, and then settled down to watch their race, accompanied by the usual knots in our stomachs.

The line up was New Zealand, Norway, Italy, Australia, and France and with the race soon under way, they were leading at every marker, closely followed by the Italians and Australia. At the line Great Britain won in a time of 5.48.57; they had put in a huge effort and had done it once again; gold for Great Britain, silver for Australia, and Bronze for Italy. This time next year, God willing, we would all be at the Olympics in Sydney and we began to wonder if Steve would manage to stay healthy and be able to achieve his 5th Olympic Gold medal; the one he now wanted so badly.

The whole family was elated; we went in search for our boy, to congratulate him and to celebrate. We had lunch with Ann and Steve and the kids and then returned to the cottage to pack for our return journey to the UK. Later that day Steve and Sophie took us to the airport while Natalie and Ann took care of Zak. The three children were staying on with their parents for a holiday all together which they had planned to spend by a lake further north in Canada. We said our goodbyes and boarded our plane back to the UK.

We had an uneventful, if somewhat cramped flight home and on our arrival at Gatwick we discovered that our luggage hadn't arrived; we were told that it had been lost on route, we hoped, not over the Atlantic. Jane, waiting at Gatwick to meet us, had begun to think that we had missed the flight, as we had taken so long to get through customs to the waiting area. The following day, after a few phone calls to the airline, our cases were located; they were still in Montreal. We were told that our cases would be delivered to us at 4pm that afternoon but as we had already planned on leaving Marlow Bottom to catch the 5 pm. ferry back to France; we were forced to alter our plans. In the end, we finally left Jane's home at 5pm in order to catch our ferry from Dover at 8.15pm; this we only just made.

We drove back to Spain, with the intention of putting the final seal on the sale of our villa. Our first job was to sell all the furniture that we had left in the villa for its summer rental; the remainder we donated to The Red Cross, a charity shop in our local town. Finally, and at 3pm on the 6th September 1999, we signed the necessary papers and our Spanish home of ten years was passed over to Mr and Mrs Dean; it was quite a sad moment really, a lot of water had passed beneath our family's bridge in that decade. It was a strange feeling too, as we were now homeless. We went to spend a couple of days with Pam and Peter, our good friends and near neighbours, in the Jalon valley. Here it was planned that we would leave the camper at their villa while we returned to England for a short time. Our intention on this trip to the UK was to purchase a house, firstly as an investment but secondly one which we could let out while we travelled. We soon found a house near to Christine, so she could keep an eye on it while we were away. It was a very good deal, the vendors wanted a quick sale as they had already found a house which they desperately wanted and to make this purchase even more tempting, there was no chain involved that might hold things up; we went ahead and in just six short weeks we had become the new owners. We set to work immediately cleaning, decorating and furnishing our new purchase from top to bottom. Geoff and I, with Chris and Edward's help decorated, tidied the garden and laid a new front path and within 3 weeks it was put up for rent. We had already promised to return to Spain to take care of Pam and Peter's villa and to dog sit for them while they went on holiday to Germany and so, leaving the property rental in Christine's capable hands, we flew back to Spain to take a much needed rest. After the exhausting whirlwind of the previous few weeks it was truly wonderful to just spend our time swimming, reading, and taking long lazy strolls walking the dog in the autumn sunshine.

When Pam and Peter returned from their holiday, we said our goodbyes and moved south, in our camper, to La Manga near Murcia on Spain's south-eastern Costa Cálida. Here, it had been arranged, that we would meet up with Steve, Ann and the three children. Steve had been asked to attend a celebrity golf tournament being held at the La Manga Club to play alongside Bruce Forsyth, the British showman and entertainer and Colin Montgomerie 'Monty' the Scottish professional golfer. We were going to help out with the children and hopefully would get to watch some great golf into the bargain. It was really nice to meet all the celebrities and to spend a few days with Steve and family. At the end of the tournament we continued south to Malaga and dropped in to see Joan and Ray Cook, in **Rincon de la Victoria,** where they now lived. Joan was Robert Haley's mum, Steve school and rowing friend who had tragically died. Joan had moved out to Spain, some years before, to be near her daughter Andrea. Andrea had married a Spaniard and they had a son whom they had called Roberto after his late uncle.

Portugal was our next destination and, once again, we had planned to visit some old friends from Marlow Bottom who now lived there, and who we had not seen for sixteen years. John and Dawn Badrick had run the local newsagents in Marlow Bottom. John, an expert welder, had kindly made a custom roof rack so that Steve could carry his boat on top of his car. The couple had moved to Portugal and had opened two restaurants; both of their son's were trained Chef's. The whole family was extremely hospitable to us and we had a great time, spending four days with them exploring the Algarve, the southernmost region of mainland Portugal. The weather was superb as we travelled along some of the Algarve's 200 mile coastline.

Amongst the places we visited were Albufeira, a thriving seaport and now a favourite holiday destination, famous for its beautiful beaches, and the town of Carvoeiro, long considered as an excellent area for tourists to acquire property due to this areas many small sandy beaches which are surrounded by high cliffs, most of which have been eroded to create dark caves accessible only at low tide. The costal city of Lagos was next, where Vasco da Gama sailed from in 1499 on his historic and epic voyage of discovery. We had come here on a family holiday in the 60's, many years before, when our children were still young. The place had changed somewhat in those thirty odd years and a beautiful new marina had now been constructed but the ancient part of the city has been well preserved and there were still many sign of its ancient past even a building dating originally back to around 1445 which is recorded as being Europe's first building used as a slave market.

We said goodbye to Dawn and John and drove on towards Lisbon, through the beautiful mountain area of 'Sierra de Monchique'. After stopping 115 miles south of Lisbon, to mend a puncture on the camper, we found a lovely spot called Vila Nova de Milfontes, which was cornered between the Atlantic Ocean and the Mira River, the estuary of which for centuries has provided shelter from the Atlantic for Portuguese fishing fleets. It had soft white-sand beaches that lined both sides of the river. It was delightful and we decided to stay here for a couple of days, before travelling on to Lisbon.

Lisbon was next on our schedule, the westernmost capital in mainland Europe, located in the west Portugal on the Atlantic Ocean coast where the river Tagus flows into the Atlantic Ocean. We stayed here for a week, taking tours around this interesting city that had in the past been ruled by Romans, Christians and Moors; it's been Portugal's capital since 1147. All of these ancient civilisations had left their mark and some beautiful architecture and gardens still survived in the old quarters with their typical tile covered building facades and narrow medieval streets.

We travelled on to Sinta, a beautiful place, with lush wooded areas, way up in the mountains but with fantastic views of the coastline. The autumn colours made it very pretty and we explored the area by taking a ride in one of the many horse-pulled Landau's seeing the marvellous manor-houses that were located within the grounds of century old farms. We were very impressed by Pena Palace, a royal residence, and also the art and toy museums. The surrounding area was becoming quite well known as an excellent winegrowing region and we noticed a few quarries that produced marble; we were most impressed.

Travelling west across the country, and inland, to lake **Barragem de Odivelas, we arrived at this** very remote natural park miles from city-life and in a very quiet and beautiful landscape. We camped lakeside and were fascinated by the extensive bird life here; there were storks, egrets, herons and many more that I couldn't identify. Geoff tried out his fishing skills and he caught two, quite large fish, we weren't sure what they were but we prepared them and then cooked them on the barbecue; I don't think that Geoff was too impressed with their taste. While staying here, we met a man from Henley, who turned out to be Mathew Pinsent hairdresser; what a small world it is.

After a week relaxing in the sunshine, by this lovely lake, we moved south, to a town called Arronches near Portalegre. As we traveled through this area, it seemed extremely rural and quite poor, as did most of the Portuguese inland municipalities. Here the local people relied on agriculture, with cork growing and production being their main source of income. The region was also famous for its tapestry, and we visited a tapestry workshop, but as today was Sunday, we found that they were only open for sales, and sadly, no demonstrations were taking place. Their intricate handiwork was expensive but really lovely. Before we left Portugal, we stopped at the town of Elvas, which sits just seven and a half miles east of the Spanish border. This is one of the greatest and most heavily fortified frontier towns in Europe, with 17th century military fortifications that are among the most sophisticated and best preserved in the continent. We parked the camper under the towering 'Amoreira Aqueduct', the city's most famous sight, completed in 1622. Lying outside the city walls, this incredible feat of engineering, at four and a half miles in length, took over 100 years to complete and has no less than 843 arches, in some places rising to over 100ft; to this day it still brings water to town. We browsed around a local market, and wondered through the narrow streets of the old town.

Later that day, we left Portugal near Bragança and once again entered Spain, just south of the Culebra Mountains. We had now climbed to an elevation of 700m and the weather was turning very cold and frosty; we had traveled over 500 km from Lisbon. Central Spain can have extremes of weather and here the climate, influenced by the distance from the coast and the elevation, meant long rigorous winters were normal and snow in winter was very common; it could last for several days with winter temperatures dipping to well below zero: at least we were warm and cozy in our well insulated German camper that had be manufactured especially made for the European winters.

This was wild country too and here wildlife in the shape of golden eagles, falcons, wolves, otters and wild boar still enjoyed their freedom. The change in scenery was stunning and we marvelled at the incredible views as we drove through the mountains. As we descended and drove higher up into Northern Spain, the weather turned quite wet. Once in France we hit stormy weather, and so with Geoff putting his foot down, over the next two days, we headed for the cross channel ferry at Calais. We eventually took a late night ferry but headed into a force eight gale; later crossings were suspended. We were really glad to be on dry land once again, and from Dover, we headed back to Furze Farm, arriving in Marlow Bottom during the early hours.

With Christmas now almost upon us, Christine and Edward, on the 19th December, gave another one of their parties, organising all the children in the family to put on a show for us and their parents; this year it was entitled. 'The 20th Century'. It was really good and the kids all enjoyed dressing up and doing little sketches and singing songs from each of the decades of the now fading century.

We were by now temporarily living in the camper at the farm. We had decided not to settle down again in Britain just yet, as we had plans to go out to Australia next spring to spend the six months leading up to the 2000 Olympics touring around and visiting my family near Sydney. On December 21st, we had quite a heavy fall of snow, making it difficult to get up and down our steep drive. Steve Ann and their children left for a skiing holiday over Christmas and we moved into their house to look after the dog and the parrot. Chris and Edward also went away for a few days, and so we enjoyed our Christmas Day at Jane and David's home celebrating with them and the twins.

Steve and family returned from skiing on December 30th; the children were really excited because they still had all of their Christmas presents to open. On New Years Eve, Steve, Ann, and Natalie, had been invited to the Millennium Dome in London, along with other celebrities, to see the building officially opened and to welcome in the new Millennium. The large dome-shaped building, the largest of its type in the world, had been built to house the Millennium Experience, a major exhibition celebrating the beginning of the third millennium. It was a really grand affair, with the Queen and her family in attendance; Natalie loved it, I think it was the latest she had ever been allowed to stay up. Located on the Greenwich Peninsula in South East London, the exhibition opened to the public the following day, on 1st January 2000 was planned to run until 31 December 2000. The dome appears as a large white marquee with twelve 100 m-high yellow support towers, one for each month of the year, or each hour of the clock face, representing the role played by Greenwich Mean Time. In plan view it is circular, 365 m in diameter, one metre for each day of the year, with scalloped edges. It has become one of the United Kingdom's most recognizable landmarks and can easily be seen on aerial photographs of London. Its exterior is reminiscent of the Dome of Discovery built for the Festival of Britain in 1951 which Geoff and I had attended with our good friends Queenie and Arthur.

Apart from the dome itself, the project had included the reclamation of the entire Greenwich Peninsula. This land was previously derelict and contaminated by toxic sludge from an earlier gasworks that had operated from 1889 to 1985. The clean-up operation was seen by the then Conservative Deputy Prime Minister, Michael Heseltine, as an investment that would add a large area of useful land to the crowded capital. This was billed as part of a larger plan to regenerate a large, sparsely populated area to the east of London and south of the River Thames, an area initially called the East Thames Corridor but latterly marketed as the "Thames Gateway". The incoming Labour government elected in 1997 under Tony Blair greatly expanded the size, scope and funding of the project. It also significantly increased expectations of what would be delivered. Just before its opening Blair claimed the Dome would be "a triumph of confidence over cynicism, boldness over blandness, excellence over mediocrity".

That evening, Geoff and I, Sophie, and Zak, all went to a party at Jane's home. We all had a great evening, seeing the old year out, and the new one in. It was a special one for us, for two reasons. One, we were moving into the year 2000 and two, it was also the Sydney Olympics this autumn. As usual, our thoughts were of course with all our family but especially with Steve, would he be able to pull of his dream of a 5$^{th}$ gold medal; if his sheer determination and the support of his entire family had any thing to do with it, he surely could.

# Chapter Twenty Two
## The Millennium 2000

### *Meet the Family*

We were especially excited about this New Year, we had made our decision to travel out to Australia at the beginning of April, therefore organizing our trip was high on our 'to do' list. There wasn't now much time left to book our flights, including a stop on the way there and on our way back, to break up the long flight. We had to organise our transport for when we got there and most importantly, try and book the accommodation ahead, for all the family when they came out to stay with us during the Olympics. As well as this, we also wanted to book flights and some accommodation and plan our route, for a three week tour around New Zealand, which we had decided would be a good idea to include on this mammoth trip, since we were in that part of the world.

The 30th January brought some very sad news; firstly it was the death of Queenie's father, Fred, who had been such a nice man and whom I had known since I was a teenager. The same day Jane's best friend, Jackie Sherry got in touch with her, to tell the family of her partner, Rod's sudden death, having suffered a fatal heart attack. Rod had been only fifty two years old and he had been Godfather to the twins, Ben, and Steph. Rods death hit us all really hard, he had been such a nice guy, the twins had loved him, and he had been an avid follower of Steve's career; he had felt like one of the family. Jackie and Rod had planned to go to Australia with Jane, David and the twins later that year to visit the Sydney Olympics to support Steve; we were devastated, we would really miss him.

Ann celebrated her 40th birthday on the 8th February, and so, on the following Saturday, the 12th February, she held a party in a large marquee on the lawn at their home in Marlow Bottom. The party had a 70's theme and everyone got into the spirit of things and had dressed up wearing floral shirts and wide flared trousers; Steve wore a Rod Stewart wig and nobody recognised him. There was a live band and a disco and dancing that went into the night with lots of their rowing friends in attendance. Just after midnight and while we were dancing to 'Walking on the Moon' by The Police, the real police arrived to ask if we could turn the music volume down as a neighbour had complained.

Our trip to Australia was booked for 2nd April; we had chosen to go out via Singapore, including a few days for a stopover there, and we would return, six months later, via Hong Kong. A lot of organisation had taken place, pre-booking our Olympic tickets for us and the family, a few months trip up the east coast of Australia before the games were due to start, our transport in several locations, our long term health insurance, our accommodation for six months, even down to what we should pack. As usual we had a disagreement about this last item, as Geoff would always say that I taken too much, where ever we went, even if I had been able to fit it all in a shoe box - be prepared, that's my motto. He was right though, it was better to travel light, and of course we could buy anything that we needed, once we had arrived.

Finally we set off to Heathrow, driven by Jane, with Ben, Steph, and Christine, there to see us off. We had already said our goodbyes to Steve and family, as due to the Easter holidays, they had already flown out to Spain on holiday. At the airport, we were soon called through to the departure lounge and so we said our final farewell to our daughters and grandchildren. It didn't feel so bad parting this time, even though we were to be away a long time, but I think that was because everyone was so excited about coming out to Australia too, in just five months time; today, everyone's frame of mind was positive. Our flight to Singapore would take about thirteen hours, so we settled down to read, and then to sleep. It was a pleasant and uneventful trip, and we arrived at 6.15pm, not feeling too exhausted. We had no delay getting through customs and we were promptly met by our driver and taken to our hotel. We tried to stay awake a while longer by taking a stroll around the hotel; we had a light snack and then we fell into bed and enyoyed another eight hours sleep.

The following morning, now feeling much brighter, we booked a city tour. We felt that this would be the best way to get an overview of this interesting city and to feel the contrast of the old and the new, the blend of east and west, especially as our time here was short. Our tour began with a visit to the Chinatown Heritage Centre where we discovered the journeys, beliefs and the myths of early Chinese migrants who had made their way to Singapore, giving us a keen insight into the lives of these people and the hardships that they endured living in the dark and cramped quarters they had built in Chinatown.

We then visited The Singapore Botanic Gardens, the 'green lung', as they put it, of this city centre. Here we experienced a little of the calm and serenity of this huge 52 hectares garden. Located within the grounds of this park was the National Orchid Garden and here we were amazed by the wide variety and colours of Orchids on display; they were really beautiful. We then stopped for something to eat.

After lunch we visited Changi Prison Museum and viewed the replica of the Chapel which was used during World War II; en-route our guide had recounted the darkest times of the war. We made an interesting tour of the cells, and heard stories of the war years and the British imprisonment under the Japanese. We also saw the Tampines Chinese Temple that houses 9 deities and the oldest Hindu Temple in Singapore, the magnificent Sri Mariamman Temple.

The following morning, 5th April was our 48th wedding anniversary, and day two of our tour, this time called "Round the Island tour', we were first taken to see the colourful city fruit and vegetable markets. We then travelled to the West Coast of Singapore to the Ming Village, the cultural & heritage centre of China, and the only one remaining of it is kind. Here we were fascinated to watch the whole pottery making process of these beautiful vases, from making the mould to firing. We then watched the artists skilfully working, using their intricate brushwork, on plates, vases and various pots in all shapes and sizes, reproducing original designs from centuries ago.

Next we visited the largest and one of the oldest, Chinese temples in Singapore, the Thien Hock Keng Temple which was more than 160 years old. Unfortunately, here we were only allowed to look around the outside, as this was during a week of special prayers; it was incredible to think that this unique wooden structure and wood carvings were built and assembled without using any nails.

Changi war memorial was our next stop, a homage paid to the 23,000 troops and civilians who had lost their lives when the Japanese had invaded unexpectedly, by the back door. They had approached through jungle and swampland that was thought to be impenetrable; then the Japanese had cut off their water supply. We saw the Alexander Military hospital built for British military personnel from British Malaya, Singapore and the Far East, where 250 patients and staff members had been bayoneted and massacred on 14 February 1942 by Japanese Imperial Forces. Among the patients in the Hospital were a four Company force nicknamed the Plymouth Argylls who were survivors of the 'Prince of Wales' and 'Repulse' which were sunk by Japanese torpedo bombers off the coast of Kuantan, Pahang, on 10 December 1941. The British troops had tried to surrender when a lieutenant had carried a white flag to meet the Japanese; The Japanese had killed him, then removed about 400 patients and staff and locked them up in a staff bungalow nearby. Next day these people were taken out in small groups and shot. The bodies were buried in a mass grave. On 15 February when Japanese General Yamashita nicknamed "The Tiger of Malaya".heard of the massacre in the Hospital, he went round the beds of the remaining patients and saluted them; he apologized profusely for the shocking conduct of his soldiers. He brought some crates of canned fruits and opened them with his bayonet and served the fruit to the patients. Later when he learnt that some Japanese soldiers were looting the Hospital he ordered them to be executed; the Japanese responsible were beheaded; we were told that seven days later Singapore had fallen to the invaders.

After that most sobering visit, we were taken to a Malay village. The Malays had been the native inhabitants of Singapore but after the British dispersed the Malay floating village at the mouth of the Singapore River in the 1840s, the Malays, together with the large influx of Malaysians and Indonesians, congregated in Geylang. In the early 1920s, Kampong Gelam's Malay population moved out en-mass to Geylang Serai as a consequence of the keen competition for land. We saw for ourselves that the Malay influence was still strong in Geylang Serai and was reflected in the restaurants and shops specialising in Malay cuisine and ethnic goods, arts and crafts. We then returned to Changi to take a bay trip by boat to see the fish farms there. All the workers lived on the water and after catching their daily haul of fish would hang them out to dry, ready for packing and selling, the boats we were taken out on, had been originally, tugs that had been used to unload ships before the docks had been built. We both thought that the tours had been very interesting and had really given us an insight into the lives of the people of Singapore; our one regret, there hadn't been time for an anniversay 'Singapore Sling' at Raffels. On returning to our hotel, we only just had time for a quick shower and a light meal, before we were off again to catch our next flight to Cairns for a five day, and by now, much needed holiday.

Our flight touched down in Darwin, the capital city of the Northern Territory, Australia to refuel and then we flew on to Cairns a regional city in Far North Queensland, on the east coat, 1500 miles north of Sydney. On arrival at our hotel, we were told to stay in our room as a cyclone was imminent, the second in two weeks. On our journey from the airport we could see that there had been a lot of damage done to trees, in the area, and our five days spent in this tropical region were mostly wet and warm. We were told that the wet season here, bringing tropical monsoons, usually ran from December to April, with a relatively dry season from May to November; we were just a little early. We had heard that the Monsoon that had passed through in February had been called 'Cyclone Steve', which we thought was a good omen. It had caused major flooding, uprooting trees and powerlines; the sugar cane damage alone had been estimated at $20 million Australian Dollars. A record flood level of 12.4m (41ft) had been reached at nearby Mareeba; we hoped that later this year our Steve would cause a storm too, not here, but in Sydney. Later that day our cyclone was downgraded to a tropical storm so we thought that perhaps tomorrow we would be able to get out and about.

After a good long rest on our first day here, the following morning we took a trip up the local Barron River by boat, supposedly, to see the crocodiles. We were told that they must have moved out of the area due to the storms so, most unusually, we didn't catch sight of any that day. After Captain James Cook's discovery in 1770, it took a further 100 years before white settlement took a firm hold in the region, due in no small part to the dense vegetation, severe cyclones and the associated wet season, treacherous reefs, disease and dangerous animals such as crocodiles. The town of Cairns had started life in 1876 as a 'tent city'; the first structures to be built were wharves and sheds on the sheltered port provided by Trinity Bay. There were many Chinese and Malaysian immigrants living in the area then as they had come to work in the gold fields and the copper and tin mines, and as the towns grew they developed their own businesses and living areas. The development of a railway line that serviced the Atherton Tableland taking up workers and supplies and bringing back tin and timber was a feat in its own right as Cairns is surrounded by a very steep and densely vegetated mountain range which made travel to and from the coast almost impossible; the railway solved this and Cairns was established. The town continued to grow, and fishing and pearling became large industries and due to its rich soil the flat coastal lands became major sugar growing plantations and still today sugar cane farms dominate the entire North Queensland coastal strip.

Next we took a trip to Kuranda Village, the picturesque mountain retreat, 25km northwest of Cairns. We went by train on Kuranda's Historic Scenic Railway, taking us through the World Heritage Rainforest, crossing narrow gorges, with at times some magnificent views; at one point we saw Green Island out on the Barrier Reef. The track twisted and turned through the mountain, at times you could see the engine and the last carriage at the same time; it was a magnificent fete of engineering completed in1891and still everything had been kept very smart and in the Victorian style.

Once at the top we wandered around the shops with their exotically handcrafted goods, some Aboriginal artefacts; there was also some restaurants and coffee shops. To complete the trip we descended again, this time over the rainforest on the Skyrail Rainforest Cableway;

another great experience, just above the tops of the trees. We stopped off half way down to walk around and view the famous giant water fall of Barron Falls from the board walks through the trees.

North Queensland has continued to grow and develop and after World War II it started to become popular as a holiday destination for other Australians. Awareness of the Great Barrier Reef had sparked a tourism growth and in 1984 an international airport opened in Cairns and a major tourism boom began which converted this sleepy regional town to the thriving city of today. We thought that we couldn't leave here without making a visit ourselves to The Reef so the following day we made a full day's trip to Green Island, with meal provided on board a catamaran. I'm not a great sailor and enjoy swimming in the sea even less, so when we had a choice of activity, I chose the glass bottomed boat to view the pretty coloured fish and coral and Geoff tried the snorkelling. He really enjoyed himself but had to admit that it was not as easy as it looked. Afterwards, we sat on the beach for a while, but soon it became too hot and as I could feel that we were in danger of sunburn we climbed back on board for a barbecued lunch and shelter from the fierce sun. Delivered safely back to the mainland and having suffered no seasickness we felt that it had been a lovely day. We set about packing as tomorrow, with our five day's over, we would once again be back on a plane, this time to Sydney. Our expected rest had not materialised, as there had been so much to see and do; perhaps we could get some rest in Sydney

I was feeling quite excited on our flight to Sydney, as this would be the first time that I had met my relatives. My mother's sister Gladys had emigrated from Birmingham in The Midlands to Sydney, Australia at the tender age of eighteen; to the other side of the world. She had made this epic voyage all alone, after six of her friends had all backed out of the trip at the last minute; a very courageous thing to do for such a young woman to do in 1925. Once in Australia she had soon met, and later married, her husband Frank and they'd gone on to have six children, five boys and one girl, whom they'd called Joan. Joan, one year my senior and I had corresponded regularly, ever since I was thirteen years old, and so now aged 69, I was really looking forward to meeting her at last, and of course her husband Bert, and her three children, Warren, Wendy, and Glenn.

On the 11$^{th}$ April 2000, as we came into land, we had an amazing view of Sydney; just below us were Darling Harbour, The Sydney Bridge and the docks and the most iconic sight of all, The Sydney Opera House. On landing we collected our luggage, and as we walked up a very long ramp, at the top, through the glass screen, I could see four people waiting together, standing side by side. Although I had not met my family in person before there was no mistaking them from the photographs we had been sent over the years. We were all so excited, we kissed and hugged and could not stop talking.

Joan and Bert lived with their son Glen; a two hour drive south of Sydney, on the coast, at a place called Dapto, a developing residential area on the western shore of Lake Illawarra and thought to be named from the Aboriginal word meaning "water plenty". The village of Dapto had once been a small mining, timber cutting and farming community but now had developed into a large town with shops and beautiful parks. We stopped at a few places on route along the coast, to see the magnificent views. Geoff had met Joan previously, when he had called in to see my family whilst he was travelling with the Merchant Navy. They had both been about nineteen then, it was just after we had met. They both remembered each other from then and Joan said how little Geoff had changed in 50 years.

Wendy, Joan's, daughter, lived not far away from her parents, and had a lovely house on Lake Illawarra, a large coastal lagoon, near the city of Wollongong about 100 km south of Sydney, New South Wales. We were to stay here at her house as she had the most space and we were made extremely comfortable, being given our own en-suite bedroom and lounge. Lake Illawarra has a narrow tidal entrance to the sea at Windang and the huge 14 square mile lake itself is very shallow, with an average depth of only 2.5 metres. There was a huge variety of birds here at the lake including pelicans, cormorants, black swans, black ducks, grey teal ducks, herons, ibises and spoonbills to name but a few; an ornithologists dream. The lake is also used for a variety of water sports, including sailing, canoeing, water skiing and fishing and a great place for walks and cycling.

Wendy's family consisted of her husband Wally, their two boys, Paul,

Scott, and one daughter, Danielle. Paul, and Danielle, both lived away from home, Scot, their youngest, at just sixteen years old and still living at home. When Scot wasn't at school, he was out surfing and spear fishing along the coast; a true Aussie. Paul their eldest son, still single, had a shop in Penrith, up in the Blue Mountains close to where the Olympic Rowing course was to be. Danielle, their daughter, was expecting her first baby shortly.

Wally, Wendy's husband, was of Dutch decent, and had emigrated here with his family when he was eight years old, along with his nine brothers and one sister. He had worked as a minor all his working life, as most men in this area did, but just like the British mining industry had suffered, it too was beginning to fall into decline. He felt that regular work would not last for many more years; the company that he worked for had already talked about closing down completely, from the way that he spoke, redundancy could not come soon enough for him.; it was a hard life. The only other industry in this area, along the coast at Wollongong, was the Steel works, but this too was also in decline.

After settling in, we were at last able to take the rest we were longing for and we really began to relax. After a few days, Joan and Bert, suggested a trip south, down the coast, to Batemans Bay. This is where their eldest son Warren lived, with his wife Maureen, and their children, Lisa, Alice and Greg. They lived in a lovely property with land that ran down to the river, where, during the summer, they boated and swam. While we were here we met one of Joan's brothers, my cousin Brian, and his wife June. They lived in Moruya, a nearby town, and had two grown up children, Michael, and Karon, both now married with two children a piece; my Aussie family was growing by the day. The name of Moruya apparently came from the Aboriginal name 'Mherroyah' meaning resting place of black swans, which were very common in the district.

My Aunt Gladys and Uncle Frank had, many years before, purchased a sixty three acre farm, in New South Wales, which they had named Bimbimby Farm. It was fairly remote and out in the 'bush' and even had an old gold mine on it. They had used the farm as a week end retreat and had spent as much time as they could there, finally moving there totally, when they retired. The whole family now used it regularly and they all seemed to have plans to move here in their retirement too. The farm had now been split between two of the sons, Brian, and John. John already lived on the farm in his parents' old bungalow which had originally been a coach house and post office from the early days of British settlement, and was said to be haunted. We heard some of the family stories of events that had taken place particularly while they had all still been children, and which seemed to have no logical explanation.

Brian was planning for the day when he could build his new house on his half of the farm, which was for now, mainly covered in Eucalyptus, 'Gum' trees as they called them; a lot of the trees had already been cleared a while ago and sold for timber. Through the entire length of their land ran a stream, near to the old gold mine, and this they had dammed, at one spot, to form a pond, which they used for swimming during the hot summer months. It reminded me of that scene from 'Crocodile Dundee' when the girl bends down to the water's edge to splash her face and the enormous crocodile came from nowhere to grab her necklace and tries to pull her in; I'm not sure I wanted to swim.

We stayed with Brian and June in Moruya, and visited the family farm most days. Every weekend, all of the family and their kids would turn up and we would spend time chatting and finding out about each others lives, while eating feshly cooked food from improvised barbecue fires made from twigs and dead tree branches which Geoff was put in charge of lighting. We were shown such hospitality by my folks and they really spoilt us too, taking us out to various places up and down the east coast not far from Sydney. With our expert local guides we got to explore the whole area and in such perfect weather too.

Australia was now approaching its autumn, but the weather we were experiencing was really nice and it was, at times, still quite hot. We were told that the Sydney area had a mild, sunny, Mediterranean-like climate and in November to March the temperatures could regularly hit 35°C. They expected their wettest months to be mainly between April and June when, they said, a waterproof jacket was useful but most winter days were pleasantly warm. Even in mid-winter, an overcoat was not necessary during the day, when temperatures regularly were in the region of 21-27°C. They told us not to get fooled by this though as some winters days could be damp and chilly and winter nights were very likely to be cold. It was strange to think that everything was turned on its head, here 'downunder'.

After a couple of weeks we returned 'up country' to Dapto, and we began to look around for a hire vehicle in order to travel further up the east coast. We wanted to see as much as we could while we were here and we still had a few months before we'd have to be back in Sydney for the Olympics. We found a company that hired out small camper vans, and sealed a deal to hire one for a couple of months. First we decided, before starting our trip north, we'd like to take a closer look at this beautiful city of Sydney and before it got too busy with the influx of tourists expected for the games; we booked to stay in the city for three days at the Mackenzie Hotel.

We had a really great time here, just being 'regular' tourists. We spent a little time being entertained by the many buskers along Central Quay, wandered the Harbour area and took a tour of the famous Sydney Opera house. We had great fun exploring the historic area of the city, known as 'The Rocks', with its cobblestone streets and old pubs. This was where the first settlers who arrived in Sydney had lived and worked and a lot of the original sandstone buildings from that time had been preserved and had now been turned into museums, shops, and cafes.

One day, while we were strolling around the city we came across a large parade of all the Australian Armed Forces that had just returned from a deployment in East Timor, a politically troubled island which lies off the northern coast of Western Australia. It was a really colourful site and local school children had been bussed in to the city to line the streets and wave their Australian flags in recognition of their troops' efforts.

Once Back in Illawarra, after gathering together with the family for a few more trips and barbecues, we started the preparation for our journey by catching the train to Sydney and taking a taxi to the hire company. Once we had looked over, the camper van we signed all the necessary insurance papers and finding our way out of the city drove back to Dapto to spend our last day with Joan while loading the camper for our trip up north.

Our expedition would take us north of Sydney so we could explore the rest of New South Wales and Queensland, Australia's second largest state, directly north of N.S.W and bordered to the east by the Pacific Ocean and the Coral Sea. This marginal sea encompasses the Great Barrier Reef, the world's largest coral reef system with its 900 islands stretching for over 1,600 miles and some of this we were determined to see.

On Sunday the 7$^{th}$ May 2000, we set off driving north through Sydney and taking the main coast road, The Pacific Highway. Our first stop was at a place called Mooney Mooney, a beautiful spot on the river, so we decided to take a break and have some lunch. While we were here we noticed a road sign for a town sign to Toukley and Geoff remembered that this was a town where a friend of his lived. Although they hadn't been in touch for some years, as we had his address with us, we decided to call in as we passed and pay him a visit. When we arrived at his house, no one was at home but a neighbour saw us knocking and came to speak with us. He told us that sadly Geoff's friend had recently died and his wife was away, in The Blue Mountains, visiting their daughter, who was just about to have a baby. We made a decision to call in again here later, on our way back down the coast or, we thought, better still to call in at the daughter's house in the Blue Mountains later, as that was the place where our rented house would be during the Olympics in September.

We resumed our journey hugging the coast, arriving at Swansea where we booked into our first camp for the night; we were allocated a spot right on the edge of the lake Macquarie by Pelican Inlet which is notable for, well, its pelicans. There were many other birds here too which we had not seen before like storks and egrets and it was fascinating to see that some of the Pelicans had built their nests on top of tall street lamps. It looked almost impossible for these large nests to be stable so far up in the air and subject, at times, to the strong winds coming in from the sea but we were told that this was a common occurrence and that the Pelicans would lay their eggs in these high rise nests, on these substitute trees, and safely hatch them out probably assisted by the heat of the lamps.

The following day 9th May, we made a stop in the town of Newcastle to do some shopping. This area was famous for its great surfing beaches and we were coming into The Hunter Valley region, noted for its wine growing. During the afternoon the weather took a turn for the worse and we thought it best that we pulled over and stoped for the night at Port Macquarie. This town had been founded as a convict settlement in 1821 and was one of the oldest towns in the state; it was now a major holiday resort.

Moving on the next day, we arrived at Coffs Harbour, a banana growing area and we calculated that we had travelled over 550 km north of Sydney. This was a very good place for shopping with huge retail areas just off the motorway so we stopped to top up our larder. Afterwards, while we sat drinking a cup of tea, we could see a storm in the distance, heading for the shore, moving in from the sea. We quickly moved on again hoping to miss it and as we left the outskirts, just north of the city and still on The Pacific Highway, we came across the biggest banana I had ever seen, an enormous yellow concrete structure and one of Australia's 'Big' icons. We later learned that there are over 150 of these 'Big Things', as they are called in Australia; we were to see a few of them on this trip. They had started out as a tourist draw and have now become something of a cult phenomenon and are now being heritage-listed. The Big Banana was the first to be built in 1964 and is the biggest at 13m x 5m.

Before long it started to get dark and it was by now almost impossible to see the road ahead due to the lashing rain so we dived in to the nearest lay-by and camped there for the night. In the morning we awoke and peered out of the camper and felt that we had somehow mysteriously been transported to India during the night; there in front of us was an enormous building just like the Taj Mahal, a spectacular pure white Temple, with golden domes. We had found our way to the town of Woolgoolga or Woopi, as it is affectionately known by the locals. We discovered that 50% of the local population here was Sikh, and that they owned 90% of the local banana farms. The early Sikh migrants had come here in the 1940's to pre-Federation Australia as free settlers when there was no restrictive immigration policy; leaving their families behind they came to make their fortune. Some returned home when they made good but the majority of them developed a love and attachment to this country and its people and had remained to lay the foundations for the Australian Sikh community. Initially they worked as labourers on the banana plantations, but later acquired leasehold and freehold to banana plantations and their descendants had now become local solicitors, teachers, doctors, accountants and policemen.

After breakfast we moved about 30 miles further up the coast and came across a little town named Corindi Beach, a few miles off the main highway. This looked like a lovely place to stay for a while so we booked into the small local campsite which was perched right on the cliff tops, over looking the beach and beautiful blue sea. We spent a lazy few days here just resting. We walked the beach each morning after breakfast and every afternoon after lunch, collecting shells, watching the dolphins playing in the surf and sitting in the sunshine on the beach reading books. While here, we met another camper, a Dutch woman who stayed here every winter in her caravan. She told us some really interesting stories of the days, when she had been a teenager in Indonesia, under Japanese occupation and had been in a prison camp; she now lived in Sydney during the summer months. We would regularly listen to the local radio each day and we heard a report of sharks that were chasing shoals of fish towards the beach, and the fish were jumping out of the water on to the sand and being picked up by the locals; an easy way of collecting supper we thought but it gave us no encouragement to take a swim.

After almost a week of just lazing about, we thought we had better get on the road again. Sometime after travelling through the beautiful beach areas of Byron Beach and Coolangatta, known as the gateway to Australia's world famous Gold Coast region, we crossed the state border into south east Queensland. We drove on through Brisbane making for Bribie Island, connected to the main land by a long bridge that had been built in 1963. It had been named after a convict by the name of

Bribie who was the first European to establish a settlement on the land and it was home to over 350 species of birds, as well as other wildlife such as dolphins, dugongs, and turtles. It was a secluded island and we could easily see why it offered the perfect getaway for the city dwellers of Brisbane as it was only an hour's dive away.

We met and chatted to lots of the local people here; we were beginning to find out that Australians were a very friendly bunch, most willing to take the time to spend a few moments chatting to obvious visitors to their country; it seemed to be their main past time. They were really amazing, we learned from them of places we should visit and things that we could do. One attraction here for us, was the local Bowls Club where, each evening, we enjoyed a cooked meal for just two dollars per head. The only down side that we could see to Bribie was that the sea was infested with large blue jelly fish, to be found both in the water and washed up on the beach. We were told that they had been washed in by the bad storms that we had been experiencing.

At the local library in Bribie, we read a notice that was offering a free course of computer lessons to all-comers so we signed up; this was to be our first introduction to the delights of e-mail which has since proved to be very useful at home and on our travels. We took daily outings to places of interest and amongst others drove out to The Glass House Mountains named by Captain Cook in 1770 as he felt that the 25 million year old rock formation resembled a glass house. It is recorded that he came ashore and climbed Mount Beerburrum from which he surveyed the whole of Moreton Bay. The mountains are fantastic volcanic crags set amidst a National Park; the area holds a rich Aboriginal history and is really popular amongst walkers and climbers. We enjoyed this scenic trip passing, as we did, through small old fashioned villages, with souvenir shops and museums.

On another day we drove out to Beerwah to visit Steve Irwin's Australian Zoo. Steve Irwin 'the crocodile hunter', apparently grew up loving all wildlife, especially reptiles; he had caught his first venomous snake (a Common Brown) at the tender age of six. In the 80s Steve had spent months on end living in the most remote areas of far North Queensland catching problem crocodiles before they ended up shot by a poacher's bullet. He developed crocodile capture and management techniques that are now utilised with crocodilians around the world and in 1992 he took over the wildlife zoo that his parents had started. The main attraction on the day we visited was the crocodile feeding show, in the spacious 'Crocoseum'. We watched as fearsome, man eating, enormous salt water crocodiles were fed by hand with whole oven-ready chickens, while Steve pranced around the enclosure putting on his show, narrowly missing their enormous jaws by inches. He showcased these fabulous creatures and made them as visible as possible so the public could appreciate them while learning of their habits and their place in nature's chain.

About 100 km north of Brisbane, the temperature now beginning to feel quite tropical, was the town of Woombye, an aboriginal name for a black snake. Here we saw another 'Big Thing', this time, The Big Pineapple, as this area had once been surrounded by pineapple farms. We visited one of the few remaining plantation and took a guided tour, learning about the history of the area and the techniques used in growing this tropical fruit. They also had Macadamia nut groves here and we visited their shop which was selling a variety of produce made from, that's right, you guessed it, nuts and pineapple.

On the road again, and now following the Bruce Highway north, we stopped off at Buderim to visit another famous Australian tourist attraction, 'The Ginger Factory'. Here we were taken on a fully escorted factory tour through the sixty year history of the ginger industry, from start to finish. We learnt about the planting and harvesting, the processing and packing and were able to see some of the most advanced processing techniques that had lead to what they claimed were the finest ginger products in the world. It was a really interesting day, seeing this multi- million dollar business in action with its shop and a museum. We took a ride on an old 1902 sugar cane train, around the whole plantation; it **was** a ginger-lover's paradise, with a tasting session of ginger-inspired snacks at the end of our tour, ending up in the company shop with a large selection of ginger products for sale.

Our next campsite stop was at Rainbow beach situated on Wide Bay; it was Geoff's birthday 70th birthday today 2nd June. Rainbow Beach had originally been known as Back Beach and had at one time been home to a large sand mining industry until 1976; the current name came from the rainbow coloured cliffs. In an Aboriginal legend, the cliffs were coloured when Yiningie, the spirit of the Gods representing the Rainbow, was killed in a fight, spreading his 'colourful' spirits across the cliffs. This small town was set on the edge of these rainbow coloured sand cliffs, overlooking wonderful Rainbow Beach, down below. You could drive along the beach here, but you had to beware of quick sand in places; one shop in town had dozens of photographs of vehicles that had been caught in the tide, after getting stuck in the sand.

We felt really fortunate to be driving through these fantastic landscapes. Just north of Rainbow Beach, we came across the small town of Tin Can Bay, located on the Fraser Coast, just opposite the southern tip of Fraser Island. The attraction here we had been told, was the early morning visits made by Pacific Humpback Dolphins; these are slightly different in shape to the well known Bottlenose Dolphins. We had heard that you could feed these delightful creatures by hand when they swam in close to the beach each day. We arrived early and bought a pot of fish from Barnacles Bait and Cafe and spent a truly wonderful time feeding the five dolphins that came in that morning. It was a really special experience and a very rare one as this place was one of only three around the whole of Australia, where you could officially hand feed the dolphins in the wild.

Hervey Bay (pronounced Harvey) was our next stopping place. With the urban area stretching from Gatakers Bay in the north to River Heads in the south, it was now known as one of the fastest growing cities in Australia with industries in sugarcane, non-orchard fruit and citrus, livestock (mostly beef cattle) and fishing. Aboriginal people had occupied the area before European settlement in 1850, and we noticed that many of the streets had Aboriginal names. Today was 4th June and we decided to make camp here for a few days as this seemed like an interesting place and so we camped on a site situated right on the beach. Captain Cook first discovered the Hervey Bay area in 1770 when he had explored most of this coastline and he had proclaimed the area "Herveys Bay" after his boss, Augustus Hervey, Lord of the Admiralty. We really enjoyed our rest and it was delightful taking our daily stroll along the beach, especially on these warm tropical evenings. We discovered Hervey Bay was becoming known as Australia's whale watching capital, as each year from late July through to early November, tourists would flock to catch site of the mighty humpback whales taking time out from their annual migration for a bit of R&R in the protected waters of the bay; sadly it was too early in the year for us to see any of these magnificent creatures. From the beach, Frazer Island was just visible across the water and at 123km x 22km is the world's largest Sand Island; one of the rare places where rainforest grows on sand. Its **World Heritage listing** apparently ranks it along with Australia's Uluru (Ayers Rock), Kakadu National Park in the Northern Territory of Australia and the Great Barrier Reef. The island's Aboriginal name, 'K'Gari', means paradise and we were told that over 325 species of birds and several species of wallaby, possums, flying foxes, echidnas and eastern Australia's purest population of dingo were living here as well as rare, vulnerable and endangered species like dugong, the incredibly strange looking herbivorous marine mammal sometimes called the sea cows; we promised ourselves a visit to the island on our next trip to Australia; there was so much to see in the awesome country.

After a few days we broke camp and on 7th June we moved on, still travelling the Bruce Highway. Further up the coast we visited Bundaberg, most famous for its rum, a product of local sugar cane production. We saw yet another of Australia's 'Big Things' here; an enormous bottle of rum, towering 6m tall with a one meter diameter. We took a tour of the distillery here and saw the whole process, starting with sticky molasses being mixed with yeast and water and ending up with the double fermented rum; the tour ended with the opportunity to taste the end product, the famous 'Bundy Rum'. Bundaberg Rum originated because the local sugar mills had a problem with what to do with the waste molasses after the sugar was extracted. It was heavy, difficult to transport and the costs of converting it to stock feed were rarely worth the effort. A group of local sugar mill owners got together and Bundy Rum was born. Bundaberg Rum has recently been labelled the drink for 'yobbos' after some bars reported that "bundy drinkers are a lot louder, and more disruptive than other patrons. Not quite considering ourselves to be yobbos, we bought some of the rum to take back as presents.

We visited the Bundaberg Botanic Gardens in North Bundaberg. The centrepiece of these gardens was the lagoons filled with colourful water lilies and we crossed on a boardwalk, admiring the gardens with their mix of native and exotic plants. This peaceful setting was noted as attracting over 100 species of bird. Overlooking the lagoons is Hinkler House an aviation museum. Bert Hinkler, Bundaberg's most famous son, was the first aviator to fly solo from England to Australia, flying from London to Sydney in sixteen days in 1928. His English home had been transported, brick by brick, from Southampton, England, back to Bundaberg in 1983 and now stands as a memorial to him and where as a boy he sat and studied the ibis in flight. Bert Hinkler had a brief forty years of lifetime being eventually killed in an air crash trying to break another record flying to Italy. The Bundaberg & District Historical Museum was also in the Gardens and was a fascinating record of the district's sugar industry pioneers and their lives. An old building, Fairymead House, built in 1890 had been moved to its current site in the Gardens and was now home to the Sugar Museum.

The Bundaberg area has over 140 kilometres of unspoiled beaches and all are boasted to be stinger (jelly fish) free and range from surf to calm water. We continued to travel north up this beautiful coast to Rockhampton. The further north we got the more the scenery was beginning to change; this was becoming really wild country up here. With grazing being the dominant industry and with two of Queensland's largest abattoirs, Rockhampton promoted itself as the Beef Capital of Australia. Rockhampton, on the banks of Fitzroy River, experiences a humid subtropical climate and the city is situated right on the Tropic of Capricorn. One day, we unknowingly took our vehicle off road, as we wanted to explore outside the city and found ourselves having to travel over 400 kms on dirt roads, miles from anywhere with only kangaroos and cattle for company. Occasionally we would come across what seemed like miles of track leading off into the distance to a remote cattle farm. The only other vehicles we came across during this outback trek were a few enormous cattle trucks, all travelling at normal speeds, as if they were on tarmac roads. We'd pull over when we saw one of these monsters approaching, trying to get as far off the dirt track as possible, and then we'd turn our heads away and close our eyes as they thundered by, showering us in a hale of stones and clouds of dust. We felt quite fortunate that we only suffered from a few dents in the body work of the vehicle and escaped without getting our windscreen broken. After our little 'off road' adventure we decided, as it was so remote up here and as we had experienced a little a taste of the outback, that we would travel back south towards Hervey Bay and civilization. We called in on a few small coastal towns along the way but we didn't stay for long.

The first morning back at the same campsite in Hervey Bay, and where we had stayed previously, I wandered to the ladies block to take a shower and met a young woman there who seemed to be quite frightened. She told me not to go into one particular cubicle as she had seen a Redback spider. The Redback is a potentially dangerous spider native to Australia. The female, the most venomous, has a round black body about the size of large pea with an obvious orange/red longitudinal stripe sometimes broken like small red dots on the upper abdomen and long, slender legs. Its bite contains a neurotoxic venom which is toxic to humans and can cause severe pain. Most bites occur in the warmer months between December and April; it was now June and I guessed that I was pretty safe, but I wasn't taking any chances and offered my services by taking off my shoes ready to strike. She immediately said, 'no don't do that they can jump', and went to fetch the caretaker. When he arrived he didn't seem too keen on taking a closer look either but he took my shoe and dispatched the intruder. I later learned that the initial bite may be painful but sometimes might only feel like a pin prick or a mild burning sensation but within an hour victims would generally develop more severe local pain with possible sweating, nausea, vomiting, abdominal or chest pain. The spiders have very interesting sex lives too, where the male has been found to actively assist the female in sexual cannibalism. In the process of mating, the much smaller male somersaults to place his abdomen over the female's mouthparts then the female consumes the male while mating continues. We had been warned about these spiders, being told to always look underneath loo seats, where the spiders could be lurking; I didn't need telling twice; I'm petrified of spiders.

The weather had now turned rainy as we moved south along the coast.

Today was 16th June and we were about 135 km north of Brisbane, and about to pass Coolum Bay. At the last minute we decided to drop in to see what the largest beach side resort on Queensland's southern Sunshine Coast looked like just as the Olympic Torch relay was passing through the town; a huge coincidence I thought and another good omen. We watched as an old athlete carried the torch through the town, helped by some young ladies; it was really good to watch and it reminded us of why we had come to Australia. The first Europeans to pass through Coolum were castaways and shipwrecked sailors and the origin of the name Coolum appears to be derived from the Aboriginal word 'kulum' meaning 'headless'. This is assumed to refer to the shape of Mount Coolum, which has no peak. According to Aboriginal legend, Ninderry knocked off Coolum's head and it fell into the ocean and is now Mudjimba Island. We were still in Queensland's sugar cane growing area, which had first started in Coolum in 1881. Since then, considerable expansion of the sugarcane industry had taken place and cane farming provided the main source of financial stability in the district until the advent of tourism in the 1960s.

Having driven on in the rain, at the end of the day we pulled into a '24hr free' camp site. We had our meal then took an after dinner stroll and got chatting to a few other travellers. We met a young couple who were moving 'lock stock and barrel' to Darwin to live. They were travelling in a car and pulling a trailer containing all of their belongings plus their dog. He was a very large husky-looking dog but he had just been shaved ready for the heat up north. This evening it was wet and cold and the poor dog whimpered all night long as he lay underneath the trailer; we felt really sorry for him but most dogs in Australia seem to sleep out side, all the year round.

Later that night we were woken by the sound of vehicles and could see the blue flashing lights of a Police car and an Ambulance. In the half light we saw them take away somebody on a stretcher from a camper close to us; we heard no more till the morning when we were told that it had been the dead body of a camper who had apparently been there for over a week. I was shocked that someone could go unnoticed for that length of time but relieved in a way that we hadn't made the discovery on our previous evenings stroll.

315

Crossing the state border back into New South Wales, we made a return visit to Corindi Beach and headed straight for the same camping ground where we had enjoyed our stay so much before. The Dutch woman that we had met last time was still here and we went to see her and had a chat about all the places we had visited that she had so kindly recommended to us. The weather had improved and so we enjoyed a good rest in this lovely place, relaxing with our books and taking walks along the beach, admiring all the unusual shore and sea birds.

On 21st June we pulled into Swansea again. Although there were plenty of camp sites here to choose from, it seemed prudent to stay in the same one as before as it has been so good. Geoff tried his hand at fishing while we were here, but with no luck. Again the wonderful and varied bird life here was a real joy to observe.

Returning once again to Mooney Mooney village, Geoff tried fishing the Hawkesbury River; this time his luck was in and he got a bite. His catch turned out to be a puffer fish which, as he hauled it in, began to puff up to twice its size. Puffers have the ability to inflate rapidly, filling their extremely elastic stomachs with water (or air when outside the water) until they are almost spherical in shape. Some puffers also produce a powerful neurotoxin called tetrodotoxin in their internal organs, making them an unpleasant and possibly lethal meal for any predatory fish that eats one. It has almost sandpaper-like spines and its scientific name, Tetraodontidae, refers to the four large teeth which are used for crushing the shells of crustaceans and mollusks, their natural prey. Puffer fish are the second most poisonous vertebrate in the world as their skin and certain internal organs are highly toxic to humans. This doesn't stop it being considered a delicacy in both Japan (as fugu) and Korea (as bok). If one is caught while fishing, it is recommended that thick gloves be worn to avoid poisoning and getting bitten when removing the hook; needless to say it very quickly went back in the river. It had probably been swimming in this area looking for its supper as this was known as succulent oyster territory, which was a local industry. The camp site where we were staying was situated, just below the northern approach to the Sydney-Newcastle Expressway Bridge crossing and we had quite a disturbed night here, listening to the sirens of the police cars and ambulances due to a multiple pile up over head.

The following day we heard all about it on the radio as we travelled back to Sydney.

We returned to Wendy and Wally's house on 26<sup>th</sup> June and spent the next few days recounting our adventures, packing our suitcases and cleaning up the camper van as we were to return the vehicle to the hire company which was close to the airport, just before catching our flight out to New Zealand on the next leg of our trip on 1<sup>st</sup> July.

# Chapter Twenty Three
## New Zealand

*Yis Jif*

In the south-western Pacific Ocean, New Zealand lies between 37 and 47 degrees south of the Tropic of Capricorn and its climate is dominated by two main geographical features: the mountains and the sea. A little bigger than the UK in area, it is made up of two separate, elongated and relatively narrow landmasses, North Island and South Island, and on average, as most of the country lies close to its 9,500 miles of coast it usually has relatively mild temperatures, moderate rainfall, and abundant sunshine. While the far north has subtropical weather during summer, the alpine areas of the South Island can be as cold as -10 C in winter.

We were visiting New Zealand, beginning our journey in the South Island, smack bang in the middle of their winter which runs from June to August. Due to this fact, and particularly while travelling in the South Island, we had been advised to pack warm winter clothing and to hire a car and use motels for our accommodation. This was opposed to hiring a camper van, which we had planned to do in The North Island; a car would make for easier handling in the, quite possibly, snowy conditions. On the plus side while the South Island has cooler winter temperatures, some areas of the island experience little rainfall in winter and so we were told that this was an excellent time to visit the glaciers and the mountain regions; we were looking forward to exploring as much of this country as we could during our three week 'whistle stop' tour.

Landing in Christchurch, the largest city in the South Island, located in the region of Canterbury, one third of the way down the east coast; we picked up our car, and drove to our first hotel. We had planned to stay here for two days and once we had recovered from our journey, the following day, we visited the city markets, some interesting museums, and of course the shops. There were trams in the city centre that had been originally introduced in 1905 but had ceased operating fifty years later, but since 1995, and mainly due to tourism, they had returned to the inner city making this a good way to get around. As we wandered around this garden city enjoying the sights we were beginning to feel the cold after the mild Australian weather we had just left behind.

Moving on now, driving on the superb uncluttered roads in the Waitaki District we took the coast road heading south; the deep blue Pacific on our left. We would stop off along the way at anywhere remotely interesting to take a closer look, but really just enjoyed the drive along the coast, through these lovely, lush green, rolling hills. At around five o clock we found ourselves driving into Oamaru and looked around for a Motel. We had read that this area was famous for its historical white stone architecture and it's Blue Penguin Colony. Checking in at our Motel, we got talking to the owner about the area. He said, 'You must see the Penguins come ashore', and told us all about the evening show.

We arrived at the outdoor viewing grandstand, and listened to an informative commentary about The Oamaru Blue Penguins. It was getting very dark and cold now but suddenly out of the blackness, from the direction of the sea, came the birds returning home from their days fishing. They made their way onto the beach, up a stony ramp, and crossed into the Colony. At this time of year apparently, they had begun to re-establish their pair bonds and were building their nests, by digging a burrow into the sand or a crevice amongst the rocks, mating and laying their eggs. We were told that they were only active on land at night and that they left the colony early in the morning before sun-rise, and would return after dark. They were very vocal as they came ashore, quacking to keep the small groups of penguins together. Some small penguins started to come up the beach, in two's and three's, they then seemed to wait in a group until a larger one took over and would lead them across the open area and on into the darkness and their nests. They were really amusing, the next group came along and the large one came back to lead the next group across the open area to the nesting place. It made me think of men wearing DJ's, being shown to their seats in a theatre. We learned that Blue Penguins could dive up to 60 meters and hold their breath for up to 2 minutes when fishing and that they could bite fiercely and would use their wings to beat their opponent when fighting during the breeding season while defending themselves and their nest sites. It had been well worth the wait in the cold and afterwards we retuned to our motel to thaw out in our spa bath.

The following day we continued along the coastal waters of the Pacific towards the Southern Alps in the direction of Dunedin, passing through some stunning scenery. This area had been settled by Scottish migrants in the 19th century, a heritage that is evident in the areas well-preserved architecture. Arriving in this bustling University City, we parked and wandered around the compact city centre. Located in the Otago region and edged by the sea, Dunedin, spread around a sheltered harbour, was New Zealand's oldest city and well-known for its Victorian and Edwardian architecture as well as its close proximity to some amazing wildlife having the only mainland breeding colony of the royal albatross and some rare New Zealand sea lions.

Continuing our drive south we were surrounded by fertile farming land dotted with sheep. The first Sheep were landed in New Zealand by Captain Cook in 1773. After that the sheep population gradually grew and was estimated to be over 70 million in 1982. From then on it had slowly declined to almost half that number now mainly due to declining profits compared to other types of farming but it still represented 12 sheep for every person in New Zealand. This area was now developing a fruit growing industry concentrating on stone fruit such as peaches and apricots. We now turned right and headed cross country towards Queenstown. As we drove on in the afternoon gradually climbing into skiing country, the roads became narrow and winding.

This area had been host to the biggest gold rush ever seen in the 1860's and had opened up Queenstown. One pair of prospectors, trying to rescue their dog from the river, had found 11 kg. of gold in rock crevices here in a single day, giving the Shotover River its then name of 'the richest river in the world'. That evening we stayed at a motel in Queenstown and went out to a local pub for our dinner and found ourselves surrounded by après skiers, all having a good time. The roads here were very icy and the side of the roads were piled high with snow.

In the morning we got a better view of the place and saw how pretty the town was, nestled on the shores of Lake Wakatipu and surrounded by the majestic peaks of the Southern Alps called 'The Remarkables', which were covered in fir trees. Queenstown had been named because "it was fit for Queen Victoria". Today Queenstown is recognised as New Zealand's premier visitor destination and as one of the friendliest cities in the world, we could vouch for that. Queenstown's reputation as an 'Adventure Capital' was growing but we thought that we would pass on the extreme bungy jumping today.

Our mornings had been frosty but were clear and crisp, gradually warming up during the day, but the cold would always return each night. The air was remarkably clean which somehow made the colours look brighter; we were told that this was due to this part of New Zealand having little or no pollution. Today we would continue crossing over to the west coast and the roads here seemed to narrow even more the closer we got to Franz Joseph. We had forgotten to fill up with fuel before leaving Queenstown, so we had a hair-raising journey to the next petrol station, wondering if we would make it. With our lesson learnt we began to realise that petrol stations were few and far between up here.

At lunch time we found a trading station, selling all sorts of unusual things; amusingly, in the Ladies loo, the door was kept shut by an old boot on a rope. After a good lunch, we wandered across the road to look in another shop and noticed that they were advertising scenic air flights around the area. We imagined that here in this beautiful mountainous area this just had to be the best way to see everything. We booked up and a while later the pilot came out to greet us. He indicated to us that we should go and get into the red plane that was parked on the small grass runway at the rear of the building. He asked us if we would mind if he brought along two young lads who were the son's of his friend; he had promised them a flight next time he took the plane up and we gladly agreed to the company.

In we all climbed and the pilot tried to start it up. The engine sputtered into life but very quickly died again, after trying it a few times he told us to climb out again and he would try the yellow plane and proceeded to get this one out of the wooden hangar. I had given Geoff a few worried looks at this point but he didn't seem at all unnerved. We all climbed in the yellow plane and immediately sped off across the rather bumpy field, turned round and shot off at high speed, leaving my stomach somewhere on the ground. As soon as we were in the air, I forgot my fear; it was fantastic. We could see below us the lowland rainforest of Westland National Park. The views were unbelievable as we circled the peak of Mount Cook and swooped down across the two mighty glaciers of Fox and Franz Josef.

Through our headsets we could hear the pilot as he told us about the glaciers that cut through the dramatic glacial valleys to flow into the temperate rainforest. While many glaciers world-wide have been retreating, these glaciers still flowed almost to sea level, making them unique relics of the last Ice Age. They flowed over large bedrock steps on the valley floors causing the ice to extend and break up, forming steep icefalls that became mazes of crevasses and pinnacles of ice. We had such a spectacular view from up here in our little yellow plane; I still felt rather pleased that the pilot hadn't been able to start the red one. Returning to terra firma once again, our plane scattered all the sheep on landing and we taxied along the bumpy field, coming to a final halt, back at the wooden hangar; it had been a truly exhilarating experience.

We waved goodbye to the lads and the pilot and got back on the road once again, now heading north along the west coast. As we were travelling along a narrow and winding road we suddenly hit a rock that had fallen into the road, Geoff tried to swerve and just clipped it, avoiding any damage to the car but we noticed that the car in front of us now stopped on the road ahead had been caught the same way but with a larger rock which had broken his axle. We stopped and tried to help but he thanked us saying that help was already on the way; they were waiting for a recovery truck. We were later told that this regularly happened at this time of year as the rock on the steep sides of the road was washed down in rain storms or just broke away in the frost; we counted ourselves as lucky. As it was now dark and the weather was closing in, we decided to make a night's stop at the very next motel we came to. We stayed the night in a really grotty small hotel on the way to Greymouth.

We made an early start, there was nothing keeping us here, and continued our journey towards Greymouth, which when we arrived turned out to be an unremarkable industrial area, a main centre for coal and timber. Here on the west coast we had something of a shock to find that there were several unguarded, combined road and rail bridges. The Arahura Bridge has carried road and rail traffic for over 100 years and is part of the Greymouth-Hokitika railway and is part of the highway that links Hokitika to both Greymouth and the east coast. The survival of the two road-rail bridges on this part of the West Coast adds to the character of the area but it is still mighty unnerving when you encounter an oncoming train while driving across a bridge.

We were now travelling along the west coast, a narrow strip of land, hemmed in on our left side by the Tasman Sea and on the right by the Southern Alps; the scenery was magnificent with the snow-capped mountains towering above us. This area was the centre of many gold mines in the 1860's and there were places we passed advertising 'Try your hand at panning for gold'; we may have given it a go if we'd had more time on our hands. They had very high rain fall in this area, caused by westerly winds coming in off the sea and condensing on the mountains, accounting for this regions lush vegetation. We were told that conveniently, most rain fell at night, the clouds parting during the day to reveal clear sparkling skies. Today was no exception; it was crisp but amazingly clear.

We drove on through The Paparoa National Park which was different yet again. Once again the views were stunning from the road, which ran close to the coast, and we looked down from the 300m high costal cliffs to the deep blue Tasman Sea below us. The roadsides were covered in sub-tropical vegetation with masses of tangled vines and palms; it was beautiful. Passing through Murchison and then on to the Nelson Lakes National Park, we decided to make our final overnight stop here and so we booked into a lovely lake side hotel, making up for the previous night. The lakes here were beautiful surrounded with beech forests and craggy peaks; it must have looked stunning during the summer and later during the autumn months when the leaves changed colours. After a comfortable nights rest, we headed towards Marlborough and the small port of Picton, at the head of Queen Charlotte Sound; this was our last day in the South Island.

Today, we were due to catch the ferry to the North Island and Wellington, the nation's capital city, and we arrived in good time to take a little look around. Picton is the main link between the South and North Island, with a scheduled ferry service over Cook Strait. We took the Roll-on/roll-off Interislander ferry that uses the Tory Channel which is one of the drowned valleys that form the Marlborough Sounds. The Marlborough Sounds are an extensive network of sea-drowned valleys, created by a combination of land subsidence and rising sea levels. According to Māori mythology, the sounds are the prows of the sunken Waka (canoe) of Aoraki.

Mount Cook, New Zealand's highest mountain is called Aoraki by the Maori and according to legend, Aoraki and his three brothers were the sons of Rakinui, the Sky Father. They were on a voyage around Papatuanuku, the Earth Mother, when their canoe was stranded after striking a reef in the ocean. Aoraki and his brothers climbed on the top side of their canoe. The cold south wind hit them, froze them, and turned them into stone. The legend says their canoe became New Zealand's South Island which was then called Te Waka o Aoraki. Aoraki, the tallest of the brothers, gave his name to the highest peak (Mount Cook) and his brothers and members of his crew became the mountains of the Southern Alps.

The main channels of the Marlborough Sounds have calm water and are really popular for sailing. Cook Strait, however, is infamous for its strong currents and rough waters, especially when the wind is from the south or north. Because of this, some of the narrow channels closer to the Strait are dangerous. I am not a good sailor at the best of times, so today, I was hoping for a smooth crossing.

My prayers were answered, and we landed in Lambton Harbour in calm waters, earlier than expected, making our way directly to the city centre. Wellington is known for three things, a huge harbour, steep hills and ferocious winds. It's known as the windy city as the funnel effect of the Cook Straits can produce winds of over 100kph; very bracing indeed. Today was fine; it was breezy but quite comfortable really for mid winter. The city put me in mind of San Francisco in the USA with its steep surrounding streets lined with wooden clapboard houses. The city itself now lies partly on reclaimed land and the original waterfront streets are now much higher and dryer and now in the middle of the business district. We could see that the city was a centre for culture, with plenty going on such as the advertised programmes from The Royal New Zealand Ballet and the New Zealand Symphony Orchestra but the general vibrancy of the city struck me with its cosmopolitan range of cafes bars and restaurants. We visited the recently opened Te Papa Museum which reflected the bicultural heritage and identity of New Zealand; this was a fascinating place and our short time here didn't do it justice.

Lake Taupo, at the centre of North Island was our next stop; it was getting dark when we arrived here, so we immediately looked for a motel. Today had been cold and frosty but we had driven through some beautiful scenery on route. The following morning we awoke to a fabulous view. Shrouded in the morning mist and surrounded by stunning volcanoes and bush clad mountains lay the largest freshwater lake in New Zealand and the Southern Hemisphere, Lake Taupo. This ancient volcanic craters 40 x30 kms expanse of water was stunningly blue and here the air felt fresh and unpolluted. We were told that some of the best trout fishing in the world has international anglers flocking to the area while the mighty mountain peaks drew skiers and adventurers to experience this pristine environment. After breakfast we drove through the town of Taupo on Tapaueharuru Bay at the north-eastern corner of the lake with its bustling shops and cafes and made our way to Hamilton, where we would be leaving our car and collecting our camper van.

In Hamilton, with the temperature feeling more spring-like, we stopped for lunch. Here, in the largest inland city in New Zealand, we wandered the boulevard-style streets with their trendy cafes and restaurants. It was an attractive city with the Waikato River winding through its heart with the parks and gardens on both banks, linked by footpaths and bridges. After a good lunch, we tested out our newly found skills, using the e-mail facilities in one of the cafes.

We drove on to Auckland, stopping every now and then to admire the scenery and wonderful beaches along the way. Near Auckland airport we dropped off our hire car and collected our camper van and driving north, we found a campsite not far from Whangarei, New Zealand's northernmost city at the small town of Ruakaka located on a subtropical peninsula at the entrance to Whangarei Harbour. It had been raining and the ground underfoot was a little muddy but we camped for the night at One Tree Point, a lovely spot, where the sandstone cliffs stretched from inside the harbour right along the white sands of Bream Bay. We were told that the local shellfish found along the coastline at Ruakaka was the best in New Zealand. Across the harbour from Ruakaka we could see Whangarei Heads, with its picturesque coves and bays; Whangarei was the Maori word for cherished harbour and we could see why it had been given that name.

After a good nights sleep, in the morning after breakfast we packed up and were about to pull away only to find that we were stuck fast in the mud. The camper van just didn't have the traction to pull us out. There was nothing we could do on our own, and so we had to resort to asking for help and were kindly towed out of our predicament by the owner of the campsite; he told us not to worry as he said that he regularly was asked to help out.

Safely back on tarmac roads, we were now travelling up the narrow 240km long peninsula known as Northland that runs north from Auckland towards the equator. The mild climate up here has earned it the name of 'the winterless north' and it really was beginning to feel a much more pleasant temperature. The east coast was indented with numerous bays with small harbours and little islands with sandy beaches. This was known as 'The Bay of Islands'. The west cost by contrast was lined with sweeping beaches pounded by surf from the Tasman Sea. Here the magnificent Ninety Mile Beach, officially designated a road, swept in a single unbroken stretch of shimmering sand, up towards Cape Reinga, at the very tip of the peninsula. Cape Reinga is traditionally revered by the Maori people as the last stepping stone for the spirits of the dead on their journey back north to 'Hawaiki', a mythical place where their ancestors are thought to have originally come from.

When we reached Cape Reinga, we parked up for lunch and as we ate we watched a man working outside repairing a billboard, opposite our camper. As he moved around he seemed to be holding on to anything he could, it looked quite amusing, but when Geoff stepped out of the camper after lunch to take a look around, he realized that the man's struggle had been because of the strong wind, it was gusting so powerfully that he had to hold on to something or be blown away. We took a few photos and then drove back along the dirt roads that we had come in on. We stopped off at various small places on route finding a very nice Wool Shop that sold sheep skins, rugs, gloves and slippers all of which were very nice and not to expensive, but sadly we couldn't carry any of this extra luggage back home.

Back in Hamilton once again, we looked up some of our old rowing friends that we had first met in the 1980s in Hazewinkle in Belgium. Their names were Tim and Teresa Clark and they had both been rowers. They had then been travelling the U K and Europe with their daughter Beth and had dropped into Hazewinkle to watch Tim's sister Robin Clark compete in the double sculls with her partner Stephanie Foster. We'd met them in the spectators stand and they were camped close to our pitch. Robin had been very successful and had won a gold medal for New Zealand. We finally found their home and dropped in on the off chance; they were at home and really excited to see us. We immediately got chatting about rowing as we had heard on the radio that very morning that Steve's crew, who were competing in the 3rd race that season of the 'World Cup Series' in Lucerne, had lost: the only race they had conceded in some years. The final order had been Italy 1st New Zealand 2nd, Australia 3rd, and Great Britain 4th. As we had only just heard this result we, of course, had not had chance to speak to Steve to find out what had gone wrong. It had come as a shock to us and I started to worry that he might be having problems with his health again. We got in touch later that day and were reassured that everything was OK. Steve said the crew seemed to just suffer from a blip and had just run out of steam; Steve said that there was nothing to worry about. We later read Dan Topolski reporting 'the post-race analysis by coach Gröbler and the crew was that their punishing racing programme - more than any of their rivals - was the culprit, depleting their glycogen levels. 'They were tired and over trained,' said Gröbler. 'My fault, they need a break.' We were relieved to hear this; it put our minds at rest.

We had so much to talk about with our old friends who seemed to be doing fine. Tim and Teresa now had their own house that they had built themselves, and they'd had two more children since we last had met. Tim was now a lawyer, and Teresa was working too. Beth, the little two year old toddler that we had met in Belgium, was now a nineteen year old student. They told us of various interesting places in the area that we should try to visit. Not far from here was Otorohanga and the Kiwi House and Native Bird Park so we went in search of New Zealand's native symbol the endangered Kiwi. Here we enjoyed a stroll through a large outdoor aviary containing almost 300 species of birds native to this country. We only caught a quick glimpse of a couple of Kiwi, who are notoriously shy, nocturnal creatures. They are about the size of a domestic chicken, and of all birds, lay the largest egg in relation to their body size; about six times the size of a chicken's egg. They have a highly developed sense of smell, unusual in a bird, and are the only birds with nostrils at the end of their long beak which help them to locate insects and worms underground without actually seeing or feeling them, due to their keen sense of smell.

Our next stop was the fascinating town of Rotorua, where we camped for a couple of nights. Rotorua is at the heart of the volcanic plateau and is built around a series of spouting geysers, hissing fumaroles and bubbling pools of mud. There was a constant pungent odour in the air, which we gradually got used to. We were told it was due to the emissions of hydrogen sulphide from thermal areas and that its nickname was 'sulphur city'. It had been first developed as a spa town at the end of the last century and the bathhouse built in 1908 still existed and was now a museum. While we were here we visited nearby Whakarewarewa, Waka as the locals called it, with its fascinating boiling mud pools, steam vents and terraces of silica. The main part of this reserve had some active geysers and we waited and watched as mighty Pohutu shot 30m into the air. Our guide was quite funny and he told us how they used to cook in these underground ovens heated by the steam from the ground but he said that he much preferred a McDonald's. We watched a show of some Maori dancers performing the Haka, the traditional posture dance performed with vigorous movements and stamping of the feet with rhythmically shouted accompaniment including facial contortions showing the whites of their eyes and poking out their tongues; it was great fun to watch

The Maori are the indigenous people of New Zealand and are Polynesian. Maoritanga is their native language which is related to Tahitian and Hawaiian; it's believed that the Maori migrated from Polynesia in canoes between the 9th - 13th centuries AD. The Dutch navigator Abel Tasman was the first European to encounter the Maori when four members of his crew were killed in a bloody encounter in 1642 but later in 1769 British explorer James Cook established friendly relations with some Maori but war and disease took their toll till eventually the Maori population dropped to about 100,000. In 1840 representatives of Britain and Maori chiefs signed the Treaty of Waitangi. This treaty established British rule, granted the Maori British citizenship, and recognized Maori land rights. Today many of the treaty's provisions are disputed and there is an effort from the New Zealand Government to recompense Maori for land that was illegally confiscated. The present Maori population is around 600,000 or 14% of the population, and the Maori live in all parts of New Zealand, but predominately here in the North Island where the climate is warmer. It seemed like a similar story to the Aboriginal people of Australia.

On 20th July we started to make our way back to Auckland as we were due to fly back to Australia two days later. That night we pulled into a lay-by in order to park overnight as we hadn't been able to find a camp site. We got chatting to a local New Zealander who invited us back to his house and said that we could park our camper in his drive overnight and that he would hook us up to the electric supply. I wasn't sure we should go but Geoff seemed to think that the man was genuine, so we followed him back to his home and meet his wife, who kindly cooked us an evening meal; they even took us to a local hot spring spa the following day so we could try swimming in the natural hot thermal outdoor mineral pools supposed to be very good for arthritis. That afternoon on our way back to Auckland to return our camper we discussed our three week visit to New Zealand. We had found it to be an astonishingly beautiful and unspoilt country with such a varied landscape with its great open spaces and empty roads an increasingly rare quality in this generally overcrowded world.

# Chapter Twenty Four
## Australia

### *Fair Dinkum*

On Saturday 22<sup>nd</sup> July we flew from Auckland back to Sydney, where at the previous hire company, we hired yet another small camper and returned to my family and our base at Dapto. We spent a few days with Joan, Bert and Glen recounting our adventures in New Zealand. After getting the camper ready and loaded with provisions, we set off south, once again returning to Brian and June's house at Moruya.

We spent the next few days sharing our time between the farm and their home in Moruya. One afternoon, Bryan suggested that we have fish and chips for supper from a local shop that he said fried really good shark at Burmagui, famous for its deep sea and big-game fishing; he said this was just down the road. We discovered that 'just down the road' meant a one hour journey. Travelling great distances seems like nothing to an Aussie, I guess, with such a big county it's just the way folks think; the shark was delicious and well worth our long trip.

On Tuesday 1<sup>st</sup> August, we set off on the next part of our expedition, this time to Australia's capital city, Canberra. Travelling south from Moruya down the South Pacific Ocean coast road we headed slightly inland at Bermagui and took the Princes Highway to Bega; a **major centre famous for its rich dairy country.** Here we headed further inland on The Snowy Mountain Highway, then north on the Monaro Highway to Cooma which was very cold and windy. We had been warned to top up our petrol before setting out on this stretch of the trip as the fuel stops were few and far between.

On arrival in Canberra, having already decided to stay here a few days as there seemed so much to see; we found our campsite and settled in. Over the next few days we took bus tours and walks around this garden city, taking in the sights. Canberra's design incorporates large areas of natural vegetation that have earned Canberra the title "bush capital". The city is located at the northern end of the Australian Capital Territory (ACT), about 170 miles south-west of Sydney, and 410 miles north-east of Melbourne. The site of Canberra had been selected for the location of the nation's capital in 1908 as a compromise between these two rivals, Sydney and Melbourne, Australia's two largest cities. It is an entirely planned city and was designed by American husband and wife architects, Walter and Marion Griffin in 1913 and the major roads here followed a wheel-and-spoke pattern rather than the usual grid. We visited the War memorial, Australia's national memorial to the members of all its armed forces, with its extensive national military museum. As the seat of the government of Australia, Canberra is the site of Parliament House, the High Court of Australia and numerous government departments and agencies. We went up the Telstra Tower, located in a beautiful nature reserve, and we got a fantastic, 360-degree view of Canberra with its circular roads and the surrounding bush.

On 5th August, we moved south west along the Hume Highway to Wagga Wagga in the Riverina region; it made us think of Dick Bentley, the Australian comedian from way back, who would always begin his act by saying he came from there. We took a guided tour here of the award-winning cheese factory and the commercial winery facilities at the Charles Sturt University campus; over 2,500 students attended the university at Wagga Wagga. This set up allowed students to gain valuable work experience through projects and traineeships in a commercial environment. Our guide told us that they'd had a visitor from the UK a few weeks before; the Duke of Edinburgh. I said that I had read a newspaper reporting that, when asked, he had refused to wear a hair net for hygiene reasons and the report had said that the cheese batch that was being made that day had been ruined. She told us that the report had been nonsense; the reason the cheese batch had been ruined was because of the sniffer dogs that had been used to safety check everywhere immediately prior to his visit. We tasted lots of their products, and bought some to take with us on our journey.

Next on our site seeing agenda was The Snowy Mountains Scheme a hydroelectricity and irrigation complex. We checked into a campsite close by and booked tickets for a tour of the facility for the following day. Our guide told us that the waters of the Snowy River and its tributary were captured at high elevations and diverted inland to the Murray River and the Murrumbidgee River, through two tunnel systems driven through the Snowy Mountains. The water fell 800 metres and traveled through large hydro-electric power stations which generated peak-load power for consumption by the huge areas of the Australian Capital Territory, New South Wales and Victoria. Built mostly in the 50's, it had been completed in1974 after 25 years of construction and had been the largest engineering project ever undertaken in Australia. Workers had come from thirty two different countries to work on this massive project; Geoff had known a few fellow merchant sailors who had jumped ship in Sydney to come to work here in 1949. These foreign workers had been allowed to stay and take Australia citizenship and this had a significant effect on the cultural mix of the country.

A strange sight out here was a double-decker bus and our tour guide told us that it had been used for some publicity photos, as the pipes that carried the water from the dam to the plant were so big, a double decker bus could be driven through them. We all had to wear protective clothing and hard hats; it was so noisy in the turbine plant but we had microphones in the helmets that enabled us to hear the guide. He told us how the electric was produced and stored, and how the whole plant was now run by a handful of staff. The camp site where we were staying was situated on the banks of a river and so Geoff tried fishing once again, only to end with the usual result - I think he must have been using the wrong bait.

After a couple of pleasantly warm days and nights on 7th August, we moved south along the Northern Highway to Bendigo, in central Victoria, 82 miles from the state capital of Melbourne. Bendigo had many magnificent ornate buildings in a late Victorian colonial style; a legacy of the gold boom. Here we took a ride on the famous Vintage Talking Tram Tour and as it trundled its way through the streets of the city, there was an automatically activated commentary telling wonderful stories of days gone by, including the history of the town and the world's richest goldfields. Just to prove again what a small world it is, we got talking to a fellow passenger who turned out to be Alex Beavers second cousin; a rower from Marlow Rowing Club.

After the tram ride we went down an authentic deep-shaft mine at the Central Deborah Gold Mine. It was very dark and scary as we descended 61 metres underground in a miners' cage. We had been dressed in safety gear complete with a hard hat with miner's lamp and we were guided through the dimly lit honeycomb of tunnels and were told what conditions, as a miner, had been really like during the harsh gold rush era. When gold was first discovered in Bendigo in 1851 it had sparked off decades of gold mining, worth billions of dollars. Central Deborah Gold Mine was one of the last two commercial mines to cease operation in the wealthy Bendigo goldfields, operating, as it had, for just 15 years between 1939 and 1954. Although a relatively short time frame, during this period the mine had produced 929kg of gold. It felt very claustrophobic down there and it was very cold, damp and noisy too, when the drills were demonstrated; I began to realise what working life might have been like for Wally, no wonder he couldn't wait for his retirement.

Moving south on the Midland Highway, and still in the gold fields of Victoria, we arrived in Ballarat which lies at the foothills of the Great Dividing Range in Central Western Victoria; we were now about 65 miles north west of Melbourne. Just outside Ballarat, a name derived from a local Aboriginal dialect meaning 'resting place', was where gold was discovered in 1851, and the influx of over 10,000 miners in less than a year transformed it from a pastoral town into Victoria's largest settlement and much of its Victorian heritage still remained. We camped here and made a visit to Sovereign Hill, a recreated goldfield township set in over 25 hectares which formed part of the richest alluvial goldfields the world has ever seen. Here the costumed staff, dressed in the mid-19th century style, showed us just how things were done during this time in history; they seemed to take great pride in their presentation and role play, portraying some of the behaviours and prejudices of the 1850s. The activities on offer were, panning for real gold in the stream at The Red Hill Gully Diggings and a 10-minute, self-guided underground tour of the Red Hill Mine which depicted the discovery of the 69kg 'Welcome Nugget', the second largest gold nugget ever found. There were regular demonstrations and street theatre performances by the staff and actors. There were around 50 working horses here, including Clydesdales & Percherons, and we rode in a stage coach around the town and watched craftsmen at work in traditional 1850s trades; there was some 1850s-style shopping too. It was a really interesting and fun day out but I'm sad to say that we didn't find any gold, although we were told that there are still thought to be large, undiscovered gold reserves around the Ballarat region.

As we were leaving Ballarat on the Western Highway heading for Adelaide, Geoff asked me if I would like to spend my birthday in Alice Springs. I thought that this was a great suggestion and so we set off for the Northern Territory. First, we had to travel through the state of South Australia and as we were passing close by we went into the city of Adelaide to take a look around. Adelaide's location belies the fact that beyond the rolling hills lie huge tracts of desert. The city itself is compact, laid out in grid form, and easily negotiated on foot. The sheltering curve of Gulf St Vincent creates calm waters and it has more than 60 klm of quiet sandy beaches. Add to this a near perfect, dry and warm Mediterranean climate and one can see why this is a seaside holiday destination. The good food and wine is well known in this area too with its European-style farmland and close proximity to the Barossa Valley wine region.

Later that afternoon we drove north on the A1, through Port Pirie on the tidal saltwater inlet from Spencer Gulf. It looked quite industrial as the main industries here were the smelting of metals, which had earned the locals the nickname of 'Lead-Heads'. We drove further north to Port Augusta, known as the southern gateway to the Northern Territory and we camped here but had quite a disturbed night as it was very windy, buffeting the van around.

The following morning we topped up with petrol, water and food, as we had been advised to, and set off on our three day trek driving to Alice Springs across the Great Victoria Desert. Travelling north on the A87, the Stuart Highway, at Kingoonya, a small settlement reputed to have the widest main street in Australia and where cricket matches have been played, we took a right fork to Coober Pedy.

Coober Pedy is known as 'the opal capital of the world' because of the quantity of precious opals that are mined there. As we passed through it was more moonscape than landscape and we saw mounds of earth that looked like lots of small excavation. We later found out from the family, that most residents here lived below ground, mostly in old refurbished mines, due to the scorching daytime heat. The name 'Coober Pedy' comes from the local Aboriginal term kupa-piti, which means 'Boys Waterhole'. The first tree ever seen in this town was welded together from scrap iron and, still standing, sits on a hilltop overlooking the town. The local golf course - mostly played at night with glowing balls, to avoid daytime temperatures - is completely free of grass and golfers take a small piece of "turf" around to use for teeing off. It was really desolate out here and we quite believed it when we were told that one of the Mad Max films had been shot here, using the locals as film extras. We had driven over 500 kms from Port Augusta with another 700kms to Alice.

The main vehicles on the long straight roads we were travelling were the 'road trains' that are used to move bulky loads efficiently. They are used for transporting all manner of materials, with livestock fuel, mineral ores and general freight the most common but loads can sometimes include up to 100 head of cattle. These massive trucks with three or more trailers seem to stop for nothing; hence so many dead kangaroos on the roadside; in fact, during the whole of our trip, we saw more dead kangaroos than live ones. One day we saw a dead cow on the side of the road, with its legs in the air; cattle out here, just seemed to freely roam about grazing and these vehicles stopped for nothing. Strict regulations regarding licensing, registration , weights and experience apply to all operators of road trains throughout Australia Their cost-effective transport has played a huge part in the economic development of remote areas, with some communities totally reliant on a regular service; out here we could see why.

Overtaking a road train can be quite difficult, when patience, assistance from the driver, and large amounts of clear road are required. On the unsealed outback roads, like these, the road trains create huge amounts of dust that need to be reckoned with when overtaking. To avoid driving through populated areas, when the road train gets close to cities, the multiple dog-trailers are unhooked, the dolly's removed and then they are connected individually to other single trucks at "assembly" yards. When the flat-top trailers of a road train need to be transported empty, it is common practice to stack them. This is commonly referred to as 'doubling-up' and if many trailers are required to be moved at the one time, they will be tripled stacked, or "tripled-up"; we kept well out of their way.

At the end of our third day, on the 12th August, we arrive at Alice Springs; it was about 6pm. We found a nice campsite, immediately took a very welcome shower and had a meal. We were now back in a good signal range for our mobile phone so we made our calls to the family and then dropped into our bed for a good nights sleep. The following morning Sunday 13th August, was my birthday, and we were invited to have breakfast pancakes by the camp team; this gave us the opportunity to meet the other travellers, which is always interesting.

Alice Springs is the second largest city in the Northern Territory, popularly known as "the Alice" or simply "Alice". Alice Springs is situated in the geographic centre of Australia near the southern border of the Northern Territory and is nearly equidistant from Adelaide and Darwin. It is the traditional home of the Arrernte Aboriginal people who have lived here for more than 50,000 years. The region here was known as Central Australia, or the Red Centre, and its arid environment consists of several different deserts. The town began with the construction of an overland telegraph station in 1871 and was now home to 28,000 people. We were told that the temperatures here during the summer could reach the mid 40's (114° F), with winter minimum temperature being as low as 7.5 °C (45.5 °F); quite a difference.

The town of Alice Springs straddles the usually dry Todd River on the northern side of the MacDonnell Ranges and due to a nearby water hole was optimistically named Alice Springs after the wife of the former Postmaster General of South Australia, Sir Charles Todd. The Todd River was named after Sir Charles himself. A unique sporting event, held annually here, links Alice to Henley Regatta in the UK, it's called the Henley-on-Todd Regatta, also known as the Todd River Race. It's a sand river race with bottomless boats and crews run along the river bed, holding their boats on shoulder straps, in fours, eights and singles, just like at Henley. It remains the only dry river regatta in the world; the Aussies do have a good sense of humour. Another unusual sporting event is the Camel Cup which is also held annually at the local racetrack, Blatherskite Park. It is a full day event featuring a series of races using camels instead of horses. Alice is also famous for its school of the Royal Flying Doctor service; it is not until you see for yourself the road distances involved getting here, that you begin to realize just how much such an isolated community must need these services.

After viewing all the places of interest in Alice on 14th August we moved south to Ayres Rock, now known by its Aboriginal name, Uluru. This sandstone monolith is one of the 7 natural wonders of the world and is in the Uluru-Kata Tjuta National Park, some 335kms south west of Alice in the southern part of the Northern Territory. Uluru is sacred to the Aboriginal people of the area. It has many springs, waterholes, rock caves and ancient paintings and is now listed as a World Heritage Site. It's one of Australia's most recognizable natural icons and stands 348 m (1,142 ft) high,with most of its bulk below the ground, and measures 9.4 km (5.8 mi) in circumference. The land all around the rock is flat, and therefore the rock can be seen for miles. Weathering of iron-bearing minerals in the sandstone, by the process of oxidation, gives the outer surface layer of rock a red-brown rusty colour. Geoff climbed the rock, while I, not having a good head for heights, waited below. Uluru is notable for appearing to change colour as the different light strikes it at different times of the day and year, with sunset a particularly remarkable sight when it briefly glows red. We returned that evening and were surprised by how many viewers had turned up to see the sunset. It was spectacular, as the sun sank the colour of the rock changed, and then to our surprise, the moon came up from behind it; it was a very special moment.

It was now very dark as we made our way out of The National Park; there were no campsites here. Whilst driving the camper, we nearly ran into three camels galloping across the road; not an unusual sight here in the desert. The first camel in Australia was imported from the Canary Islands in 1840 and an estimated 12,000 camels were imported into Australia between 1860 and 1907 and were used as draft and riding animals by people pioneering the dry interior. Camel studs were set up in 1866 and operated for about fifty years and provided high class breeding stock. Working camels bred in Australia were of superior quality to those imported. The camels brought into Australia were almost exclusively the one-humped camels (Camelus dromedarius) dromedaries, which are found in hot desert areas and are highly suited to the climate in Australia. Central Australia used camels in the construction of the Overland Telegraph line, the supply of goods to Alice Springs and to cattle and sheep stations, missions and Aboriginal communities. Camels hauled wagons, loaded with wool to the railhead at Oodnadatta; they pulled scoops and ploughs to build dams or performed other heavy jobs. Most of the camels were released in the mid 1920s, when motor vehicles began operating in the central areas of Australia and they established free-ranging herds in the semi-arid desert areas. In the late 1960s renewed interest occurred in camels and by 1970 Australia had two camel tourist businesses, both operating in Alice Springs; we later learned that the camels were often let free to roam at night, lucky for them we weren't a Road Train.

It was getting a little hazardous driving at night so we stopped in the next lay-by and bedded down. Over the next two days, we drove non-stop by day, changing drivers every few hours, only stopping for food and drinks. We made good time and we arrived back in Port Augusta on Wednesday the 16th August; this had been a diversion well worth taking if only for the spectacular view of Uluru at sunset.

On 17th August and on our way back towards Adelaide the weather began to change and it was becoming very windy, so strong at times, we had, in the end, to shelter behind a line of trees, which we used as a wind break; it was too dangerous to drive as the wind just pushed the vehicle all over the road. The clips that held the pop top down were being pulled out of their sockets and so we had to tie the roof down with rope and we waited for things to quieten down. Luckily our vehicle hire company had a depot in Adelaide so we called in there as we were passing for some repairs.

Back on the Princes Highway going south and hugging the Southern Ocean coast we stopped for the night at Mount Gambier, 460kms south east of Adelaide. Set on the slopes of an extinct volcano and in the centre of the largest softwood pine plantation in the Commonwealth, Mount Gambier was beautiful and just within the border of South Australia. Here the rich volcanic soil of the surrounding plain supported the areas farming, viticulture and dairy herds. This region was called "The Limestone Coast" and the white Mount Gambier stone was used when building the city.

Today we crossed back into the state of Victoria and headed for Melbourne. Along the way, we came across Geelong, and stopped here to take a look around. Belinda (Steve's former girlfriend) and Melanie, (Belinda's sister and now Steve's secretary), had spent their early years here. The city is located on Corio Bay and the Barwon River and is just 75 kms south-west of the state's capital, Melbourne. In 1840 Geelong had became the port for the wool industry and the gold rush in Ballarat saw the population increase to 22,000 by the mid 1850s. It was still windy and cold; we could see that this would have been a nice place to stay had the weather been better. We moved up the coast and camped at a 'Big4' camp site just out side of Melbourne.

On 20th August we took a full day trip into the city of Melbourne. The city's metropolitan area is located on a large natural bay known as Port Phillip. Noted for a blend of contemporary and Victorian architecture, expansive parks and gardens and diverse multicultural society, Melbourne is also home to the world's largest tram network. First we visited 'The Queen Victoria Market', an enormous market spread over some seven hectares with more than 600 individual retailers which seemed to sell everything from fruit and vegetables to local and imported gourmet foods, fashion and general merchandise. The Aboriginal art here was very interesting too, there was also several different sizes of beautifully carved and decorated didgeridoos, I would have loved to have bought one but unfortunately we couldn't carry anything as large as this back to the UK. We sat for a while in the main street and watched some very talented kids perform on their BMX bikes but it had begun to drizzle and so we moved on. We wandered around some of the main streets, taking in some of the sights and sounds of the city but as today was wet and cold, we were soon glad to return to our little camper to warm up again; perhaps not the best time of year to see this coast.

The following day we carried on along the coast road in the direction of Sydney. We found ourselves travelling beside Ninety Mile Beach a sandy stretch of the south-eastern coastline of Victoria which separates the Gippsland Lakes region from Bass Strait; the stretch of water between mainland Australia and Tasmania. This 94 mile beach is believed to be the third longest uninterrupted beach in the world and is known as the Gippsland Lakes Coastal Park. After a three hours drive, east of Melbourne we reached Lakes Entrance, a tourist resort and fishing port whose main beach front is a safe harbour for many major commercial fishing and recreational water sport operations; the weather was beginning to improve a little and we decided to camp here over night.

We woke the following morning to lovely weather, we were now approaching the end of August and there were signs of spring in the air; the weather was improving daily. Today we crossed the state border into New South Wales again, and we headed for Eden, a place we had visited before with Bryan and had liked very much. Eden had been founded in whaling days, when there had been a huge whaling industry in these southern oceans but now it was a major whale watching area and the most important fishing port on the south coast. It was a lovely little town with nice beaches and we decided to stay here in a campsite with an indoor swimming pool for a few days, to rest after our hectic journey.

On 29th August we made a five hour journey back to Brian and June's farm; it was great to see them all again and as usual we were made to feel very welcome. The following morning while walking around the farm, we came across a baby wallaby all alone nestling in the grass. Bryan said that it was possible that it had been abandoned by its mother as sometimes if a dog chases the adult wallaby; it has a tendency to lead the dog away from its baby but then may not return. We gently picked him up and wrapped him in a cosy jacket to keep him warm; he seemed quite happy and relaxed just to cuddle up. Brian made a telephone call to the local wild life protection agency and they came later that day to pick him up, saying that they would take good care of him.

After checking with the agency the following day, we were invited out to their sanctuary to come and see all the other animals that they were taking care of. It was really interesting as there was a variety of rescued animals to see. There were kangaroos, large and small, and some wombats too. Two of the larger kangaroos had been brought up here and recently released back into the wild but they still returned each day for their food. There was a wombat that had been rescued because he had broken teeth and couldn't feed on his usual diet of grass. He was huge and very heavy and we watched, fascinated, as the lady keeper struggled to left him up. Bryan's grandchildren wanted to stroke him but they were advised not to as apparently wombats weren't to be trusted and might give a nasty bite: even with broken teeth.

Our little wallaby turned out to be a female Red Necked Wallaby and was taking the special milk that they were feeding her with extremely well. He was sleeping in a special sheepskin pouch/bag which was now hanging in the ladies bedroom so she could feed him during the night. She told us that he had been out of his pouch and had climbed back in without any help so she thought that he would happily thrive in his new home. We had given him a name; we had called him Bimby, as Bryan's farm was called Bimbimby. The weather had improved a lot and we spent a few more very peasant days at the farm, enjoying midday barbeques before finally leaving for Dapto on the 4th September. We said our final farewell to Bryan, June and family; they had been perfect hosts.

Steve and Ann and the children had now arrived in Queensland for the pre-Olympic training camp. Jane David, Ben and Steph had also left England and were taking a 'round the world' trip on their way to Australia. They were flying eastward from London to begin their trip in San Francisco and from there they'd be stopping off at the Hawaiian Islands and then the Barrier Reef off Queensland before travelling on to Sydney for the Olympics. Their plans were to fly back to the UK stopping off in Hong Kong making the complete trip something that they would all remember. Ben and Steph had needed to obtain special permission to miss the start of their school term and this had been granted due to the fact that their Uncle Steve was making a once-in-a-life-time attempt at achieving five consecutive Olympic gold medals; the whole trip was deemed to be an education in itself.

Christine had originally planned on being at home during the Olympics as she had not thought that she would be able to afford the trip. Edward had surprised her with a last minute offer to pay for their flights and they were now both planning to join us too; we were so pleased that the whole family would be here to support Steve. Edward had pushed the boat out and was flying with Chris via Tokyo to Brisbane, where they would be hiring a camper and touring the east coast for a few weeks prior to arriving in the Blue Mountains, where we would all be staying during the Olympics. Afterwards they had planned to drive the camper inland, for a visit to Canberra, returning to Sydney via Bateman's Bay. Their flight back to the UK would take them to Osaka in Japan; a five weeks trip in all.

Geoff and I spent a few days with Joan, Bert and Glen and Wendy and Wally and their family before making our way back to Sydney. Bert had just come out of hospital and was recovering well. Danielle, Wendy's daughter had just given birth to a baby boy; he was to be called Kalani and both mother and son were doing well. We were really pleased too as we had just heard that all of my Australian family had arranged to visit us at our rented house at Wentworth Falls in the Blue Mountain on the Sunday following Steve's final; we really hoped we would all have something to celebrate.

# Chapter Twenty Five
## The 2000 Sydney Olympic Games

### *Guts, Glory and Gold*

We left Dapto on the 9th September; it hadn't been the sad farewell that I had expected due to the news that we would all be getting together for one more family gathering before we finally left Australia. We made our way through Sydney to Botany Bay which was close to the vehicle hire company where we'd be retuning the camper the following morning; we stayed here for the night. Sydney Airport, Australia's largest airport, sits on north-western side of the bay Botany Bay and land was reclaimed from the bay to extend its first north-south runway and also to build a second one parallel to it. From where we were camped we could see the planes taking off and landing, which was quite noisy but it somehow added to our building excitement and anticipation of everything that was to come over the next few weeks. In the morning, we swapped our camper for an estate car, our vehicle for our last few weeks in Australia, and headed for the Blue Mountains and Wentworth Falls.

Wentworth Falls, we'd been told, was one of the most beautiful towns within the Blue Mountains, and its proximity, close to Penrith Lakes and the Olympic Rowing venue, made it an ideal base for our family to stay. It was on the main railway line to Sydney too, which made it a good place to be for the days between rowing when we may all want to go into the city to do some sightseeing. We had booked our stay here over six months ago and we'd had no contact with the owners, while on our travels. It had been arranged that we would take over the property today, Sunday 10th September. We imagined that someone would be at the property to meet us but when we arrived, no one was there: not even a note saying where we might collect the key. The only phone number we had for the owners, was a business telephone number, and of course being Sunday no was answering; I began to panic. We asked either neighbour but neither had a clue. After re-checking the address and spending sometime discussing what we might now do if we weren't able to get in, we began to search the garden and the sheds trying to imagine where a spare key might have been secreted. About to give up and as a last resort, Geoff lifted the lid of the kettle barbeque on the patio and there inside was a bunch of keys; we immediately tried the front door and to our amazement it opened.

We let ourselves in and what a wonderful surprise we had. The house had looked lovely from the outside; it was in a Canadian lodge style but inside was even more impressive. The house was enormous and beautifully decorated with modern furniture and polished wooden floors. It had a very large modern kitchen/diner which must have been 40ft long, with double patio door leading to the large patio and the lawn below. The dining area had a very long table that would easily seat us all. At the sitting room end was a large screen TV and there were several large sofas and arm chairs in a semi-circle around a large wood burning fire, ready stacked with logs for burning; it was all extremely pleasant. Upstairs were five large bedrooms and two bathrooms. We unpacked and then sat down to enjoy a meal. It was luxury being in a king sized bed after sleeping in a small camper for almost six months and we fell asleep while watching the TV in our bedroom.

On Monday 11th September, we had arranged to meet Ann and the children at Sydney airport as they were flying in from Brisbane. We hadn't seen them all for six months and we felt very excited. At the airport the kids all came running through to meet us they were as excited as we had been. Once back at the house the kids soon made themselves at home and began to run around and play while I got a meal and Ann brought us up to speed on the last six months events. She said that Steve was well and the lads had enjoyed a good training camp in Brisbane. Ann spent the night with us, mainly to get the children settled in, before catching the train to Sydney, the following morning, to rejoin the rowing squad at the Olympic Village.

It felt wonderful to be with our grandchildren again; we'd really missed them and we were both amazed at how much they had grown. Once we had dropped Ann at the station we continued to walk over the railway bridge into Sinclair Crescent which we found lead through a corridor of trees to the beautiful Wentworth Falls Lake. Beside the lake was a children's playground and all three of them happily played on the swings and had fun feeding the geese and ducks.

On Thursday 14th September, Paul, Wendy's son came to visit us for the day, bringing his two dogs with him; this really pleased the kids. He was a lovely lad who lived and worked close by in Penrith where he owned a local grocery store and newsagents; he had left his staff to hold the fort and had taken a day off. After settling the children down to sleep, we too had an early night as we knew that we had to be up early as the following morning; Geoff had arranged to meet Jane, David, Ben and Steph at Sydney airport as they were flying in from Cairns; I stayed at home with the kids as Christine and Edward were due to arrive too that day in their camper.

Friday 15th September dawned and we felt the air of excitement beginning to build as today was the Sydney Olympic Games opening ceremony: it was taking place at 7pm this evening. After breakfast, Geoff set off on foot for the train station as he was picking up a hire car and then meeting Jane, David Ben, and Steph, from the airport. The vehicle hire company had given them an upgrade to a 4x4 so there was now plenty of room for them and their luggage. Christine and Edward arrived in their hired camper and parked on the large lawn at the side of the house. Everyone was pleased to be finally here and we all enjoyed a big family meal together; the first for six months. The children had a great time exploring the house and garden. There were lots of places to play hide and seek and lots of toys had been left in the house for them to play with. Zak seemed to follow Ben everywhere; I guess he looked up to his older cousin.

We had eaten our evening meal early so that we would all be able to gather around the television to watch the Opening Ceremony together. We had decided to watch this on the television at home as it was too far away and was too late for the children, as it didn't start till 7pm. From our previous experience at these events, although fantastic to watch, they are not really the place to take small children. With the children all bathed and ready for bed, we settled down to watch the Opening Ceremony; Australian style.

For us watching on Australian TV, The **Games of the XXVII Olympiad opened being** hosted by Australia's Channel Seven's newsreader Chris Bath, while seven months pregnant with her first child; live on stage in the stadium. The Opening Ceremony had a cast of over twelve thousand people and represented everything Australian, from sea creatures and flora and fauna to lawn mowers and other Australian cultural icons. The mascots for the Sydney Olympics were "Olly", a kookaburra, "Syd", a platypus; and "Millie", an echidna, all three native Australian animals representing the earth, the air and water. There were segments covering Australia's Aboriginal past and others showcasing the Australian outback, wildlife and flora. Various fire performers, jugglers and breathers, moved across the stadium floor, symbolizing the advance of a bushfire. Tap dancers danced on the corrugated iron sheets, with umbrellas made up to look like giant cogs and wheels to represent the industrial growth of Australia.

There were various musical performances, including of course "Waltzing Matilda". Next was the stiring stuff of the massed Millennium Marching Band. Two thousand musicians performed both Australian and international classics. The band was made up of 1000 Australian musicians, with the remaining 1000 musicians being from other countries around the world. The massed band was so large that six conductors were required for this segment. The band members wore the famous Driza-Bone riding coats which had been especially modified for them. The band was the only live sound that night; later we learned that all other sounds, including the tap dancers' taps, had been pre-recorded to ensure top quality sound on the night. A large model of the Sydney Harbour Bridge, composed of sparklers, was set off in the middle of the stadium with the word "Eternity" shown in the middle of the bridge.

The athletes then entered the stadium, in alphabetical order as usual. This time it was Mathew, who carried the flag for Great Britain, he looked so proud with his arm outstretched carrying the flag ahead of the Great Britain team, who were all looking really good in their uniforms. Most remarkable was the entering of North Korea and South Korea as one team, using a specially designed flag. Four athletes from East Timor also marched in the parade of nations; this country-to-be had no National Olympic Committee yet, but they were allowed to compete under the Olympic Flag. For these Games, a record 199 nations entered the stadium. The Australian pop stars John Farnham and Olivia Newton-John walked among the Olympic competitors next and sang the song "Dare to Dream", which had been written especially for the occasion.

IOC President Juan Antonio Samaranch then described the ceremony as 'the most beautiful ceremony the world has ever seen'. His poor wife was seriously ill and was not able to accompany her husband to the Olympics (she died the following day, from cancer). Samaranch had invited former Australian Olympic Champion swimmer, Dawn Fraser, to accompany him at the ceremony. The Governor-General, Sir William Deane, opened the games; this was the first occasion that a Summer Olympics held in a Commonwealth nation was not opened by the monarch or member of the Royal Family

The opening ceremony concluded with the lighting of the Olympic Flame. Pop star Tina Arena and the Sydney Children's Choir performed 'The Flame' before former Australian Olympic champion Herb Elliott brought the Olympic Flame into the stadium. Then, celebrating 100 years of women's participation in the Olympic Games, former Australian women Olympic champions brought the torch through the stadium, finally handing it over to Cathy Freeman, a major role model for Aborigines in Australia. Cathy then climbed a long set of stairs towards a circular pond and walked into the middle of the water and ignited the cauldron around her feet in a circle of fire. The planned spectacular climax to the ceremony was delayed by the technical glitch of a computer switch, which had malfunctioned, causing the sequence to shut down by giving a false reading. This meant that the Olympic flame was suspended in mid-air for about four minutes, rather than immediately rising up a water-covered ramp to the top of the stadium. When the cause of the problem was discovered, the program was overridden and the cauldron continued its course, and then the ceremony concluded with a spectacular fireworks display as the aerial camera panned back to show a view of Sydney Harbour Bridge and The Sydney Opera House. It had been a very long ceremony which we'd all felt emotional watching. Needless to say some of the children didn't see it all; a few had nodded off long before the fireworks.

On Saturday 16th September we all had a quiet day. Racing would start tomorrow and we all had to be up early to catch the train to Penrith. We bought some Australian newspapers to read about the opening ceremony and spent a lazy afternoon and evening reading and watching TV while the children played. The first medals of the Games were awarded in the women's 10 meter air rifle competition, which was won by Nancy Johnson of the United States. The Triathlon made its Olympic debut with the women's race. Set in the surroundings of the Sydney Opera House, Brigitte McMahon of Switzerland swam, cycled and ran to the first gold medal in the sport, beating the favoured home athletes. We all watched as the amazing Ian Thorpe, the 17-year-old Australian swimmer; first set a new World Record in the 400 m freestyle final before competing in an exciting 4 x 100 m freestyle final. Swimming the last leg, Thorpe passed the leading Americans and arrived in a new World Record time, two tenths of a second ahead of the Americans. The IOC president Juan Antonio Samaranch, at his last Olympics, had to leave for home, as his wife was severely ill. Upon his arrival, he sadly found that his wife had already passed away; Samaranch returned to Sydney four days later.

Today was Sunday 17th September and it was Steve's first heat. We were all up early and raring to go; it didn't seem to matter to any of us that it was 5am and still dark. We all trouped off, en masse, to the local railway station and waited on the platform in the cold morning air; we could see our own breath as we chatted excitedly to each other and stamped our feet to keep warm. We didn't have long to wait before the train to Penrith pulled in and we all scrambled aboard. It was like the old saying 'I met a man with seven wives'; there was eleven of us altogether, adults, kids, pushchairs, bags and flags.

On the train already, and there to greet us, were Ann's family who were staying further up the rail line at Katcoomba; the bunch of British supporters were growing, we were now sixteen strong. There was June, Ann's mother, Pattie, June's friend, Sue, Ann's youngest sister and her husband Cameron with their baby girl Paige: our youngest supporter at just a few months old. The train took about forty five minutes to get to Penrith and during this journey we watched from the window as the new day dawned; the passing fields misty in the weak morning sunshine. When we arrived in Penrith, we found it all very well organised with Olympic volunteers guiding our way, ushering us into line for the waiting busses that would transport us to the rowing course. When we finally arrived at the course, we all lined up once more to pass through the security systems where our bags were searched. We then had quite a walk to get to our seats in the stands but by 8.30am we were marking out our territory by tying our flags to the railings. We knew that some of the Australian family would be here today but their tickets would have taken them to the other side of the rowing course; we scanned the crowds trying to spot them but it was too far away and there were throngs of people; it was hard to pick out individuals.

It was beginning to warm up now and the water was sparkling in the sunshine. Some of the men were already drinking beer and coke and eating a belated breakfast of hotdogs and burgers. We'd got our steaming cups of coffee and the kids were munching on crisps; we were feeling good and ready to take on the world.

Rowing started on time with the Women's Single sculls, Alison Mowbray for GB and this was followed by Men's single sculls, with our sculler Mathew Wells. The Women's Coxless Pairs heats with Dorothy Blackie, and Catharine Bishop for Great Britain and The Men's Coxless Pairs with Edward Coode and Greg Searle. Ed had rowed in the Coxless Four with our lads in Canada, and Greg was already an Olympic gold medallist from Barcelona in 1992. We watched the Women's Double Scull heats, with Francis Houghton, and Sarah Winkless for G B and the Men's Double Sculls, which this year had no British entry.

Our lads were up next; our stomachs were beginning their usual somersaults. The Great Britain Men's Coxless Four included Steve, James Cracknell, Matthew Pinsent and, we were pleased to say, Tim Foster, who was back now to full fitness after his back injury; this would be their first heat. Their draw today was: Slovenia, lane 1, Romania, lane 2, Great Britain lane 3, Australia, lane 4, Yugoslavia, lane 5. We sat huddled in our seats, our fingers were crossed. I had found some four leaved clover a few days ago and I had carefully pressed the leaves into my diary pages, one on each of the days that Steve would be rowing; today and hopefully Thursday in the semi-finals and Saturday in the finals, but I wouldn't let myself think that far ahead yet.

There was not too much banter at this point and from where we were sitting. We could clearly see down the entire course; it was too distant to pick anyone out. The commentary began and we eagerly watched the big screen; they'd made a positive start and had taken a small lead. At the thousand meter mark, they were holding their lead. At the 1500 metre mark we could see they were well out in front and they crossed the line in first place to a huge cheer from their supporters. We were all elated; it was a wonderful feeling to know that they had got this one firmly in the bag. We watched the rest of the races that morning feeling quite relaxed; it was all over by 12'oclock. We slowly made our way with the crowds out of the enclosure; we weren't sure how we were going to find my Aussie family in this mass of people. Once over the other side of the lake, I suddenly heard some shouts of 'Sheila', and was really surprised to see Peter McConnell running up to me. It was lovely to see him; Peter had been in the Great Marlow School crew with Steve all those years ago. He told me that he felt that he couldn't miss the Olympics for anything and had travelled over to Australia with some friends particularly to come here and support Steve. We chatted for a while before he returned to his friends; it was really heart-warming to think that his old school friends and colleagues had come to the other side of the world to see him compete.

Then we caught a glimpse of Joan and Wendy and the rest of their family. Even Bert had come along; what a sport he was, but the poor man didn't look too well. We were shocked when we got closer to Joan whose face was looking really bruised. She had taken a tumble on her way into the spectator's enclosure and had fallen over a low barrier; she already looked as if she had done a couple of rounds with Mike Tyson. The family had taken her to have first aid and the paramedics had patched her up but she looked very shaken and bruised. We had a chat all together over coffee, then we went our separate ways; they drove to Paul's house and we made our way back to the trains and returned to Wentworth Falls.

On Monday 18<sup>th</sup> September Geoff, Jane, David, Ben, Steph, Chris, and Edward, had booked ahead to do the Sydney Bridge Climb, a 3 ½ hour guided journey to the top of the Sydney Harbour Bridge. The bridge at 134m above Sydney Harbour was a little too high for my vertigo but I had a good excuse; the younger kids couldn't go they were too young as the lower age limit was 13years old. The Sydney Harbour Bridge opened in 1932, may not be the longest steel-arch Bridge in the world, but it is the largest and widest at 48.8 metres (151.3 feet) wide, making it the widest single-span Bridge in the world. They told me later that they had all been kitted out with special all-in-one jump suit and a cap and had first completed a compulsory training course before being allowed on the actual climb. Their climb had taken them along the outer arch of the Bridge on catwalks and ladders all the way to the summit; a slider clip attached to a static line on the bridge ensuring they felt safe. They were told that the pylons were made of concrete faced in granite, which had been quarried near Moruya, 300km from Sydney and was where my cousin Bryan came from. They couldn't stop talking about their fantastic experience with the 360 degree views of Sydney, including the Harbour city surrounds, Sydney Opera House and out west to the Blue Mountains. At the end of their Climb, they received a commemorative Climber Certificate and a complimentary group photograph of them all standing together with huge smiles in the sunshine with Sydney Opera House as the backdrop way below.

I had spent a more sedentary day, taking Natalie, Sophie and Zak to The Sydney Children's Museum. It had been very good, focusing on providing a number of hands-on activities for kids. There was an exhibit on anatomy that began with a walk through a giant mouth, an area that tested their sense of smell, an exhibit on electricity and a display of vintage toys, all in very good condition. We had really enjoyed our morning and after lunch we met up with the climbers and Geoff and I had then taken the young ones back to the house, while the others had stayed in Sydney to do some more sightseeing. Back at the house the kids played in the garden while Geoff and I settled down to watch some more of the Olympic events on TV.

On Tuesday morning, Geoff woke up not feeling very well; there was a nasty flu going round. Ann came over later that day and gave us all flue jabs, as she had already done with all the rowers. Natalie had been invited to do a television interview by the team from the BBC's children news programme 'Newsround'; we had arranged to meet the reporter that morning in Darling harbour. Natalie sat on a wall by the harbour and told the reporter what is was like to have a famous father. She also said that she didn't get to see him during the competition and that she was sure that he would retire after the Sydney Games; she did really well. Sophie didn't speak at all and Zak just smiled and kicked his heels against his push chair. Putting the microphone in front of Zak, the reporter asked him what he would shout during his dad's race. Natalie whispered in Zak's ear and then he loudly chanted Dad-dy, Dad-dy, it was really amusing. Geoff had not joined us today; he was feeling a little rough and hoped that by staying in bed for a couple of days, he would feel better for the lad's semi-final on Thursday. After Natalie's interview, we all went on to visit the Sydney Aquarium.

Sydney Aquarium was close at hand and was just the other side of Darling Harbour. It was very impressive and the kids were really fascinated by the huge variety of Australian aquatic life we saw as we walked through a series of underwater, see-through, acrylic glass tunnels where sharks, rays and other fish swam above the visitors in a recreation of a Great Barrier Reef coral environment. The rest of us returned to the house while Jane and family went to the airport to meet their friend Jackie Sherry, who was flying in today to join our party for the rest of the Olympics.

Wednesday 20th September was a quiet day for Geoff and I. He was still not feeling great but we had high hopes that tomorrow would see him fit enough to join us at Penrith Lakes. The weather was still good and the kids were enjoying the garden so I left Geoff in charge while I popped out for some grocery shopping. The adults had all gone into Sydney to have lunch at The Sydney Tower which standing at 305 meters tall is the second tallest building in Australia. They enjoyed their dining experience in the Sydney Tower Restaurant with its revolving floor and 360-degree panoramic views of Sydney. The menu, amongst other things, had included Ostrich, Crocodile and Kangaroo. On their way back Jane and Chris had called into the supermarket too and so we ended up with an absolute mountain of food and wine, enough to last us the entire holiday.

On Thursday morning Geoff, who was still not at all well, reluctantly stayed behind; he must have been bad to have missed such an important race. We asked Paul to join us at the last minute; it would be great to see him again and he could use Geoff's ticket. We all set off at the crack of dawn again taking the train and bus to the rowing course; the weather today was really good. Jackie had bought some small union jack transfers and she had applied these to all the kids faces including herself. Armed with our flags we took our seats in the stand; there wasn't long to wait before our boys lined up. They were in the first semi-final of The Men's Coxless Fours with the line up as follows: lane 1 Germany, 2 U S A, 3 France, 4 Great Britain, 5 Slovenia, 6 Romania.

Great Britain got their bows out in front before the 250 meter mark and as the commentator announced this, a great cheer went up; they'd taken the lead. By the 1,000 meter mark they were ahead by half a boat length and continued to the finish in the same position. They'd made it to the final; what a relief. It was hard for us to imagine that we would not see him achieve his final goal; but I couldn't go there, it would be tempting fate. Also through to Saturday's final from the lad's heat, was Slovenia and USA; France, Germany, and Romania would go to the B final.

We watched the second semi-final with Egypt, Australia, Italy, New Zealand, Norway and Yugoslavia. This was a cracking good race with the home crowd yelling for their team. The race was between Australia and Italy most of the way with Italy a few feet in front. Australia made a final push and took the lead almost on the line; cheered on by the crowd they had won by a very small margin. It had been a faster time than the first semi-final due mainly to the fact that Australia was being pushed all the way. The line up for Steve's final on Saturday had been decided, it would be Great Britain, Slovenia, USA, Australia, Italy and New Zealand.

After the rowing had finished we all decided to travel into Sydney on the train and visit the Taronga zoo; Paul joined us too which was great. We took the train to Circular Quay and then boarded a ferry across Sydney Harbour to Taronga Ferry wharf. The weather was fabulous today and as we ploughed across the deep blue waters of the Bay, the brilliant sun glinting on the water, we got a amazing view of The Sydney Opera House and Harbour Bridge; it took just 12 minutes. Once we had landed we then took the Sky Safari cable car which took us to Taronga Zoo at the top of the cliffs over looking the bay; the scenery was almost unbelievable and the weather couldn't have been better; we were all on a high. The children really loved seeing the Australian birds and animals that they had not seen before like the Laughing Kookaburra, the Platypus, the Kangaroos and Dingoes and the cuddly Koalas clinging to their gum trees while sleeping in the sunshine. At the end of the day, I think that we all fell asleep on the train going back to Wentworth Falls, where with renewed energy; the kids excitedly told their granddad about their adventures. Geoff, who was feeling a little better today, had watched Steve's race on television from the comfort of his armchair.

Friday, Christine and Edward went to look round the area and Jane, David, Ben, Steph, and Jackie went to meet some friends in Sydney, Geoff and I, and the children, had a quiet morning and after lunch went down to Penrith shopping centre. The children were really well behaved but seemed a little tired from their long day yesterday so we planned an early night for everyone as we had to make another early start tomorrow for the final; I think we all went to bed saying a little prayer.

Saturday 23rd September started much the same as every other day really. Geoff was only just beginning to feel a little better but today I think that he would have dragged himself from his death bed to be there to see Steve race. We had the usual scramble to make sure everyone had some breakfast, we got the kids washed and dressed and we gathered together all that we needed to take for the day ahead. We made the station just in time to catch the 7.05am train. With so much to think about and with so much to carry, I had given our big union jack to Jane to look after. This was one of our lucky charms which we'd had since Steve early days of rowing and had taken to all of his races.

355

By the time we got to the course, Jane had lost the flag, she didn't know where it could be, she thought that she may have left it on the train; we couldn't go back now. We managed without it and I must say, there was no shortage of flags; union jacks were all around us and again Jackie and Jane had transferred union flags onto all our cheeks. We found our seats and settled down, David and Edward went to buy drinks for everyone. The air was a little nippy this morning but the sun was climbing higher and I could feel its rays already warming my back. Zak was still a bit sleepy and as he was at on my lap being cuddled, he fell asleep. I was sitting in an aisle seat and a man opposite had set up his camera next to me. We chatted a while and he told me that he was Australian and that he was making a video; he said that he had followed Steve's career and would send me a copy. I thought that was nice of him but I thought no more about it; I had other things on my mind.

The rowing started, but I couldn't say now what order things happened in; my mind is a bit of a blur. I do remember hearing the start of the Pairs race called. Ed Coode and Greg Searle were in this one and we got to our feet and cheered them along. They led to the 1,250 meter mark but were then overtaken by the French pair; in the final seconds of the race they were engulfed by the USA and Australia too. It must have been a terrible disappointment for them; fourth place after leading early on. Zak had woken up by now with all the shouting, so I sat back down with him on my lap again and let him wake up properly; every one was disappointed for Ed and Greg and every thing had quietened down.

During this lull my thoughts went out to my son; if that happened to him next, how would he cope; this was surely his last Olympics. I reminded myself to stay positive; my stomach was beginning to churn. All the pressure he had taken and the pain he had suffered along the way to reach this pinnacle of his career; if it all went wrong today, I couldn't bear to see this happen to him, it would be a massive blow. I looked at Geoff; he gave a shrug and mouthed 'He'll be OK'.

Ann arrived then; she wanted to be with us for this race. She sounded and looked good and was smiling as she always did, but I knew she would be feeling just as anxious as me. They would do it; they were the best and strongest team in the world.

Geoff is a very quiet man; Steve is like his father in many ways neither of them finds it easy to show their feelings. Some people may think that Geoff is dispassionate, but he's not at all, he's an extremely emotional man under the cool exterior; I know he would have crawled on his hands and knees to be here to support his son today. Natalie was by my side, as she has always been for the big races and Zak was now fully awake and seemed full of beans. Sophie was with Geoff. Their race was being called now at the starting pontoons and we could clearly see them up on the big screen as they sat on the start line waiting for the off. The line up for the final of the Men's Coxless Fours were as follows: lane 1 USA, lane 2 Slovenia, lane 3 Great Britain, lane 4 Australia, lane 5 Italy, lane 6 New Zealand; our boys were flanked by their two biggest rivals.

A final thought, in these last seconds, kept running through my mind; in their semi-final they hadn't been pressured. Please God give them the strength to win this one. The commentator called, 'They are off to a clean start'; I thanked God; no false start. At the 250 meter mark our lads had managed to get their bows out in front, and at the 500 meter mark they were in front of the field by half a boat length with Italy in second position and Australia in third. Steve had always said to me 'If I'm in contention at the one thousand metre mark, then the race is mine'. With just 250 meters left to go their lead was down to a third of a boat length, and the Italians were closing fast. With a call from Steve, Mathew raised their rate to 44. We were all on our feet and yelling so loud that it was deafening, the children we screaming too Dad-dy, Dad-dy Dad-dy. It was down to a canvas at one hundred metres from the line; we were all shouting our heads off, as if the louder we shouted the faster they might go, we almost lost sight of them as the tears flowed down our cheeks. As they crossed the line, the mixed nationality crowd of 22,000 rose to their feet and cheered in unison, I wasn't totally sure they had won. Natalie thinking that her Dad had lost the race had started to cry. Then it flashed up on the big screen; they had done it, by a hair's breath; 38/100$^{th}$ of one second. It was incredible, Great Britain had taken the Gold in 5.56.24, Italy, the Silver in 5.56.62 and Australia, the Bronze in 5.57.61. Great Britain had the gold, Steve had his Fifth Gold Medal, achieved over Five consecutive Olympics; what a man.

Mathew had taken his third Olympic gold, Tim and James their first. We watched as Mathew crawled over Tim and back along the boat to congratulate Steve, they hugged each other, then Mathew had fallen overboard into the water, they were all so elated but we could see their exhaustion too. Mathew clung to the boat as they rowed over to the pontoon so he could get back into the boat, but they all got out of the boat and hugged each other, then they got back in and rowed off to wind down. All this time there were continuous cheers going up, from both sides of the lake. The lads rowed back towards the rostrum to receive their medals. Our crowd was very animated and talking non-stop; everybody showing huge signs of relief, faces still damp with tears. Ann held Natalie who by now had calmed down, knowing her Dad had won. Every body was still cheering, whooping and whistling as they climbed out of their boats and again congratulated each other, the Italians, and Australians all shook their hands and seemed pleased with their final medal positions. The absolute icing on the cake was that Princess Ann was there to present them with their medals, accompanied by David Osborne, IOC Chairman, and Juan Antonio Samaranch the IOC President; what an honour.

Princess Ann came forward to give them their gold medals, James was first in line, but indicated to the Princess that she should give the first medal to Steve, which she did, I thought this was a really nice gesture by James. The Princess finished presenting the medals, to Italy, then to Australia. Next David Osborne gave each team member their winners flower bouquet and then Juan Antonio Samaranch, presented Steve a special gold pin for achievements in rowing in five Olympics and said, "He is an athlete who is really in the golden book of the history of the Olympic Games."

Five consecutive Olympic Gold Medals; this was the first time this had ever been achieved in an endurance sport. It brought tears to our eyes; it was such a special moment for both Geoff and me. Our son, from a working class back ground, with all his medical problems suffering from debilitating colitis and insulin-dependent diabetes and his childhood dyslexia, he had overcome all this and achieved so much. We were all so very proud and gratified, knowing that his entire family had been here to witness this ultimate event and had shared in his triumph; it had been a truly remarkable journey.

Directly after the medal ceremony Steve came over to us and kissed Natalie and gave her his flowers, he had hugged and kissed Sophie and scooped Zak up in his arms and had hugged and kissed Ann. It was so lovely to see the happiness on all of their faces. After lots of interviews and congratulations, we wandered about meeting other spectators that we knew in the crowd. Roxanne, Steve's publicity agent, came to tell us that we had all been invited to a photo shoot and reception which was being given by The News of the World; it was being held at a hotel in Sydney and we would be taken their in taxis.

When we all arrived at the hotel, we were taken into a large conference room where food and champagne was served to us while we watched the crew set up for their photo session. We were then all individually interviewed and then included in a group photos; Steve with his five medals around his neck. Afterwards we travelled home by train leaving Steve and his crew to be whisked off for more meetings, interviews and photo shoots. Ann had to return to the Olympic village as she was still officially working especially as there would still rowing tomorrow and she would have to take care of the crews. It had been arranged that my entire Australian family would join us in The Blue Mountains on Sunday for a lunchtime barbeque and that Steve and Ann would be joining us too when Ann had officially clocked off after the rowing had finished. We later heard that a British television audience of 7.5 million had sat up till after midnight to watch Steve's final race.

The Rowing on Sunday had brought two more medals for Great Britain. The Women's quad won silver; it was a first for British women's rowing. The crew were Guin Batten, Gillian Lindsay, Katharine Granger, and Miriam Batten, Guinn was Miriam's younger sister; we had watched them over the years. The girl's parents had also followed their careers but sadly their mother had died a few years before and I guessed that the girls would be thinking of her that today. The quad had been coached by Mike Spracklen, Steve's first professional coach, so we were very pleased for him too. Less than an hour later the British Men's Eight had rowed to gold, with a crew of, Andrew Lindsay, Ben Hunt-Davis, Simon Dennis, Louis Attrill, Luka Grubor, Kieran West, Fred Scarlett, Steve Trapmore and cox Rowley Douglas; not since 1912 had a British eight won gold and so it had been a superb achievement and would be a big boost to the squad four years later in Athens. In terms of the British Rowing squad, Sydney had been a huge success.

We hadn't forgotten the huge influence and dedicated input by Jürgen Gröbler; Steve and his crew owed their coach 'big time'. We wanted to pay our own special tribute to Jürgen for the way he had steadfastly stood by Steve throughout the ups and downs of Steve's illness: he never stopped believing in Steve and we wanted to thanks him for that. Later, we were so pleased to see that he would become nationally recognised for his enormous efforts and dedication to British Rowing when, later in 2000, he would win the BBC Sports Personality of the Year Coach Award, and in March 2006 he would be presented with an honorary Order of the British Empire (OBE) by Culture Secretary Tessa Jowell for his contribution to British sport.

With the Olympics now over for us, it was time to turn our attentions to celebrating properly and this was to include a huge gathering of all my Australian family too; we had invited every last one of them for a barbeque lunch on Sunday 24th September. Unfortunately, Jane, David, Ben, Steph, and Jackie were leaving for Hong Kong today on the next leg of their world trip before heading home to the UK; they would sadly not be around to meet everyone. Christine, who had, by this morning, completely lost her voice from yelling so much yesterday and was not even being able to utter one squeak, helped me with the food.

There would be thirty from the Australian contingent arriving for lunch, including, my cousins, their children and their grandchildren; I was so excited. Ann's family would be joining us too and Steve and Ann would be arriving after today's rowing had finished. It was a gorgeous day, the sun was shining and the champagne flowed. Wally had volunteered to be in charge of the 'barbie' and there was a mountain of food to consume. We had a grand day, one that I will always remember. During the afternoon, Chris gathered everyone together for some group photos so that we would all be able to keep a record of this great gathering of the clans. Joan, Bert, Wendy, Wally, Danielle, Rob, baby Kalani and brothers Paul and Glen, and Michael and his family all stayed till quite late in the evening. Brian and June stayed with us over night as they had the furthest too travel.

The house seemed quite empty on Monday morning but there was still a huge amount of food left over and a lot of clearing up to do. After breakfast we said our final sad farewell to Brian and June; they had a long trip back to Batemans Bay 300 kms south of Sydney. I loaded them up with copious amounts of food to take home but we still had so much left; Steve and Ann sorted that out for us later when they came over for lunch and helped to polish off the rest. They had been loaned a lovely large apartment in Darling Harbour for the last week of the games; now perhaps they could start to relax as a family and enjoy their week together. We felt really proud when we heard that Steve had been given the honour of carrying the GB flag at the closing ceremony; a fitting end to his Olympic career.

After lunch, Christine and Edward packed up their camper and waved goodbye as they went off for another week of sightseeing before their return to the UK. Now there was just Geoff and me to deal with the final clean up. We were due to vacate the house the following morning when we would return our vehicle to the hire company, before going on to the airport; our six months here in Australia had finally come to an end. We'd spent such a memorable six months in this beautiful country and had loved every minute; we were already hatching plans to return very soon but this time to see much more of Australia. We would go on to make our return five years later in 2005; this time spending twelve month travelling the entire coastline of Australia.

Late the following evening, Tuesday 25<sup>th</sup> September we dropped off our vehicle to the hire company after office hours; posting the key through their letterbox as pre-arranged. We caught a taxi to the airport only to find that our late flight had been severely delayed and would now, not be departing until the following morning. As we had unfortunately already returned our car and with no way of retrieving it, we had no choice but to wait at the airport so we looked around for somewhere to wait; it was now 11.30pm. The next blow we received was being told that the airport completely closed down for the night at midnight and would not re-open until check-in began at 4pm.

With quite a few other people caught up in this delay, the airport staff offered to take us all into an area of the airport where we would be allowed to wait. This turned out to be a very drafty corridor where we settled down as best we could till 4pm the following morning. We had been under the impression that all international airports stayed open 24 hours a day but obviously not; this felt like a very long night. At 4am we were finally allowed to check our luggage in and then we went off in search of some much needed coffee and breakfast. Later while going through security, we managed to somehow loose Geoff's anorak, which contained his favourite Australian leather coin purse; we didn't discover the loss until we reached Hong Kong. We asked the airline staff to check with Sydney but it could not be found.

On our arrival in Hong Kong, although feeling somewhat weary we managed to take a day tour around the island including taking a boat trip around Repulse bay. The former British Crown colony was now, officially since 1997, the Hong Kong Special Administrative Region of the People's Republic of China. It still had a high degree of autonomy in all areas except foreign affairs and defence. Hong Kong, a global city and international financial centre with a highly developed capitalist economy is renowned for its expansive skyline and deep natural harbour, and its identity as a cosmopolitan centre where east meets west is reflected in its cuisine and traditions. Hong Kong which means "fragrant harbour" is located on China's south coast, 37 miles east of Macau on the opposite side of the Pearl River Delta, and its location, just south of the Tropic of Cancer, gives it a humid subtropical climate. Our drive to The Peak took us high above the city giving us a superb view of the Central district, the harbour and Kowloon. The following day we wandered around the shops, looking for last minute gifts to take home and later that evening we arrived back at Chek Lap Kok Airport, about to embark on the last leg of our trip.

We had just boarded our flight and found our economy seats, when one of the flight attendants came to us and enquired if we were Mr & Mrs Redgrave, Steve's mum and dad. She told us that she lived in Marlow and that the airline would like to offer to upgrade us to first class. In all of Steve's long career we have never had a treat like this before and we quickly gathered our belongings together before they changed their mind. Up front in first class, we had wonderful seats, which collapsed down into full length beds and our own mini

T V screens. After take-off, we were given Champagne and then later we were invited to the cockpit to meet the Captain. Everyone was very pleasant to us and we were made to feel like VIPs; it was the most comfortable trip to Heathrow that we have ever had. As we came into land, we could see the River Thames and it brought to mind memories of where it had all started for our son. Never in our wildest dreams had we imagined the enormous success he would have in his rowing career which had now spanned more than twenty five years. We could see St Paul's Cathedral below us where he had married Ann and where subsequently all of his children had been christened, Buckingham Palace where he had received his MBE and CBE; it felt like his whole life was unfolding before our eyes. I turned to look at my husband, Geoff; I had tears in my eyes and so had he.

The house we rented in St Catharine's Canada for the World
Championships 1999

St Catharine's Canada for the World Championships 1999. View
overlooking the rowing course from the lounge of rented house.

St Catharine's Canada for the World Championships 1999. Visit to Niagara Falls - on board the Maid of the Mist. Sheila and Geoff

Four generations Australian Family Aunt Gladys, left to right Wendy (2nd cousin) Aunt Gladys (Aunt), Joan (cousin), Danielle (3rd cousin)

Brian Gray (my Australian cousin) & wife June and their Grandchildren
Jarrod and Rachel

Aunt Gladys Haunted House at Bimbimby Farm, New South Wales,
Australia.

Sheila with abandoned Wallaby at Bimbimby Farm, New South Wales, Australia.

Sidney Opera House, Sydney, Australia taken from Central Quay

Four Seasons (rented house) Wentworth Falls, Blue Mountains Sydney
Olympics 2000

Sidney Harbour Bridge Walk, back row left to right - Ben, David, Edward,
Christine, Stephanie front row - Geoff and Jane during Sydney Olympics
2000

Sydney Olympics 2000 -After the Race - back row Left to Right - David, Edward, Christine, Jane, June, Geoff, Steph, Sue, Cameron, baby Paige, Jackie. Middle row - Natalie, Ben, Sheila, Steve with 5 gold medals, Pattie, front row – Ann, Zak & Sophie.

Aussie and British Family Clan - too many to mention. In garden at Wentworth Fall, after Sydney Olympics 2000

Henley Royal Regatta July 2000 - The Coxless Four – The Steward's
Challenge Cup win.
Tim Foster, Steve Redgrave, Matthew Pinsent, James Cracknell.

'Stars in their Lives' The Green Room, Charlton TV Show, 2000. Back row;
Roger Hatfield, Ian Desmond, Arthur Johns, Nick Baatz, Joan Pritchard,
Jane Evans, Craig Gibbins, David Evans, Derek Pritchard, Liz Spicer.
Bottom row; Sophie Redgrave, Queenie Johns, Steph Evans, Ben Evans,
Ann Redgrave, Natalie Redgrave, Sheila Redgrave, Edward Spicer, Geoff
Redgrave.

Homecoming Bus Ride, Marlow Bottom after Sydney Olympics 2000

Homecoming Bus Ride, Crowds in Marlow High Street, after Sydney Olympics 2000

Sir Steve and Lady Ann Redgrave after Knighthood Ceremony 2001

Steve chatting with Francis Smith his first coach. Francis put Steve's foot on
the first rung of the ladder

Erection of the bronze statue of Steve in Higginson Park Marlow, 2002

Her Majesty The Queen Elizabeth II talking to Sophie and Zak – Left to Right Geoff, Sheila, Matthew, James, Tim, Jürgen, Steve, Ann and Hugh McNearnie. The official unveiling by the Queen of Steve's Statue in Higginson Park, Marlow. May 2002

The Family With Steve's Statue. Back row: Edward, David, Ben. Front row: Jane, June, Ann, Sophie, Steve, Zak, Geoff, Sheila, Aunt Doris, Christine & Stephanie. Higginson Park, Marlow. May 2002.

Our Grandchildren, Christmas 2006 Left to Right Stephanie, Ben, Sophie, Natalie, and Zak.

# Chapter Twenty Six
## Welcome home

### *The Hero's Return*

Our plane landed and taxied in; we'd had a wonderfully comfortable flight. As we gathered our belongings together, the crew all said goodbye and shook our hands. As we collected our luggage from the carousel, we wondered if Jane and the children would be here to collect us as arranged. We had no idea whether they had arrived home safely as we had not been able to be in touch since they'd left the Blue Mountains. Coming through the doors from customs into the arrivals hall, there they all were waiting to greet us. After hugs and kisses, on our way back to the car park, Jane excitedly told us how the folks of Marlow Bottom had decked the village out with bunting and flags and that on the wall of the local farmers barn, in large gold pained letters, had been written 'Welcome Home Steve', with the Olympic rings underneath. She told us that most of the houses in the valley had decorated their front gardens with hand written signs and flags; at that my tears started once again.

On the following day, Friday the 29th September, Ben and Steph had their thirteenth birthday and it had been arranged that we would all go out to a restaurant to celebrate on Sunday. Lots of friends were dropping in to Jane's home today, to see the twins, and so it acted as a sort of home coming for us too. Every one was offering their congratulation and wanting to chat about our experiences in Australia. The day whizzed by and by late evening we were exhausted and were very glad to drop into our bed.

Monday 2nd October was spent decorating Steve's house and drive with flags and banners and welcome home signs. I did a lot of baking and food preparation for the following day as Steve, Ann and the kids were coming home. On Tuesday 3ʳᵈ October, Roxanne, Steve's agent, had made arrangements for chauffeur driven cars to collect us all from home and take us to Heathrow airport where the whole Olympic team would be arriving at 7.30am. We were all up early the next morning at 4.30am., and when we arrived at the airport, television film crews and dozens of newspaper reporters were already there in strength ready to interview the athletes on their arrival.

All the British Olympic teams were arriving on the same flight, so with parents and supporters to meet them, you couldn't move; some rowing supporters had been there all night. The nearest we could get was several rows of people back from the barriers in the arrivals hall. The atmosphere was unbelievable; with people waving flags and holding up banners; you had to shout to be heard above the din. The whole team had attended a press conference first before coming into the arrivals hall but as the athletes came through the doors everyone cheered. It was wonderful to witness the great reception they all received. Suddenly a huge cheer went up that almost raised the roof. I could barely see them but I knew that it was the coxless four. I recognised different people from various rowing clubs all milling around wanting to shake their hands and get their autographs. Reporters were thrusting microphones into their faces and almost getting crushed in the rush. Then I saw Ann and the children pushing their luggage trolley and Natalie shouted 'There's Nan', the people in front of me turned around and opened up a path for us to get to the barriers and I leaned over and kissed the children; they were so excited to see us. Then I looked up and Steve was there with the rest of the lads; he gave me a hug and said 'This is great mum, I've never had a reception like this before'; he was so happy it was wonderful to see.

His supporters around us all got his autograph while telling him that they had been here since midnight; his smile said it all and my hanky had started to get soggy again. Jane and Christine kissed him and took some photos of him with the lads. Steve shook hands with his Dad; I think Geoff was too full of emotion to say too much. Next Steve greeted Ben, Steph, David and Edward, and then signed some more autographs; what a home coming and so well deserved. We all moved out side to where Ann had arranged a huge surprise for her husband. Out side the building and parked at the kerb was a beautiful, brand-spanking new silver Jaguar XJR; apparently they didn't make it in gold. The press photographers were squabbling so much over their positions, elbowing each other out of the way, just to get a shot of him with his new car; a fight was about to break out so the police had to intervene. Steve had always wanted a car like this; we couldn't wait to see his face. With the crowds milling around him he hadn't seen the car but as Ann handed him the keys, with his eyes nearly popping out of his head, he said, 'Is this for me'. He kissed her and they had their photo taken by the TV and newspapers; his smile took a long time to disappear that day.

We all got back into our chauffeured cars and made our way back to Marlow Bottom. As our cars turned in to the valley there were more surprises. The valley residents were out in force, flag waving and cheering and hooting their car horns. We came to a standstill by the farm barn bearing its welcome home sign and there were more crowds of people; it was really overwhelming for us all. Finally, we arrived at Steve's house where he found sacks of mail had been delivered. This was a very different home coming to all the others; he was really being recognised for all his efforts.

We were only just beginning to realise what a large part the BBC had played in Steve's recognition when they had broadcast the lads video diary programme 'Gold Fever', leading up to the Olympics. We had not seen any of these programmes, having been away from the UK for six months. We knew that the lads had all carried a small video camera each with them for most of the time  during the last four years but we hadn't had a chance to watch the recoded tapes of these that Christine had kept for us. We did later watch all of the episodes and were amazed that the lads had recorded their hopes and thoughts directly to camera. It showed their highs and their lows leading up to the Sydney Olympics and it had then been edited and broadcast a mini series of programmes showing the reality of the very tough road they had all had to travel. The series had been really successful and had informed the wider public of their individual struggles. It had created such an interest so much so that over seven million people had stayed awake to watch their final race. We'd heard later that some pubs in Marlow had obtained a late licence that day to be able to show the lads race on their big screens; it had created a respect for their sport

The broadcasting of 'Gold Fever' had given the public a window into their world of training and competition and the hard work and heartache that the sport involved. As Richard Phelps said in his article prior to the Sydney Games 'It chronicled how the four-time gold medal winner, long-time partner Matthew Pinsent plus James Cracknell and Tim Foster as the quartet built towards the millennium games. All four members of the crew, plus super-sub Ed Coode, made entries into video diaries which recorded the highs and lows of their professional and personal lives. For Redgrave that meant a battle with diabetes, a condition he was diagnosed with during the period covered, as well as an addition to his family. Foster had two major injuries, one of them self-inflicted after an accident with a window at a party and the other a career-threatening back problem. His absence brought Coode into the boat for the 1999 season, and left him and Foster facing a selection dilemma handled by coach Jürgen Gröbler - another key player in this drama. Cracknell faced up to making decisions between his sport and his long-term girlfriend. Meanwhile Pinsent came over as the rock on which the others depended - with little more dramatic than moving house taking place for him off the water. It all added up to a fascinating soap opera with high class sport thrown in as a bonus, and has left anyone who viewed it in the UK even more determined to support the four at Sydney'; Gold Fever had made the lads British Heroes.

Steve's first job after returning home was to attend the ceremony for the erection of a new village sign at the entrance to Marlow Bottom. The sign had been the creation of a young artist, who lived in the village, and was accepted by the village committee as the official Marlow Bottom Village sign. The design was of a Woodpecker, cast in wrought iron and Steve had the honour, along with village elders, Gwen and Harry Watson, of dedicating the sign. Steve was able to take this opportunity to thanks the local crowds for the support they had given him over his career.

The next big event was a Super Sprint Regatta, Grand Prix which was being held on the 14th October. It had been Steve's idea to bring International crews over to Britain to compete over a short sprint course of 500 meters: very fast and exciting competition. This had been done nationally before but now with other countries competing it would make good viewing as an international grand prix. The Great Britain team was made up of Miriam Batten and Gillian Lindsay would row in the double sculls event, James Cracknell and Andrew Lindsay would take on the single sculls event. Steve and Mathew and Ben Hunt-Davis and Simon Dennis would compete as separate pairs. The International teams participating were Great Britain, Russia, Netherlands, Norway, Denmark, U S A, and Germany. There was a great turn out, at Dorney Lake's modern world-class rowing centre when almost ten thousand people were there to see the Olympic teams perform. Officials had to close the gates at mid morning as they had reached capacity and cars were queuing for miles. The weather had been dull but the rowing was really exciting.

Racing had started with Ben-Hunt Davis and Simon Dennis, rowing in the pairs and they won their heat against the Netherlands, Denmark, and Russia; these lads had been in the gold medal winning eight in Sydney. In Heat two Steve and Mathew raced against the Olympic sliver medal crews from U S A, Germany, and Norway. As Steve and Mathew rowed to the start the roars went up from the supporting crowds and they took the time to wave to the crowds to show their appreciation. As 'kings of the pairs' from past years, they didn't want to lose this race and they led all the way and were encouraged along the way by their fans coming home for a good win.

James Cracknell was up next, a very tough task going from a sweep oar, to sculling. Like some of the others he had not raced in sculls for a very long time. Still you could see the determination and true grit of a winner as he took second place in his heat, making the final. Gillian and Miriam won their heat and then came third in their final with Russia in first place and the Netherlands in second. The next few events were schools, and collages, then university races, and domestic races and relays and all were very hotly contested.

The final was the International relay; James started with the first leg, in his single scull and came home first to give Gillian and Miriam in the double scull a small headway on the second leg. This leg the girls won giving Steve and Mathew a good start on the final leg and they raced to the finish giving a home win and creating much excitement for the supporting crowds. The final Grand Prix was won by Great Britain followed by Russia, the Netherlands, Norway, Denmark, and the U S A. The crowds all stayed to see the prize giving; it had been a very successful event.

We were now looking forward to the following week when Marlow and High Wycombe were giving a reception for Steve and his crew. The day began at Steven's house when all the family gathered together. We boarded the usual open top bus at the bottom of Steve's road meeting councillors from High Wycombe and Marlow and the Mayor of Marlow; there were lots of press reporters and photographers too. Unfortunately, the weather was cold and damp as it had rained earlier that morning but it didn't keep the crowds away who were out in force, lining the roads as the bus slowly made its way out of the valley and towards Marlow.

Tim Foster and Miriam Batten were the only other athletes to have made it today but happily Jürgen Gröbler, Steve's coach was there with his wife Angela. With Steve, Ann, Natalie, Sophie and Zak standing up front, the bus moved slowly along Marlow Bottom road with people lining each side of the road, all waving their flags and shouting their congratulations, then falling in, to walk behind. The first stop was the village store, opposite the local pub, where another crowd of people were already milling, awaiting his arrival. We all got off the bus and speeches were made to which Steve responded and photographs were taken. It brought a lump to my throat to see how much everybody seemed to adore and admire him. Back on the bus again we were now joined by the Marlow Town Band; they were following the bus on the back of a lorry. As the precession moved slowly away I caught a glimpse of a man who had climbed onto the roof of the shop to wave his flag. We next stopped at Patches Field, The Residential Flats for retired people where Steve, Tim and Miriam went to meet the old folks who couldn't leave their homes.

We slowly wended our way into Marlow, all the time gathering more people who would walk behind us; it was like the Pied Piper. One unscheduled but very necessary stop was at The Plough, when Zak, needing the toilet, had to be rushed inside for a call of nature. We were joined here by Members of Marlow Rowing Club, dressed in their cardinal red club colours; they carried their oars as a guard of honour walking on either side of the bus. It was here that all traffic had been stopped and the crowds suddenly grew bigger; it was later estimated to be thirty two thousand people had turned up to see Steve that day. It was truly overwhelming and at this point we could only smile and wave to the crowds. What a home coming it was with flags and bunting strung across the street and with all the shops and pubs decorated with rowing memorabilia. I was amused by the display in the sandwich bar in Marlow, where the centre piece in the window was a large French stick, with oars either side and toy figures rowing as an eight.

We had a musical accompaniment all the way as the following band played tunes like, When the Saints Come Marching In, The March of the Athletes and Congratulations. Once we reached the bottom of the High Street there was just one seething mass of people as every one had filled the road and they all followed the bus into Higginson Park gate. The Lord Lieutenant of Buckinghamshire was waiting to greet Steve, Tim and Miriam, and he shook our hands too. The park was full of people, we later learned, that some had waited for four hours in the cold and damp just to get his autograph. It must have taken an hour and a half, to walk the 700 meters to Court Gardens, where the reception was being held. The organisers of the event eventually had to call a halt to this and ushered us all inside for some waiting hot drinks. Steve felt sorry for all these people who had gathered on such a cold day and promised to return later.

Welcome speeches were made and it was announced that Marlow Council had decided to give an annual bursary of one thousand pounds to help the most promising athlete from the town; it was to be called 'The Steve Redgrave Bursary'. Steve was particularly pleased with this as he had really struggled in his early years without sponsorship. There was a very special champagne buffet banquet and a huge cake with 'Welcome Home Steve'. Afterwards Steve, Tim and Miriam returned to the park to sign more autographs as promised. It was a wonderful day. Steve had met up with lots of old friends, his first coach, Francis Smith, had been there and all the boys from the first school crew. The whole family rounded off the day at a local restaurant; what a day for Geoff and I to remember, it had to have been seen to be believed.

On Wednesday 1st November Steve and Mathew were invited to appear on the cookery programme 'Ready Steady Cook' which they thoroughly enjoyed; this was to be broadcast on Wednesday 20th December. A few days after their recording Steve and Ann flew off to Hong Kong for a few days and we looked after the children.

On Tuesday 21st November, the entire family was up early because today a camera crew was arriving to film Geoff and I, and Chris and Jane for a programme called "Stars and Their Lives". This was to be kept as a secret from Steve. Geoff and I completed our piece to camera, and then the camera crew visited Chris to interview and film her at home, followed by an interview and filming with Jane at her home; these were to be small video clips that would be played back during the show, which was to go to air live on Monday evening, 11th December. It was a very exciting time for us all as we never quite knew what the next day would bring.

Steve had been kept really busy since he had returned from Sydney and the next significant event in his diary was the 'BBC Sports Personality of the Year'. Steve and Mathew had previously won the Team Sports Personality of the year in 1996 after their Atlanta Gold medal and they firmly felt that they may be in the running for it again this year with the Coxed Four gold medal win in Sydney. Steve and Ann left for the show and in the early evening Geoff and I settled down in front of the TV with the children to watch their dad.. The programme started with an introduction of all the medallists from the Sydney Olympics, each one getting their acclaim. The Men's Eight, the Women's Coxless four etc. ending up with Steve last; they all received a standing ovation from their fellow athletes in the audience. It had been a very healthy medal tally overall, both from the Sydney Olympics and from the 2000 Paralympic competitors. The presenters continued showcasing the sporting events of this year but by now it was getting late for the children to still be up. I suggested that it might be bedtime but I was soon worn down by all the pleas from both of the girls, to be allowed to stay up. Zak by this time had fallen asleep anyway, so I relented and allowed them to continue watching. The coach of the year came next and with great admiration, we watched as Jürgen Gröbler collected his award; he deserved this so much and all the lads respected him greatly.

There were then various clips from athletes who had not done so well; funny clips but still all receiving great applause from the audience. Steve Ryder then introduced Alan Shearer, who was to present the awards. Alan was in my opinion the best footballer Britain had ever seen. He had just retired from playing internationally but was still playing football, for Newcastle.

Steve Ryder started with 'Sports Personality Team of the Year' and Alan presented this award to Mathew who was representing the entire British Rowing Team; they had all performed so well. Next, came the 'Sports Personality of the Year' awards in reverse order. Third place went to Tanni Grey-Thompson, a really great Paralympic athlete, who had won four gold medals at the Sydney Paralympic games; what an huge achievement. Denise Lewis was awarded second place, she looked so beautiful tonight; it was well deserved, the stamina required for her Heptathlon event was enormous. We all held our breath as Steve Ryder said, 'and the BBC's Sports Personality for 2000 is, Steve Redgrave', the whole studio erupted and his fellow athletes gave Steve a standing ovation; it seemed to go for ages. It was fabulous, the kids started leaping about, Zak woke up and as we all cheered, the tears streamed down our faces. As he stepped forward to the microphone I thought quickly back to 1984 when he'd given his first speech at the first 'Welcome Home' reception in Marlow; he had been so shy then. Geoff and I were about to be blown away by the speech that Steve gave. Once the applause had died down he started by saying, 'I have been coming here for sixteen years, and had to hint that I was retiring, before I got this award', every one thought this was very funny.

He went on to thank the people he had rowed with and then especially singled out Mathew, by saying what a great athlete he was and how without him such success would not have been possible. He then thanked the people who had coached him, first Francis Smith, who had coached him, from thirteen to seventeen, Mike Spracklen who had taken over and helped take him to two Olympic gold's and a bronze, and several world gold medals too, then he turned his attention to Jürgen Gröbler who had coached him to three Olympic gold medals and he stressed that the respect that he felt for these three men was immense. He added that he had been especially pleased to see Jürgen receive the 'Sports Personality Coach of the Year' award. At the end of his speech Steve received yet another standing ovation; it was fantastic to watch his respected fellow athletes pay homage. He had made one faux pas during his speech though, he had missed out the one person who means more to him than any of the others; Ann his wife. Without her care, immense patience and understanding it might have been a very different story. It was a huge blunder to have made and he remembered as soon as he had left the stage but then it was too late. She forgave him; what a lucky guy.

On Monday 11th Dec the programme 'Stars in their Lives' presented by Carol Vorderman, was to be broadcast live. The whole family had been taken to the Charlton TV studios and were given coffee and cakes in the Green Room. We were then all ushered to tiered seats to one side of the stage before the cameras started to roll. Carol Vorderman introduced her guest celebrity by first giving the audience clues to his identity. She showed a clip of a still photo of Steve as a young boy and followed this by a few video clips of well known people talking about what they thought of Steve but without saying his name. These included the Prime Minister Tony Blair, Heptathlete Denise Lewis, and president of the International Olympic Committee Juan Antonio Samaranch. Carol then introduced him as Sir Steven Redgrave, as Steve walked through the double sliding doors at the top of the stairs. It was the first time that this news had been broadcast, all of the family already knew this wonderful news; we had found out a few days before but we had been sworn to secrecy as the recipients are usually not revealed until the Honours List was printed in the newspapers on 31$^{st}$ December. We could only assume that a researcher on the programme had been able to obtain prior knowledge from somewhere.

He walked down onto the set and sat next to Carol while she interviewed him in her relaxed style. A replay of the highlights of The Coxed Four race at the Sydney Olympics was played followed by a small video clip of each of his crew speaking about him; then the doors opened again and then in they all walked onto the set together. Each crew member then took it in turn to say a few words about Steve. It was quite funny when Carol spoke to Matthew about their ten years together saying 'You spent so much time together it must have felt like a marriage'. Mathew replied 'I'm not married yet, but if that's what it's like I don't think I want to be', every one in the audience laughed. There was another video clip from Tony Blair who spoke of Steve as being an excellent roll model for all children, including his own, and how he admired his determination to win through against all the odds. Juan Antonio Samaranch, then spoke again, on video, of how Steve had made Olympic history that day in Sydney. It was Ann's turn to speak and she said how emotional she had felt after the race was over and how she couldn't explain why she had just kept welling up and constantly bursting into tears for about two days afterwards.

Carol came to me next and I mentioned the time when at the Atlanta Church service, an Australian man at the back of the church had said that we were being modest about our son and that Steve was, without doubt, the best oarsman in the world; how that had brought both Geoff and I to tears. Next the two doctors who had treated Steve with both the Colitis and the Diabetes had spoken individually, of Steve's struggle with the illness and how extremely difficult it had been for him at times while training and competing. This was followed by an introduction of the gold medal winning British Men's Eight from Sydney and the British Women who had won a silver medal.

Next Francis Smith Steve's school master who had first introduced him to rowing spoke of how Steve had recently arranged with his sponsors to purchase a coxed four boat for the school when Steve had learned that his old school club no longer had the necessary funds to carry on rowing and how, because of this, they had been forced to drop rowing from the school curriculum; it had now started up again and hopefully would produce another Olympian. Steve replied to this by saying how pleased he had been to have been able to give something back to his school. The programme was brought to a close by a special appearance by a distant relative, Vanessa Redgrave, the actress. It was a really wonderful programme and everyone was pleased that the profile of the sport of rowing had once more been brought to public awareness.

On the 19th of December, I was asked to appear on the **Ester Ranson** show, 'Famous Mothers'. Geoff came along too and sat in the audience; I joined the other Mothers' on stage. There was Eve Pollard, author, journalist and former tabloid editor and mother of Claudia Winkleman the television and radio presenter and journalist and several mothers of other famous people such as Darren Campbell the British Olympic, World, European and Commonwealth sprint athlete, Diarmuid Gavin Irish garden designer and television personality, Scott Chisholm, the British actor, Kacey Ainsworth the English actress, best known for playing the long-suffering Little Mo in the BBC soap opera EastEnders. Julie Teasdale, TV actress and Karen O'Shea, of Redroofs Theatre School. I was a little nervous as were some of the other mothers but Ester had made us all feel much more relaxed once the show got underway. It was quite interesting to hear how Daren Campbell's mum, who encouraged and supported her son, was always too nervous to watch him compete. Mrs Gavin told how she had worried about Diarmuid when he was young, not knowing what he would do with his life but how buying a few packets of seeds had sparked his interest in growing and how now, having become a very successful gardener, he had won many medals at the Chelsea Flower Show. I spoke about how Steve had first become interested in rowing, about the way dyslexia had affected him at school and his huge determination to become the best rowing athlete in the world. It made a very interesting programme, giving an insight into the background of these now famous people. It was hard to come to terms with the fact that now my son was one of them; a household name. We later watched the video recording that Chris had made and it was amusing and a little disconcerting, watching myself on television.

Christmas soon followed and the whole family gathered at Steve and Ann's house this year for lunch on Christmas Day. A lovely lunch had been cooked by Cameron, Ann's brother-in-law who was a chef with the RAF and twenty of us sat down around the large dining table to eat; slightly less than the usual battalion I supposed.

# Chapter Twenty Seven
## The Knighthood

### *Arise Sir Steve*

On Friday 29th December, a press conference was called at Steve's home. Fifteen cars had turned up that morning with reporters and photographers so, we imagined, there would be some good press coverage, announcing his Knighthood at the weekend. We'd had a sprinkling of snow the day before so the photographers wanted to take most of their shots outside. We got the impression that it had been a popular choice, as the press and TV had been suggesting it, ever since that day in Sydney when he had won his fifth gold medal. Steve was absolutely bowled over by his forthcoming investiture which was scheduled to take place on 1st May 2001.

The Flora London Marathon would be coming up in the spring and both Steve and Ann were entering. Steve had made an announcement after his win in Sydney, promising to raise five million pounds for charity over the next five years; part of his fund raising effort would be achieved during this event. There was much preparation and training to be done beforehand; running a marathon was quite different to rowing a boat; especially for a big man. Flora sent out a doctor and some nurses to Steve's home to do some blood tests for a 'before and after' advert campaign. It was decided to test the whole family and everyone was invited to take part. Our blood pressure and cholesterol readings were taken to establish how fit we all were. Christine had high cholesterol but her blood pressure was normal, both readings of Jane's were in the average range, as were mine and Steve's. Geoff discovered that he had really high blood pressure which came as a shock as he had been showing no symptoms; he immediately made an appointment to see his doctor. The evening before the Marathon, we stayed at the London Tower Hotel, to take care of the children while Steve and Ann took part in the event.

Steve's first marathon on Sunday 22$^{nd}$ April turned out to be a great success; Steve had been asked to be the official starter. Many people had turned out to cheer them on and most of them wanted to shake his hand. Their official time was, Steve: 04:55:36 and Ann 04:55:37, although I believe they crossed the line together. Their time might have been better, if they had not had to stop so many times along the way to sign autographs. They had both really enjoyed themselves but their poor feet were a mess. Steve lost some toe nails and Ann had massive blisters which took weeks to properly heal. We took the kids down to the finishing line just before their mum and dad got there and the kids were then allowed to run the last 30 meters with their parents. The children had all made stickers that they wore on their chests, which read 'Go Mummy' and 'Go Daddy'. Sophie had been really poorly that day and was suffering with a very bad throat but she had been a really good girl all day even though she hadn't been able to eat much; she used her last drop of energy running to the finishing line. After their race had finished, and with Zak sitting on top of his shoulders, Steve was interviewed by Sue Barker for TV. He was wearing the number one on his T-shirt, but he said that he didn't think he really deserved that number, especially as it had taken him almost 5 hours to complete.

On Tuesday 1$^{st}$ May, the day we had all waited for had arrived; today was Steve's investiture at Buckingham Palace. With only three guests allowed to attend the ceremony, Ann had made the very unselfish sacrifice of letting me go in her place; I will always be grateful to her for this kind gesture, especially as it would be my second visit. Geoff and I would take Sophie with us on this occasion, as Natalie had been to Buckingham Palace with Jane and Chris when Steve had received his CBE.

This time was just as wonderful as my first visit to the palace and delightful music played by the Coldstream Guards, drifted over the guest from the minstrel's gallery above. Steve was the second person to be knighted, with just two people receiving Knighthoods that day. As his name was announced and he walked into the ballroom, Geoff and I felt so very proud to see our son looking so smart in this morning suit approaching his Queen. He walked forward and then turned to face the Queen, stepped forward and knelt down in front of her. The Queen was then handed the ceremonial sword and she lightly tapped him with it on each of his shoulders. He rose to his feet, smiled at her and then they chatted together for a short while; he bowed and stepped backwards and turning to his right, and walked out as Sir Steven Redgrave. Ann of course would be now known as Lady Redgrave; they had both earned this well deserved honour. Mathew came next receiving the CBE and James and Tim received the MBE, for their services to rowing; it was a wonderful moment for them all.

Later Steve had told us that after the Queen dubbed him a Knight Bachelor, she had asked him "How are your feet?"; a reference to his recent participation in the London Marathon. He said he'd replied, "I told the Queen I still had a couple of blisters and my legs were so stiff that I had to walk downstairs backwards," He told us that it was a wonderful feeling to be honoured by his country. At Christmas that year, The Queen featured pictures of his victory in Sydney in her Christmas message to the nation.

After all the investitures had taken place we walked back to the foyer where Ann, Natalie and Zak had been allowed to wait. We had our official photographs taken and then we were driven in chauffeured cars to the celebrated Swiss chef, Anton Mosimann's private dining club in a beautifully converted 19th century church in Belgravia .We were greeted and taken through the club to The Library where a huge and very beautifully laid, lunch table awaited. This felt right for such an important occasion. We had been joined for this exquisite lunch by June, Ann's mother, Jürgen and his wife, Angela, Jane, Christine and Edward. Sadly missing from our family gathering today were Ben and Steph, who had important exams at school today, and their father David who had not been able to take time from work. We had champagne on arrival followed by a delicious lunch accompanied by exemplary wines and a bespoke service second to none; a fitting way to celebrate such an auspicious occasion.

Towards the end of May we took a four week holiday in Spain; we were looking after a friend's villa and were joined by our friends Queenie and Arthur. During this time Steve was kept constantly busy, attending lots of different events which had kept him in the public eye. Mathew had made a decision to carry on rowing and had already returned to training, with the aim of competing in the 2004 Olympics in Athens. To begin with James and Matthew rowed together as a pair but later they joined Ed Coode and Steve Williams in a coxless four. Tim had chosen to retire from competitive rowing due to his long term back injury and was now coaching; we wished them well.

# Chapter Twenty Eight
## The Statue

### *Cast in Bronze*

During the spring of 2001, it was suggested that a permanent tribute to Steve should be made by the town; something to honour his achievements. A committee from Marlow and Marlow Bottom was formed to launch an appeal to raise enough money to commission and erect a bronze statue of Steve which was to be sited in Higginson Park, in Marlow, and most appropriately, overlooking the river where Steve had first learned his craft.

The Patron of The Marlow Redgrave Tribute Appeal was Sir Nigel Mobbs KstJ JP, Lord Lieutenant of Buckinghamshire and the Vice Patrons were Lady Dr Ann Redgrave, Sir Keith Stuart and Sir Raymond Whitney OBE MP. The Chairman of the Appeal Committee, Hugh McNearnie, worked tirelessly to raise money with his team, which included, Alan Coster, Hon Treasurer, Peter Hunt, Chairman of Marlow Rowing Club, Marlow Town Councillor Maurice Oram, and Mike Williams from Marlow Bottom Residents' Association. There were also to be four members of a special Selection Committee, who would make the final choice from the proposed designs. These included, Hugh McNearnie, David Messum, of Messum's Fine Art dealers of Mayfair, Marlow Town Councillor Maurice Oram and Steve's dad, Geoff Redgrave. Geoff had been really pleased to have been invited to be involved in the selection of this lasting tribute to his son.

Hugh McNearnie had said to the press, "We felt we needed something that would reflect Marlow's civic pride in Sir Steve, something tangible and also something to provide inspiration and encouragement to others." Peter Hunt, a member of the appeal committee and chairman of Marlow Rowing Club, had said: "We have Sir Steve's tacit agreement. I think he was not all that keen and he was more eager to see money spent on the town but there are some things you just can't avoid." Hugh added "There is going to be a great deal to organise between now and then. It is not just a sculpture but planning permission, a plinth, possibly railings, designs, unveiling and so on."

The group, now faced with raising funds for the project, began to approach local businesses and town's people to help raise the cash. The **Royal Society of British Sculptors** acted as consultants, and in due course, Neale Andrew won the commission; one of six concept proposals from acclaimed sculptors. Neale's studio was in Nottingham; a good omen, we thought, as many of Steve's national and international triumphs had taken place in this city.

Neale Andrew had an already impressive list of completed commissions to his name; particularly of famous sportsmen. Some of these portrait heads had included footballers, Bobby Moore and Gary Lineker, cricketers, Sir Garfield Sobers and Geoffrey Boycott and golfer Tony Jacklin; he now had the 16ft figure of Sir Steve Redgrave, five times Olympic medallist to grapple with. The icing on the cake was for us, the announcement that Her Majesty the Queen would be officially unveiling Steve's statue, in May, on a visit to Marlow during her Golden Jubilee year of 2002.

The one and a half life-size bronze statue was to be cast locally, at a foundry at Loudwater, near High Wycombe in Buckinghamshire. Burleighfield Arts, had a good reputation in its field, producing high quality work and casting for top artists throughout Europe; they also came highly recommended having worked for organisations such as the Tate Gallery. The business had been established for almost 30years and Paul Dimishky, the owner, had taken over the company from his father-in-law Eric Gibbard and was carrying on the family tradition; Paul's wife was, coincidentally, a teacher at Herries School in Cookham, which was the school that all Steve's children attended.

Bronze had been the material of choice, being judged the most versatile.

Cast bronze is capable of reproducing the finest level of detail that is present in the surface form of the original sculpture. A well made bronze sculpture is less likely to be chipped or damaged accidentally than other materials, and can last hundreds or even thousands of years. If carefully made and given an appropriate patina, the sculpture will 'come alive' and will look better than the original sculpture; there is a huge amount of skilled manual work involved in producing a bronze but bronze is beautiful and was deemed to be appropriate for its subject.

Neale made a series of visit's to Steve's home for sittings and on one occasion, nearing completion, Neale, travelling to Marlow in his car, had needed to make an emergency stop to avoid an accident. The almost finished sculpture of Steve's head apparently had rolled onto the car floor, flattening one side of his face; luckily all was not lost and with a few adjustments Neale was able to repair the damage. Steve later joked that it had been a good job that the head hadn't rolled out of the car as the other motorist might have thought that he had actually decapitated the rower.

The day arrived for the cast to be poured, and I had been invited to see this part of the process, along with Geoff and the rest of the committee; it was really interesting to see how it was done. They were also working on some other castings of well know figures that day including one of Cardinal Basil Hume which was to be erected in his home town of Newcastle and unveiled by the Queen in 2002.

My next visit to the foundry was with Geoff, to see the completed bronze statue of our son, holding the 16ft oar in his hand, hoisted up and loaded on to the back of a long flat bed lorry. This procedure took a lot of time, patience, and the effort of several strong men but eventually, lying on its side, covered in blankets and bubble wrap, and still looking awfully precarious, it was settled onto the flatbed, ready for its, hopefully steady, eight mile journey to Marlow.

Christine and Jane had driven us to the foundry and we all retuned to the car to slowly follow the precious cargo to Higginson Park. We all stood on the lawns at the back of Court Gardens and watched and took photos, as the reverse procedure took place and the bronze was secured onto its plinth. There he stood in all his glory, in a very tight and revealing pair of Bronze rowing shorts, with one hand raised in triumph, facing the River Thames and Marlow Rowing Club, where it had all started twenty-eight years before.

The 10th May 2002, now ranks as the proudest day in our lives, when as Steve's parents, we were introduced, by our son, to Queen Elizabeth II, That spring morning, Higginson Park was full to capacity, marquees had been erected on the lawned slopes of Court Garden House and crowds of townsfolk and school children had gathered behind the enormous cordoned-off area surrounding the statue, which prior to the ceremony, had been completely covered with an opaque golden veil. It had been arranged this way so that as many people as possible could get a clear view, when later, the Queen would step down from Court Garden terrace, to unveil Steve's statue.

Her majesty, Queen Elizabeth, and Prince Philip, Duke of Edinburgh were visiting Marlow as part of the Queen's Golden Jubilee celebrations. The whole of our family had been invited as special guests and would be allowed at close quarters during the unveiling ceremony. The royal couple were due to arrive in separate helicopters with a planned landing on the cricket pitch in front of Court Garden House; we all eagerly awaited their arrival. Hundreds of local school children were there to greet them, all armed and ready to wave their flags. The Sea Cadets were smartly dressed in uniform and had formed a Guard of Honour either side of the landing pad. Her Majesty was the first to arrive accompanied by her Lady-in-Waiting. She looked stunning in a matching Strawberry coloured straw hat and woollen coat and slowly made her way along the line of children, occasionally stopping to chat to someone. While this was happening The Duke arrived in his helicopter, and dressed in a smart dark suit and raincoat, stepped out of the aircraft looking extremely sprightly for eighty years of age.

The Royal couple were escorted to the entrance of Court Garden House, the beautiful Georgian Mansion set on the edge of Higginson Park, where they were introduced to Steve and Ann and the County and Town dignitaries, and then they disappeared out of view, inside to have their lunch. The family were then taken, with other guests, to another room in the building which overlooked the gardens for a lovely buffet lunch. While we ate our sandwiches and sipped our champagne, we gazed out of the windows at the descending view over the River Thames and to the tall golden-covered statue, waiting to be unveiled.

Lots of people who had been involved with Steve's rowing career were with us today. Some of them included Steve's crew, Mathew, Tim and James, Steve's coach Jürgen and his wife, Angela, Frances Smith, Steve's rowing school master and his wife and many members of Marlow Rowing Club. Steve's children, Zak and Sophie, were here with us, but Natalie was at Bisham Abbey, on the opposite side of the river. Her school, along with others in the area, were rehearsing a pageant that they were later performing for the Queen; Her Majesty would be visiting the Abbey after the unveiling as she was meeting some of the England football team who were training there. Melanie, Steve's P.A. collected Natalie at the last minute so she could be here to watch the unveiling and to meet the Queen.

At 1.45pm after we had enjoyed our lunch, the organiser came to tell us that we should take our places in a line by the statue. As we came out onto the lawns, we noticed how much the crowd had grown; they were now filling the park. From Court Garden House, right down to the river bank, there was a sea of faces all looking in our direction which made it was hard to make anyone out. In front of the cordon was a line of people in wheelchairs who had been given a front row seat and inside the marquee, the OAP's were sitting down ready for their afternoon tea and a slice of cake, once the Queen had cut the specially decorated Golden Jubilee cake.

A 4ft. wide red carpet had been laid from the bottom of the terrace steps, along the lawn to in front of the statue. With most family members standing on the terrace and Aunt Doris sitting down on a bench to one side, Geoff and I stood in line to meet the Queen. From the bottom of the terrace steps, shoulder to shoulder were Jürgen, Mathew, Tim, Natalie, Sophie, Zak and myself, with Geoff last in the line, right next to the statue. As the Queen emerged into the afternoon sunlight, the crowds let out a huge cheer. She was closely followed by Steve, then The Duke and next Ann. They all paused while the National Anthem was played by the town band.

A young boy who had entered a Marlow Schools poetry competition had won the honour of presenting the Queen with a bouquet of flowers, and as she reached the last step, he came forward, bowed and proffered the flowers. Young Zak had skilfully made a paper crown at school which he had painstakingly coloured and decorated and now wore on his head, replacing his school cap; he was very proud of his handiwork.

As they progressed along the line, Steve first introduced Jürgen, and then each crewmember in turn, the Queen stopped to have a little chat with each one. Steve then introduced his two daughters, Natalie, and Sophie. Zak was next in line, the Queen bent forward and said, "Oh you have a crown on, that's nice", at this Zak snatched his crown from his head and quickly replaced his school cap, looking amused at this the Queen said, "Oh he's put his cap on", Zak gave her a big grin which she returned. Steve then said "this is my mother your majesty", we shook hands and she said, "You must be very proud of your son", and I murmured "yes your majesty", then Steve introduced his father, Geoff, feeling overwhelmed by the moment, Geoff couldn't remember later, what she had said to him but as that was the end of the line, The Queen then turned towards the crowds who were still cheering, and stood next to the veiled statue. Hugh McNearnie had been held up and was not quite there on cue, the Queen obviously feeling a lull in the proceedings turned to Geoff and asked, "What should I do next", and Geoff replied 'I don't know, we'll have to ask Hugh', thankfully, at that precise moment Hugh suddenly appeared and quickly handed her the unveiling cord and indicated that she should just pull it; this she did and with out a hitch the golden shroud fell to the floor revealing Steve's statue and the crowds loudly cheered and waved their flags.

The Duke strolled by smiling and chatting to us all and the Queen moved over to speak to the people sitting in their wheelchairs. The Royal couple entered the marquee, chatted with the OAP's and then the Queen cut the cake. While this was taking place we were all entertained by the Sea Cadets Band and Natalie was whisked back to the Abbey in time for her performance. The Queen and the Duke then wandered down towards the river bank, chatting to people along the way, and then boarded a launch and were taken over the river to Bisham Abby, with crowds cheering and waving them on their way.

The family, the officials and their guests returned to the theatre hall which was beautifully decorated in Golden Jubilee colours. Steve cut the cake, speeches were made, bouquets were presented to me and to Ann, and some ladies who had helped with the day. Afternoon tea was then served, while entertainment was provided by the excellent Sir **William Borlase's** Grammar School Jazz Band and Choir. During the afternoon Steve gave an interview to the local paper and when asked what he felt about being immortalised in bronze replied "To have had a statue of myself unveiled by the Queen in my home town is very, very special. It's a very good likeness, but to be honest it could have done with a few less pounds around the middle."

With formalities now over, Steve had a chance to relax and enjoy his reception; it was a chance for him to catch up with a few old friends. For us it was time to reflect on the wonderful memories that, through his sport, Steve had been able to bring to us and the rest of his family. We will hold these memories with us forever and cherish the wonderful moments that we have been so fortunate to share.

# Chapter Twenty Nine
## The Epilogue

Now, almost ten years have passed since that wonderful morning in Sydney. Mathew and crew managed to win gold in the Athens Olympics, in 2004; Steve was at long last allowed to enjoy the Olympics as a spectator and to be with his family. He had been invited by the BBC to give commentary on the rowing events there but he had been free in the afternoon to enjoy the other sporting events. In Beijing he was again asked to join the BBC commentary team but the rowing was in the afternoon so he didn't get to see as many other sporting events as he would have liked but he'd told me that it was still fantastic to have been part of the Olympics even if he hadn't been competing.

Steve has been seen back in a boat just a few more times since then too. In 2007 and in the following year 2008, he entered Henley Veterans and won so he now has a few more Henley medals to add to his tally. He also now has a few other responsibilities; he's an Acting Steward of Henley Royal Regatta, President of The Amateur Rowing Association, Vice President of The British Olympic Association, Deputy Lord Lieutenant of Buckinghamshire and Freeman of the Waterman and Lighterman of the River Thames.

He has also gone on to raise millions of pounds for charity in his role as President for 'The Steve Redgrave Fund' which aims to support school projects

such as providing indoor rowing machines (complete with teacher training) designed to reach children between the ages of 11 and 16 in the UK (including special schools)  providing a cross-curricular tool and helping to provide a solution to problems including fitness, obesity, social inclusion, and confidence.

He works tirelessly as Vice President for 'Sparks', the children's medical research charity and for 'Diabetes UK'. He is Patron of 'Kids Out', a charity for disadvantaged and disabled children, 'Cry', Cardiac Risk in the Young and 'CEDAR', Centre for Endocrinology Diabetes and Research. He is a Trustee for 'Comic Relief', 'Stewards' Charitable Trust', a Steering Committee Member for 'Sports Relief' and Ambassador for the 'Talented Athlete Scholarship Scheme'.

A very sad event took place while he was away on holiday in the spring of 2007. His home was broken into and jewellery, laptops, watches and some of his prize trophies were taken; luckily not his medals which are now kept in a safe. It was loosing the irreplaceable and sentimental ones that hurt him the most; his Grandfathers retirement presentation gold watch was one of these; it had been presented to Harold Stevenson, my dad, after forty years of service, driving for the Birmingham City Transport Department. I had given the watch to Steve on my father's death as he had been the only grandson. Also taken were Steve's three trophies from the BBC Sports Personality Awards. Steve appealed directly to the burglars who broke into his home, asking them to return the irreplaceable and sentimental items that they had stolen but none have been recovered. When asked recently what he did with his medals nowadays he said, "Now they're locked away in a safe. They've done the rounds over the years but they're getting a little bit bruised and battered now."

His eldest daughter Natalie now eighteen years old, is at Oxford University and has many sporting interests including netball and skiing. Two years she took part in a school girls skiing competition and so Steve now has had a taste of what it feels like to be a supporting parent and has experienced the stomach wrenching nerves that go with this role. His middle daughter Sophie, now fifteen years old, is studying hard for her forthcoming GCSE's and her interests include cookery, drama and child care. Steve's Son Zak at eleven years old enjoys most sports but especially cricket and also is skilled at computer games. All three of Steve's children along with their father are passionate supporters of Chelsea Football Club.

We have been extremely fortunate to have been the parents of such a close and loving family, we will be forever grateful for these blessings and hope that our children and grandchildren will have as much happiness in their lives as Geoff and I have shared.

There have been some wonderful articles written in the newspapers about the moment when Steve took his 5th Gold Medal and I'd like to share a few of my favourites:

## Kevin Mitchell in The Observer

As Princess Anne put the gold around Redgrave's tired old shoulders; there were not many Britons present who were not thinking: Arise, Sir Steve. If there is a safer bet for the next Honours List, none is immediately apparent. Hell, Sir Steve might even finally win the BBC Sports Personality of the Year award.

**According to the Times newspaper**, after the race Redgrave said to his crewmates, "Remember these six minutes for the rest of your lives. Listen to the crowd and take it all in. This is the stuff of dreams."

## Dan Topolski in The Observer: Sunday 24th September 2000

A CBE, an MBE, an Honoris causa Doctorate of Civil Law, and vice president of the charity Sparks have propelled him into prominence and he carries his celebrity well. He remains down to earth, serious, but accessible - unless race day is imminent, when he becomes unapproachable. He doesn't suffer fools easily, but he's learnt diplomacy and public speaking.

**James Lawton salutes a seminal moment of sheer sporting guts.**

## *Monday, 13 July 2009 The Independent*

It still looks ridiculous when you write it down: 0.38 of a

second, then measure it against 2,000 metres of the glassy lake in Australia on that September morning nine years ago. That dawn when the flags of the Olympic nations hung limp and the tension rose with the brilliant sun burning away the mist - and then you remember the near-death agony of the winners and losers before they could celebrate or grieve the micro moment that was now gone for ever. Nought point 38. . . You cannot take half a breath in such a grain of time, you cannot formulate a thought. Maybe it is an age in the Olympic blue riband, the 100-yard dash. In rowing, it can be no more than a single convulsion.

## Richard Williams    Saturday 23 September 2000 guardian.co.uk

Redgrave's achievements will always be in his deeds and not in his memories. The fifth gold medal, which was presented to him by the president of the International Olympic Committee, Juan Antonio Samaranch, will, one imagines, go where the other four have gone into a display case in the the Henley rowing museum. But somewhere deep in that warrior's heart perhaps one day he will feel a glow of pride in his immense, unexampled conquests.

## Richard Phelps Saturday, 23 September, 2000

Bookmaker William Hill meanwhile immediately quoted Redgrave at 1/10 favourite to win the BBC Sports Personality of the Year Award - and 20/1 to win Olympic gold again in 2004.

## Nick Pitt Sunday Times 24th September

And if training is pain upon pain, as dull and deadening as a long prison sentence, racing is a concentrated, exquisite form of self-punishment. Long before halfway on a 2,000m course,

401

lungs and legs scream for mercy; but the brain must deny and ignore them, for each stroke, although wrenched with furious effort, has to be sweet and in harmony.

## Brian Cazeneuve October 09, 2000
## sportsillustrated.cnn.com

Few athletes have pursued their craft with Redgrave's desire. He took up rowing at 14 and dropped out of school at 16, beginning a 22-year run of six-day-a-week, five-hour-a-day training sessions. That's 22 years of watching the dawn break, replenishing sturdy legs with lactic acid and parting with breakfast over the side of the boat. Why? "It has given me my passion," Redgrave says of rowing. "Everyone should have a passion."

## Neil Drysdale    Scotland On Sunday    24 September 2000

"I've never been bored, never thought about giving up, but there have been times when I thought the sport was giving me up," said Redgrave. "I struggled in late 1997, early 98, and February 99, and the early part of this year was also very difficult, but going on as long as I have, there are bound to be days where you feel like walking away. I mean, I'm not stupid, I know that life is not only about competing in the Olympics and that there are bigger things to worry about. "Because, in years to come, when we are all dead and buried, someone will pick up a history book and say 'Oh, he did well, didn't he'. But it won't really mean anything to them. I'll be some distant memory by then and maybe that's as it should be. Basically, I have now got five golds, I wouldn't change a thing, and I'm thrilled at what we have achieved in Australia, but there are other things out there and it will be nice to be in charge of my life again. I want to go on holiday. I want to go skiing. Hell, I want to go and play golf with some old farts down at the local club."

# The Independent - London  October 8, 2000
## NICK TOWNSEND

IT WAS triumph only of the fittest. Where strong arms and bulky torsos won the day. "Oi, f****** get down," bellowed one belligerent character. "Don't you f****** push me," snarled another smooth- talker as the cacophony outside Heathrow Terminal 4 reached a crescendo. Never, ever could Steve Redgrave have imagined it. Press photographers squabbling so vociferously over places to picture him with the new £51,000 Jaguar XJR bought for him by wife Ann that police officers had to intervene? "It's crazy," he mutters three days later as he sprawls across his favourite armchair

## Australian Associated Press Prior to the Sydney Olympics

By now, he will have begun to experience the inner turmoil. Imperceptibly, at first, as he and his crew complete their training on Australia's Gold Coast, an appropriate enough venue for Britain's greatest Olympian. But then, as they mentally pencil off the hours to their moment of destiny, the coxless fours final on 23 September, he will undergo a water torture unique to the man who always travels to an Olympic Games strictly on business, never as a tourist.

# About the Author

Sheila Redgrave was inspired to write this book by her only son Sir Steven Redgrave, the five times Olympic Gold Medallist. "The Sonshine of our Lives", is not a typo (although dyslexia does run in the family), but refers to the fact that Steve is her son, and that he has always been the sunshine of his parents' lives. Sheila has used Steve's thirty year rowing career as the background to the story of the lives of her family members during these years and has taken the facts from the pages of her diaries which she religiously writes each and every day. She was born in Birmingham in 1931 to Ada and Harold Stevenson, the youngest daughter of a close and loving family. Sheila married her husband Geoffrey in 1952 and had three children, two girls, Christine and Jane and a son, her youngest. Sheila and Geoff supported and followed Steve to each and every rowing event that he entered in his long career - in later years, taking care of his children, being their 'nanny' in both senses of the word and allowing Steve and his wife Ann, to single-mindedly pursue their careers within Sport and Sports Medicine. Sheila's lifelong friends Queenie and Joan, whose husbands Arthur and Derek are Steve's Godfathers, all moved to Marlow Bottom in the 1950's and are still firm friends. Sheila has five grandchildren, Benjamin, Stephanie, Natalie, Sophie and Zak. The book recounts the Redgrave family history from 1975 to the turn of the millennium.

Lightning Source UK Ltd.
Milton Keynes UK
19 April 2010

153047UK00001B/73/P